T0189924

Lecture Notes in Computer Science 9718

Commenced Publication in 1973
Founding and Former Series Editors:
Gerhard Goos, Juris Hartmanis, and Jan van Leeuwen

More information about this series at http://www.springer.com/series/7408

Jose Julio Alferes · Leopoldo Bertossi
Guido Governatori · Paul Fodor
Dumitru Roman (Eds.)

Rule Technologies

Research, Tools, and Applications

10th International Symposium, RuleML 2016
Stony Brook, NY, USA, July 6–9, 2016
Proceedings

 Springer

Editors
Jose Julio Alferes
Universidade Nova de Lisboa
Lisboa
Portugal

Leopoldo Bertossi
Carleton University
Ottawa, ON
Canada

Guido Governatori
NICTA Queensland
Brisbane, QLD
Australia

Paul Fodor
Stony Brook University
Stony Brook, NY
USA

Dumitru Roman
SINTEF/University of Oslo
Oslo
Norway

ISSN 0302-9743   ISSN 1611-3349   (electronic)
Lecture Notes in Computer Science
ISBN 978-3-319-42018-9   ISBN 978-3-319-42019-6   (eBook)
DOI 10.1007/978-3-319-42019-6

Library of Congress Control Number: 2016943419

LNCS Sublibrary: SL2 – Programming and Software Engineering

Printed on acid-free paper

This Springer imprint is published by Springer Nature
The registered company is Springer International Publishing AG Switzerland

Preface

The annual International Web Rule Symposium (RuleML) is an international conference on research, applications, languages, and standards for rule technologies. It has evolved from an annual series of international workshops since 2002, international conferences in 2005 and 2006, and international symposia since 2007. RuleML 2016 was the 10th symposium of this series, co-located in New York State with the 25th International Joint Conference on Artificial Intelligence (July 9–15, 2016) and the Joint Multi-Conference on Human-Level Artificial Intelligence 2016 (July 16–19, 2016).

RuleML is a leading conference aiming to build bridges between academia and industry in the field of rules and its applications, especially as part of the semantic technology stack. It is devoted to rule-based programming and rule-based systems including production rule systems, logic programming rule engines, and business rule engines and business rule management systems, Semantic Web rule languages and rule standards (e.g., RuleML, SWRL, RIF, PRR, SBVR, DMN, CL, Prolog), rule-based event processing languages (EPLs) and technologies, and research on inference rules, transformation rules, decision rules, and ECA rules.

This annual symposium is the flagship event of RuleML. The RuleML Initiative (http://ruleml.org) is a non-profit umbrella organization with a Steering Committee, an advisory board, taskforces, and technical groups, whose participants from academia, industry, and government work on rule technology and its applications. Its aim is to promote the study, research, and use of rules in heterogeneous distributed environments such as the Web. RuleML maintains effective links with other major international societies and acts as intermediary between various "specialized" rule vendors, applications, industrial and academic research groups, as well as standardization efforts from, e.g., W3C, OMG, OASIS, and ISO. One of its major contributions is the unifying RuleML system of families of rule languages, serialized in XML and spanning across all industrially relevant kinds of Web rules.

The technical program of RuleML 2016 included presentations of novel rule-based technologies, such as Semantic Web rule languages and standards, rule engines, formal and operational semantics, rule-based systems, as well as new emerging topics relevant to rules. Besides the regular research track, RuleML 2016 included six special research tracks: Smart Contracts, Blockchain, and Rules; Constraint Handling Rules; Event-Driven Architectures and Active Database Systems; Legal Rules and Reasoning; Rule- and Ontology-Based Data Access and Transformation; Rule Induction and Learning. These tracks reflect the significant role of rules in several research and application areas, which include: blockchains and smart contract, ontology-based data access, active databases and rules, legal rules, constraint handling rule, and rule induction and learning.

After a successful industry track at RuleML 2015, RuleML 2016 again included such a track, describing practical applications of rules, and aspects of the state of the art of rule-based business cases.

The highlights of this year's RuleML Symposium included the following invited presentations:

Two keynote talks:

- Richard Waldinger, from Artificial Intelligence Center, SRI International, USA, presenting "Natural Language Access to Data: It Needs Reasoning"
- Bruce Silver from Bruce Silver Associates, presenting "DMN as a Decision Modeling Language"

Two tutorials:

- "Programming in Picat" by Neng-Fa Zhou, City University of New York
- "Practical Knowledge Representation and Reasoning in Ergo" by Michael Kifer, Theresa Swift and Benjamin Grosof (Coherent Knowledge Systems)

A RuleML standards talk:

- "The RuleML Knowledge-Interoperation Hub" by Harold Boley, Faculty of Computer Science, University of New Brunswick

In addition, the program included the 10th International Rule Challenge, dedicated to practical experiences with rule-based applications, the 6th RuleML Doctoral Consortium, which focused on PhD research in the area of rules, and finally, the DecisionCAMP 2016.

The contributions in this volume include a set of invited papers and research track papers. Invited presentations include two full papers and three abstracts for the keynotes, tutorials, and standards talk. Research papers include a selection of 20 papers, which were presented during the technical program of RuleML 2016. The research papers were selected from 36 submissions through a peer-review process. Each paper was reviewed by at least three members of the Program Committee.

RuleML 2016, like its predecessors, offered a high-quality technical and applications program, which was the result of the joint effort of the members of the RuleML 2016 Program Committee.

Special thanks are due to the Track Chairs, the excellent Program Committee, and the additional reviewers for their hard work in reviewing the submitted papers. Their criticisms and very useful comments and suggestions were instrumental in achieving a high-quality publication. We also thank the symposium authors for submitting high-quality papers, responding to the reviewers' comments, and abiding by our production schedule. We further wish to thank the invited speakers for contributing their inspiring presentations. RuleML 2016 was financially supported by industrial companies and scientific journals and was technically supported by several professional societies. We wish to thank our sponsors, whose financial support helped us to offer this event, and whose technical support allowed us to attract high-quality submissions. Last, but not least, we would like to thank the development team of the EasyChair conference management system and our publisher, Springer, for their support in the preparation of this volume and the publication of the proceedings.

May 2016   Jose Julio Alferes
                                                          Leopoldo Bertossi
                                                          Guido Governatori
                                                                 Paul Fodor
                                                              Dumitru Roman

Organization

General Chair

Paul Fodor   Stony Brook University, USA

Scientific Program Co-chairs

Jose Julio Alferes   Universidade Nova de Lisboa, Portugal
Leopoldo Bertossi   Carleton University, Canada
Guido Governatori   NICTA, Australia

Track Chairs

Smart Contracts, Blockchain, and Rules Track

Sudhir Agarwal   Stanford University, USA
Alex Oberhauser   Sigimera, USA
Dumitru Roman   SINTEF/University of Oslo, Norway

Event-Driven Architectures and Active Database Systems Track

Darko Anicic   Siemens AG, Germany
Chitta Baral   Arizona State University, USA

Constraint Handling Rules Track

Thom Fruehwirth   University of Ulm, Germany

Legal Rules and Reasoning Track

Monica Palmirani   Università di Bologna, Italy
Shashishekar Ramakrishna   Freie Universität Berlin, Germany

Rule- and Ontology-Based Data Access and Transformation Track

Andrea Cali   University of London, Birkbeck College, UK
Martin Giese   University of Oslo, Norway

Rule Induction and Learning Track

Cèsar Ferri Ramirez   Technical University of Valencia, Spain
Maria José Ramirez   Universidad Politécnica de Valencia (UPV), Spain
  Quintana

Industry Track

Tara Athan   Athan Services, USA
Marc Proctor   Red Hat, UK

Proceedings Chair

Dumitru Roman   SINTEF/University of Oslo, Norway

Doctoral Workshop Chair

Kia Teymourian   Rice University, USA

10th International Rule Challenge Co-chairs

Adrian Giurca   Brandenburg University of Technology
                              Cottbus–Senftenberg, Germany
William Van Woensel   Dalhousie University, Canada
Rolf Grütter   Swiss Federal Research Institute, Switzerland

DecisionCAMP

Jacob Feldman   Open Rules, USA

Web Chair

Tiantian Gao   Stony Brook University, USA

Local and Finance Chair

Christine Cesaria   Stony Brook University, USA

Program Committee

Slim Abdennadher   German University in Cairo, Egypt
Martin Atzmueller   University of Kassel, Germany
Ebrahim Bagheri   Ryerson University, Canada
Christopher Baker   UNB Saint John, Canada
Nick Bassiliades   Aristotle University of Thessaloniki, Greece
Bernhard Bauer   University of Augsburg, Germany
Andrea Bracciali   University of Stirling, UK
Lars Braubach   University of Hamburg, Germany
Christoph Bussler   Oracle Corporation, USA
Jean-Paul Calbimonte   EPFL, Switzerland
Henning Christiansen   Roskilde University, Denmark
Gökhan Coskun   Universität Bonn, Germany

Andrew Miller	University of Wollongong, Australia
Angelo Montanari	University of Udine, Italy
Grzegorz J. Nalepa	AGH University of Science and Technology, Poland
Sergey Nazarov	SmartContract.com, USA
Alex Norta	Tallinn University of Technology, Estonia
Philipp Obermeier	University of Postdam, Germany
Jose Ignacio Panach Navarrete	Universitat de València, Spain
Gareth W. Peters	University College London, UK
Andreas Pieris	Vienna University of Technology, Austria
Zbigniew Ras	University of North Carolina, USA
Oliver Ray	University of Bristol, UK
Fabrizio Riguzzi	University of Ferrara, Italy
Mariano Rodríguez Muro	IBM Research, USA
Fariba Sadri	Imperial College London, UK
Giovanni Sartor	EUI/CIRSFID, Italy
Uli Sattler	University of Manchester, UK
Ute Schmid	Universität Bamberg, Germany
Rolf Schwitter	Macquarie University, Australia
Ralph Schäfermeierz	Freie Universität Berlin, Germany
Omair Shafiq	University of Calgary, Canada
Rishabh Singh	MIT, USA
Martin G. Skjæveland	University of Oslo, Norway
Ahmet Soylu	University of Oslo, Norway
Francois Levy	LIPN, University of Paris, France
Petros Stefaneas	National Technical University of Athens, Greece
Christian De Sainte Marie	IBM, Paris, France
Giorgos Stoilos	National Technical University of Athens, Greece
Umberto Straccia	ISTI-CNR, Italy
Olga Streibel	National Institute of Informatics, Russia
Martin Sulzmann	Karlsruhe University of Applied Sciences, Germany
Melanie Swan	IEET, USA
Ioan Toma	STI Innsbruck, Austria
David Toman	University of Waterloo, Canada
Emilio Tuosto	University of Leicester, UK
Wamberto Vasconcelos	University of Aberdeen, UK
George Vouros	University of Piraeus, Greece
Renata Wassermann	University of São Paulo, Brazil
Frank Wolter	University of Liverpool, UK
Adam Wyner	University of Aberdeen, UK
Michael Zakharyaschev	Birkbeck College London, UK
Amal Zouaq	Royal Military College of Canada, Canada
Leon van der Torre	University of Luxembourg, Luxembourg
Özgür Lütfü Özcep	Institute of Information Systems, University of Lübeck, Germany

Additional Reviewers

Leif Harald Karlsen
Francesco Parisi
Riccardo Zese
Nada Sharaf

Kalliopi Kravari
Marcelo Finger
Elena Bellodi
Amira Zaki

RuleML 2016 Sponsors

Invited Papers Abstracts

Natural Language Access to Data:
It Needs Reasoning

Richard Waldinger

Artificial Intelligence Center, SRI International

Researchers have been working on natural language access to data for decades. We argue that to do a good job, we must have knowledge of the subject domain and the ability to reason with that knowledge. We are interested in queries for which the answer does not exist explicitly in any one data source but must be deduced or computed from information provided by many sources. Furthermore, we consider queries which are not be expressed in a single question but are distributed over a sequence of questions, each one refining or elaborating on earlier ones. We have adopted a deductive approach to this problem, in which the query is translated into a logical form, which is submitted as a conjecture to a theorem prover; answers are extracted from proofs. A proof is conducted over an axiomatic theory of the subject domain; symbols in the theory are linked to tables in appropriate databases, which may be consulted as the proof is underway. Reasoning is necessary to link the query to the relevant databases, to compose answers from information provided by those databases, and to resolve ambiguities in the English query. We illustrate the approach with the SAP Quest system, which answers questions in a business enterprise domain.

DMN as a Decision Modeling Language

Bruce Silver

Bruce Silver Associates

Decision Model and Notation (DMN) is a relatively new decision modeling standard maintained by the Object Management Group. Based on a formal metamodel, it combines a business-oriented graphical notation with precise rule-based decision logic semantics. As such, DMN tools allow non-technical users to define, validate, and maintain executable decision logic themselves, as opposed to the traditional error-prone approach of writing business requirements for programmers. In the notation, the dependencies of a complex decision on other supporting decisions and input data are represented graphically by a Decision Requirements Diagram (DRD). The decision logic of each decision node in the DRD is defined by a variety of tabular formats called boxed expressions, and DMN also specifies a new expression language, FEEL, used in the boxed expressions. In combination, the DRD, boxed expressions, and FEEL constitute a powerful decision modeling language standard. In fact, the XML serialization of a DMN model captures all the essential semantic details of the notation, so that it can be validated for completeness and consistency, and supplied with input data values directly executed on a suitable engine.

This keynote talk reviews the structure and key features of DMN 1.1 as a decision modeling language.

Programming in Picat

Neng-Fa Zhou

CUNY Brooklyn College and Graduate Center, Brooklyn, USA
zhou@sci.brooklyn.cuny.edu

Abstract. Picat (picat-lang.org) is a logic-based multi-paradigm programming language that integrates logic programming, functional programming, constraint programming, and scripting. Picat takes many features from other languages, including logic variables, unification, backtracking, pattern-matching rules, functions, list/array comprehensions, loops, assignments, tabling for dynamic programming and planning, and constraint solving with CP (constraint programming), SAT (satisfiability), and MIP (mixed integer programming). These features make Picat more convenient than Prolog for scripting and modeling, and more suitable than functional languages (such as Haskell and F#) and scripting languages (such as Python and Ruby) for symbolic computations. This article provides a quick introduction to Picat using examples from Google Code Jam (GCJ).

Practical Knowledge Representation and Reasoning in Ergo

Michael Kifer, Theresa Swift, and Benjamin N. Grosof

Coherent Knowledge Systems, LLC

This tutorial covers the latest progress in Ergo[1], a cutting-edge practical knowledge representation and reasoning system. Ergo is the most complete and highly optimized implementation of Rulelog, an expressive yet scalable extension of Datalog and logic programs. Some of the salient (and often unique) features of Ergo include:

- *frame-based* object syntax [5]
- *higher-order* statements [3, 12]
- support for *general quantification and general formulas* [4]
- *dynamically* evolving knowledge [2]
- *hypothetical* reasoning
- *modularity*
- argumentation-based *defeasible reasoning* [10, 11]
- *user-defined functions*, which provide a limited form of functional programming
- *ErgoText*, which relates controlled natural language phrases (sprinkled with variables and other syntactic elements) to logic sentences
- *explanations* that are fully detailed, interactively navigable, and presented in natural language – understandable by those who are not expert in logic or programming [1]
- flexible probabilistic reasoning, including distribution semantics [9], evidential probability [6], and tight integration with inductive machine learning

Ergo also has connectors for fast loading of data, SQL and SPARQL querying, graph databases, Java and C interfaces, and more. Probabilistic uncertainty and machine learning capabilities are under development. In case studies, Ergo enables cost-effective, agile development of knowledge bases for automated decisions/analytics support in finance, defense, e-commerce, health, and in domains that utilize complex knowledge such as terminology mappings, policies, regulations, contracts, and science.

Much of this tutorial will be dedicated to Ergos development environment, *Ergo Studio*, especially to its unique advanced support for debugging knowledge. For instance, execution of Ergo queries can be paused and the state of the evaluation examined. Information that can be gleaned at that point includes the various statistics as well as indication of whether the query may be inefficient or even that it might not terminate. Ergos *Terminyzer* [7, 8] is a tool that performs a more detailed analysis and can point to the specific parts of the knowledge base that are likely to cause objectionable behavior. The user can also set up various *tripwires*, which would trigger

---

[1] Ergo is a product of Coherent Knowledge (coherentknowledge.com). It is available free of charge to selected academic researchers.

various actions if certain conditions are met. Last, but not least, Ergo can be asked to explain the answers it returns as well as the answers it does not return. These explanations can use either logical expressions or English sentences (through ErgoText).

In conclusion, we will also briefly discuss key frontiers for research, including probabilistic, machine learning, natural language, and multi-processor inferencing.

This tutorial requires prerequisite knowledge of neither Ergo nor Rulelog. However, familiarity with logic rules, semantic technology, and logic programming is very desirable.

References

1. Andersen, C., Benyo, B., Calejo, M., Dean, M., Fodor, P., Grosof, B.N., Kifer, M., Liang, S., Swift, T.: Advanced knowledge base debugging for rulelog. In: Joint Proceedings of the 7th International Rule Challenge, the Special Track on Human Language Technology and the 3rd RuleML Doctoral Consortium, Seattle, USA, July 11–13, 2013 (2013). http://ceur-ws.org/Vol-1004/paper8.pdf
2. Bonner, A., Kifer, M.: Transaction logic: Unifying declarative and procedural knowledge (1993), manuscript
3. Chen, W., Kifer, M., Warren, D.: HiLog: a foundation for higher-order logic programming. J. Logic Program. **15**(3), 187–230 (1993)
4. Grosof, B.: Rapid text-based authoring of defeasible higher-order logic formulas, via textual logic and rulelog. In: Morgenstern, L., Stefaneas, P., Lvy, F., Wyner, A., Paschke, A. (eds.) RuleML 2013, LNCS 8035, pp. 2–11. Springer, Heidelberg (2013). http://dx.doi.org/10.1007/978-3-642-39617-5_2
5. Kifer, M., Lausen, G., Wu, J.: Logical foundations of object-oriented and frame-based languages. J. ACM **42**, 741–843 (1995)
6. Kyburg, H., Teng, C.: Uncertain Inference. Cambridge University Press (2001)
7. Liang, S., Kifer, M.: A practical analysis of non-termination in large logic programs. Theor. Pract. Logic Program. **13**, 705–719 (2013)
8. Liang, S., Kifer, M.: Terminyzer: an automatic non-termination analyzer for large logic programs. In: Sagonas, K. (ed.) PADL 2013, LNCS 7752, pp. 173–189. Springer, Heidelberg (2013)
9. Riguzzi, F., Swift, T.: Well-definedness and efficient inference for probabilistic logic programming under the distribution semantics. Theor. Pract. Logic Program. **13**(2), 279–302 (2013)
10. Wan, H., Grosof, B., Kifer, M., Fodor, P., Liang, S.: Logic programming with defaults and argumentation theories. In: Hill, P.M., Warren, D.S. (eds.) ICLP 2009, LNCS 5649, pp. 432–448. Springer, Heidelberg (2009)
11. Wan, H., Kifer, M., Grosof, B.: Defeasibility in answer set programs with defaults and argumentation rules. Semant. Web J. (2014)
12. Yang, G., Kifer, M.: Reasoning about anonymous resources and meta statements on the Semantic Web. In: Spaccapietra et al. (eds.) Journal on Data Semantics 1, LNCS 2800, pp. 69–98. Springer, Heidelberg (2003)

The RuleML Knowledge-Interoperation Hub

Harold Boley

Faculty of Computer Science, University of New Brunswick, Fredericton,
Canada
harold[DT]boley[AT]unb[DT]ca

Abstract. The RuleML knowledge-interoperation hub provides for syntactic/
semantic representation and internal/external transformation of formal knowledge. The representation system permits the configuration of textbook and
enriched Relax NG syntax as well as the association of syntax with semantics.
The transformation tool suite includes serialized formatters (normalizers and
compactifiers), polarized parsers and generators (the RuleML↔POSL tool and
the RuleML→PSOA/PS generator and PSOA/PS→AST parser), as well as
importers and exporters (the importer from Dexlog to Naf Datalog RuleML and
the exporter from FOL RuleML languages to TPTP). An N3-PSOA-Flora
knowledge-interoperation use case is introduced for illustration.

Contents

Invited Papers

Programming in Picat

Neng-Fa Zhou[✉]

CUNY Brooklyn College and Graduate Center, Brooklyn, USA
zhou@sci.brooklyn.cuny.edu

Abstract. Picat (picat-lang.org) is a logic-based multi-paradigm programming language that integrates logic programming, functional programming, constraint programming, and scripting. Picat takes many features from other languages, including logic variables, unification, backtracking, pattern-matching rules, functions, list/array comprehensions, loops, assignments, tabling for dynamic programming and planning, and constraint solving with CP (constraint programming), SAT (satisfiability), and MIP (mixed integer programming). These features make Picat more convenient than Prolog for scripting and modeling, and more suitable than functional languages (such as Haskell and F#) and scripting languages (such as Python and Ruby) for symbolic computations. This article provides a quick introduction to Picat using examples from Google Code Jam (GCJ).

1 Introduction

Picat is a simple, and yet powerful, logic-based multi-paradigm programming language. The desire for a logic-based general-purpose programming language that is as powerful as Python for scripting, and on a par with OPL [8] and MiniZinc [11] for modeling combinatorial problems, led to the design of Picat. Early attempts to introduce arrays and loops into Prolog for modeling failed to produce a satisfactory language: most noticeably, array accesses are treated as functions only in certain contexts; and loops require the declaration of global variables in ECLiPSe [14] and local variables in B-Prolog [16].

Picat departs from Prolog in many aspects, including the successful introduction of arrays and loops. Picat uses pattern-matching rather than unification in the selection of rules. Unification might be a natural choice in Horn clause resolution [9] for theorem proving, but its power is rarely needed for general programming tasks. Pattern-matching rules are fully indexed, and therefore Picat can be more scalable than Prolog. Unification can be considered as an equation over terms [4], and just like constraints over finite domains, Picat supports unification as an explicit call.

Non-determinism, a powerful feature of logic programming, makes concise solutions possible for many problems, including simulation of non-deterministic automata, parsers of ambiguous grammars, and search problems. Nevertheless, non-determinism is not needed for deterministic computations. In Prolog, Horn clauses are backtrackable by default. As it is undecidable to detect determinism in general [5], programmers tend to excessively use the cut operator to

© Springer International Publishing Switzerland 2016
J.J. Alferes et al. (Eds.): RuleML 2016, LNCS 9718, pp. 3–18, 2016.
DOI: 10.1007/978-3-319-42019-6_1

prune unnecessary clauses. Picat supports explicit non-determinism, which renders the cut operator unnecessary. Rules are deterministic unless they are explicitly denoted as backtrackable.

Picat supports functions, like many other logic-based languages, such as Curry [7], Erlang [2], and Mozart-Oz [13]. In Prolog, it's often that queries fail, but the system gives no clue about the source of the failure. Functions should be used instead of relations, unless multiple answers are required. Functions are more convenient to use than predicates because (1) functions are guaranteed to succeed with a return value; (2) function calls can be nested; and (3) the directionality of functions enhances the readability.

Many combinatorial problems can be formulated as constraint satisfaction problems (CSPs). There are three kinds of systematic solvers for solving CSPs, namely, Constraint Programming (CP), Mixed Integer Programming (MIP), and SAT solving. CP uses constraint propagation to prune search spaces, and uses heuristics to guide search [12]. MIP relies on LP relaxation and branch-and-cut to find optimal integer solutions [1]. SAT performs unit propagation and clause learning to prune search spaces, and employs heuristics and learned clauses to perform non-chronological backtracking [10]. No solver is superior all the time; sometimes, extensive experimentation is necessary to find a suitable solver.

Picat provides a common interface with CP, SAT, and MIP solvers for solving CSPs. For each solver, Picat provides a separate module of built-ins for creating decision variables, specifying constraints, and invoking the solver. The common interface allows for seamless switching from one solver to another. The basic language constructs, such as arrays and loops, make Picat a powerful modeling language for these solvers.

The PicatSAT compiler [20] employs hybrid encodings to translate finite-domain variables and constraints into compact and efficient CNF (conjunctive-normal-form) codes. The SAT module is superior to the CP module for not only Boolean problems but also many problems that involve arithmetic and global constraints.

Tabling [15] can be employed to cache the results of certain calculations in memory and reuse them in subsequent calculations through a quick table lookup. As computer memory grows, tabling is becoming increasingly important for offering dynamic programming solutions for many problems. Picat's tabling system is inherited from B-Prolog [22].

Picat has a planner module. For a planning problem, the programmer only needs to specify conditions on the final states and the set of actions, and to call the planner on an initial state to find a plan or an optimal plan. The planner, which is implemented by the use of tabling, performs a state-space search and tables every state that is encountered during search.

A joint effort by the system and the programmer is needed to deal with the state explosion problem. The Picat system stores all structured ground terms in a table, so ground terms that are shared by states are only tabled once. The enhanced *hash-consing* technique [19] also stores hash codes in order to speed up computation of hash codes and equality tests of terms. The Picat system also performs *resource-bounded tabled search*, which prunes parts of the search space that cannot lead to acceptable plans. In order to exploit these techniques, the programmer needs to design a good representation for states that facilitates sharing and removes symmetries. For certain problems, the programmer can also employ domain knowledge and heuristics to help prune the search space.

Picat's planner has produced surprising and encouraging results [3,17]. It overwhelmingly outperforms the cutting-edge ASP and PDDL planners on many benchmarks used in recent ASP and IPC competitions.

This paper gives programs in Picat for several Google Code Jam (GCJ) practice problems. The objective is to provide a quick introduction to the Picat language, the library, and the programming techniques. More details of the Picat language can be found in the User's Guide [18]. The constraint programming and planning modules are detailed in the book [21], which includes a short account, by Agostino Dovier, of the history of logic programming that led to the design of Picat. Solutions in Picat for several GCJ problems that utilize tabling and constraints can be found in [6]. Many more programs for GCJ problems can be found at:

   http://picat-lang.org/gcj/index.html

2   Store Credit

Store Credit is another easy practice problem[1]. A test case consists of an integer C, which is the store credit you receive, and a sequence of integers, which are prices of the available items. The output for a test case consists of the indices, i and j $(i < j)$, of the two items whose prices add up to the store credit. It is assumed that each test case will have exactly one solution.

```
main =>
    T = read_int(),
    foreach (TC in 1..T)
        C = read_int(),
        N = read_int(),
        Items = {read_int() : _ in 1..N},
        do_case(TC, C, Items)
    end.

do_case(TC, C, Items),
    between(1, len(Items)-1, I),
    between(I+1, len(Items), J),
    C == Items[I]+Items[J]
=>
    printf("Case #%w: %w %w\n", TC, I, J).
```

---

[1] https://code.google.com/codejam/contest/351101/dashboard#s=p0.

The function `read_int()` reads an integer from the standard input `stdin`. The `main` predicate reads T, the number of test cases. For each test case number TC, the `foreach` loop reads the store credit C, the number of available items N, and the sequence of prices of the items `Items`. For each test case, the predicate `do_case` searches for two indices, I and J (I < J), that satisfies the condition C == `Items[I]+Items[J]`, and prints out the answer.

The expression `{read_int() : _ in 1..N}` is called an *array comprehension*, which returns an array consisting of N integers read from `stdin`.

The array comprehension `{read_int() : _ in 1..N}` is equivalent to:

```
[read_int() : _ in 1..N].to_array()
```

which creates a list using a list comprehension, and converts the list to an array. Since the array comprehension creates a temporary list, the following code is more efficient:

```
Items = new_array(N),
foreach (I in 1..N)
    Items[I] = read_int()
end,
```

The function `new_array(N)` returns a new array of N elements. Initially, all the elements are distinct variables. The `foreach` loop fills in the array with integers from the input.

In Picat, the function `len(L)` returns the length of L, and the index operator `L[I]` returns the Ith element of L. While `len(L)` and `L[I]` take constant time when L is an array, they take linear time when L is a list. For this reason the program uses an array, rather than a list, to store the prices.

The `do_case` predicate uses a *failure-driven loop* to enumerate I, over the range `1..len(Items)-1`, and J, over the range `I+1..len(Items)`, until a pair of indices is found that satisfies the condition C == `Items[I]+Items[J]`. It encodes the *generate-and-test* algorithm. The predicate call `between(From, To, X)` is a *choice point*, which non-deterministically selects a value from the range $From..To$ for X. It first binds X to $From$. When execution backtracks to the call, it binds X to $From + 1$ if $From + 1$ is not greater than To. Execution can backtrack to the call as long as there are untried values in the range. The call fails when execution backtracks to it, and all values have been tried. When this calls fails, execution will continue to backtrack to another call that is a choice point.

The operator == tests if two terms are identical, and the operator = performs *unification* on two terms. The *unification* $T_1 = T_2$ is true if term T_1 and term T_2 can be made identical by binding some of the variables to values.

The `do_case` predicate can be implemented as follows using a `foreach` loop:

```
do_case(TC, C, Items) =>
    foreach(I in 1..len(Items)-1, J in I+1..len(Items))
        if (C == Items[I]+Items[J]) then
            printf("Case #%w: %w %w\n", TC, I, J)
        end
    end.
```

Nevertheless, this implementation is not as preferable as the failure-driven loop, because the `foreach` loop continues to check all the remaining pairs, even after a satisfying pair has been found. Picat does not provide statements like the `break` or `return` statements in procedural languages that can terminate loops early.

The above program takes $O(n^2)$ time, where n is the number of items. It can be improved by using a map to speed up search. The following gives an improved version:

```
main =>
    T = read_int(),
    foreach (TC in 1..T)
        C = read_int(),
        N = read_int(),
        Items = {read_int() : _ in 1..N},
        Map = new_map(),
        foreach (I in N..-1..1)
            Is = Map.get(Items[I], []),
            Map.put(Items[I],[I|Is])
        end,
        do_case(TC, C, Items, Map)
    end.

do_case(TC, C, Items, Map),
    between(1, len(Items)-1, I),
    Js = Map.get(C-Items[I], []),
    member(J, Js),
    I < J
=>
    printf("Case #%w: %w %w\n", TC, I, J).
```

The function `new_map()` returns a new map. The function put(*Map, Key, Value*) puts the pair (*Key, Value*) into *Map*. The function get(*Map, Key, DefaultVal*) returns the value associated with *Key* in *Map*; it returns *DefaultVal* if *Map* does not contain *Key*.

The `foreach` loop below `new_map()` inserts a key-value pair for each price into the map, where the key is the price, and the value is a list of indices at which the price occurs in the array. Note that the loop iterates over the indices from N down to 1. The indices associated with each price are added to the front of the list, from the largest to the smallest. In this way, the resulting list of indices for each price will be sorted in ascending order.

The `do_case` predicate does the following: For each I in 1..len(Items)-1, and for each J in Js (which is the list of indices associated with the value C-Items[I]), if I < J, then (I, J) is a satisfying pair of indices. The call member(J, Js) non-deterministically selects a value from Js for J.

3   Minimum Scalar Product

This problem is from Round 1 A 2008[2]. Given two vectors $v_1 = (x_1, x_2, \ldots, x_n)$ and $v_2 = (y_1, y_2, \ldots, y_n)$, the problem is to choose a permutation of v_1 and a permutation of v_2 such that the scalar product of these two permutations is the smallest possible, and output that minimum scalar product.

Like many other GCJ problems, this problem requires insightful reasoning. The brute-force approach that enumerates all of the permutations cannot be scaled to handle large vectors. Let $v_1 = (x_1, x_2)$ and $v_2 = (y_1, y_2)$. Assume $x_1 \leq x_2$ and $y_1 \leq y_2$. It is not difficult to prove that

$$x_1 \times y_2 + x_2 \times y_1 \leq x_1 \times y_1 + x_2 \times y_2.$$

In general, in order to get the minimum product, we can sort v_1 in ascending order and sort v_2 is descending order, and multiply the sorted vectors.

```
main =>
    T = read_int(),
    foreach (I in 1..T)
        do_case(I)
    end.

do_case(TC) =>
    N = read_int(),
    V1 = [read_int() : _ in 1..N].sort(),
    V2 = [read_int() : _ in 1..N].sort_down(),
    Prod = sum([E1*E2 : {E1,E2} in zip(V1,V2)]),
    printf("Case #%w: %w%n", TC, Prod).
```

The sort(L) function returns a sorted list of L in ascending order, and the sort_down(L) function returns a sorted list of L is descending order. These sort functions can be utilized to sort a list of any terms. The expression

```
sum([E1*E2 : {E1,E2} in zip(V1,V2)])
```

gives the product of the two vectors V1 and V2. The function zip(V1,V2) returns a zipped list of pairs from V1 and V2. For example, zip([1,2],[3,4]) returns a list of two pairs: {1,3} and {2,4}. This expression sums E1*E2 for each pair {E1,E2} in the zipped list of V1 and V2. For this expression, the Picat compiler generates code for evaluating the expression without actually creating a zipped list or a list for the list comprehension.

Let's see how to implement the brute-force algorithm for the problem. We don't need to try all permutations of both vectors. We can fix v_1 and choose a permutation of v_2 such that the product of v_1 and the permutation is minimum. This brute-force algorithm is not efficient, but it can handle the small test.

---

[2] https://code.google.com/codejam/contest/32016/dashboard#s=p0.

```
import util.

main =>
    T = read_int(),
    foreach (I in 1..T)
        do_case(I)
    end.

do_case(Case) =>
    N = read_int(),
    V1 = [read_int() : _ in 1..N],
    V2 = [read_int() : _ in 1..N],
    minof(scalar_prod(V1,V2,Prod),Prod),
    printf("Case #%w: %w%n", Case, Prod).

scalar_prod(V1,V2,Prod) =>
    permutation(V2,V22),
    Prod = sum([E1*E2 : {E1,E2} in zip(V1,V22)]).
```

The predicate permutation(V2,V22), which is defined in the util module, non-deterministically binds V22 to a permutation of V2. For a permutation V22 of V2, the predicate scalar_prod(V1,V2,Prod) binds Prod to the product of V1 and V22. Since the permutation predicate is non-deterministic, the scalar_prod predicate is also non-deterministic. The built-in predicate minof(scalar_prod(V1,V2,Prod),Prod) returns an instance of the predicate call scalar_prod(V1,V2,Prod) that has the smallest Prod[3].

It is also possible to iterate over all of the permutations to find the best permutation that gives the minimum product[4]. Nevertheless, the backtracking-based approach is more memory efficient than the iterative approach, since it does not use any memory to store all the permutations.

The following shows how the permutation predicate is implemented in Picat:

```
permutation([], P) => P = [].
permutation(L, P) =>
    P = [X|P1],
    select(X, L, L1),
    permutation(L1, P1).

select(X, [Y|L], L1) ?=> Y = X, L1 = L.
select(X, [Y|L], L1) => L1 = [Y|L2], select(X, L, L2).
```

---

[3] The minof predicate, which takes another predicate call as the first argument, is called a higher-order predicate. Picat provides several higher-order built-ins. For example, maxof(*Goal,Exp*), find_all(*Template,Goal*), and count_all(*Goal*).

[4] The function permutations(*L*), which is defined in the util module, returns a list of permutations of *L*.

This implementation utilizes pattern-matching rules, where the heads contain non-variable patterns. The first rule states that the permutation of [] is []. For a non-empty list L, the second rule is applied. The call P = [X|P1] binds P to the list constructed by the *cons* operator [X|P1]. The call select(X, L, L1) non-deterministically selects an element X from L, resulting in a new list L1. The last call permutation(L1, P1) generates a permutation P1 of L1.

The implementation of select uses a *backtrackable* rule, as denoted by the operator ? =>. Because of the use of this backtrackable rule, this predicate becomes *non-deterministic*, and it is able to return multiple answers. For example:

```
Picat> select(X,[1,2,3],L1)
X = 1
L1 = [2,3] ?;
X = 2
L1 = [1,3] ?;
X = 3
L1 = [1,2] ?;
no
```

After Picat returns an answer, you can type a semicolon immediately after the answer to let the system backtrack; the system reports no if no answer remains.

4   Alien Numbers

This is Problem A in the set of practice problems[5]. The objective of the problem is to convert a number from one alien numeral system, called the source language, to another alien numeral system, called the target language. Each numeral system consists of a set of "digits", and the size of the set is the base.

For a number in the source language, the conversion can be done in two steps: first convert the number to a decimal number, and then convert the decimal number to the target language. For each language, we use a map in order to map the digits to their values, the first digit to 0, the second digit to 1, and so on.

```
import util.  % use split

main =>
    T = to_int(read_line()),
    foreach (TC in 1..T)
        [Num,SDs,TDs] = read_line().split(),
        do_case(TC, Num, SDs, TDs)
    end.

do_case(TC, Num, SDs, TDs) =>
    SMap = new_map(),
    SBase = len(SDs),
    foreach ({D, DVal} in zip(SDs, 0..SBase-1))
```

---

[5] https://code.google.com/codejam/contest/32003/dashboard#s=p0.

```
            SMap.put(D,DVal)
        end,
        source_to_decimal(Num, SBase, SMap, 0, SVal),
        %
        TMap = new_map(),
        TBase = len(TDs),
        foreach ({D, DVal} in zip(TDs, 0..TBase-1))
            TMap.put(DVal,D)
        end,
        decimal_to_target(SVal, TBase, TMap, TNum),
        printf("Case #%w: %s\n", TC, TNum).

source_to_decimal([], _Base, _Map, Val0, Val) => Val = Val0.
source_to_decimal([D|Ds], Base, Map, Val0, Val) =>
    source_to_decimal(Ds, Base, Map, Val0*Base+Map.get(D), Val).

decimal_to_target(0, _Base, Map, Num) => Num = [Map.get(0)].
decimal_to_target(Val, Base, Map, Num) =>
    Ds = [],
    while (Val !== 0)
        DVal := Val mod Base,
        Val := Val div Base,
        Ds := [Map.get(DVal)|Ds]
    end,
    Num = Ds.
```

Each test case consists of a number string Num, a list of digits SDs in the source language, and a list of digits TDs in the target language. For the source language, the program uses SMap to map the digits to the values, and stores the base in SBase.

Let $[D_{n-1}, D_{n-2}, \ldots, D_1, D_0]$ be a number string of the source language that has the base B. This string represents the decimal value: $D_{n-1} * B^{n-1} + D_{n-2} * B^{n-2} + \ldots + D_1 * B^1 + D_0$. The predicate source_to_decimal(Num, Base, Map, Val0, Val) uses tail recursion to convert the number string Num into decimal: If Num is empty, then the result Val is bound to the accumulator Val0; otherwise, if Num is a list [D|Ds], then it recurses on Ds using Val0*Base+Map.get(D) as the new accumulator value. The accumulator value in the initial call to source_to_decimal is 0.

Let $D_{n-1} * B^{n-1} + D_{n-2} * B^{n-2} + \ldots + D_1 * B^1 + D_0$ be the decimal value and B be the base of the target language. The digits can be extracted using the *divide-by-base* algorithm. When the value is divided by the base B, the remainder is D_0, and the quotient is $D_{n-1} * B^{n-2} + D_{n-2} * B^{n-3} + \ldots + D_1$. This division step is repeatedly applied to the value until the value becomes 0. The predicate decimal_to_target(Val, Base, Map, Num) converts the decimal value Val to a number string of the target language. If Val is 0, then the string only consists of the 0-value digit. Otherwise, the predicate uses the divide-by-base algorithm to extract the digits.

The predicate `decimal_to_target` illustrates the use of the `while` loop and the assignment operator `:=` in Picat. A while loop takes the form

```
while (Cond)
    Goal
end
```

It repeatedly executes *Goal* as long as *Cond* succeeds. For the assignment $X := Exp$, Picat introduces a new variable to hold the value of *Exp*; after that, this new variable replaces all of the occurrences of X in the scope. Because of variable cloning, no values can be returned using assignments. For example, if the unification `Num = Ds` in the `decimal_to_target` predicate were changed to `Num := Ds`, then the result would never be returned to the caller through the variable `Num`.

5 Alien Language

Alien Language involves matching words in an alien language against patterns[6]. A pattern consists of tokens, where each token is either a single lowercase letter or a group of unique lowercase letters surrounded by parentheses (and). For example: `(ab)d(dc)` means the first letter is either `a` or `b`, the second letter is definitely `d`, and the last letter is either `d` or `c`. Therefore, the pattern `(ab)d(dc)` can stand for any one of these 4 possibilities: `add`, `adc`, `bdd`, `bdc`. Each test case is a pattern. The output for the case indicates how many of the given words match the pattern.

The problem can be solved by pattern matching. For a letter in a word, if the token is also a letter, then the match succeeds iff the two letters are identical; otherwise, if the token is a group, then the match succeeds iff the letter is included in the group.

```
import util.

main =>
    [_L,D,T] = [to_int(W) : W in read_line().split()],
    Words = [read_line() : _ in 1..D],
    foreach(TC in 1..T)
        do_case(TC, Words)
    end.

do_case(TC, Words) =>
    trans_pattern(read_line(), P),
    printf("Case #%w: %w%n", TC,
                        sum([1 : Word in Words, match(Word, P)])).

trans_pattern([], P) => P = [].
```

---

[6] https://code.google.com/codejam/contest/90101/dashboard#s=p0&a=1.

```
trans_pattern(['('|S], P) =>
    P = [G|PR],
    trans_pattern_group(S, SR, G),
    trans_pattern(SR, PR).
trans_pattern([X|S], P) =>
    P = [X|PR],
    trans_pattern(S, PR).

trans_pattern_group([')'|S], SR, G) =>
    G = [], S = SR.
trans_pattern_group([X|S], SR, G) =>
    G = [X|GR],
    trans_pattern_group(S, SR, GR).

match([], []) => true.
match([A|As], [A|Ps]) =>
    match(As, Ps).
match([A|As], [L|Ps]), member(A,L) =>
    match(As, Ps).
```

The first line in the body of the main predicate reads three integers from the input: the length of each of the words _L, the number of words D, and the number of test cases T. The value _L is not used later in the program[7]. The list comprehension [read_line() : _ in 1..D] reads D lines into a list. For each test case, the do_case predicate reads the pattern, transforms the pattern into a list, and counts the words that match the pattern.

The predicate trans_pattern(S, P) transforms the pattern string S into a list P. A letter is copied into the list. For a group that is surrounded by parentheses, the call trans_pattern_group(S, SR, G) extracts the letters from the group and puts them into the list G; SR holds the remainder of S after the extraction. For example, for the pattern "(ab)d(dc)", the list obtained after transformation is [[a,b],d,[d,c]]. The matching of a word against a pattern is done by the match predicate.

Since a group is represented as a list, it takes $O(n)$ time to check if a letter is in a group of size n. The above program can be improved by using a set for each group.

```
trans_pattern([], P) => P = [].
trans_pattern(['('|S], P) =>
    P = [G|PR],
    G = new_set(),
    trans_pattern_group(S, SR, G),
    trans_pattern(SR, PR).
trans_pattern([X|S], P) =>
```

---

[7] Picat does not issue singleton variable warnings for variable names that begin with the underscore _.

```
    P = [X|PR],
    trans_pattern(S, PR).

trans_pattern_group([')'|S], SR, _G) =>  S = SR.
trans_pattern_group([X|S], SR, G) =>
    G.put(X),
    trans_pattern_group(S, SR, G).

match([], []) => true.
match([A|As], [P|Ps]), atom(P) =>
    A == P,
    match(As, Ps).
match([A|As], [G|Ps]), G.has_key(A) =>
    match(As, Ps).
```

The call new_set() returns a new empty set. For each pattern group that begins with '(', the call trans_pattern_group(S, SR, G) adds every letter X in the group into set G using the function G.put(X). The match predicate uses G.has_key(A) to test if letter A is in group G.

6   Egg Drop

Egg Drop is an optimization problem that involves three parameters: the number of floors F in a building, the number of drops D that you are allowed to perform, and the number of eggs B that you can break[8]. You are assumed to have at least D eggs. All eggs are identical in terms of the shell's strength. If an egg breaks when dropped from floor i, then all eggs are guaranteed to break when dropped from any floor $j \geq i$. Likewise, if an egg doesn't break when dropped from floor i, then all eggs are guaranteed to never break when dropped from any floor $j \leq i$. For each floor in the building, you want to know whether or not an egg dropped from that floor will break.

The problem can be posted in three different ways, depending on which parameter is to be optimized. The first variant is to determine the maximum number of floors that can be examined when D and B are given. If $D = 0$ or $B = 0$, then no floors can be examined, so $F = 0$. If $B = 1$, then what you can do is to try the floors, starting at floor 1, until the egg breaks or you have dropped D times; so $F = D$. In general, let $f(D, B)$ be the number of floors that can be examined with D drops and B breaks. There are two possible outcomes when dropping an egg from floor k, an optimal floor number to start. If the egg breaks, then the $k - 1$ floors that are below floor k need to be examined, and the number of remaining breaks becomes $B - 1$. If the egg does not break, then the floors above floor k need to be examined, and the number of remaining breaks remains to be B. The function can be defined recursively as:

---

[8] https://code.google.com/codejam/contest/32003/dashboard#s=p2.

```
f(0, _) = 0.
f(_, 0) = 0.
f(D, B) = f(D-1, B) + f(D-1, B-1) + 1.
```

This function grows exponentially, and dynamic programming can be used to speed up the computation. Since the problem requires outputting -1 if the value is greater than or equal to 2^{32} for given B and D, calls with large arguments are guaranteed to return -1, and therefore do not need to be tabled.

The second variant of the problem is to find the minimum number of drops D given F and B, and the third variant is to find the minimum number of breaks B given F and D. These variants can also be solved using dynamic programming. However, since the input values can be as large as 2 billion, the dynamic programming approach is not feasible. A more efficient approach is to use binary search to find the smallest value for which the F floors can be examined.

```
main =>
    T = read_int(),
    foreach (TC in 1..T)
        F = read_int(), D = read_int(), B = read_int(),
        do_case(TC, F, D, B)
    end.

do_case(TC, F, D, B) =>
    MF = max_f(D, B),
    min_d(F, MD, B),
    min_b(F, D, MB),
    printf("Case #%w: %w %w %w\n", TC, MF, MD, MB).

% maximize F for given D and B
max_f(D, B) = F, D >= 100000, B >= 2 =>  F = -1.
max_f(D, B) = F, D >= 10000, B >= 3 =>  F = -1.
max_f(D, B) = F, D >= 1000, B >= 4 =>  F = -1.
max_f(D, B) = F, B > D => F = max_f(D, D).
max_f(D, B) = f(D, B).

table
f(_, 0) =  0.
f(D, 1) =  D.
f(0, _) =  0.
f(1, _) =  1.
f(D, B) =  F =>
    F1 = f(D-1,B),
    F2 = f(D-1,B-1),
    if F1 == -1 ; F2 == -1 then
        F = -1
    else
        F0 = F1+F2+1,
```

```
      F = cond(F0 >= 2**32, -1, F0)
   end.

% minimize D for given F and B
min_d(F, D, B) =>
    bsearch_d(0, F, F, D, B).

bsearch_d(From, To, F, D, B), From >= To =>
    D = cond((max_f(From, B) >= F ; max_f(From, B) == -1), From, From+1).
bsearch_d(From, To, F, D, B) =>
    Mid = (From+To) div 2,
    if max_f(Mid, B) == F then
        D = Mid
    elseif max_f(Mid, B) == -1 ; max_f(Mid, B) > F then
        bsearch_d(From, Mid-1, F, D, B)
    else
        bsearch_d(Mid+1, To, F, D, B)
    end.

% minimize B for given F and D
min_b(F, D, B) =>
    bsearch_b(0, F, F, D, B).

bsearch_b(From, To, F, D, B), From >= To =>
    B = cond((max_f(D, From) >= F ; max_f(D, From) == -1), From, From+1).
bsearch_b(From, To, F, D, B) =>
    Mid = (From+To) div 2,
    if max_f(D, Mid) == F then
        B = Mid
    elseif max_f(D, Mid) == -1 ; max_f(D, Mid) > F then
        bsearch_b(From, Mid-1, F, D, B)
    else
        bsearch_b(Mid+1, To, F, D, B)
    end.
```

The function max_f(D, B) returns the maximum number of floors that can be examined with D drops and B breaks. It returns -1 for certain combinations of values of D and B, where f(D, B) $\geq 2^{32}$. It is necessary to filter out these cases because the function f(D, B) takes $O(D \times B)$ table space.

In the implementation of function f(D, B), the values from f(D-1, B) and f(D-1, B-1) are combined in such a way that -1 is returned if either value is -1 or if f(D-1, B) + f(D-1, B-1) + 1 is greater than or equal to 2^{32}.

The min_d(F, D, B) and min_b(F, D, B) predicates implement binary search for finding the minimum D and the minimum B, respectively. In Picat, $(A; B)$ is a disjunction, (A, B) is a conjunction, and cond(C, A, B) is a conditional expression, which gives the value of A if C if true and the value of B if C is false. Since ';' has lower precedence than ',', C must be parenthesized if it is a disjunction.

7   Summary

This article has provided a quick introduction to Picat using examples from GCJ. The Picat implementation is generally as fast as the Python implementation; for programs that use tail recursion, Picat can be significantly faster than Python because Picat performs tail recursion optimization.

Despite a young language, Picat has attracted considerable attention recently. Several contestants have used Picat in recent GCJ competitions. In order to perform well in a competition like GCJ, one requires a comprehensive set of skills, including reading, reasoning, coding, and testing skills. Picat's features allow for concise description of problem solutions, and can give contestants a competitive edge in coding. GCJ problems tend to have insidious smart algorithms. Picat sometimes can provide an alternative way to solve a problem in case one cannot come up with the insight during a competition.

Acknowledgement. The author would like to thank Sergii Dymchenko for bring GCJ to his attention, and the following people for giving very helpful comments on early drafts of this article: Roman Barták, Peter Bernschneider, Mike Bionchik, Jonathan Fruhman, Håkan Kjellerstrand, Annie Liu, Claudio Cesar de Sá, and Bo Yuan (Bobby) Zhou.

References

1. Appa, G.M., Pitsoulis, L., Springer, H., Williams, P.: Handbook on Modelling for Discrete Optimization. International Series in Operations Research & Management Science. Springer, New York (2010)
2. Armstrong, J.: Programming Erlang, 2nd edn. Pragmatic Press, Dallas (2013)
3. Barták, R., Dovier, A., Zhou, N.-F.: On modeling planning problems in tabled logic programming. In: Proceedings of the 17th ACM International Symposium on Principles and Practice of Declarative Programming, PPDP 2015, pp. 31–42 (2015)
4. Colmerauer, A.: Equations and inequations on finite and infinite trees. In: Proceedings of FGCS, pp. 85–99. ICOT (1984)
5. Debray, S.K.: Static inference of modes and data dependencies in logic programs. ACM Trans. Program. Lang. Syst. **11**(3), 418–450 (1989)
6. Dymchenko, S., Mykhailova, M.: Declaratively solving Google Code Jam problems with Picat. In: Pontelli, E., Son, T.C. (eds.) PADL 2015. LNCS, vol. 9131, pp. 50–57. Springer, Heidelberg (2015)
7. Hanus, M.: Functional logic programming: from theory to Curry. In: Voronkov, A., Weidenbach, C. (eds.) Programming Logics. LNCS, vol. 7797, pp. 123–168. Springer, Heidelberg (2013)
8. Van Hentenryck, P.: Constraint and integer programming in OPL. INFORMS J. Comput. **14**, 345–372 (2002)
9. Kowalski, R., Kuehner, D.: Linear resolution with selection function. Artif. Intell. **2**(3–4), 227–260 (1971)
10. Malik, S., Zhang, L.: Boolean satisfiability: from theoretical hardness to practical success. Commun. ACM **52**(8), 76–82 (2009)
11. Nethercote, N., Stuckey, P.J., Becket, R., Brand, S., Duck, G.J., Tack, G.: MiniZinc: towards a standard CP modelling language. In: CP, pp. 529–543 (2007)

12. Rossi, F., van Beek, P., Walsh, T.: Handbook of Constraint Programming. Elsevier, Amsterdam (2006)
13. Van Roy, P., Haridi, S.: Concepts, Techniques, and Models of Computer Programming. MIT Press, Cambridge (2004)
14. Schimpf, J.: Logical loops. In: Stuckey, P.J. (ed.) ICLP 2002. LNCS, vol. 2401, pp. 224–238. Springer, Heidelberg (2002)
15. Warren, D.S.: Memoing for logic programs. Commun. ACM, Special Sect. Logic Program. **35**, 93–111 (1992)
16. Zhou, N.-F.: The language features and architecture of B-Prolog. Theory Pract. Logic Program., Special Issue Prolog Syst. **12**(1–2), 189–218 (2012)
17. Zhou, N.-F., Bartak, R., Dovier, A.: Planning as tabled logic programming. Theory Pract. Logic Program. **15**, 543–558 (2015)
18. Zhou, N.-F., Fruhman, J.: A User's Guide to Picat. http://picat-lang.org
19. Zhou, N.-F., Have, C.T.: Efficient tabling of structured data with enhanced hash-consing. Theory Pract. Logic Program. **12**(4–5), 547–563 (2012)
20. Zhou, N.-F., Kjellerstrand, H.: The Picat-SAT compiler. In: Gavanelli, M., Reppy, J. (eds.) PADL 2016. LNCS, vol. 9585, pp. 48–62. Springer, Heidelberg (2016). doi:10.1007/978-3-319-28228-2_4
21. Zhou, N.-F., Kjellerstrand, H., Fruhman, J.: Constraint Solving and Planning with Picat. SpringerBriefs in Intelligent Systems. Springer, Heidelberg (2015)
22. Zhou, N.-F., Sato, T., Shen, Y.-D.: Linear tabling strategies and optimizations. Theory Pract. Logic Program. **8**(1), 81–109 (2008)

The RuleML Knowledge-Interoperation Hub

Harold Boley[✉]

Faculty of Computer Science, University of New Brunswick, Fredericton, Canada
harold.boley@unb.ca

Abstract. The RuleML knowledge-interoperation hub provides for syntactic/semantic representation and internal/external transformation of formal knowledge. The representation system permits the configuration of textbook and enriched Relax NG syntax as well as the association of syntax with semantics. The transformation tool suite includes serialized formatters (normalizers and compactifiers), polarized parsers and generators (the RuleML↔POSL tool and the RuleML→PSOA/PS generator and PSOA/PS→AST parser), as well as importers and exporters (the importer from Dexlog to Naf Datalog RuleML and the exporter from FOL RuleML languages to TPTP). An N3-PSOA-Flora knowledge-interoperation use case is introduced for illustration.

1 Introduction

RuleML focuses on structured knowledge, as used, e.g., in data, domain, and process modeling. Such knowledge is often represented with ontologies and rules, which may be combined in hybrid or homogeneous ways. Description logics, underlying various ontologies, can be homogeneously combined with the decidable Datalog$^\pm$ [1], a compact rule language including head existentials; corresponding rule engines are being increasingly used for efficient ontology reasoning [2]. Similarly, ontological subsumption axioms and rule-based mappings can be combined for uniform Rule-Based Data Access [3]. Moreover, Inductive (Functional-Logic) Programming is based on the rule paradigm, and employed in industrial applications [4]. When decidability of querying is not aimed for, knowledge-representation expressivity can be extended from Datalog, Datalog$^\pm$, and description logics to, e.g., Datalog$^+$, Horn logic, as well as FOL and higher-order rule languages.

This article presents the RuleML hub for interoperating structured knowledge formalized via a system of rule families ranging from declarative/deliberative condition-conclusion rules to stateful/reactive event-condition-action rules.

Formal rule knowledge can be collected in knowledge bases (KBs) and transformed on a network such as an intranet or the Internet, specifically the Web. Utilizing a hub and spoke model, *knowledge interoperation* benefits from a canonical knowledge-representation language allowing knowledge transformation via translators mapping through this canonical form. RuleML as an open non-profit organization has developed a series of rule specifications leading to Version 1.02[1]

---

[1] http://wiki.ruleml.org/index.php/Specification_of_RuleML_1.02.

© Springer International Publishing Switzerland 2016
J.J. Alferes et al. (Eds.): RuleML 2016, LNCS 9718, pp. 19–33, 2016.
DOI: 10.1007/978-3-319-42019-6_2

of the RuleML system, whose novel Consumer RuleML family achieves an initial integration of the main Deliberation and Reaction RuleML families.

The Web-based RuleML tools for knowledge interoperation (representation and transformation) have reached a critical mass, where synergies are becoming possible such as novel chains of translators mapping through RuleML/XML. A variety of useful interoperation tools is described on, or linked from, the categorized RuleML Wiki[2] (currently consisting of 1247 pages), although they have not yet been discussed in a synthesis article, in spite of interoperation being central to RuleML.

The current presentation thus gives a top-down account of the RuleML knowledge-interoperation hub, focusing on advances in syntactic/semantic representation and internal/external transformation. The two main knowledge-interoperation components will be expanded in Sect. 2, on knowledge representation, and Sect. 3, on knowledge transformation, followed, in Sect. 4, by a knowledge-interoperation use case and, in Sect. 5, conclusions.

2 Knowledge Representation System

The RuleML knowledge-representation architecture consists of a system of families of **languages** of XML-serialized instance documents (containing KBs and queries) specified syntactically through schemas (for Deliberation RuleML, normatively in Relax NG, from which XSD is generated) and associated with semantic **profiles** through syntax-semantics-pairing **logics** as appropriate. For each pair $logic = (language, profile)$, $language$ is predefined but $profile$ and $logic$ are predefined or user-defined (where $logic$ can be predefined only if $profile$ is).

2.1 Configuration of Textbook and Enriched Relax NG Syntax

RuleML's modular schemas permit rule interchange with high precision. Deliberation RuleML 1.0 introduced a modularization approach based on the schema language Relax NG [5], restricted to be *monotonic*: When two modules are combined, e.g. by including them both into a larger schema, the language defined by the larger schema contains both of the languages defined by the modules. Because of this monotonicity property, the more than fifty Deliberation RuleML 1.02 schema modules may be freely combined to define a fine-grained poset lattice of languages, with a partial order based on syntactic language containment.

To select from the many resulting predefined languages of the Deliberation RuleML family, the Modular sYNtax confiGurator (MYNG) application [6] was developed for providing a unified parameterized schema accessible either directly, using a REST interface, or through a GUI that exposes the REST interface.

MYNG may be used to configure a RuleML language with a set of desired features. Relax NG schemas configured using MYNG 1.02[3] may be employed

---

[2] http://wiki.ruleml.org/index.php/Special:Categories.
[3] http://deliberation.ruleml.org/1.02/myng/.

outside of MYNG for schema-aware authoring, instance validation, or parser generation through XML tools such as oXygen XML and JAXB.

All MYNG-configured RuleML languages have a unique myng-code URL. Members of the subset of *anchor languages* additionally have a (composite) name. An example from Deliberation RuleML is the anchor language Datalog$^+$ (more precisely, the language defined by its Relax NG schema[4]). Starting with its Version 1.01, an "Instructive KB"[5] has been made available including examples from [1]. This KB (with embedded queries) has acted as a Datalog$^+$ RuleML paradigm also for the Rulebase Competition 2014 held at the 8th International Rule Challenge[6], whose KBs from the RCC-geospatial, investment-regulation, and car-insurance domains, along with their descriptions in the proceedings papers, are collected in one place[7].

RuleML – as a rich knowledge modeling system supporting, e.g., Web rules – comes with supplementary features for (Semantic) Web applications such as (optional) IRIs, OIDs, types, and slots in its specification of anchor languages, including Datalog($^+$), Hornlog($^+$), and FOLog. For users who just need unsupplemented languages (where such features are not even optional), RuleML has started to introduce "textBooK" (BK) language versions without any supplementary features, including DatalogBK($^+$), HornlogBK($^+$), and FOLogBK. Since myng-codes for such unsupplemented languages already exist amongst the vast variety [6] of myng-codes of the language lattice, once identified, they can be easily designated as BK anchor languages.

2.2 Logics Associating Syntactic Languages with Semantic Profiles

Rather than assuming a default semantics for syntactically defined languages, RuleML 1.02 leaves their semantics unspecified by default; this is motivated by concerns for security, scalability, refinability, and application requirements.[8] Instead, each RuleML 1.02 document permits to prominently refer to a logic.

RuleML logics are *syntax-semantics* pairs, associating a syntactic language with a semantic profile. The *syntax* is a predefined language as MYNG-configured in Sect. 2.1. The *semantics* is defined by a profile of descriptors including: (a) a classification distinguishing Proof(-theoretic) vs. Model(-theoretic), with the former being subclassified as Resolution vs. ASP etc., the latter as Herbrand vs. Tarski, all of which can be further qualified by fine distinctions; (b) a reference to a Web-published semantics and a mapping between its syntax and RuleML/XML syntax.

The two components constituting a logic allow for many-to-many relationships, where multiple syntaxes can have one semantics (see Sect. 3), and one syntax can have multiple semantics, as exemplified next.

---

[4] http://deliberation.ruleml.org/1.02/relaxng/datalogplus_min_relaxed.rnc.
[5] http://deliberation.ruleml.org/1.02/exa/DatalogPlus/datalogplus_min.ruleml.
[6] http://2014.ruleml.org/challenge.
[7] http://deliberation.ruleml.org/1.02/exa/RulebaseCompetition2014/.
[8] http://wiki.ruleml.org/index.php/Specification_of_RuleML_1.02.

The *predefined logics* of RuleML 1.02 include Horn-Herbrand, associating the Hornlog RuleML syntax with Herbrand semantics. For a user group requiring Tarski models, this logic can be complemented by a *user-defined logic* Horn-Tarski, associating the same syntax with Tarski semantics (in a future RuleML version, this might also become predefined). Moreover, both components of Horn-Herbrand can be refined, e.g. for negation-as-failure, leading to, e.g., NafHorn-HerbrandWF (Naf with Well-Founded semantics) or to NafHorn-HerbrandSM (Naf with Stable Model semantics).

Positional-Slotted, Object-Applicative RuleML (PSOA RuleML) [7,8][9] uses psoa atoms which permit the application of a predicate (acting as a relation) to be [in an *oidless / oidful* dimension] without or with an Object IDentifier (OID) – typed by the predicate (acting as a class) – and the predicate's arguments to be [in an orthogonal dimension] *positional, slotted,* or *combined.*

PSOA RuleML's presentation syntax PSOA/PS [7] was complemented by an XML syntax [8] defined by an XSD schema[10], which can be translated to a Relax NG schema called HornPSOA.

PSOA RuleML has a Tarski semantics [7], which could be complemented by a Herbrand semantics. Both semantics provide a model theory for PSOA RuleML, whose object identifiers lead to (head-)existential rules (which can be Skolemized to Horn rules). While the Tarski semantics of PSOA RuleML refers to the online version of [7], its Herbrand semantics could refer to a direct definition or to a definition with the domain of a PSOA RuleML semantic structure in [7] becoming the set of all equivalence classes over the Herbrand PSOA RuleML universe, adapting the Herbrand RIF-FLD Subframework[11].

The resulting predefined logic HornPSOA-Tarski could be complemented by a user-defined logic HornPSOA-Herbrand (in a future RuleML version, this might also become predefined).

An interoperation use case for bidirectional SQL-PSOA-SPARQL transformation (schema/ontology mapping) of – flat and nested – addresses is developed in the PSOA RuleML tutorial [8]. For a geospatial use case see [9].

3   Knowledge Transformation Tool Suite

Based on the RuleML knowledge representation of Sect. 2, we now proceed to the suite of tools for (semantics-preserving) knowledge transformation (Rule-ML/XML is the 'machine-oriented' RuleML serialization syntax; *RuleML/short* stands for 'human-oriented' RuleML shorthand syntaxes such as POSL and PSOA/PS; *foreign* stands for non-RuleML syntaxes such as Prolog and RIF/PS):

---

[9] http://wiki.ruleml.org/index.php/PSOA_RuleML.
[10] http://wiki.ruleml.org/index.php/PSOA_RuleML_API.
[11] https://www.w3.org/TR/rif-fld/#Appendix:_A_Subframework_for_Herbrand_ Semantic_Structures.

– Internal: RuleML-to-RuleML
  • Serialized: RuleML/XML-to-RuleML/XML
    * Upgraders (e.g., to Version 1.02[12])
    * Formatters (e.g., for Version 1.02[13])
      · Normalizer (Sect. 3.1)
      · Compactifiers (Sect. 3.1)
  • Polarized (Sect. 3.2): Between-RuleML/XML-and-*RuleML/short*
    * Parsers: *RuleML/short*-to-RuleML/XML
    * Generators: RuleML/XML-to-*RuleML/short*
– External: Between-RuleML/XML-and-*foreign*[14]
  • Importers (Sect. 3.3): *foreign*-to-RuleML/XML
  • Exporters (Sect. 3.3): RuleML/XML-to-*foreign*

On the top-level, this tool-suite taxonomy distinguishes transformations that are Internal to RuleML from those that are External in the sense of mapping – in either direction – between RuleML and foreign syntaxes. The more deeply differentiated Internal branch is then divided into Serialized transformations (staying within the XML syntax of RuleML) and Polarized transformations (having both a RuleML/XML and a *RuleML/short* side). The Parsers and Generators under the Polarized sub-branch of the Internal branch as well as the Importers and Exporters of the External branch can be composed. This creates transformation chains mapping through RuleML/XML as in the following compositions, where POSL and PSOA/PS are two 'shorthand' syntaxes for a Deliberation RuleML subset,[15] while Dexlog [10] and TPTP refer to subsets of two 'foreign' syntaxes:

– Internal-Internal: POSL⟶RuleML/XML⟶PSOA/PS
– External-External: Dexlog⟶RuleML/XML⟶TPTP
– Internal-External: POSL⟶RuleML/XML⟶TPTP
– External-Internal: Dexlog⟶RuleML/XML⟶PSOA/PS

The following subsections will traverse this taxonomy, expanding on a selection of its leaf nodes.

3.1   Serialized Formatters

Normalizer. RuleML has always allowed abbreviated serialization (skipped edge tags) and some freedom in the ordering of elements. XSLT stylesheets have been developed[16] for normalizing the syntax used in a given Version 1.02 instance, filling in any skipped edges and sorting elements into a canonical order.

---

[12] http://wiki.ruleml.org/index.php/Specification_of_Deliberation_RuleML_1.02# XSLT-Based_Upgrader.

[13] http://wiki.ruleml.org/index.php/Specification_of_Deliberation_RuleML_1.02# XSLT-Based_Formatters.

[14] External transformations should be defined via the normative RuleML/XML, rather than via any *RuleML/short*, while *foreign* may be any normative XML or other format.

[15] On the other hand, Prova is a shorthand syntax for a Reaction RuleML subset.

[16] http://deliberation.ruleml.org/1.02/xslt/normalizer/.

The goals of the RuleML Normalizer include the following:

- Reconstruct all skipped edge tags to produce a fully striped form [since edge tags correspond to (RDF) properties, this simplifies interoperation between RuleML/XML and directed labeled (RDF) graphs]
- Perform canonical ordering of sibling elements [this reduces the complexity of equality comparison across RuleML/XML serializations, for both humans and machines]

As a first example, the Existential Datalog$^+$ rule

```
<Forall>
  <Var>H</Var>
  <Implies>
    <Atom>
      <Rel>human</Rel>
      <Var>H</Var>
    </Atom>
    <Exists>
      <Var>M</Var>
      <Atom>
        <Rel>hasMother</Rel>
        <Var>H</Var>
        <Var>M</Var>
      </Atom>
    </Exists>
  </Implies>
</Forall>
```

is normalized to

```
<Forall>
  <declare><Var>H</Var></declare>
  <formula>
    <Implies>
      <if>
        <Atom>
          <op><Rel>human</Rel></op>
          <arg index="1"><Var>H</Var></arg>
        </Atom>
      </if>
      <then>
        <Exists>
          <declare><Var>M</Var></declare>
          <formula>
            <Atom>
              <op><Rel>hasMother</Rel></op>
              <arg index="1"><Var>H</Var></arg>
              <arg index="2"><Var>M</Var></arg>
            </Atom>
          </formula>
```

```
      </Exists>
     </then>
    </Implies>
   </formula>
</Forall>
```

As a second example, the compact version[17] of the Datalog$^+$ example is normalized to the expanded version[18].

Normalization is a preparatory step for many other transformations such as the compactifiers (cf. Sect. 3.1) and the TPTP exporters (cf. Sect. 3.3).

Compactifiers. The compactifier XSLTs[19] specify formatting into a compact serialization, which has fewer elements (i.e. is more compact) than the normalized serialization.

Two variations of this formatter specification are provided due to some limitations of XSD schemas. Both first apply the normalizer of Sect. 3.1 to sort the child nodesets into the canonical order. Then the "full" compactifier specifies the removal of all skippable RuleML stripes, while the "ifthen" compactifier retains <if> and <then> edges to provide disambiguating contexts for certain elements.

For example, as two inversions of the first example in Sect. 3.1, the full and ifthen compactifiers transform the expanded version to their compact versions without (shown there) and with retained <if> and <then> edges, respectively.

3.2 Polarized Parsers and Generators

RuleML↔POSL Parser & Generator Tool. The POsitional-SLotted (POSL) shorthand syntax of Hornlog RuleML combines the essence of Prolog's positional and F-logic's slotted syntaxes [11][20].

A pair of inverse translators has been developed for polarized internal transformation under a common GUI: A parser building RuleML-serialization syntax from POSL-shorthand syntax and a generator working in the opposite direction. Currently in Version 1.0, the tool is available online through its "Java Web Start" implementation.[21]

These translators have enabled writing KBs in the POSL shorthand while deploying them in the RuleML/XML serialization, as well as getting RuleML/XML rendered as POSL. Several Hornlog KBs[22] have been built in POSL and serialized with the RuleML←POSL parser, initializing the RuleML knowledge hub.

---

[17] http://deliberation.ruleml.org/1.02/exa/DatalogPlus/datalogplus_min.ruleml.
[18] http://deliberation.ruleml.org/1.02/exa/DatalogPlus/datalogplus_min_normal. ruleml.
[19] http://deliberation.ruleml.org/1.02/xslt/compactifier/.
[20] http://ruleml.org/submission/ruleml-shortation.html.
[21] http://www.jdrew.org/oojdrew/demo.html.
[22] http://wiki.ruleml.org/index.php/Rulebases:Master.

RuleML→PSOA/PS Generator and PSOA/PS→AST Parser. The RIF-like presentation syntax of PSOA RuleML (PSOA/PS) is a shorthand that goes beyond RIF/PS by capturing PSOA RuleML's integration of, e.g., relationships and frames [7,8].

The PSOA RuleML API[23] supports creating and manipulating abstract syntax objects (ASOs) using factory-based Java methods. These are employed to read the XML-based concrete syntax (serialization) of PSOA RuleML into ASOs, and render ASOs as PSOA/PS. This read-render composition, developed with the API, amounts to a generator of the presentation syntax from PSOA RuleML's XML syntax. The PSOA RuleML API is wrapped into an online demo Web application[24], which shows a list of PSOA RuleML/XML rulebases[25] and generates their equivalent forms in the presentation syntax.

For the inverse direction, RuleML←PSOA/PS, the PSOATransRun implementation[26] of PSOA RuleML provides a parser of PSOA/PS into ANTLR abstract syntax trees (ASTs). From there, it generates either TPTP [12] or Prolog but does not currently transform ASTs into RuleML/XML, although this should be easy, since XML trees are structurally similar to the ASTs themselves.

3.3 Importers and Exporters

Importer from Dexlog to Naf Datalog RuleML. Dexter [10][27] is a browser-based, domain-independent data explorer for the everyday user.

Dexter among other things allows to create, edit and query tables locally in the browser, to define (integrity and derivation) rules in Dexlog, an extension of Datalog using negation-as-failure, sets, tuples, aggregates, and built-in arithmetic and comparison operators, as well as to import data, and export data and rules.

One Dexter export format (which becomes imported to RuleML) is Naf Datalog RuleML/XML. It was developed in a joint effort by the Stanford Logic Group and RuleML.[28] The JavaScript-implemented translator maps tables and rules from a subset of Dexlog to a subset of Naf Datalog RuleML.

For example, the Dexlog rules (without negation-as-failure etc.)

```
ancestor(X, Y) :- parent(X, Y)
ancestor(X, Y) :- parent(X, Z) & ancestor(Z, Y)
```

are translated to the following rules, valid w.r.t. Naf Datalog RuleML (which can be strengthened to validity w.r.t. RuleML's Datalog and BinDatalog and to their textbook versions – according to Sect. 2.1 – DatalogBK and BinDatalogBK):

---

[23] http://wiki.ruleml.org/index.php/PSOA_RuleML_API.

[24] http://psoa-rulemlapi.rhcloud.com/psoaxml2ps/.

[25] http://wiki.ruleml.org/index.php/PSOA_RuleML#Test_Cases.

[26] http://wiki.ruleml.org/index.php/PSOA_RuleML#PSOATransRun.

[27] http://dexter.stanford.edu.

[28] http://wiki.ruleml.org/index.php/Dexter_and_RuleML.

```
<?xml version="1.0" encoding="UTF-8"?>
<?xml-model href="http://deliberation.ruleml.org/1.01/xsd/nafdatalog.xsd"?>
<RuleML xmlns="http://ruleml.org/spec">
  <Assert>
    <Forall>
      <Var>X</Var>
      <Var>Y</Var>
      <Implies>
        <Atom>
          <Rel>parent</Rel>
          <Var>X</Var>
          <Var>Y</Var>
        </Atom>
        <Atom>
          <Rel>ancestor</Rel>
          <Var>X</Var>
          <Var>Y</Var>
        </Atom>
      </Implies>
    </Forall>
    <Forall>
      <Var>X</Var>
      <Var>Z</Var>
      <Var>Y</Var>
      <Implies>
        <And>
          <Atom>
            <Rel>parent</Rel>
            <Var>X</Var>
            <Var>Z</Var>
          </Atom>
          <Atom>
            <Rel>ancestor</Rel>
            <Var>Z</Var>
            <Var>Y</Var>
          </Atom>
        </And>
        <Atom>
          <Rel>ancestor</Rel>
          <Var>X</Var>
          <Var>Y</Var>
        </Atom>
      </Implies>
    </Forall>
  </Assert>
</RuleML>
```

An inverse translator, from a subset of Naf Datalog RuleML to a subset of Dexlog, could be built with the PSOA RuleML API of Sect. 3.2, where the generation of PSOA/PS is replaced with Dexlog generation.

Exporters from Datalog$^+$/Hornlog$^+$/FOL RuleML to TPTP. "Thousands of Problems for Theorem Provers" (TPTP [12][29]) is a widely used syn-

---
[29] http://www.cs.miami.edu/~tptp/.

tax and library for Automated Theorem Proving (ATP) test/benchmark problems. RuleML2TPTP[30] is an XSLT 2.0-based translator from Deliberation RuleML/XML 1.01 to TPTP. Originally implemented for Datalog$^+$ RuleML, it was later extended to Hornlog$^+$ RuleML, and then to all of FOL RuleML (with Equality).

RuleML2TPTP first uses the RuleML Normalizer (cf. Sect. 3.1) to transform Deliberation RuleML/XML to its normalized version. With the fully striped normalization avoiding conditional branching between stripe-skipped and striped forms, the XSLT stylesheet[31] then performs recursive case analysis to linearize XML trees to TPTP texts. The generated TPTP can finally be validated and executed with an ATP system via the "System on TPTP" page[32] such as with Vampire and the E prover.

For instance, the first example's input in Sect. 3.1 will be normalized to the output shown there. This is then transformed to the following TPTP:

```
fof(example,axiom,(
  ! [H] :
    ( human(H) =>
    ? [M] : hasMother(H,M) ) )).
```

RuleML2TPTP has been used, e.g., to translate the "Instructive KB" for Datalog$^+$ in Sect. 2.1 to TPTP;[33] also, on an OpenRuleBench-derived RuleML version of the well-known Wine Ontology, generating a TPTP KB for the Semantic Web.[34]

Preparatory planning for an inverse translator, TPTP2RuleML[35], has started, whose implementation is intended as a joint endeavor of the RuleML and TPTP communities.

4   N3-PSOA-Flora Knowledge-Interoperation Use Case

While Sect. 3 discussed various interoperation test cases under the perspective of the tool-suite taxonomy, the present section proposes a use case bridging the gap between two languages of particular relevance to the rule-based Semantic Web, both also supporting the (light-weight-)ontology-based Semantic Web: N3 [13] and Flora-2/F-logic [14][36]. The N3-PSOA-Flora use case is focusing on the interoperation from N3 to Flora-2/F-logic, although the opposite direction can be easily constructed from the alignment provided. This also demonstrates the role of PSOA RuleML [7,8] as an intermediate (canonical) format that

---

[30] http://wiki.ruleml.org/index.php/TPTP_RuleML.
[31] https://github.com/RuleML/RuleML2TPTP/archive/v1.02.zip.
[32] http://www.cs.miami.edu/~tptp/cgi-bin/SystemOnTPTP.
[33] http://deliberation.ruleml.org/1.01/exa/DatalogPlus/datalogplus_min/.
[34] http://ruleml.org/usecases/wineonto#Step%204:%20RuleML%201.
     0%20-%20RuleML%201.01%20Conversion.
[35] http://wiki.ruleml.org/index.php/TPTP_RuleML#TPTP2RuleML.
[36] With "Flora-2/F-logic" we refer to the current F-logic version as part of Flora-2.

focuses entirely on the knowledge-representation layer rather than programming-language details, but makes syntactic assumptions (e.g. quantifiers) explicit. After having introduced the central rule of this use case in (controlled) English, the rule and a fact will be given as the N3 source, as the Flora-2/F-logic target, and as three variants of the PSOA RuleML canonical form.

English: "If the relation addressRel holds between a name, a street, and a town, then there exists an object, addressObj, with a name slot and a place slot for which there exists an object, placeObj, with a street slot and a town slot."

Source: N3 fact and rule, where the default namespace (N3's ":" prefix) is RuleML's GeospatialRules [9] and `rel:arglist` is an N3 property defined in the PSOA RuleML namespace for an N3 vocabulary that emulates relations:

```
@prefix : <http://psoa.ruleml.org/GeospatialRules#>.
@prefix rel: <http://psoa.ruleml.org/n3/vocab/rel#>.

[a :addressRel;
 rel:arglist ("Computer Science" "Engineering Dr" "Stony Brook, NY 11794")].

{
 [a :addressRel;
  rel:arglist (?Name ?Street ?Town)]
}
=>
{
 [a :addressObj;
  :name ?Name;
  :place [a :placeObj;
          :street ?Street;
          :town ?Town]]
}.
```

Target: Flora-2/F-logic fact and rule, where the compiler option for experts enables the use of the embedded ISA-literal (Flora-2's ":" infix) in the rule head, as described in [14], Sect. 48:

```
:- compiler_options{expert=on}.

addressRel('Computer Science','Engineering Dr','Stony Brook, NY 11794').

\#(?Name,?Street,?Town):addressObj[
    name->?Name,
    place->\#(?Name,?Street,?Town):placeObj[
      street->?Street,
      town->?Town]] :-
    addressRel(?Name,?Street,?Town).
```

Canonical, presentation syntax: PSOA RuleML/PS fact and rule, where the rule, from [8], uses FOL-style explicit quantifiers (adapted from FOL RuleML/XML as well as W3C RIF/XML and RIF/PS):

```
addressRel("Computer Science" "Engineering Dr" "Stony Brook, NY 11794")

Forall ?Name ?Street ?Town (
  Exists ?O1 ?O2 ( ?O1#addressObj(name->?Name
                                  place->?O2#placeObj(street->?Street
                                                      town->?Town)) )  :-
    addressRel(?Name ?Street ?Town)
                   )
```

Canonical, compact serialization: Stripe-skipped PSOA RuleML/XML for the fact and rule:

```xml
<Atom>
  <Rel>addressRel</Rel>
  <Data>Computer Science</Data>
  <Data>Engineering Dr</Data>
  <Data>Stony Brook, NY 11794</Data>
</Atom>

<Forall>
  <Var>Name</Var>
  <Var>Street</Var>
  <Var>Town</Var>
  <Implies>
    <Atom>
      <Rel>addressRel</Rel>
      <Var>Name</Var>
      <Var>Street</Var>
      <Var>Town</Var>
    </Atom>
    <Exists>
      <Var>O1</Var>
      <Var>O2</Var>
      <Atom>
        <oid><Var>O1</Var>></oid>
        <Rel>addressObj</Rel>
        <slot><Ind>name</Ind><Var>Name</Var></slot>
        <slot>
          <Ind>place</Ind>
          <Atom>
            <oid><Var>O2</Var></oid>
            <Rel>placeObj</Rel>
            <slot><Ind>street</Ind><Var>Street</Var></slot>
            <slot><Ind>town</Ind><Var>Town</Var></slot>
          </Atom>
        </slot>
      </Atom>
    </Exists>
  </Implies>
</Forall>
```

Canonical, normalized serialization:[37] Fully striped PSOA RuleML/XML:

```
<Atom>
  <op><Rel>addressRel</Rel></op>
  <arg><Data>Computer Science</Data></arg>
  <arg><Data>Engineering Dr</Data></arg>
  <arg><Data>Stony Brook, NY 11794</Data></arg>
</Atom>

<Forall>
  <declare><Var>Name</Var></declare>
  <declare><Var>Street</Var></declare>
  <declare><Var>Town</Var></declare>
  <formula>
    <Implies>
      <if>
        <Atom>
          <op><Rel>addressRel</Rel></op>
          <arg><Var>Name</Var></arg>
          <arg><Var>Street</Var></arg>
          <arg><Var>Town</Var></arg>
        </Atom>
      </if>
      <then>
        <Exists>
          <declare><Var>O1</Var></declare>
          <declare><Var>O2</Var></declare>
          <formula>
            <Atom>
              <oid><Var>O1</Var></oid>
              <op><Rel>addressObj</Rel></op>
              <slot><Ind>name</Ind><Var>Name</Var></slot>
              <slot>
                <Ind>place</Ind>
                <Atom>
                  <oid><Var>O2</Var></oid>
                  <op><Rel>placeObj</Rel></op>
                  <slot><Ind>street</Ind><Var>Street</Var></slot>
                  <slot><Ind>town</Ind><Var>Town</Var></slot>
                </Atom>
              </slot>
            </Atom>
          </formula>
        </Exists>
      </then>
    </Implies>
  </formula>
</Forall>
```

---

[37] Normalization here refers to PSOA RuleML (edge-)stripe reconstruction etc. like in RuleML 1.02, rather than to unnesting using PSOATransRun 1.1 (cf. footnote 9).

The central rule of this use case also clarifies a point – shown in parts (A) and (B) – that may be surprising to readers new to the rule-based Semantic Web:[38]

(A) The rule can (1) be enriched by light-weight-ontological knowledge in the form of taxomic subsumptions – using PSOA's "##" infix – such as `addressObj##` `geoObj` and `placeObj##geoObj` and (2) be employed to align (transform) given facts/instances populating a *relational* address ontology such as the `addressRel` fact/instance from above with (into) derivable facts/instances for populating an *object-centered* address ontology such as the following derivable fact/instance:

```
skolem1#addressObj(name->"Computer Science"
              place->
                      skolem2#placeObj(street->"Engineering Dr"
                                       town->"Stony Brook, NY 11794"))
```

(B) But, following up on Sect. 3, such a rule, e.g. in the above normalized serialization variant, is itself the subject of interoperation, e.g. using XSLT for transformation. Moreover, the rule-transformation rules, e.g. XSLT templates, could again be interoperated. This could also be done based on the RuleML hub technology by encoding the RuleML rules as RuleML facts[39] and transcribing the XSLT templates into RuleML metarules translating those rule-encoding facts. Since XSLT templates can be conceived as term-rewriting rules over XML trees, this could employ Functional RuleML[40].

5   Conclusions

RuleML has become a hub for the interoperation of formal knowledge by providing a foundational representation layer topped by a transformation layer. Ongoing representation work includes Deliberation RuleML's PSOA, Higher-Order, Modal, and Defeasible subfamilies as well as the further formalization – and transition from XSD to Relax NG – of Reaction RuleML. Novel transformation chains are already emerging from unexpected translator compositions such as between subsets of Dexlog, Datalog RuleML/XML, and TPTP. Future development of the hub should give rise to further interoperation pathways for knowledge sharing and reuse. Readers are invited to consult the links and references about some of the RuleML features and tools not detailed in this article.

Acknowledgements. Thanks to my RuleML 1.02 Taskforce colleagues Tara Athan and Adrian Paschke, as well as to Gen Zou, Sadnan Al Manir, Adrian Giurca, Alexandre Riazanov, Michael Genesereth, Sudhir Agarwal, Marcel Ball, Meng Luan, Leah Bidlake, and many others, for their contributions leading to the RuleML hub. Thanks also to Paul Fodor and the entire Organizing Committee chairing RuleML 2016.

---

[38] The canonical PSOA RuleML format, presentation variant, is employed here, from which the other two formats can be obtained via their alignments.

[39] http://ruleml.org/indoo/indoo.html#Programs-as-Data.

[40] http://ruleml.org/fun/.

References

1. Cali, A., Gottlob, G., Lukasiewicz, T.: A general Datalog-based framework for tractable query answering over ontologies. J. Web Semant. **14**, 57–83 (2012)
2. Nenov, Y., Piro, R., Motik, B., Horrocks, I., Wu, Z., Banerjee, J.: RDFox: a highly-scalable RDF store. In: Arenas, M., et al. (eds.) ISWC 2015. LNCS, vol. 9367, pp. 3–20. Springer, Heidelberg (2015). doi:10.1007/978-3-319-25010-6_1
3. Boley, H., Grütter, R., Zou, G., Athan, T., Etzold, S.: A Datalog$^+$ RuleML 1.01 architecture for rule-based data access in ecosystem research. In: Bikakis, A., Fodor, P., Roman, D. (eds.) RuleML 2014. LNCS, vol. 8620, pp. 112–126. Springer, Heidelberg (2014)
4. Hernández-Orallo, J., Muggleton, S.H., Schmid, U., Zorn, B.: Approaches and applications of inductive programming (Dagstuhl seminar 15442). Dagstuhl Rep. **5**(10), 89–111 (2016)
5. Athan, T., Boley, H.: Design and implementation of highly modular schemas for XML: customization of RuleML in Relax NG. In: Palmirani, M. (ed.) RuleML 2011 - America. LNCS, vol. 7018, pp. 17–32. Springer, Heidelberg (2011)
6. Athan, T., Boley, H.: The MYNG 1.01 suite for Deliberation RuleML 1.01: Taming the language lattice. In: Patkos, T., Wyner, A., Giurca, A. (eds.) Proceedings of the RuleML 2014 Challenge, at the 8th International Web Rule Symposium. CEUR, vol. 1211, August 2014
7. Boley, H.: A RIF-style semantics for RuleML-integrated positional-slotted, object-applicative rules. In: Bassiliades, N., Governatori, G., Paschke, A. (eds.) RuleML 2011 - Europe. LNCS, vol. 6826, pp. 194–211. Springer, Heidelberg (2011)
8. Boley, H.: PSOA RuleML: integrated object-relational data and rules. In: Faber, W., Paschke, A. (eds.) Reasoning Web 2015. LNCS, vol. 9203, pp. 114–150. Springer, Heidelberg (2015)
9. Zou, G.: PSOA RuleML integration of relational and object-centered geospatial data. In: Bassiliades, N., Fodor, P., Giurca, A., Gottlob, G., Kliegr, T., Nalepa, G.J., Palmirani, M., Paschke, A., Proctor, M., Roman, D., Sadri, F., Stojanovic, N. (eds.) Proceedings of the RuleML 2015 Challenge, Berlin, Germany, 2–5 August 2015. CEUR Workshop Proceedings, vol. 1417. CEUR-WS.org (2015)
10. Agarwal, S., Mohapatra, A., Genesereth, M., Boley, H.: Rule-based exploration of structured data in the browser. In: Bassiliades, N., Gottlob, G., Sadri, F., Paschke, A., Roman, D. (eds.) RuleML 2015. LNCS, vol. 9202, pp. 161–175. Springer, Heidelberg (2015)
11. Boley, H.: Integrating positional and slotted knowledge on the Semantic Web. J. Emerg. Technol. Web Intell. **4**(2), 343–353 (2010)
12. Sutcliffe, G.: The TPTP problem library and associated infrastructure. J. Autom. Reason. **43**(4), 337–362 (2009)
13. Berners-Lee, T., Connolly, D., Kagal, L., Scharf, Y., Hendler, J.: N3Logic: A logical framework for the World Wide Web. Theory Pract. Logic Program. (TPLP) **8**(3), 249–269 (2008)
14. Kifer, M., Yang, G., Wan, H., Zhao, C.: $\mathcal{E}RGO^{Lite}$ (a.k.a. $\mathcal{F}$lora-2): User's Manual, v1.1 (2015). http://flora.sourceforge.net/docs/floraManual.pdf

General RuleML Track

Handling Complex Process Models Conditions Using First-Order Horn Clauses

Stefano Ferilli[✉]

University of Bari, Bari, Italy
stefano.ferilli@uniba.it

Abstract. WorkFlow Management Systems provide automatic support to learn process models or to check compliance of process enactment to correct models. The expressive power of the adopted formalism for representing process models is fundamental to determine the effectiveness or even feasibility of a correct model. In particular, a desirable feature is the possibility of expressing complex conditions on some elements of the model. The formalism used in the WoMan framework for workflow management, based on First-Order Logic, is more expressive than standard formalisms adopted in the literature. It allows tight integration between the activity flow and the conditions, and it allows one to express conditions that take into account contextual information and various kinds of relationships among the involved entities. This paper discusses such a formalism, especially concerning conditions, and provides an explicative example of how this can be applied in practice.

Keywords: Business process modeling · Process mining · Logic programming

1 Introduction

Critical processes, of which our society is pervaded, are typically very complex. WorkFlow Management Systems (WFMSs for short) are designed to help, supported by computers, in accomplishing several process-related tasks of interest. E.g., they may supervise process enactment to check whether it is compliant to the expected behavior, or they may simulate process enactment to show possible behaviors that may be expected from a process, or they may guess which are the next activities that will be performed in a certain status of the process execution. To carry out these tasks, WFMSs require some kind of formal model of the process to be available. Due to the said complexity of the processes, corresponding models are in turn very hard to set up and to formalize manually [13]. Skilled experts are needed to make such a formalization, which means that it is a costly activity. Even worse, the resulting model might not be the correct one, both due to human errors and because the perspective of experts on a given process may be different than that of the practitioners that actually carry out

© Springer International Publishing Switzerland 2016
J.J. Alferes et al. (Eds.): RuleML 2016, LNCS 9718, pp. 37–52, 2016.
DOI: 10.1007/978-3-319-42019-6_3

the involved activities. This problem motivated a further task in Workflow Management concerned with automatically learning a model from sample executions of a process (known as *Process Mining* [25]).

In this landscape, the importance of defining and using suitable representation formalisms for expressing process models is already apparent. Nevertheless, it becomes even more crucial if one considers that the formalism may enforce, or prevent, the fulfillment of several desirable properties proposed in the literature for the models. A process model should indeed be *complete* (i.e., able to recognize or generate all sample executions used to build it), *irredundant* (able to recognize or generate as few executions as possible that are different from the sample executions used to build it), and *minimal* (as simple and compact as possible) [1,4,13,25]. *Accuracy* (i.e., completeness and irredundancy [4]) is typically in contrast with minimality (more compact models are more general, and thus tend to recognize or generate more executions).

To express the models of complex processes, powerful representation formalisms are needed. While most research on this topic focused on the flow of activities, little attention was paid to the possibility of setting conditions along the model to determine if and when activating its components. Since conditions may prevent undesired executions of activities, they provide further support to irredundancy. The few works that introduced this topic proposed to model the conditions using decision trees. These are some of their shortcomings: (1) they do not provide any specific contribution to, nor strict integration with, the process model representation aspects; (2) they are based on propositional approaches, which are unable to represent and handle relationships; (3) conditions have been usually associated with tasks because they have been considered as expressing causal dependencies between tasks, but also other elements of a process may be associated with conditions. All these aspects are very important for condition handling, especially in real-world, complex domains. When determining and checking conditions, one should be able to: (1) take into account the whole history of process enactment; (2) consider interactions among the involved entities and their properties, possibly at different time points, and the history of process enactment; (3) have a more fine-grained control of the process enactment.

This paper deals with the above shortcomings and needs. It proposes a process modeling formalism based on a fragment of First-Order Logic (FOL for short) that tightly integrates both the activity flow aspects and the conditions aspects in a single framework. It extends the formalism proposed in [2,8,10] with the capability of handling agents, to generalize sequential information, and to express new types of pre-and post-conditions. The integrated formalism, alone, significantly improves the support to the desirable properties of process models. Moreover, the use of the FOL setting for the conditions further enhances the power of this representation. While increasing the power and expressiveness of the models, this poses some new problems that were not investigated in previous literature. This paper proposes a way to overcome these problems, as well.

After introducing basic concepts and related work in Sect. 2, Sect. 3 reports the details of the representational framework. Then, Sect. 4 shows how the proposed formalism is applied in practice. It can be used as a running example, taken from a Process Mining task, to better understand Sect. 3. Finally, Sect. 5 concludes the paper and outlines future work issues.

2   Background and Related Work

Let us first quickly introduce some process-related concepts and their definitions, and then review relevant literature concerning the formalisms for process modeling and the use of conditions.

A *process* consists of a combination of different, inter-related tasks performed by agents (humans or artifacts). A *task* is a generic piece of work to be executed. An *activity* is the actual execution of a task by an agent. Activities spanning some significant period of time are represented by the interval between their start and end events. A *case* is a particular execution of tasks according to a given workflow. Case *traces* are lists of events associated with *steps* (time points). Events of several traces may be collected and interleaved in *logs*. A process model (or *workflow*) is a formal specification of how a set of tasks can be composed to result in valid processes. Allowed compositional schemes include sequential, concurrent, conditional, or iterative execution. Especially relevant for determining the complexity of a model is whether it is purely *sequential* or it allows a *concurrent* flow, and whether many activities referred to the same task are allowed or not. Further complexity is introduced by the presence of synchronization among tasks and of invisible or duplicate tasks. Using the above terminology, Process Mining aims at using a set of sample case traces to infer process models automatically. An overview of the current state-of-the-art on Process Mining can be found in [15,22].

Several models have been proposed in the literature for representing processes. In Finite State Machines [5], nodes are associated with states, and edges represent activities. In Hidden Markov Models [11], states represent nodes, and activities correspond to output symbols. Neither of these formalisms can model concurrency, which is a serious limitation. A more specialized formalism that distinguishes several types of nodes (Begin, End, Activity, Decision, Split, Join) connected by edges was proposed in [12,14]. Activity nodes are associated with tasks and edges can be labeled with probabilities and/or conditions. More recent works have established *Petri nets*, or a restriction thereof, called *WorkFlow nets* (WF-nets) [21], as the current standard formalism to represent process models. In fact, they were purposely developed to express the control flow in a process. E.g., models in the form of WF-nets are learned in [21,25]; 'sound *Structured WF-nets*' (a further, very limited restriction of WF-nets that can handle parallelism between pairs of tasks only and does not permit synchronization between tasks) are learned in [26]; Petri nets which do not involve duplicate tasks nor more than one place with the same input and output tasks are learned in [6].

Declarative Process Mining is specifically concerned with logic formalisms for process specification. Instead of completely specifying process flow, it imposes only a (minimal) set of constraints that must be satisfied when executing the process activities. This approach has been recognized to be very important when dealing with particularly complex models and domains [19]. Interesting works in this field proposed the Declarative Process Model Learner [16], and its incremental version [3]. In particular, the latter supports the usefulness of model refinement with respect to batch learning in this field.

A few works in the literature considered the possibility of handling simple Boolean conditions, that determine whether a task is to be executed or not depending on the particular situation that holds at that moment in the specific execution. Preconditions must be satisfied in the current state of the world to enable the execution of a task. Postconditions must hold after the task execution. Triggers are additional external conditions that, if satisfied in the current state of a case, cause the execution of a task. Triggers can be *automatic*, if the task is triggered just because it is enabled, or determined by some kind of *user* interaction, or by a *message* notifying an external event, or by a clock reaching a pre-determined *time* [21]. Specifically, [1,12,20] propose the use of decision trees as classification models, and corresponding learning techniques. However, only [20] provides some details about this issue. Using decision trees means focusing on propositional approaches, based on attribute-value representations to describe the status on which the decision is to be taken, i.e., whether a given activity is to be carried out or not is determined according to the content of feature vectors describing the status of the execution when the decision is to be carried out. This is a significant limitation, because fixed-size feature vectors cannot capture variability in the number of objects involved in the observations, and relationships among them and between situations. FOL can do this.

Strictly related to the question of condition handling are two current 'hot' topics in the process mining field: the need to consider contextual information [23] and the importance of efficient and declarative approaches [18]. Conditions can be based on the current state of the process and/or on the context in which the decision is to be taken. Especially the contextual perspective is very important, because it allows one to consider, and to include in the model, external factors that are outside the realm of pure activity flow.

Recently, the WoMan framework for workflow learning and management has been introduced [8,10]. Incrementality, expressiveness, and efficiency are its most outstanding features. Incremental learning allows one to refine a given model as long as new evidence becomes available, without starting each time from scratch. This yields much efficiency, but is more complex, because only partial knowledge is available for learning at any given time. This is why little work can be found in the literature on this kind of approach, especially in the FOL setting. WoMan's input, output, and internal representations are all based on the Logic Programming formalism [17] (which is, syntactically, a fragment of FOL). In particular, WoMan models include both the activity flow and associated conditions, both expressed using this formalism. So, WoMan naturally overcomes some of the limitations of past works in the workflow management literature, by allowing to describe and handle in the same framework not only information about tasks and control flow, but relevant contextual observations as well. Of course, also the conditions must be learned incrementally. For this purpose WoMan embeds InTheLEx [7], an incremental learner of FOL rules.

3   The WoMan Formalism

The Logic Programming formalism [17] is based on *Horn clauses*, i.e., implications represented in Prolog style as $l_0 \text{ :- } l_1, \ldots, l_n.$, where l_0 (called the *head*) is the conclusion and $l_1, \ldots, l_n$ (called the *body*) is a conjunction of pre-conditions. Each l_i is an *atom*, i.e., a predicate applied to terms as arguments. WoMan works in Datalog, which allows only constants or variables as terms. Clauses having only the head are called *facts*, and represented as just l_0. Clauses having both the head and the body are called *rules*.

According to foundational literature, trace elements can be considered as 6-tuples $\langle T, E, W, P, A, O \rangle$, where: T is the event timestamp, E is the type of the event (**begin_process**, **begin_activity**, **end_activity**, or **end_process**[1]), W is the name of the workflow the process refers to, P is a unique identifier for each process execution, A is the name of the activity, and O is the progressive number of occurrence of that activity in that process [1,13]. An optional field, R, can be added to specify the agent that carries out activity A. They are represented in WoMan as facts

$$\text{entry}(T, E, W, P, A, O, R).$$

To describe also the context in which the activities take place, WoMan exploits a further kind of event, **context_description**. When $E = $ **context_description**, A is a FOL description of the context at time T consisting of a set of atoms built on domain-specific predicates.

WoMan models are expressed as sets of facts built on four predicates:

task(t, C): task t occurred in training cases C.

transition(I, O, p, C): transition[2] p, occurred in training cases C, is enabled if all input tasks in $I = [t'_1, \ldots, t'_n]$ are active; if fired, after stopping the execution of all tasks in I (in any order), the execution of all output tasks in $O = [t''_1, \ldots, t''_m]$ is started (again, in any order). Transitions represent the allowed connections between activities. If several instances of a task can be active at the same time, I and O are multisets, and application of a transition consists of closing as many instances of active tasks as specified in I and of opening as many activations of new tasks as specified in O.

task_agent(t, R): task t can be carried out by an agent matching one of the roles[3] in R.

---

[1] Specifically, task start and end events are needed to properly handle time span and parallelism of tasks [24].

[2] Note that this interpretation differs from the one given in Petri Nets, where 'transitions' represent tasks.

[3] In an obvious representation, R may be a simple set of roles, but other kinds of representation formalism can be used as well (e.g., intensional description, reference to hierarchies, etc.).

transition_agent$([R'_1, \ldots, R'_n], [R''_1, \ldots, R''_m], p, C, q)$: transition p, involving input tasks $I = [t'_1, \ldots, t'_n]$ and output tasks $O = [t''_1, \ldots, t''_m]$, may occur provided that each task $t'_i \in I, i = 1, \ldots, n$ is carried out by an agent matching one of the roles in R'_i, and that each task $t''_j \in O, j = 1, \ldots, m$ is carried out by an agent matching one of the roles in R''_j; several combinations can be allowed, numbered by progressive q, each encountered in cases C.

Argument C in these predicates is the multiset of identifiers of the cases in which the associated task/transition occurred. It is a multiset because a task or transition may occur several times in the same case. When supervising process executions, it is useful in at least 3 ways:

1. It allows one to check that the whole flow of activities that are taking place was encountered in at least one training/sample case. In this way, it is possible to avoid recognizing as valid a new execution that mixes partial execution flows taken from different sample cases.
2. It allows one to set limits on the number of repetitions of loops. Indeed, when loops are enacted, one may check that the new execution does not repeat the involved tasks/transitions more times than seen in sample/training cases.
3. It allows one to compute statistics. Given a model involving overall n sample/training cases, if a task or transition t is associated with cases C_t, then its probability may be approximated by its relative frequency $|C_t|/n$.

WoMan models can specify conditions on three kinds of items: tasks (in general), transitions, and tasks within transitions. Conditions on tasks (resp., transitions) define what must be true in general for carrying out those tasks (resp., transitions). Conditions on tasks in transitions specify further constraints for allowing a task to be run in the context of a specific transition (provided that its general conditions are met), and may be applied only to output tasks of transitions. It is possible to specify pre-conditions, post-conditions, and triggers, but only pre- and post-conditions are learned automatically. Indeed, pre-conditions express permission, post-conditions express constraints that can be checked posterior to process execution, and triggers express obligation. So, while pre- and post-conditions can be learned autonomously by the system from observations of what happens before and after tasks or transitions, triggers require a supervisor that purposely indicates when a task or transition is to be immediately applied. Since WoMan performs unsupervised learning, in the following we will focus on pre- and post-conditions only.

WoMan expresses conditions as FOL rules. The rule head predicate specifies the task, transition, or task within a transition for which the condition is set, applied to an argument expressing the moment at which the test is carried out. For transitions, this is the step at which the first output activity is started. The rule body expresses the actual condition using the following predicates:

act_start(s): at step s the case execution begins;
act_stop(s): at step s the case execution terminates;
activity(s, t, a): at step s task t is executed by agent a;

after$(s', s'', [n', n''], [m', m''])$: step s'' follows step s' after a number of steps ranging between n' and n'', and after a time ranging between m' and m'';

after$(c', c'',$ **context**$, [n', n''], [m', m''])$: contextual step c'' follows contextual step c' after a number of contextual steps ranging between n' and n'', and after a time ranging between m' and m'';

context(s, c): the activity associated with step s is carried out in context c;

act_A(a): a denotes activity A;

agent_A(a): a denotes agent A;

suitable domain-dependent predicates (different from the previous ones) that describe the context in which the various activities take place in terms of the entities involved, their properties, and the relationships that come into play among entities, among steps, and between entities and steps.

Each (activity or context) step is denoted by a unique identifier. Predicates `after/4` and `after/5`, borrowed from the formalism used in InTheLEx to handle sequential information [9], describe two different dimensions (for activities and contexts flow, respectively), and induce ordering relationships on the corresponding sets of steps. The flow-of-activities dimension, associated with `after/4` atoms, may involve concurrent executions, possibly nested. The beginning of a concurrent execution corresponds to several `after/4` atoms having the same s', while several `after/4` atoms having the same s'' correspond to the end of some concurrent activities. Due to concurrency, `after/4` induces a partial ordering. Conversely, `after/5` atoms induce a total ordering, because the flow-of-contexts dimension is a strictly linear flow. Together with `activity/3`, `after/4` allows one to describe the flow of activities in a case. So, they ensure seamless integration of the flow-of-activity part of the model with the conditions part.

An example to learn or test a condition consists of a label (expressing the occurrence of a task, transition, or task-in-transition) referred to an observation. The observation uses the above predicates to provide a (complete or partial) account of the flow of activities, along with the relevant context(s) for that flow of activities. Observations are automatically built from the log events as follows.

The **begin_process** event generates a unique activity step s_b, and introduces in the observation description an atom:

$$\texttt{act\_start}(s_b)$$

Events of type **begin_activity** or **end_activity** are used to build the flow of activities account. Each **begin_activity** event, reporting that activity t is carried out by agent a, generates a unique activity step s, and introduces in the observation description three atoms:

$$\texttt{activity}(s, t, a), \ \texttt{act\_T}(t), \ \texttt{agent\_A}(a)$$

where T and A are replaced by the names of the activity and of the agent, respectively, which are domain-dependent. It also generates example labels for the task, transition, or task-in-transition that is taking place. Suppose that the above activity t is carried out in transition p; then, the following labels/examples are generated:

$$\text{act\_}T(s), \ \text{act\_}T\_\text{p}(s)$$

Moreover, if t is the first output activity of p, also the following label/example is generated:

$$\text{p}(s)$$

Whenever an activity t', associated with step s', is followed by another activity t'', associated with step s'' (meaning, in a nutshell, that the **begin_activity** event of the latter is successive to the **end_activity** event of the former, and that there is no other activity whose **begin_activity** and **end_activity** events are both in the middle) an atom:

$$\text{after}(s', s'', [1,1], [d,d])$$

is introduced in the observation description, where d expresses some kind of distance between the two activities (e.g., the clock time between them)[4].

The **end_process** event generates a unique activity step s_e, and introduces in the observation description an atom:

$$\text{act\_stop}(s_e)$$

For all activities a, associated with step s, such that the current description does not contain an atom $\text{after}(s, s', [1,1], [d,d])$ (i.e., the latest concurrent activities in the current process enactment), an atom:

$$\text{after}(s, s_e, [1,1], [d,d])$$

is introduced in the observation description, where d has the same meaning as above[5]. This is sufficient to provide an account of the flow of actions that take place in the process enactment.

Concerning the contexts, each event of type **context_description** generates a unique context step c, and introduces in the observation description an atom[6]:

$$\text{after}(c', c, \text{context}, \ [1,1], [d,d])$$

where c' is the step associated with the previous event of type **context_description** (if any). This context will be associated with any subsequent activities, until the next **context_description** event is encountered, through atoms of the form:

$$\text{context}(s, c)$$

meaning that the activity carried out at step s took place in the context c. Moreover, the list of atoms reported in parameter A of the **context_description** log entry is added to the description. To allow the linking of contextual descriptions

---

[4] Actually, in its internal representation, WoMan uses a simplified notation $\text{next}(s', s'', d)$ with exactly the same meaning.

[5] Again, the simplified notation $\text{next}(s, s_e, d)$ is actually used.

[6] In this case, the simplified notation $\text{next}(c', c, \text{context}, \ d)$ is actually used.

to the steps, the system automatically replaces any occurrence of the substring timestamp in the constants by the context step name c.

Depending on the specific experimental needs, examples descriptions can be reduced, filtering out useless or irrelevant information. E.g., only the most recent context and activity steps might be considered, along with the associated information. The choice about whether filtering the descriptions, and about what to filter out, is of course context-dependent. During the supervision stage, whenever an activity is carried out, corresponding examples for the task and task-in-transition conditions (and, if the activity starts a transition, also for the transition condition) are generated and checked for compliance with the currently available model. During the learning stage, InTheLEx is run to revise the currently available model for conditions according to these examples. The availability of negative examples is not standard in process mining [6], because only actual executions of a process are logged by process management systems, and they are assumed to be correct. Otherwise, traces should be manually labeled as positive or negative, which may be unrealistic in some domains. While most machine learning systems are unable to learn if provided with positive examples only (without negative examples to impose some kind of biases to prevent over-generalization, they would learn models that just accept everything), InTheLEx embeds a generalization operator that tries to keep as much information as possible in the model, and has shown to be able to effectively learn conditions for process models from positive examples only [2].

4 Sample Application

This section shows a practical application of the WoMan formalism on a toy problem. To give an idea of how a model reflects a set of cases, the example is taken from a Process Mining task. The same model might be considered as an abstract specification of a workflow by just ignoring the training cases and how it is built from them. In such a case, the case identifiers in the model would represent different kinds of allowed behavior, and their occurrences would reflect the frequency of these behaviors. Figure 1 shows the possible flows of activities for a hypothetical 'afternoon' smart environment process, aimed at supporting the user in his afternoon routines. It involves many complex features for most process mining systems: short loops ('videogame'/'phone'), duplicated tasks ('football' and 'eat'), concurrent activities (e.g., 'clean', 'radio', and 'cook'). Albeit not apparent in the graph, there are optional tasks, in that, between 'videogame' and 'bed', 'football' or 'play_cards' may or may not be carried out.

Figure 2 reports the log of a hypothetical case 'day4' of the smart environment process in Fig. 1 (only the first two events expressing contextual descriptions are reported). Here, all activities are carried out by agent 'steve'. Concurrency is evident in activities that begin when previous activities have not ended yet.

The process model underlying Fig. 1 can be easily represented in WoMan formalism as reported in Fig. 3 (the part concerning agents has been stripped). In Fig. 3 it is associated with 5 sample cases (corresponding to training cases if the

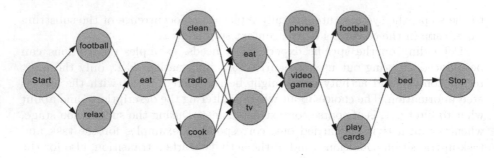

Fig. 1. Activity flow for an 'afternoon' smart environment process.

entry(201509281400, begin_process, afternoon, day4, start, 1, steve).
entry(201509281401, context_description, afternoon, day4,
    [good_weather(timestamp), status(h12,timestamp, status_h12_timestamp),
    off(status_h12_timestamp), heater(h12), ...],1).
entry(201509281404, begin_activity, afternoon, day4, football, 1, steve).
entry(201509281600, end_activity, afternoon, day4, football, 1, steve).
entry(201509281645, begin_activity, afternoon, day4, eat, 1, steve).
entry(201509281715, end_activity, afternoon, day4, eat, 1, steve).
entry(201509281718, context_description, afternoon, day4,
    [bad_weather(timestamp), status(h12,timestamp,status_h12_timestamp),
    off(status_h12_timestamp), heater(h12), ...], 1).
entry(201509281720, begin_activity, afternoon, day4, radio, 1, steve).
entry(201509281727, begin_activity, afternoon, day4, cook, 1, steve).
entry(201509281743, begin_activity, afternoon, day4, clean, 1, steve).
entry(201509281801, end_activity, afternoon, day4, cook, 1, steve).
entry(201509281822, end_activity, afternoon, day4, clean, 1, steve).
entry(201509281823, end_activity, afternoon, day4, radio, 1, steve).
entry(201509281825, begin_activity, afternoon, day4, tv, 1, steve).
entry(201509281834, begin_activity, afternoon, day4, eat, 2, steve).
entry(201509281926, end_activity, afternoon, day4, eat, 2, steve).
entry(201509281931, end_activity, afternoon, day4, tv, 1, steve).
entry(201509281938, begin_activity, afternoon, day4, videogame, 1, steve).
entry(201509282156, end_activity, afternoon, day4, videogame, 1, steve).
entry(201509282219, begin_activity, afternoon, day4, bed, 1, steve).
entry(201509290700, end_activity, afternoon, day4, bed, 1, steve).
entry(201509290700, end_process, afternoon, day4, stop, 1, steve).

Fig. 2. Event-based representation of a case.

model was learned from examples), including case **day4** in Fig. 2 (corresponding
to case #4 in the model). Some tasks are carried out in all cases ('eat', 'clean',
'radio', 'cook', 'tv', 'videogame', 'bed'). All the others may or may not take
place depending on the specific process enactment. Some tasks and transitions
are carried out more than once in the same case (e.g., 'eat' is always carried out
twice; 'phone' is carried out 0, 1, or 2 times depending on the case). Transitions

task(stop,[1,2,3,4,5]).

task(play_cards,[2]).

task(relax,[2,3]).

task(bed,[1,2,3,4,5]).

task(phone,[2,2,5]).

task(videogame,[1,2,2,2,3,4,5]).

task(tv,[1,2,3,4,5]).

task(clean,[1,2,3,4,5]).

task(cook,[1,2,3,4,5]).

task(radio,[1,2,3,4,5]).

task(eat,[1,1,2,2,3,3,4,4,5,5]).

task(football,[1,2,4,5]).

task(start,[1,2,3,4,5]).

transition([start],[football],p1,[1,4]).

transition([football],[eat],p2,[1,4]).

transition([eat],[clean,radio,cook],p3,[1,2,3,4,5]).

transition([clean,radio,cook],[eat,tv],p4,[1,2,3,4,5]).

transition([eat,tv],[videogame],p5,[1,2,3,4,5]).

transition([videogame],[phone],p6,[2,2,5]).

transition([phone],[videogame],p7,[2,2,5]).

transition([videogame],[bed],p8,[1,4]).

transition([bed],[stop],p9,[1,2,3,4,5]).

transition([start],[relax],p10,[2,3]).

transition([relax],[eat],p11,[2,3]).

transition([videogame],[football],p12,[2,5]).

transition([football],[bed],p13,[2,5]).

transition([videogame],[play_cards],p14,[3]).

transition([play_cards],[bed],p15,[3]).

Fig. 3. 'Afternoon' workflow model in WoMan formalism

$p1$ and $p10$ start alternative routes: in $p1$ the user plays football, while in $p10$ he relaxes. Also transitions $p8$, $p12$, and $p14$ start alternative routes before the user goes to bed: in $p8$ he goes to bed directly, while in $p12 - p13$ he first plays football and in $p14 - p15$ he first plays cards. So, $p12 - p13$ and $p14 - p15$ express optional tasks that are not carried out in $p8$. It is possible to note that task 'phone' occurs in only 2 cases (#2,#5) out of 5, and thus has frequency 0.4. Also, it was carried out at most twice in the same case (specifically, in case #2), which can be used as an upper limit to the number of accepted executions of this task in future executions. Task 'play_cards', and associated transitions $p14$ and $p15$, occur in only 1 case out of 5, yielding a probability of 0.2.

Let us now show how condition-related information is represented, by translating an initial excerpt of the log in Fig. 2. The first event (**begin_process**) gets step $s0$, and adds to the description the following atom:

act_start(s0)

Then, the first context event is found in the log (meaning that at timestamp *201509281401* the weather is good, the status of the heater $h12$ is 'off', etc.). This piece of information generates context step identifier $c1$ associated with timestamp *201509281401*, and adds the following atoms to the observation:

good_weather(c1), status(h12,c1,status_h12_c1), off(status_h12_c1),
heater(h12), ...

Then, activities 'football' and 'eat' are carried out, associated with steps $s1$ and $s2$, respectively, and contribute to the observation with the following atoms:

next(s0,s1,4), activity(s1,football,steve), act_football(football),
next(s1,s2,161), activity(s2,eat,steve), act_eat(eat), agent_steve(steve)

where 4 is the number of minutes in between activities 'start' and 'football', and 161 is the number of minutes in between activities 'football' and 'eat'. Also, both activities (actually, their corresponding steps) are associated with context $c1$:

$$\text{context}(s1,c1), \ \text{context}(s2,c1)$$

Then, the next context-related event is found in the log. It gets context step identifier $c2$, associated with timestamp *201509281718*, and causes the following contextual information to be added to the observation:

```
next(c1,c2, context, 197), bad weather(c2), status(h12,c2,status_h12_c2),
          off(status_h12_c2), heater(h12), ...
```

meaning that in context $c2$, following context $c1$ after 197 min, the weather is bad and the status of the heater *h12* is still 'off'. And so on.

Let us show some conditions. For instance, the task precondition:

```
football(X) :-
    after(Y,X,[1,10],[3,437]), act_start(Y), context(X,C),
    good_weather(C), available(C,B), ball(B), status(C,B,S),
    inflated(S).
```

says that, in order to play football at step X, the beginning of the process, at step Y, must have happened between 1 and 10 steps, and between 3 and 437 min, before X. Indeed it is one step for the leftmost occurrence in Fig. 1, while for the rightmost occurrence it is 6 steps (if activity 'phone' was never carried out), or 8 (if 'phone' was carried out just once), or 10 (if it was carried out twice, which is the upper limit for each single case). Moreover, in the context C associated with the time of playing football, the ball B must be available, and its status S must be 'inflated'. The task post-condition:

```
football(X) :-
    after(Y,X,[1,10],[3,437]), act_start(Y), context(X,C),
    good_weather(C), available(C,B), ball(B), status(C,B,S),
    inflated(S), after(C,D,context,[1,4],[127,439]),
    clothes_hamper(H), status(D,H,T), not_empty(T).
```

say that, after playing football at step X in context C (which required the precondition for activity 'football' to be fulfilled), there will be a later context D (coming between 1 and 4 contextual steps, and between 127 and 439 min, after C) in which the clothes hamper is not empty.

As regards transitions, a precondition might be:

```
p4(X) :-
    act_stereo(R), status(X,R,S), off(S), act_oven(O),
    status(X,O,T), off(T), agent_steve(U), after(Y,X,[1,1],[38,46]),
    activity(Y,A,U), act_clean(A), after(Z,X,[1,1],[61,73]),
    activity(Z,B,U), act_radio(B), after(W,X,[1,1],[54,62]),
    activity(W,C,U), act_cook(C).
```

This rule means that transition $p4$ may be fired (i.e., either activity 'eat' or activity 'tv' may be started, possibly depending on their specific pre-conditions) at step X if both the stereo and the oven are off, and the most recent activities (step intervals $[1,1]$) terminated by user 'steve' are 'clean', 'radio' and 'cook' (i.e., the input activities required by transition $p4$), which were carried out between 38 and 46 min before ('clean'), between 61 and 73 min before ('radio'), and between 54 and 62 min before ('cook'), respectively. The post-condition of transition $p1$ might be:

```
p1(X) :-
    after(Y,X,[1,1],[3,43]), act_start(Y), context(X,C),
    good_weather(C), available(C,B), ball(B), status(C,B,S),
    inflated(S), after(X,Z,[5,5],[487,501]), activity(Y,U,V),
    act_bed(U), agent_steve(V).
```

i.e., if transition $p1$ is carried out at step X (which means playing football at step X, since this is the only output task in transition $p1$), then in a sequence of exactly 5 steps (and in a time ranging from 487 to 501 min) activity 'bed' will be carried out. This means that when football is played in the early evening, the user in the evening goes straight to bed after playing videogames, and he never uses the phone while playing videogames. Note that a special case of the general precondition for activity 'football' is specified (the step and time ranges separating Y from X are sub-ranges of those in the general precondition).

Finally, as regards the tasks in the context of specific transitions, consider task 'football' in transition $p12$. The precondition might be:

```
football_p12(X) :-
    after(Y,Z,[1,1],[6,19]), act_start(Y), after(Z,X,[7,9],[413,418]),
    activity(Z,R,U), act_relax(R), agent_steve(U), context(X,C),
    good_weather(C), available(C,B), ball(B), status(C,B,S),
    inflated(S).
```

i.e., to play football in transition $p12$, in addition to the usual preconditions, the user must have relaxed in the early afternoon (i.e., he must not have played football already). Note that the after/4 intervals in the pre-condition have been split to consider the intermediate step at which activity 'relax' was carried out. The post-condition for activity 'relax' in transition $p10$ might be:

```
relax_p10(X) :-
    after(Y,X,[1,1],[2,19]), act_start(Y), after(X,Z,[9,9],[417,425]),
    activity(Z,A,U), act_football(A), agent_steve(U), context(X,C),
    good_weather(C), available(C,B), ball(B), status(C,B,S),
    inflated(S).
relax_p10(X) :-
    after(Y,X,[1,1],[2,19]), act_start(Y), after(X,Z,[5,5],[436,452]),
    activity(Z,A,U), act_play_cards(A), agent_steve(U),
    context(X,C), bad_weather(C), available(C,B), card_deck(B).
```

50   S. Ferilli

It is expressed by two alternative rules: after relaxing, either after exactly 9 steps (and between 417 and 425 min) the user plays football if the weather is good and an inflated ball is available, or after exactly 5 steps (and between 436 and 452 min) he plays cards if the weather is bad and a card deck is available.

5 Conclusions

WorkFlow Management Systems provide automatic support to learn process models or to check compliance of process enactment to correct models. The expressive power of the adopted formalism for representing process models is fundamental to determine the effectiveness or even feasibility of a correct model. In particular, a desirable feature is the possibility of expressing complex conditions on some elements of the model. The formalism used in the WoMan framework for workflow management, based on First-Order Logic, is more expressive than standard formalisms adopted in the literature. It allows tight integration between the activity flow and the conditions, and it allows one to express conditions that take into account contextual information and various kinds of relationships among the involved entities. This paper discusses an extended version of this formalism, and provides an explicative example of its use.

Due to the increased expressive power of the proposed formalism with respect to the state-of-the-art in process mining and management systems, we could not find process logs that could fully exploit it. So, we are currently building a dataset to run experiments aimed at assessing the behavior and performance of WoMan in using all features of the proposed formalism. However, preliminary experiments carried out on the available datasets already show interesting and promising results, also concerning runtime [2] (some notes on the complexity of the proposed approach can be found in [8]). We are also exploring advanced representation and learning approaches for dealing with the generalization of agent roles involved in the process, based on a given taxonomy.

References

1. Agrawal, R., Gunopulos, D., Leymann, F.: Mining process models from workflow logs. In: Schek, H.-J., Saltor, F., Ramos, I., Alonso, G. (eds.) EDBT 1998. LNCS, vol. 1377, pp. 467–483. Springer, Heidelberg (1998)
2. De Carolis, B., Ferilli, S., Redavid, D.: Incremental learning of daily routines as workflows in a smart home environment. ACM Trans. Interact. Intell. Syst. **4**, 1–23 (2015)
3. Cattafi, M., Lamma, E., Riguzzi, F., Storari, S.: Incremental declarative process mining. In: Szczerbicki, E., Nguyen, N.T. (eds.) Smart Information and Knowledge Management. SCI, vol. 260, pp. 103–127. Springer, Heidelberg (2010)
4. Cook, J.E., Wolf, A.L.: Discovering models of software processes from event-based data. Technical Report CU-CS-819-96, Department of Computer Science, University of Colorado (1996)

5. Cook, J.E., Wolf, A.L.: Event-based detection of concurrency. Technical Report CU-CS-860-98, Department of Computer Science, University of Colorado (1998)
6. de Medeiros, A.K.A., Weijters, A.J.M.M., van der Aalst, W.M.P.: Genetic process mining: an experimental evaluation. Data Min. Knowl. Discov. **14**, 245–304 (2007)
7. Esposito, F., Semeraro, G., Fanizzi, N., Ferilli, S.: Multistrategy theory revision: induction and abduction in InTheLEx. Mach. Learn. J. **38**(1/2), 133–156 (2000)
8. Ferilli, S.: WoMan: logic-based workflow learning and management. IEEE Trans. Syst. Man Cybern. Syst. **44**, 744–756 (2014)
9. Ferilli, S., Esposito, F.: A heuristic approach to handling sequential information in incremental ILP. In: Baldoni, M., Baroglio, C., Boella, G., Micalizio, R. (eds.) AI*IA 2013. LNCS, vol. 8249, pp. 109–120. Springer, Heidelberg (2013)
10. Ferilli, S., Esposito, F.: A logic framework for incremental learning of process models. Fundamenta Informaticae **128**, 413–443 (2013)
11. Herbst, J.: Dealing with concurrency in workflow induction. In: Proceedings of the European Concurrent Engineering Conference, pp. 175–182. SCS Europe (2000)
12. Herbst, J., Karagiannis, D.: Integrating machine learning and workflow management to support acquisition and adaptation of workflow models. In: Proceedings of the 9th International Workshop on Database and Expert Systems Applications, pp. 745–752. IEEE (1998)
13. Herbst, J., Karagiannis, D.: An inductive approach to the acquisition and adaptation of workflow models. In: Proceedings of the IJCAI 1999 Workshop on Intelligent Workflow and Process Management: The New Frontier for AI in Business, pp. 52–57 (1999)
14. Herbst, J.: A machine learning approach to workflow management. In: Lopez de Mantaras, R., Plaza, E. (eds.) ECML 2000. LNCS (LNAI), vol. 1810, pp. 183–194. Springer, Heidelberg (2000)
15. van der Aalst, W., et al.: Process mining manifesto. In: Daniel, F., Barkaoui, K., Dustdar, S. (eds.) BPM Workshops 2011, Part I. LNBIP, vol. 99, pp. 169–194. Springer, Heidelberg (2012)
16. Lamma, E., Mello, P., Riguzzi, F., Storari, S.: Applying inductive logic programming to process mining. In: Blockeel, H., Ramon, J., Shavlik, J., Tadepalli, P. (eds.) ILP 2007. LNCS (LNAI), vol. 4894, pp. 132–146. Springer, Heidelberg (2008)
17. Lloyd, J.W.: Foundations of Logic Programming, 2nd edn. Springer, Heidelberg (1987)
18. Maggi, F.M., Bose, R.P.J.C., van der Aalst, W.M.P.: Efficient discovery of understandable declarative process models from event logs. In: Ralyté, J., Franch, X., Brinkkemper, S., Wrycza, S. (eds.) CAiSE 2012. LNCS, vol. 7328, pp. 270–285. Springer, Heidelberg (2012)
19. Pesic, M., van der Aalst, W.M.P.: A declarative approach for flexible business processes management. In: Eder, J., Dustdar, S. (eds.) BPM Workshops 2006. LNCS, vol. 4103, pp. 169–180. Springer, Heidelberg (2006)
20. Rozinat, A., van der Aalst, W.M.P.: Decision mining in business processes. In: WP 164, BETA Working Paper Series. Eindhoven University of Technology (2006)
21. van der Aalst, W.M.P.: The application of petri nets to workflow management. J. Circ. Syst. Comput. **8**, 21–66 (1998)
22. van der Aalst, W.M.P.: Process mining overview and opportunities. ACM Trans. Manage. Inf. Syst. **3**, 7.1–7.17 (2012)
23. van der Aalst, W.M.P., Dustdar, S.: Process mining put into context. IEEE Internet Comput. **16**, 82–86 (2012)

52   S. Ferilli

24. van der Aalst, W.M.P., Weijters, T., Maruster, L.: Workflow mining: discovering process models from event logs. IEEE Trans. Knowl. Data Eng. **16**, 1128–1142 (2004)
25. Weijters, A.J.M.M., van der Aalst, W.M.P.: Rediscovering workflow models from event-based data. In: Proceedings of 11th Dutch-Belgian Conference of Machine Learning (Benelearn 2001), pp. 93–100 (2001)
26. Wen, L., Wang, J., Sun, J.: Detecting implicit dependencies between tasks from event logs. In: Zhou, X., Li, J., Shen, H.T., Kitsuregawa, M., Zhang, Y. (eds.) APWeb 2006. LNCS, vol. 3841, pp. 591–603. Springer, Heidelberg (2006)

Business Rules Uncertainty Management with Probabilistic Relational Models

Hamza Agli[1]([✉]), Philippe Bonnard[1], Christophe Gonzales[2],
and Pierre-Henri Wuillemin[2]

[1] IBM France Lab, Gentilly, France
{hamza.agli,philippe.bonnard}@fr.ibm.com
[2] Sorbonne Universités, UPMC Univ Paris 6, CNRS, UMR 7606 LIP6, Paris, France
{christophe.gonzales,pierre-henri.wuillemin}@lip6.fr

Abstract. Object-oriented Business Rules Management Systems (OO-BRMS) are a complex applications platform that provide tools for automating day-to-day business decisions. To allow more sophisticated and realistic decision-making, these tools must enable Business Rules (BRs) to handle uncertainties in the domain. For this purpose, several approaches have been proposed, but most of them rely on heuristic models that unfortunately have shortcomings and limitations. In this paper we present a solution allowing modern OO-BRMS to effectively integrate probabilistic reasoning for uncertainty management. This solution has a coupling approach with Probabilistic Relational Models (PRMs) and facilitates the inter-operability, hence, the separation between business and probabilistic logic. We apply our approach to an existing BRMS and discuss implications of the knowledge base dynamicity on the probabilistic inference.

Keywords: Business rules management systems · Uncertainty management · Probabilistic Relational Models · Bayesian Networks

1 Introduction and Related Work

OO-BRMS are very popular tools for decision-making automation. They are considered as the evolution of rule-based expert systems. In a separation between application and business logic, these systems facilitate authoring, checking, deploying and executing day-to-day companies operational business policies. Indeed, business professionals and IT specialists can collaborate relatively independently using such systems. This is because they provide double level artifacts that align IT practices with business needs [3,9].

Whereas BRMS are well adapted to deal with structured and complete data using classical Boolean inference, they face difficulties when they take into account uncertain or incomplete data. To tackle the issue of uncertainties in the domain, three approaches are commonly used:

© Springer International Publishing Switzerland 2016
J.J. Alferes et al. (Eds.): RuleML 2016, LNCS 9718, pp. 53–67, 2016.
DOI: 10.1007/978-3-319-42019-6_4

- Heuristic models to weight rules with a degree of truth, e.g., certainty factors
(CF) and likelihood ratios (LR) [5,10]. These deal with uncertainty in the
knowledge (rules) not the data. However probabilistic interpretation given to
CF is incoherent with probability theory [11]. On the other hand, the conditional independence between evidence and rules actions in LR is rarely satisfied
in real applications and LR-based expert systems have poor performance [16].
- *Fuzzy logic* (FL) [21] to capture the uncertainty and imprecision by associating variable values to fuzzy sets, but in essence, FL is not conceived to deal
with incomplete data or to express relations between variables in the knowledge base as in OO frameworks. Besides, fuzzy logic when applied to systems
that performs chains of inference, such as BRMS may lead to inconsistent
conclusions [7].
- Bayesian techniques, which are essentially based on Bayesian Networks (BNs)
[17], to consistently model domains with uncertainty. In addition, several algorithms have been proposed to learn their graphical structure and their conditional probability tables (CPTs) parameters. Even if they are a very popular
tool to deal with uncertainty, BNs are not suited for complex systems, in which
they involve high design and maintenance costs [13,15]. Besides, they do not
support well object-oriented and dynamic systems.

One can also find hybrid approaches that combine, for instance, BNs with
CF [4,14]. Obviously these methods incur in problems discussed previously.
Moreover they are developed for specific use and cannot handle effectively the
frequent changes of business policies, where BRMS perform better. Another approach is Probabilistic Logic Programming [6]. But this is not suited for the BRs
procedural side effects and the OO-BRMS upon which we build our application.
To summarize, current BRMS uncertainty management state-of-the-art face theoretical and practical limitations, do not exploit structural information encoded
in the knowledge base and face scaling difficulties.

To overcome the previous limitations, we propose to couple BRMS with Probabilistic Relational Models (PRMs) [12,18,19], an object-oriented extension of
BNs that enables handling very large systems. Their object paradigm and relational model allow them to be a good candidate for managing uncertainty in an
OO-BRMS. In addition, PRMs are equipped with sophisticated inference engines
that enable to answer efficiently various types of probabilistic queries.

In this paper, we describe a method that allows modern OO-BRMS to reason under uncertainty using a coupling approach that separates uncertainty and
rules management. There are many reasons for this separation. First, trying to
manage PRM inference and update inside BRMS would be inefficient and difficult since the rule engine is non-monotonic and is by essence a procedural engine
on object data. Second, separating concepts and architectures simplifies the software maintaining and offers more control over the framework complexity. Last,
such a coupling gives a mathematically sound interpretation of the uncertainty
and is based on a framework that is essentially designed to cope with large and
complex systems. This work is the continuation of [1] that proves the feasibility
and describes the coupling framework.

The remainder of this paper is organized as follows: in the next section, we briefly introduce OO-BRMS and PRMs. Then, we present the coupling apporach in Sect. 3, as a solution that allows OO-BRMS to deal with uncertainty. Then Sect. 4 describes how we implemented this solution in practice. Finally, some conclusion and future works are provided in Sect. 5.

2 Preliminaries

2.1 Object-Oriented BRs

BRs are rules in the form *"IF condition THEN action"* that are exploited for reasoning by forward chaining inference engines. OO-BRRMS execute BRs against an object model (OM) that describes the application objects. Let us illustrate this through a simplified example from an insurance application. Assume the model consist of three classes representing a healthcare professional, a subscriber and a reimbursement request. Figure 1 gives a UML class diagram for this application.

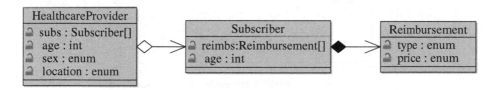

Fig. 1. UML diagram for a simplified insurance application

In a fraud detection context, we want to verify, using BRs-based approach, whether the healthcare professional is fraudulent. In such a way, anomalies that indicate fraud are detected by executing a set of rules and using scoring heuristics. For instance, if a fraud detection rule says that an excessive invoice alert must be raised on a healthcare provider who submits a high price reimbursement request for one of his subscribers, the corresponding object-oriented BR in Rule 1.1 will look for objects in the working memory (WM) that corresponds to providers with subscribers requesting reimbursements with a high price.

Rule 1.1. Detect invoice anomaly

```
1 IF hp has type HealthcareProvider & sub has type Subscriber &
      reimb has type Reimbursement & sub in hp.subs & reimb in sub.
      reimbs & reimb.price == high
2 THEN raiseAlertExceededInvoicePrice(hp)
```

Similarly, another rule says that a lens age anomaly alert must be raised on a healthcare provider who submits a lens reimbursement request for a subscriber under age 10. Rule 1.2 shows its pseudo-code.

Rule 1.2. Detect lens anomaly

```
1 IF hp has type HealthcareProvider & sub has type Subscriber &
    reimb has type Reimbursement
2       & sub in hp.subs & reimb in sub.reimbs & sub.age < 10 &
          reimb.type=lens
3 THEN raiseAlertLensAgeAnomaly(hp)
```

When the data is completely known and well adapted to classical logic paradigm, such rules are well handled using variant of pattern matching algorithms, e.g., enhanced RETE [8] or stateless sequential execution. However, in front of uncertain or missing data, such rules cannot be executed. The next paragraph introduce theoretical foundations to handle such a situation using PRMs.

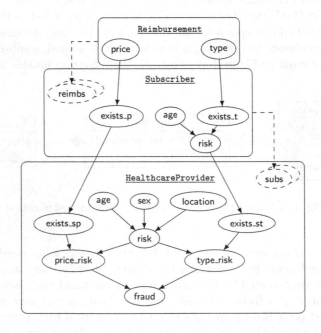

Fig. 2. PRM dependency schema for the fraud example

2.2   PRMs

One reason why standard BNs do not scale well is because they do not exploit the structure of the data. Instead, PRMs share the same class concept used in the object models. Indeed, the idea is that in complex systems, one can often identify repeated patterns, which can be abstracted as classes. Each pattern represents a fragment of a BN over its random variables. These correspond to the class descriptive attributes. PRMs also define the mechanism of reference slot allowing the navigation between attributes of different classes, and hence, the good definition of conditional probability distribution. They use aggregators to express many-to-one instance relations and get around the issue of multiple class definitions w.r.t variable number of configurations depending on relation arities. Finally, PRMs define a relational skeleton that represents the instance graph. This corresponds to the PRM system: classes that are instantiated and linked using reference slots. To sum up, a class corresponds to a set of random variables that share common relations (abstraction of repeated patterns) and are gathered in a BN fragment. Classes communicate through reference slots.

It is easy to see that the PRM can, not only represent the object model, but also the relation or causal/influence directions between the model attributes. Given an attribute, these relations are expressed through an arc connection between this attribute and its immediate predecessors, which are called "parents" in the graphical structure. In this paper, both relations and CPTs are assumed to be provided by a domain expert or obtained from a learning process.

One possible PRM representation of the fraud detection example is showed in Fig. 2. For instance, the attribute `reimbs` of class `Subscriber` is a multiple reference slot, which shows that the class points to a set of `Reimbursement`. In the running example, a divide-and-conquer approach is used to build aggregators: we first determine whether the `Subscriber` has a `Reimbursement` with a `high price` (by `exists_p` aggregator); second, we determine if the `HealthcareProvider` is linked to a `Subscriber` satisfying the previous condition (by `exists_sp`). We follow the same reasoning to generate the aggregator `exists_st`.

Figure 3 depicts an example of a relational skeleton obtained from the fraud example instances. A dashed arc stands for a reference slot, for instance `sub1` references `reimb1` and `reimb2`. Further details bout the PRMs extension used in this work might be found in [20].

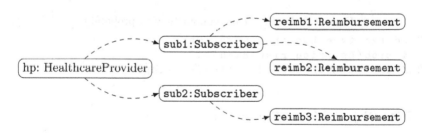

Fig. 3. An instance relational skeleton for the fraud example

3   Coupling BRs and PRMs

In the previous paragraph, we highlighted the common OO paradigm that ties OO BRMS and PRMs and we illustrated this through the fraud example. Using PRMs allows for more model abstraction, while using classical BNs methods results in

a repetition of objects creation, model dependence ins rules and inference ineffi-
ciency for large systems. In this paragraph, we suggest to extend the BRs data
meta-model, compilation and runtime to specify relations and probability model.

3.1 Probabilistic Rules

We propose to use the aforementioned similarity to invoke probabilistic instructions within the rules, e.g., marginal distribution computation and evidence posting. For this reason, probabilistic attributes in the rules are directly mapped to their
equivalent PRM attributes (see Sect. 2). Assume that the OM against which the
rules are executed is extended to include all the nodes in the dependency network
on Fig. 2 as attributes of the corresponding classes. Assume further that a `prob`
operator[1] is introduced in the syntax and allows triggering inference process of the
probabilistic engine. As we discussed previously, PRM relates attributes of different classes, and those of generated instances consequently, to permit the creation
of complex networks covering multiple instances. Although, RVs are generated
from the same classes, they should be regarded as distinct variables with their own
life-cycle. We know from Fig. 2 that `price_risk` attribute is linked to attributes
of classes `Subscriber` and `Reimbursement` in the PRM by reference mechanism,
hence, in this new extension, there is no need to evaluate conditions that can be
processed by probabilistic inference. When the engine encounters the `prob` operator, it immediately launches the probabilistic process, which queries the underlying PRM. In such an extension, probabilistic data is explicitly identified and can
be processed by PRM engines. Now, instead of Rule 1.1, which says basically, that
an alert must be raised when a healthcare provider submits a fraudulently expensive price reimbursement for a subscriber, we can have Rule 1.3 that says that an
excessive invoice alert must be raised on a healthcare provider if there is a 80 %
probability that the price of a reimbursement request is excessive.

Rule 1.3. Detect invoice anomaly with probability

```
1 IF hp has type HealthcareProvider
2    & prob(hp.price_risk=high)>.8
3 THEN raiseAlertExceededInvoicePrice(hp)
```

3.2 BRs Object Model Extension

We suggest to extend both rules, by adding new attributes as in the previous
section, and their data meta-model by adding probabilistic annotations. This
has two advantages. The first is moving probabilistic definitions from rules to
their data meta-model. In making this move, BRs can externalize probabilistic
inference and allow for separate management of business and probabilistic logic.
Second, this enables the model to be more independent w.r.t the rules, which
means an independent evolution of both. Annotations are a type of meta-data
that enriches the meta-model at hand. In this work, they are added to indicate

---

[1] For probability.

that a class contains probabilistic information, as well as that an attribute is mapped to a PRM attribute and is parametrized by its corresponding CPT and parents. If the attribute is an aggregator, annotations show its type, its domain and the concerned modalities, i.e., random variables (RVs) possible states. As we can see, such annotations allow for a natural mapping between OM and PRMs. Therefore, an OM class (resp. attribute) is mapped to a PRM class (resp. attribute) and the probabilistic data and how classes are related to each other is extracted from the OM annotations. In the OM, a restricted type represents a type whose domain is restricted, for instance an `integer` that is restricted to $\{0, 1, 2\}$. Only discrete RVs are supported in PRMs, they can be user-labeled (e.g., `state_type`) or built-in types (e.g., `boolean,int`). Thanks to these annotations, rules engine can generate the underlying PRM classes and system at compile time. Before the generation process, the model is parsed and checked. For example we check if the given list of a PRM attribute parents is valid and consistent with its CPT. This latter is also checked to verify it represents a well defined probability distribution. Actually, there are two possible modes for PRM system definition. The first is a static declaration, which assumes that all WM instances are known at compile-time. The PRM system is then generated either by directly processing the WM instance graph, or by an explicit declaration inside a special annotated class, which also specifies necessary relations. The second mode allows a dynamic definition in addition to the previous mode. Here, rules execution may also update the system by incrementally inserting new instances or modifying relations for instance. The last mode is obviously much more interesting since it reflects BRs and WM dynamic nature. The mapping we use allows the rules to generate complex probabilistic networks via the simple mechanism of class instantiation and reference slot. This power property enables the rules, for instance to handle many sets of RVs, which are obtained for free, just by means of linking instantiated classes.

4 Implementation

To illustrate all the concepts introduced in previous sections, we implemented a prototype that couples IBM Operational Decision Manager (ODM)[2] as an OO-BRMS with A Graphical Universal Model (aGrUM)[3] as a probabilistic engine. However, the methodology we applied can be easily generalized to any OO-BRMS as we showed previously. ODM execute BRs against an eXecutable OM, hereafter XOM, using the Ilog Rule Language (IRL). The latter is a Java-like language, which is also based on the OO paradigm. In practice, this model can be build from Java sources for instance. The XOM is a class model that describes the application objects and data of the WM. ODM allows also business professionals to enter rules using the Business Action Language (BAL), which describes rules[4] in a more human readable format. Finally, ODM provides an automated mapping between both BAL business and IRL technical rules[5].

---

[2] http://www-03.ibm.com/software/products/en/odm.
[3] http://agrum.lip6.fr.
[4] The series of "if-then(-else)" statements.
[5] Actually, this automation is not always defined, but may require IT specialist insight.

```
1  @PrmClass
2  public class Subscriber{
3    @PrmMultiReference
4    public Reimbursement[] reimbs;
5
6    @PrmAttribute(parents={},cpt={{.2},{.8}})
7    public AgeType age;
8
9    @PrmAgg(name="exists",attribute="reimbs.type",mod="lens")
10   public boolean exists_t;
11
12   @PrmAgg(name="exists",attribute="reimbs.price",mod="high")
13   public boolean exists_p;
14
15   @PrmAttribute(parents={"age","exists_t"},cpt
            ={{.2,.6,.5,.3},{.8,.4,.5,.7}})
16   public boolean risk;
17  }
18
19  @PrmSystemClass
20  public class System{
21    public HealthcareProvider hp = new HealthcareProvider();
22    public Reimbursement[] reimbs  = new Reimbursement[3];
23    public Subscriber[] subs = new Subscriber[2];
24
25    public System(){
26      hp.subs=subs;
27      sub[0].reimbs={reimbs[0],reimbs[1]};
28      sub[1].reimbs={reimbs[2]};
29    }
30  }
```

Fig. 4. Subscriber and System classes

To begin with, let us show the IRL classes obtained for Subscriber and the system of our running example. Consider Fig. 4 line 1, the annotation @PrmClass is a mark to express that the class contains probabilistic information. The corresponding probabilistic attributes are annotated with @PrmAttribute and carry information needed to describe their counterpart PRM attributes. For instance, age in line 7 has no parents and a CPT describing whether the subscriber is under the age of 10 is given. Note that AgeType at line 7 is an Integer restricted type. @PrmAgg marks the attribute as an aggregator. In line 15, the annotation specifies a list of the attribute parents and its CPT. In this example, we implemented the static mode. So, instances are specified as internal attributes of the system class that is annotated with @PrmSystemClass in line 19. Reference slots are set inside the class constructor at line 25. Finally, the relational skeleton in Fig. 3 is generated from this system class.

4.1   Compilation Process

The compilation process is based on a series of model rewritings. This is a powerful tool that allows ODM, not only to abstract instructions from their implementation, but also to conserve the rule paradigm. Practically, the IRL rules life-cycle is completely separated from that of BAL rules. As a consequence, changing the implementation is possible without altering every BR.

When BRs are entered using the BAL, they are first translated into IRL rules by a rewriting procedure. Second, the resulting rule-set is checked and parsed to obtain a rule-set semantic model as Abstract Syntax Tree (AST). At this level, the result may undergo recursive rewritings, on top of which one can plug different APIs. Then, the rule-set AST is compiled while taking into account the chosen algorithm. Again this phase can be parametrized by various plugins according to the algorithm to be used, e.g. RETE. The output at this stage is optimized and transformed to obtain the semantic OM. This latter is a powerful meta-model, it can be seen as an extension of the Java meta-model that allows compilation, sources processing and model definition. There is no longer semantic rule-sets here, but instead, an object model that encodes the semantics inside the generated classes and methods. Other operations may appear such as the BAL/IRL mapping and the linkage with outside application via services mechanism. The final result is persisted and jitted into an archive that can be deployed in the desired platform, e.g. Java, C# and Script. Note that this chain is executed in pipe-line and the order is controlled by the plugins execution in the chain. Our proposed prototype, called BIS for Bayesian Insight System, can be plugged on top of the rules compilation process as an additional rewriting of the rule-set. The plugging choice is motivated by our desire to take advantage of an existing compilation framework, rather than building such a process from scratch. Additionally, a plugging approach facilitates the conceptual and technical integration in the product architecture. Figure 5 depicts an overall schema of the compilation process. In particular, a compilation factory is implemented to adapt the probabilistic context to the compilation chain. The IRL-based Rule 1.4 illustrates the results after rewriting the Rule 1.3. In this example, we move from function rewriting to proper call of the probabilistic engine with current arguments.

Rule 1.4. Detect invoice anomaly with probability

```
1  rule detectInvoiceAnomaly{
2    when{
3    hp:HealthcareProvider(ProbabilisticEngine.this.
         calculateProbability(this,"price_risk", "high") > 0.8)
         ;
4      }
5    then{
6      raiseAlertExceededInvoicePrice(hp);
7      }
8  }
```

When the extended IRL is compiled, annotations serve to extract PRM attributes, CPTs and relations. When the checking is completed, the final model is written into the PRM text format and processed for inference. We give another way to introduce the probability in rules using the IRL `evaluate` operator. Rule 1.5 evaluates the risk that a `Subscriber` is participating in a fraud.

Rule 1.5. Evaluate subscriber risk with probability

```
1  rule evaluatSubscriberRisk{
2    when{
3      hp: HealthcareProvider();
4      sub: Subscriber() in hp.subs;
5      evaluate(prob(sub.risk==true)| hp.risk==true)>.8);
6    }
7    then{
8      alertRiskedSubscriber(sub);
9    }
10 }
```

The vertical bar in the rule stands for "knowing that" and corresponds formally to conditional probability of a RV. In this rule, the RV `sub.risk` is connected to `HealthcareProvider`'s attributes through the reference `subs`. In the expression `prob(sub.risk==true)| hp.risk==true)`, the conditional context is explicitly mentioned, which refers to computing the probability of `sub.risk` given some information on `hp.risk`. However, we want to simplify more the syntax by considering implicitly every fact in the WM. As a consequence, `prob` should be stateful to facilitate the rule writing without bothering oneself with the underlying PRM. Thus, the previous expression is reduced to `prob(sub.risk==true)`, which is implicitly equivalent to `prob(sub.risk==true|WM)`, where WM is simply reduced to `"hp.risk==true"`. Finally, one can similarly manage the introduction of other operators such as `likelihood` and `entropy`.

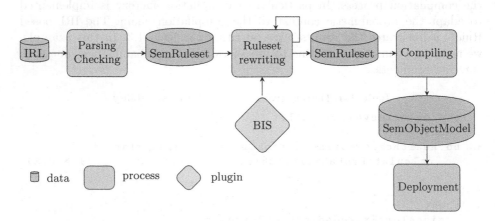

Fig. 5. ODM compiling chain

4.2   Advanced Probabilistic Rules

At rules level, one is interested in decision-making, to which the notion of *risk* is relevant[6], not in how probabilistic query is performed. So another easy, yet interesting, approach to express probability in the rules, is to parametrize the whole condition by probabilistic activation threshold while allowing the coupling introduced in Sect. 3. Doing so helps the rule engine agenda to determine which rule should be executed. In practice, we need to introduce a general probability operator that governs rules eligibility by testing if the probability of the corresponding tuple pattern matching equals or exceeds the probabilistic threshold.

Rule 1.6. Evaluate subscriber risk with probability

```
1  rule evaluatSubscriberRisk{
2    probability >= .8;
3    when{
4    hp:HealthcareProvider();
5    sub:Subscriber(sub.risk==true|hp.risk==true) in hp.subs;
6    }
7    then{
8    alertRiskedSubscriber(sub);
9    }
10 }
```

The *probability* operator in Rule 1.6 involves all the RVs occurring in the condition part. However, since PRM engines cannot directly deal with such conditions but only with variables, one must specify the rule conditions, which are really participating in computations, and identify the underlying probabilistic variables. This is a challenging task that involves a difficult compilation process. Actually, in this approach, we need to analyze rules, extract information that is relevant to probabilistic inference and avoid non probabilistic variables for instance. Then, one must transform the result into the adequate probabilistic query[7]. Many operators that are present in the compilation process are complex to evaluate and need to be detected. This means introducing new operations in the compilation in order for the probabilistic engine to deal with different conditions including different tests (variable and class conditions), aggregators and generators. Fortunately, both models share some high level operators, e.g., *min, max, for all, exists* aggregators, which can be automatically extracted from rules conditions, thanks to the compilation, and mapped to their PRM counterparts if any. Otherwise they can be used to complete the PRM definition with new attributes.

Now, using this general operator, every logical production rule can be given a probabilistic meaning by considering non probabilistic variables as a Dirac distribution and by imposing *probability* operator to be equal to 1. In this way, we can give probabilistic meaning to Rule 1.1 as showed in Rule 1.7.

---

[6] For instance, the risk of not executing a rule that should be executed (false negative).
[7] In general, one must specify how every language construct is compiled to be processed by this general operator and assure the preservation of queries operational semantic after the rewriting, but this is beyond the scope of this paper.

Rule 1.7. Detect invoice anomaly

```
1  rule detectInvoiceAnomaly{
2    probability=1;
3    when{
4     hp:HealthcareProvider();
5     sub:Subscriber() in hp.subs();
6     exists Reimbursement(price=='high') in sub.reimbs();
7    }
8    then{
9     raiseAlertExceededInvoicePrice(hp);
10   }
11 }
```

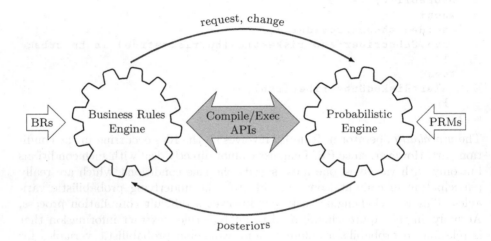

Fig. 6. BIS coupling

4.3 A Loosely Coupling-Based Execution

The declarative aspect of the rules facilitates efficient instances generation for the PRM system. At run-time, a hundred of RVs with complex relations can be easily obtained just by means of instanciation; this is an advantage over the classical BNs approach. In addition to the compilation API discussed previously, BIS is also endowed with an execution API. Both insure different services communicating following the schema shown in Fig. 6. This allows for a coupling between both BRs and probabilistic engines, which are implemented as services. Actually, our framework is not restricted to one implementation, but is open to any other probabilistic engine, which can be seen as a plugged service implementation. For instance, the current work is using aGrUM that can deal with PRMs. We have also tested JSmile[8] as a probabilistic engine, however, we were limited

---

[8] See https://dslpitt.org/genie/wiki/JSMILE_and_Smile.NET for more details.

by the lack of relations and object concepts in such a framework. Recall that the compilation part performs a rewriting from the rules semantic model, which encompasses probabilistic data, to run-time functions, which actually call the probabilistic engine. In our case the PRM is generated by XOM compilation and read by probabilistic engine. It is also possible to read both models from external files. Furthermore, our architecture allows for a good inter-operability between both engines. On the one hand, rules execution can change the state of the WM and consequently the RVs in the PRM system by posting evidence, adding, removing new instances or setting new relations. For instance, the action part of Rule 1.8, update the WM by adapting the **risk** attribute. Through additional process of rewriting and compilation, one can even discover particular variables to post soft evidence on their corresponding probabilistic ones[9].

Rule 1.8. Detect invoice anomaly with probability

```
1 rule detectInvoiceAnomaly{
2   when{
3     hp:HealthcareProvider( prob(type_risk==high)>.8) );
4     sub: Subscriber() in hp.subs;
5   }
6   then{
7     update sub{risk=true;}
8       }
9 }
```

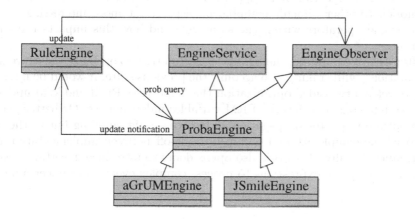

Fig. 7. PRM plugin as a service

On the other hand, when the rules trigger the inference process, the probabilistic engine computes the needed probability for the query and may also notify the WM to update some attributes for rules reevaluation.

In Fig. 7 engines are related via an observation mechanism and both are notified, through the observer, when any change occurs in the WM. That is,

---

[9] Constrains on probability distribution.

each time an incremental change, such as object or relation insertion/retraction occurs in the WM, the underlying PRM is notified for the update, e.g., reference slot change. Both probabilistic and rules engine perform inference in a lazy way. The former records every incremental WM update until the next rule query evaluation. Then it accordingly updates the PRM system to answer the probabilistic query. The latter seeks to minimize evaluations in the RETE network.

5   Conclusion

This paper introduced an effective approach to integrate probabilistic reasoning into modern BRMS. The solution we proposed couples BRMS with PRMs. We highlighted the natural mapping between both paradigms and gave an operational method to assure it. Finally we proposed a general architecture of the coupling platform prototype. The technical contribution is implemented as an embedded prototype in the ODM product.

Our work opens many other research perspectives. In particular, due to the dynamic aspect of the WM, a probabilistic inference algorithm should be developed to insure the PRM inference adaptability. For this purpose, we are currently working on an adaptation of the incremental junction tree inference algorithm, which is proposed in [2]. Moreover, as soon as we deal with aggregators/generators in the rules, e.g., `from,in`, it becomes necessary to automatically generate their PRM counterpart as and when we compile the rules. This immediately opens the issue of PRMs non-supported operators and the idea of extending this model. Another difficult compilation aspect, yet more interesting, is the use of several operators within the same rule and how this impacts the PRM construction.

After each WM update, the RETE algorithm tries to optimize the expression re-evaluations, while taking into account the previous state. It would be interesting to develop a two-sided optimization that supervises PRM and WM updates, e.g., take into consideration the PRM variables independence. Or better yet, to try to optimize updates propagation as part of a tight coupling but to the cost of algorithmic complexity and finding a trade-off between implementation and performance. Finally, this work also opens doors to introduce uncertain reasoning in rules temporal expressions to process complex events over uncertain data or events.

Acknowledgments. This work was partially supported by IBM France Lab/ANRT CIFRE under the grant #421/2014. The authors would like to thank Christian De Sainte Marie for useful discussions and insights.

References

1. Agli, H., Bonnard, P., Wuillemin, P., Gonzales, C.: Uncertain reasoning for business rules. In: Proceedings of the 8th International Web Rule Symposium Doctoral Consortium (2014)

2. Agli, H., Bonnard, P., Wuillemin, P., Gonzales, C.: Incremental junction tree inference. In: Proceedings of the 16th Information Processing and Management of Uncertainty in Knowledge-Based Systems International Conference (2016, to appear)
3. Berstel-Da Silva, B.: Verification of Business Rules Programs. Springer, Heidelberg (2014)
4. Bobek, S., Nalepa, G.J.: Compact representation of conditional probability for rule-based mobile context-aware systems. In: Bassiliades, N., Gottlob, G., Sadri, F., Paschke, A., Roman, D. (eds.) RuleML 2015. LNCS, vol. 9202, pp. 83–96. Springer, Heidelberg (2015)
5. Buchanan, B.G., Shortliffe, E.H.: Rule Based Expert Systems: The Mycin Experiments of the Stanford Heuristic Programming Project. Addison-Wesley, Reading (1984)
6. De Raedt, L., Kimmig, A.: Probabilistic (logic) programming concepts. Mach. Learn. **100**(1), 5–47 (2015)
7. Elkan, C.: The paradoxical success of fuzzy logic. In: IEEE Expert, pp. 698–703 (1993)
8. Forgy, C.L.: RETE: a fast algorithm for the many pattern/many object pattern match problem. Artif. Intell. **19**(1), 17–37 (1982)
9. Graham, I.: Business Rules Management and Service Oriented Architecture: A Pattern Language. Wiley, Chichester (2006)
10. Hart, P.E., Duda, R.O., Einaudi, M.T.: PROSPECTOR–a computer-based consultation system for mineral exploration. J. Int. Assoc. Math. Geol. **10**(5), 589–610 (1977)
11. Heckerman, D.E., Shortliffe, E.H.: From certainty factors to belief networks. Artif. Intell. Med. **4**(1), 35–52 (1992)
12. Koller, D., Pfeffer, A.: Probabilistic frame-based systems. In: Proceedings of the 15th National Conference on Artificial Intelligence (AAAI), pp. 580–587 (1998)
13. Koller, D., Pfeffer, A.: Object-oriented Bayesian networks. In: Proceedings of the Thirteenth Conference on Uncertainty in Artificial Intelligence (UAI), pp. 302–313 (1997)
14. Korver, M., Lucas, P.J.F.: Converting a rule-based expert system into a belief network. Med. Informatics **18**, 219–241 (1993)
15. Mahoney, S.M., Laskey, K.B.: Network engineering for complex belief networks. In: Proceedings of the Twelfth International Conference on Uncertainty in Artificial Intelligence (UAI), pp. 389–396 (1996)
16. Ng, K.C., Abramson, B.: Uncertainty management in expert systems. IEEE Expert Intell. Syst. Appl. **5**(2), 29–48 (1990)
17. Pearl, J.: Probabilistic Reasoning in Intelligent Systems: Networks of Plausible Inference. Morgan Kaufmann, San Mateo (1988)
18. Pfeffer, A.J.: Probabilistic Reasoning for Complex Systems. Ph.D. thesis, Stanford University (2000)
19. Torti, L., Gonzales, C., Wuillemin, P.H.: Speeding-up structured probabilistic inference using pattern mining. Int. J. Approximate Reasoning **54**(7), 900–918 (2013)
20. Wuillemin, P.H., Torti, L.: Structured probabilistic inference. Int. J. Approximate Reasoning **53**(7), 946–968 (2012)
21. Zadeh, L.A.: Fuzzy sets. Inform. Control **8**(3), 338–353 (1965)

A Declarative Semantics for a Fuzzy Logic Language Managing Similarities and Truth Degrees

Pascual Julián-Iranzo[1], Ginés Moreno[2(✉)], Jaime Penabad[3], and Carlos Vázquez[2]

[1] Department of Technologies and Information Systems, UCLM, 13071 Ciudad Real, Spain
Pascual.Julian@uclm.es
[2] Department of Computing Systems, UCLM, 02071 Albacete, Spain
{Gines.Moreno,Carlos.Vazquez}@uclm.es
[3] Department of Mathematics, UCLM, 02071 Albacete, Spain
Jaime.Penabad@uclm.es

Abstract. This work proposes a declarative semantics based on a fuzzy variant of the classical notion of least Herbrand model for the so-called FASILL language (acronym of "Fuzzy Aggregators and Similarity Into a Logic Language") which has been recently designed and implemented in our research group for coping with implicit/explicit truth degree annotations, a great variety of connectives and unification by similarity.

Keywords: Fuzzy logic programming · Similarity · Herbrand model

1 Introduction

The challenging research area of *Fuzzy Logic Programming* is devoted to introduce *fuzzy logic* concepts into *logic programming* in order to explicitly deal with vagueness in a natural way. It has provided an extensive variety of Prolog dialects along the last three decades. *Fuzzy logic languages* can be classified (among other criteria) according to the emphasis they assign to fuzzifying the original unification/resolution mechanisms of Prolog. Whereas some approaches are able to cope with similarity/proximity relations at unification time [1,6,22,24], others extend their operational principles (maintaining syntactic unification) for managing a wide variety of fuzzy connectives and truth degrees on rules/goals beyond the simpler case of *true* or *false* [13,15,19].

The first line of integration, where the syntactic unification algorithm is extended with the ability of managing similarity/proximity relations, is of special relevance for this work. Similarity/proximity relations associate the elements of a set with a certain approximation degree and serve for weakening the notion of

Work supported by the EU (FEDER), and the Spanish MINECO Ministry (*Ministerio de Economía y Competitividad*) under grant TIN2013-45732-C4-2-P.

equality and, hence, to deal with vague information. With respect to this line, the related work can be summarized as follows:

In [24], an extension of the declarative paradigm of classic logic programming is proposed by considering similarity-based computations (the weakening of the equality notion is managed by means of fuzzy similarity relations for dealing with vague information) which allows to perform approximate inferences. Also, it describes the notion of fuzzy least Herbrand model and proves the equivalence with the fixpoint semantics of logic programs with similarity. Moreover, a graded notion of logical consequence can be considered and the operational semantics is designed by introducing a modified version of SLD resolution, by using a generalized notion of most general unifier that provides a numeric value which gives a measure of the exploited approximation.

In [24] (work that extends the precedent [23]) an operational semantics and a fixpoint semantics are defined and related, as well as a fuzzy extension of the least Herbrand model is given. Also in [2], that proposes the logic programming language Likelog (*LIKEness in LOGic*) which relies on similarity too, an operational semantics and a fix-point semantics are defined.

A more general notion called proximity relation was introduced in [5] by omitting the transitivity axiom. The Bousi∼Prolog language [11] is a fuzzy logic programming language with an operational semantics which is an adaptation of the SLD resolution, incorporating a fuzzy unification algorithm based on proximity relations.

A different generalization of similarity-based logic programming is the SQLP scheme (see *S*imilarity-based reasoning in qualified logic programming, [3]), designed as an innovative extension of the QLP scheme (Quantitative Logic Programs of [25]), in which the authors show that the similarity-based logic programming approach presented in [24] can be reduced to Qualified Logic Programing in the QLP(D) scheme introduced in [21], which supports logic programming with attenuated program clauses over a parametrically given domain D. The SQCLP scheme is a notable extension of [13,25] which supports qualification values (elements of a domain of qualification), proximity relations and notions coming from CLP (Constraint Logic Programming). In this framework, the authors present a declarative semantics for SQCLP that is based on observables, providing fixpoint and proof-theoretical characterizations of least program models.

Ending this section, it is important to say that our research group has been involved both on the development of similarity-based logic programming systems and those that extend the resolution principle, as reveals the design of the Bousi∼Prolog language[1] [11,12,22], where clauses cohabit with similarity/proximity equations, and the development of the FLOPER system,[2] which manages fuzzy programs composed by rules richer than clauses [16,18]. Our unifying approach is somehow inspired by [4], but in our framework we admit a wider set of connectives inside the body of programs rules. In this paper, we propose the declarative semantics of the FASILL (acronym of "Fuzzy Aggregators and

---

[1] Two different programming environments for Bousi∼Prolog are available at http://dectau.uclm.es/bousi/.

[2] The tool is freely accessible from the Web site http://dectau.uclm.es/floper/.

Similarity Into a Logic Language") language, whose operational semantics has been recently embedded into the FLOPER system. Following the same scheme of [9,11], this paper introduces the declarative semantics of the FASILL language, since it was proposed as a pending task in [7].

The structure of this paper is as follows. Firstly, in Sect. 2 we formally define and illustrate the syntax of the FASILL language, whose operational semantics was initially presented too in [7]. Next, Sect. 3 details its declarative semantics by introducing the concept of Herbrand model and least Herbrand model of a FASILL program. Finally, in Sect. 4 we present our conclusions and future research lines.

2   The FASILL Language

FASILL is a first order language built upon a signature Σ, that contains the elements of a countably infinite set of variables $\mathcal{V}$, function symbols, and predicate symbols with an associated arity –usually expressed as pairs f/n or p/n where n represents its arity–, the implication symbol ($\leftarrow$), and a wide set of other connectives ς (t-norms, t-conorms and aggregators). The language combines the elements of Σ as terms, atoms, rules, and formulas. A *constant* c is a function symbol with arity zero. A *term* is a variable, a constant or a function symbol f/n applied to n terms $t_1, \ldots, t_n$, and is denoted as $f(t_1, \ldots, t_n)$. We allow values of a lattice L as part of the signature Σ, whose formal definition follows.

Definition 1 (Complete lattice). *A complete lattice is a partially ordered set* $(L, \leq)$ *such that every subset S of L has infimum and supremum elements. Then, it is a bounded lattice, i.e., it has bottom and top elements, denoted by $\bot$ and $\top$, respectively. L is said to be the carrier set of the lattice, and $\leq$ its ordering relation.*

More precisely, we allow the existence of a set of truth degree literals, Σ_L, as part of the signature Σ. These literals are written exactly as they have meant to be interpreted as values of a lattice of truth degrees L[3]. Therefore, a well-formed formula can be either:

- r, if $r \in \Sigma_L$ (which will be interpreted as itself, that is, as the truth degree $r \in L$),
- $p(t_1, \ldots, t_n)$, if $t_1, \ldots, t_n$ are terms and p/n is an n-ary predicate. This formula is called *atom*. Particularly, atoms containing no variables are called *ground atoms*, and atoms built from nullary predicates are called *propositional variables*,
- $\varsigma(\mathcal{F}_1, \ldots, \mathcal{F}_n)$, if $\mathcal{F}_1, \ldots, \mathcal{F}_n$ are well-formed formulas and ς is an n-ary connective.

---

[3] This convention is quite standard and even used in a pure logic language like Prolog, where the reserved words *true* and *fail* -which directly resemble the pair of elements conforming the fixed lattice of truth degrees associated to any Prolog program- can be freely used on goals and clause bodies.

The language is equipped with a set of *connectives* ς[4] interpreted on the lattice, including

- aggregators denoted by @, whose truth functions $\dot{@}$ fulfill the boundary condition: $\dot{@}(\top,\top) = \top$, $\dot{@}(\bot,\bot) = \bot$, and monotonicity: $(x_1,y_1) \leq (x_2,y_2) \Rightarrow \dot{@}(x_1,y_1) \leq \dot{@}(x_2,y_2)$.[5]
- t-norms and t-conorms [20] (also named conjunctions and disjunctions, that we denote by & and |, respectively) whose truth functions fulfill the following properties:
  · Commutative: $\quad \dot{\&}(x,y) = \dot{\&}(y,x) \qquad\qquad \dot{|}(x,y) = \dot{|}(y,x)$
  · Associative: $\quad \dot{\&}(x,\dot{\&}(y,z)) = \dot{\&}(\dot{\&}(x,y),z) \ \dot{|}(x,\dot{|}(y,z)) = \dot{|}(\dot{|}(x,y),z)$
  · Identity element: $\dot{\&}(x,\top) = x \qquad\qquad\qquad \dot{|}(x,\bot) = x$
  · Monotonicity in each argument:
  $$z \leq t \Rightarrow \begin{cases} \dot{\&}(z,y) \leq \dot{\&}(t,y) \ \dot{\&}(x,z) \leq \dot{\&}(x,t) \\ \dot{|}(z,y) \leq \dot{|}(t,y) \quad \dot{|}(x,z) \leq \dot{|}(x,t) \end{cases}$$

Example 1. In the (complete) lattice $([0,1],\leq)$, where $\leq$ is the usual ordering relation on real numbers, it is possible to consider three sets of connectives corresponding to the fuzzy logics of Gödel, Łukasiewicz and Product, defined in Fig. 1, where labels L, G and P mean respectively *Łukasiewicz logic*, *Gödel logic*, and *product logic* (with different capabilities for modeling *pessimistic*, *optimistic*, and *realistic* scenarios –see [20] for a description of these scenarios–).

$$\dot{\&}_P(x,y) \triangleq x * y \qquad \dot{|}_P(x,y) \triangleq x + y - xy \qquad Product$$
$$\dot{\&}_G(x,y) \triangleq \min(x,y) \qquad \dot{|}_G(x,y) \triangleq max(x,y) \qquad G\ddot{o}del$$
$$\dot{\&}_L(x,y) \triangleq \max(0,x+y-1) \ \dot{|}_L(x,y) \triangleq \min(x+y,1) \ \text{Łukasiewicz}$$

Fig. 1. Conjunctions and disjunctions in $[0,1]$ for *Product*, *Łukasiewicz*, and *Gödel* fuzzy logics

It is possible to include also other connectives. For instance, the arithmetical average, defined by connective $@_{aver}$ (with truth function $\dot{@}_{aver}(x,y) \triangleq \frac{x+y}{2}$), that is a stated, easy to understand connective that does not belong to a standard fuzzy logic. Connectives with arities different from 2 can also be used, like the $@_{very}$ aggregation, defined by $\dot{@}_{very}(x) \triangleq x^2$, that is a unary connective or modifier.

---

[4] Here, the connectives ς are binary operations but we usually generalize them with an arbitrary number of arguments, that is, with truth function $\dot{\varsigma}: L^n \to L$.
[5] Note that, in the antecedent of this implication we use the order for pairs, (which is defined as $(x_1,y_1) \leq (x_2,y_2)$ if, and only if, $x_1 \leq x_2$ and $y_1 \leq y_2$), while in the consequent the usual order on the interval $[0,1]$ is considered. Similarly, it is possible to extend the usual order on $[0,1]$, for n-ary connectives.

Definition 2 (Similarity relation). *Given a domain $\mathcal{U}$ and a lattice L with a fixed t-norm $\wedge$, a similarity relation $\mathcal{R}$ is a fuzzy binary relation on $\mathcal{U}$, that is a fuzzy subset on $\mathcal{U} \times \mathcal{U}$ (namely, a mapping $\mathcal{R} : \mathcal{U} \times \mathcal{U} \to L$), such that fulfils the following properties:*[6]

- *Reflexive: $\mathcal{R}(x,x) = \top, \forall x \in \mathcal{U}$,*
- *Symmetric: $\mathcal{R}(x,y) = \mathcal{R}(y,x), \forall x, y \in \mathcal{U}$,*
- *Transitive: $\mathcal{R}(x,z) \geq \mathcal{R}(x,y) \wedge \mathcal{R}(y,z), \forall x, y, z \in \mathcal{U}$.*

Certainly, we are interested in fuzzy binary relations on a syntactic domain. We primarily define similarities on the symbols of a signature, Σ, of a first order language. This makes possible to treat as indistinguishable two syntactic symbols which are related by a similarity relation $\mathcal{R}$. Moreover, a similarity relation $\mathcal{R}$ on the alphabet of a first order language can be extended to terms by structural induction in the usual way [24]. That is, the extension, $\hat{\mathcal{R}}$, of a similarity relation $\mathcal{R}$ is defined as:

1. let x be a variable, $\hat{\mathcal{R}}(x,x) = \mathcal{R}(x,x) = 1$,
2. let f and g be two n-ary function symbols and let $t_1, \ldots, t_n, s_1, \ldots, s_n$ be terms, then $\hat{\mathcal{R}}(f(t_1,\ldots,t_n), g(s_1,\ldots,s_n)) = \mathcal{R}(f,g) \wedge (\bigwedge_{i=1}^{n} \hat{\mathcal{R}}(t_i, s_i))$
3. otherwise, the approximation degree of two terms is zero.

Analogously for atomic formulas. In this work conditional formulas of the form $\mathcal{C} : A \leftarrow \mathcal{B}$, where A is an atom, have a special relevance (see below). For this kind of formulas we use a different and more restrictive notion of similarity than the one defined in [24]. The idea is that a conditional formula $\mathcal{C}$ is similar to another conditional formula $\mathcal{C}'$ if their heads are similar but maintain the same body. Hence, given $\mathcal{C} : A \leftarrow \mathcal{B}$ and $\mathcal{C}' : A' \leftarrow \mathcal{B}'$, $\hat{\mathcal{R}}(\mathcal{C},\mathcal{C}') = \hat{\mathcal{R}}(A, A')$ if $\mathcal{B} = \mathcal{B}'$; otherwise $\hat{\mathcal{R}}(\mathcal{C},\mathcal{C}') = 0$. That is, a conditional formula $\mathcal{C}$ is similar to another conditional formula $\mathcal{C}'$ in the same degree that their heads provided that they have the same body.

Note that, in the sequel, we shall not make a notational distinction between the relation $\mathcal{R}$ and its extension $\hat{\mathcal{R}}$.

Example 2. A similarity relation $\mathcal{R}$ on $\mathcal{U} = \{vanguardist, elegant, metro, taxi, bus\}$ is defined by the following matrix:

$\mathcal{R}$	vanguardist	elegant	metro	taxi	bus
vanguardist	1	0.6	0	0	0
elegant	0.6	1	0	0	0
metro	0	0	1	0.4	0.5
taxi	0	0	0.4	1	0.4
bus	0	0	0.5	0.4	1

It is easy to check that $\mathcal{R}$ fulfills the reflexive, symmetric, and transitive properties. Particularly, using the *Gödel* conjunction as the t-norm $\wedge$, we have that: $\mathcal{R}(taxi, metro) \geq \mathcal{R}(metro, bus) \wedge \mathcal{R}(bus, taxi) = 0.5 \wedge 0.4$.

---

[6] For convenience, $\mathcal{R}(x,y)$, also denoted $x\mathcal{R}y$, refers to both the syntactic expression (that symbolizes that the elements $x, y \in \mathcal{U}$ are related by $\mathcal{R}$) and the membership degree $\mu_{\mathcal{R}}(x,y)$, i.e., the affinity degree of the pair $(x,y) \in \mathcal{U} \times \mathcal{U}$ with the verbal predicate (or fuzzy predicate) $\mathcal{R}$.

Furthermore, the extension $\hat{\mathcal{R}}$ of $\mathcal{R}$ determines that the terms $elegant(taxi)$ and $vanguardist(metro)$[7] are similar: $\hat{\mathcal{R}}(elegant(taxi), vanguardist(metro)) = \mathcal{R}(elegant, vanguardist) \wedge \hat{\mathcal{R}}(taxi, metro) = 0.6 \wedge \mathcal{R}(taxi, metro) = 0.6 \wedge 0.4 = 0.4$.

Definition 3 (Rule and goal). *A* rule *has the form* $A \leftarrow \mathcal{B}$, *where* A *is an atomic formula called* head *and* $\mathcal{B}$, *called* body, *is a well-formed formula (ultimately built from atomic formulas* $B_1, \ldots, B_n$, *truth values of* L, *and connectives). In particular, when the body of a rule is* $r \in L$ *(an element of lattice* L*), this rule is called* fact *and can be written as* $A \leftarrow r$ *(or simply* A *if* $r = \top$*). A* goal *is a body submitted as a query to the system.*

Definition 4 (Program). *A* FASILL program *(or simply program) is a tuple* $\langle \Pi, \mathcal{R}, L \rangle$ *where* Π *is a set of rules,* $\mathcal{R}$ *is a similarity relation between the elements of* Σ, *and* L *is a complete lattice.*

Example 3. The set of rules Π given below, the similarity relation $\mathcal{R}$ of Example 2, and lattice $L = ([0, 1], \leq)$ of Example 1, form a program $\mathcal{P} = \langle \Pi, \mathcal{R}, L \rangle$.

$$\begin{cases} R_1 : vanguardist(hydropolis) \leftarrow 0.9 \\ R_2 : elegant(ritz) \qquad\qquad \leftarrow 0.8 \\ R_3 : close(hydropolis, taxi) \;\;\leftarrow 0.7 \\ R_4 : good\_hotel(x) \qquad\qquad \leftarrow @_{aver}(elegant(x), @_{very}(close(x, metro))) \end{cases}$$

Figs. 2 and 3 show two screenshots of an on-line work session with the FLOPER system when introducing and executing (according the operational semantics described in [7]) the program above.

3 Declarative Semantics of FASILL

In logic programming, the declarative semantics for a program is traditionally formulated on the basis of the least Herbrand model (conceived as the infimum of a set of interpretations). In this section, we formally introduce the semantic notions of Herbrand interpretation, Herbrand model and least Herbrand model for a FASILL program $\mathcal{P}$, in order to characterize the declarative semantics for this kind of fuzzy programs. The process follows the guidelines of [14] and also generalizes the model-theoretic semantics defined in [9] for multi-adjoint logic programs and in [17] for X-MALP programs.[8] That is, if L is a multi-adjoint lattice and $\mathcal{P}$ is a multi-adjoint program (see [8,15] for a description of these concepts), or L is a complete lattice and $\mathcal{P}$ is a X-MALP program, it is easy to see that our Herbrand model $\mathcal{I}$ coincides with the one corresponding to this framework.

---

[7] Note that *elegant(taxi)* and *vanguardist(metro)* are 1-ary predicates, whereas that *taxi, metro* are terms with arity 0, i.e. constants.

[8] Note that, X-MALP programs do not rely on *adjoint pairs*.

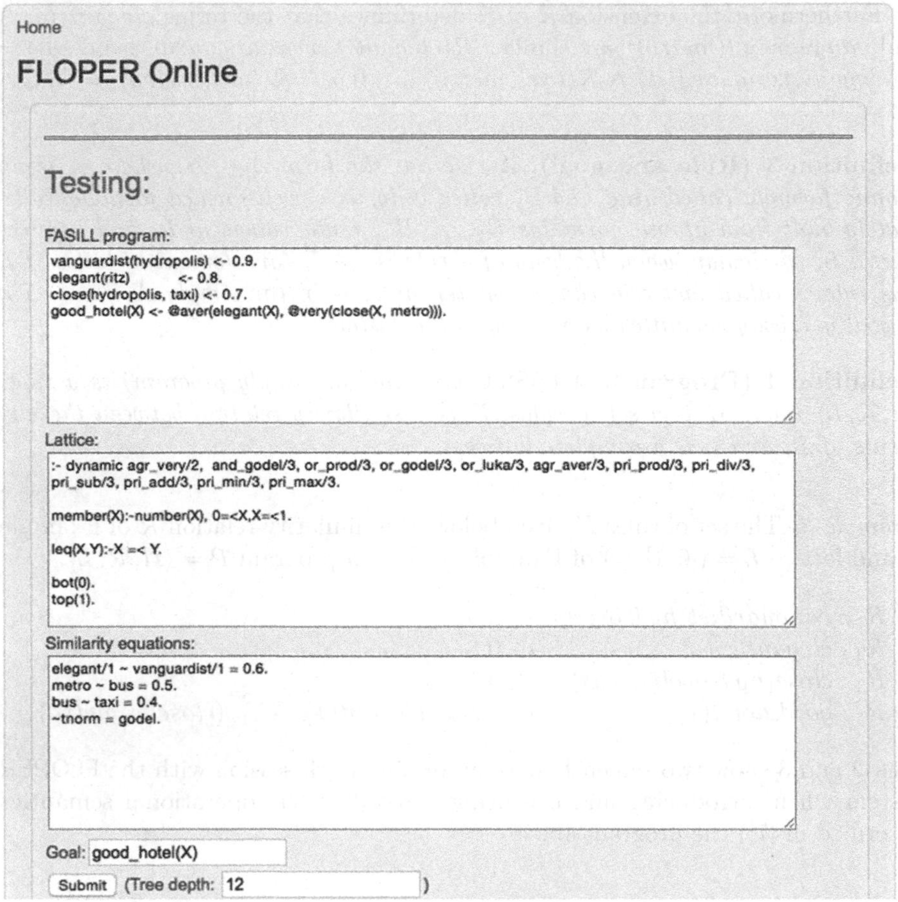

Home

FLOPER Online

Testing:

FASILL program:

```
vanguardist(hydropolis) <- 0.9.
elegant(ritz)          <- 0.8.
close(hydropolis, taxi) <- 0.7.
good_hotel(X) <- @aver(elegant(X), @very(close(X, metro))).
```

Lattice:

```
:- dynamic agr_very/2, and_godel/3, or_prod/3, or_godel/3, or_luka/3, agr_aver/3, pri_prod/3, pri_div/3,
pri_sub/3, pri_add/3, pri_min/3, pri_max/3.

member(X):-number(X), 0=<X,X=<1.

leq(X,Y):-X =< Y.

bot(0).
top(1).
```

Similarity equations:

```
elegant/1 ~ vanguardist/1 = 0.6.
metro ~ bus = 0.5.
bus ~ taxi = 0.4.
~tnorm = godel.
```

Goal: good_hotel(X)

[Submit] (Tree depth: 12   )

Fig. 2. Screenshot of the FLOPER online tool input

In what follows, we will consider that $\mathcal{B}_{\mathcal{P}}$ is the Herbrand base of the FASILL program $\mathcal{P}$, that is, the set of all ground atoms which can be formed by using the symbols in Π and in the similarity relation $\mathcal{R}$ of $\mathcal{P}$.

Definition 5 (Herbrand Interpretation). *Let* $\mathcal{P} = \langle \Pi, \mathcal{R}, L \rangle$ *be a FASILL program. A Herbrand interpretation is a mapping* $\mathcal{I} : \mathcal{B}_{\mathcal{P}} \to L$, *where* $\mathcal{B}_{\mathcal{P}}$ *is the Herbrand base of* $\mathcal{P}$.

Let $\mathcal{H}$ be the set of Herbrand interpretations whose order is induced from the order of L, $\mathcal{I}_1 \leq \mathcal{I}_2 \iff \mathcal{I}_1(A) \leq \mathcal{I}_2(A), \forall A \in \mathcal{B}_{\mathcal{P}}$. It is trivial to check that $(\mathcal{H}, \leq)$ inherits the structure of complete lattice from $(L, \leq)$.

A Herbrand interpretation $\mathcal{I}$ can be extended in a natural way to the set of ground formulae of the language by simply making use of the following definition:

$$\mathcal{I}(\varsigma(A_1, \ldots, A_n)) = \dot{\varsigma}(\mathcal{I}(A_1), \ldots, \mathcal{I}(A_n))$$

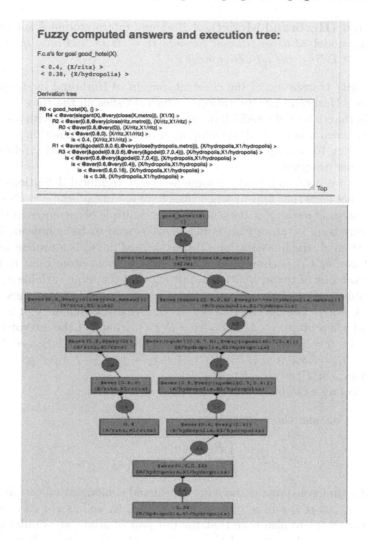

Fig. 3. Screenshot of the FLOPER online tool output

where ς is an arbitrary connective and $A_1, \ldots, A_n$ ground atoms. Note that, by abuse of language we use the same symbol for the Herbrand interpretation and its extension.

In order to interpret a non ground (closed and universally quantified) formula $\forall A$, it suffices to take

$$\mathcal{I}(\forall A) = \inf\{\mathcal{I}(A\vartheta) : \vartheta \text{ is a variable assignment}\}$$

where a *variable assignment* ϑ is a ground substitution that applied to a syntactic expression $\mathcal{E}$ transforms it into a ground instance $\mathcal{E}\vartheta$.

Moreover, in order to interpret a conditional formula we give the following definition.

Definition 6 (Herbrand Model). *A Herbrand interpretation $\mathcal{I}$ satisfies or is a Herbrand model of a conditional formula $H \leftarrow \mathcal{B}$ if, and only if, it verifies that $\mathcal{I}(H\vartheta) \geq \mathcal{I}(\mathcal{B}\vartheta)$, for all assignment ϑ.*

A direct naive translation of the classical concept of Herbrand model of a program $\mathcal{P}$ (as a Herbrand interpretation $\mathcal{I}$ which satisfies all the rules in $\mathcal{P}$) does not work in the context of a FASILL program, since it is equipped with a similarity relation. We need a new definition supported by an extended notion of program which are going to contain the meaning introduced by a similarity relation into the core of the program.

But first, we need to introduce some necessary technical definitions to cope with some problems that appear when rules have nonlinear atoms in their heads. A term or atom is *linear* if it does not contain multiple occurrences of the same variable. Any term or atom that is not linear is said to be nonlinear. Given a nonlinear atom A, the linearization of A (as defined in [3]) is a process by which the structure $\langle A_l, C_l \rangle$ is computed, where: A_l is a linear atom built from A by replacing each one of the n_i multiple occurrences of the same variable x_i by new fresh variables $y_k (1 \leq k \leq n_i)$; and C_l is a set of similarity constrains $x_i \sim y_k$ (with $1 \leq k \leq n_i$). The operator "$s \sim t$" is asserting the similarity of two terms s and t and when interpreted, $\mathcal{I}(s \sim t) = \mathcal{R}(s, t)$, whatever the interpretation $\mathcal{I}$ of $\mathcal{L}$. Now, let $R = A \leftarrow \mathcal{B}$ be a rule and $\langle A_l, C_l \rangle$ be the linearization of A, where $C_l = \{x_1 \sim y_1, \ldots, x_n \sim y_n\}$, $lin(R) = A_l \leftarrow x_1 \sim y_1 \wedge \cdots \wedge x_n \sim y_n \wedge \mathcal{B}$. For a set Γ of rules, $lin(\Gamma) = \{lin(R) : R \in \Gamma\}$.

The following example discusses the need of linearization.

Example 4. Consider the program

$$\Pi = \begin{cases} R_1 : & p(a) \\ R_2 : & q(x, x) \leftarrow p(x) \end{cases}$$

Assume also that constants a and b are considered similar with a certain degree. This implies that $p(a)$ and $p(b)$ are similar atoms, as well as $q(a, a)$ and $q(b, b)$. But it is important to also note that the last pair of atoms are similar again to $q(a, b)$ and $q(b, a)$ (obviously, all the atoms mentioned so far conform the Herbrand base of the program). As we are going to see in what follows, this last couple of atoms must necessarily be included in the minimal Herbrand model of the program, which will previously require to linearize the second program rule for obtaining $lin(q(x, x) \leftarrow p(x)) = q(y_1, y_2) \leftarrow x \sim y_1 \wedge x \sim y_2 \wedge p(x)$.

At this point, we wish to recall from [10] our notion of *"Similarity-based Strict Equality"* (*sse* in brief) which is strongly connected with the $\sim$ operator used when linearizing rules. In fact, we can conceive the new predicate *sse* as a high level implementation of $\sim$ in the sense that a set of FASILL rules coding *sse* suffices for emulating the behavior of $\sim$ when using the FLOPER system.

For instance, assuming in our example that the similarity relation $\mathcal{R}$ is described by the condition $\mathcal{R}(a, b) = 0.8$, then the following set of FASILL facts are enough to model *sse* in our case: $sse(a, a) \leftarrow 1$, $sse(a, b) \leftarrow 0.8$, $sse(b, a) \leftarrow 0.8$

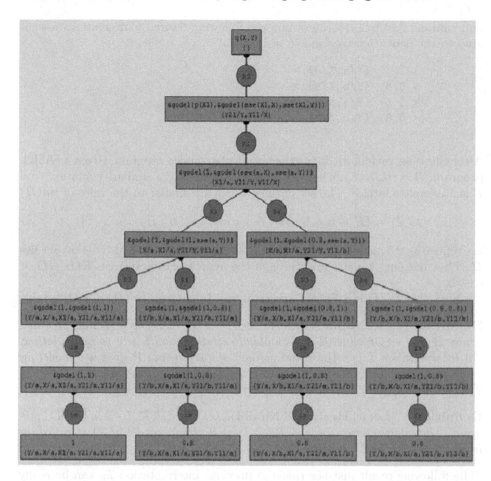

Fig. 4. Screen-shot of FLOPER managing a linearized FASILL program

and $sse(b,b) \leftarrow 1$. And now, rule R_2 can be linearized by using sse to become $q(y_1, y_2) \leftarrow sse(x, y_1) \wedge sse(x, y_2) \wedge p(x)$.

For putting in practice all these ideas with FLOPER in the previous rule we assign the Gödel conjunction to $\wedge$ and we also delay the calls to sse at the end of the body for gaining efficiency (see [10] for details). So, after loading the following program into the system:

```
p(a).
q(Y1,Y2) <- p(X) &godel sse(X,Y1) &godel sse(X,Y2).
sse(a,a) <- 1.
sse(a,b) <- 0.8.
sse(b,a) <- 0.8.
sse(b,b) <- 1.
```

and running goal p(X,Y), we obtain the following desired four solutions associated to the derivation tree shown in Fig. 4:

```
< 1,    {Y/a,X/a} >
< 0.8,  {Y/b,X/a} >
< 0.8,  {Y/a,X/b} >
< 0.8,  {Y/b,X/b} >
```

After this observation, we define the notion of extended program. Given a FASILL
program, $\mathcal{P} = \langle \Pi, \mathcal{R}, L \rangle$, where Π is a set of rules, $\mathcal{R}$ is a similarity relation, and
L is a complete lattice. The set of rules which are similar to the rules in $lin(\Pi)$

$$\mathcal{K}(\Pi) = \{H' \leftarrow \alpha \wedge \mathcal{B} : H \leftarrow \mathcal{B} \in lin(\Pi), \mathcal{R}(H', H) = \alpha > \bot\}$$

are reflecting the meaning induced by the similarity relation $\mathcal{R}$ into the set of rules
Π. That meaning is measured through the approximation degrees $\mathcal{R}(H', H) = \alpha \in L$.

Note that $\mathcal{K}(\Pi)$ is a FASILL program too. In general, $lin(\Pi) \subseteq \mathcal{K}(\Pi)$.

Definition 7 (Herbrand Model). *Let $\mathcal{P} = \langle \Pi, \mathcal{R}, L \rangle$ be a FASILL program,
where Π is a set of rules, $\mathcal{R}$ is a similarity relation, and L is a complete lattice.
An interpretation $\mathcal{I}$ is a* Herbrand model[9] *of the program $\mathcal{P}$ iff it is a model for
each ground instance $H'\vartheta \leftarrow \alpha \wedge \mathcal{B}\vartheta$ of a rule in $\mathcal{K}(\Pi)$. That is, $\alpha \wedge \mathcal{I}(\mathcal{B}\vartheta) \leq
\mathcal{I}(H'\vartheta)$ for each assignment ϑ and rule in $\mathcal{K}(\Pi)$.*

Definition 8 (Least Herbrand Model). *Let $\mathcal{P} = \langle \Pi, \mathcal{R}, L \rangle$ be a FASILL program. The interpretation $\mathcal{I}_\mathcal{P} = inf\{\mathcal{I}_j : \mathcal{I}_j$ is Herbrand model of $\mathcal{P}\}$ is called the
least fuzzy Herbrand[10] model of $\mathcal{P}$.*

The following result justifies that the previous interpretation $\mathcal{I}_\mathcal{P}$ can be really
understood as the least fuzzy Herbrand model.

Theorem 1. *Let $\mathcal{P} = \langle \Pi, \mathcal{R}, L \rangle$ be a FASILL program. The Herbrand interpretation $\mathcal{I}_\mathcal{P} = inf\{\mathcal{I}_j : \mathcal{I}_j$ is a Herbrand model of $\mathcal{P}\}$ is the least Herbrand model
of $\mathcal{P}$.*

Proof. Let $\mathcal{M}$ be the set of Herbrand models of $\mathcal{P}$, that is, $\mathcal{M} = \{\mathcal{I}_j : \mathcal{I}_j$ is a
Herbrand model of $\mathcal{P}\}$. $\mathcal{M}$ is not empty, being as the Herbrand interpretation
$\mathcal{I} = sup(\mathcal{H})$, defined on each $A \in \mathcal{B}_\mathcal{P}$ by $\mathcal{I}(A) = sup(L)$, is a Herbrand model
of $\mathcal{P}$.

Then, if we denote $\mathcal{I}_\mathcal{P} = \inf(\mathcal{M})$, $\mathcal{I}_\mathcal{P}$ is a Herbrand interpretation: since
$(\mathcal{H}, \leq)$ is a complete lattice, there exists the infimum of the subset $\mathcal{M} \subset \mathcal{H}$ and
it is a member of $\mathcal{H}$. We will prove that $\mathcal{I}_\mathcal{P}$ is a Herbrand model of $\mathcal{P}$, that
is, it satisfies all rules of $\mathcal{P}$. Consider a rule $R = H' \leftarrow \alpha \wedge \mathcal{B} \in \mathcal{K}(\Pi)$, where
$\mathcal{R}(H, H') = \alpha$ and H is a head of rule in Π, and $\mathcal{I}_j \in \mathcal{M}$ ($\mathcal{I}_j$ is a model of

---

[9] Sometimes we will abbreviate writing "fuzzy model" or simply "model".

[10] Sometimes we will abbreviate writing "least fuzzy model" or simply "least model".

$\mathcal{P}$). Since $\mathcal{I_P}$ is the infimum of $\mathcal{M}$, $\mathcal{I_P} \leq \mathcal{I}_j$, for all model $\mathcal{I}_j$ of $\mathcal{P}$. Therefore, $\mathcal{I_P}(A) \leq \mathcal{I}_j(A)$ for each atom $A \in \mathcal{B_P}$.

Moreover, given that $\mathcal{I}_j$ is a Herbrand model of $\mathcal{P}$, $\mathcal{I}_j$ is a Herbrand model of R, that is, by Definition 7: if H' is an atom such that $\mathcal{R}(H, H') = r$, then $\mathcal{I}_j(H'\theta) \geq r \wedge \mathcal{I}_j(\mathcal{B}\theta)$, for all ground instances $H\theta, H'\theta$ of H and H'; in particular, $\mathcal{I}_j(H) \geq \mathcal{I}_j(\mathcal{B})$.

Consider, then, an atom H' verifying $\mathcal{R}(H, H') = r$. Using the monotonicity of (truth function of) $\wedge$,

$$\begin{aligned}
\mathcal{I_P}(H'\theta) &= inf\{\mathcal{I}_j(H'\theta) : \mathcal{I}_j \text{ is a Herbrand model of } \mathcal{P}\} \\
&\geq inf\{r \wedge \mathcal{I}_j(\mathcal{B}\theta) : \mathcal{I}_j \text{ is a Herbrand model of } \mathcal{P}\} \\
&\geq r \wedge inf\{\mathcal{I}_j(\mathcal{B}\theta) : \mathcal{I}_j \text{ is a Herbrand model of } \mathcal{P}\} = r \wedge \mathcal{I_P}(\mathcal{B}\theta)
\end{aligned}$$

So, as the condition $\mathcal{I_P}(H'\theta) \geq r \wedge \mathcal{I_P}(\mathcal{B}\theta)$ is fulfilled, $\mathcal{I_P}$ is a Herbrand model of the rule $R \in \mathcal{K}(\Pi)$ and (since it analogously is a Herbrand model of all rules in $\mathcal{P}$) it is a Herbrand model of $\mathcal{P}$, as we expected. Finally, since $\mathcal{I_P} = \inf(\mathcal{M})$, using again the definition of infimum, $\mathcal{I_P} \leq \mathcal{I}_j, \forall j$, so $\mathcal{I_P}$ is the least Herbrand model of $\mathcal{P}$, which concludes the proof.

The need for linearizing the program Π in order to obtain the suitable least Herbrand model is suggested in Example 4. Indeed, given the set of rules Π of that example, as well as the similarity relation $\mathcal{R}$ described by the condition $\mathcal{R}(a, b) = 0.8$, if the linearization process is omitted, the least Herbrand model of the program $\mathcal{P} = \langle \Pi, \mathcal{R}, [0, 1] \rangle$ is the interpretation $\mathcal{I}$ that fulfills the following conditions

$$\mathcal{I}(p(a)) = 1 \quad \mathcal{I}(p(b)) = 0.8 \quad \mathcal{I}(q(a, a)) = 1 \quad \mathcal{I}(q(b, b)) = 0.8.$$

On the other hand, with linearization, the least Herbrand model of $\mathcal{P}$ is the interpretation $\mathcal{I}$ which, in addition to the above conditions, satisfies that $\mathcal{I}(q(a, b)) = 0.8$ and $\mathcal{I}(q(b, a)) = 0.8$.

In the next example we illustrate how to calculate the least Herbrand model $\mathcal{I_P}$ of a FASILL program and, in general, how to calculate a Herbrand model $\mathcal{I}$ of program $\mathcal{P}$.

Example 5. Let $\mathcal{P} = \langle \Pi, \mathcal{R}, L \rangle$ be a FASILL program, where Π and the lattice $(L, \leq)$ are given in the following diagram $((L, \leq)$ is stated by its Hasse diagram) and the relation $\mathcal{R}$ is the one establishing that $\mathcal{R}(a, a') = \alpha$ and $\mathcal{R}(b, b') = \beta$.

If we assume that the truth function $\dot{\vee}_\mathsf{G}$ for connective $\vee_\mathsf{G}$ is defined by $\dot{\vee}_\mathsf{G}(x, y) = \sup\{x, y\}$, the least Herbrand model $\mathcal{I_P}$ is determined by $\mathcal{I_P}(p(a)) = \gamma$, $\mathcal{I_P}(p(b)) = \delta$, $\mathcal{I_P}(p(a')) = \alpha$, $\mathcal{I_P}(p(b')) = \beta$, $\mathcal{I_P}(q(a)) = \gamma$, $\mathcal{I_P}(q(a')) = \alpha$, $\mathcal{I_P}(r(b)) = \delta$, $\mathcal{I_P}(r(b')) = \beta$, as shown in the next table (where atoms interpreted as $\bot$ have been omitted).

$$\Pi = \begin{cases} R_1 : r(b) \leftarrow \delta \\ R_2 : q(a) \leftarrow \gamma \\ R_3 : p(x) \leftarrow q(x) \vee_\mathsf{G} r(x) \end{cases}$$

$$\mathcal{K}(\Pi) = \begin{cases} R_1 : r(b) \leftarrow \delta \\ R_1' : r(b') \leftarrow \beta \wedge \delta \\ R_2 : q(a) \leftarrow \gamma \\ R_2' : q(a') \leftarrow \alpha \wedge \gamma \\ R_3 : p(x) \leftarrow q(x) \vee_\mathsf{G} r(x) \end{cases}$$

	$p(a)$	$p(a')$	$p(b)$	$p(b')$	$q(a)$	$q(a')$	$r(b)$	$r(b')$
$\mathcal{I}_\mathcal{P}$	γ	α	δ	β	γ	α	δ	β

Indeed, by Definition 7 (note that in this example $lin(\Pi) = \Pi$),

· $\mathcal{I}$ is Herbrand model of R_1 iff $\mathcal{I}(r(b)) \geq \delta$
· $\mathcal{I}$ is Herbrand model of R_1' iff $\mathcal{I}(r(b')) \geq \beta \dot{\wedge} \delta = \beta$
· $\mathcal{I}$ is Herbrand model of R_2 iff $\mathcal{I}(q(a)) \geq \gamma$
· $\mathcal{I}$ is Herbrand model of R_2' iff $\mathcal{I}(q(a')) \geq \alpha \dot{\wedge} \gamma = \alpha$

· $\mathcal{I}$ is Herbrand model of R_3 iff $\begin{cases} \mathcal{I}(p(a)) \geq \mathcal{I}(q(a) \vee r(a)) = \mathcal{I}(q(a)) \dot{\vee} \mathcal{I}(r(a)) \\ \mathcal{I}(p(b)) \geq \mathcal{I}(q(b) \vee r(b)) = \mathcal{I}(q(b)) \dot{\vee} \mathcal{I}(r(b)) \\ \mathcal{I}(p(a')) \geq \mathcal{R}(a,a') \dot{\wedge} \mathcal{I}(q(a)) \dot{\vee} \mathcal{I}(r(a)) \\ \mathcal{I}(p(b')) \geq \mathcal{R}(b,b') \dot{\wedge} \mathcal{I}(q(b)) \dot{\vee} \mathcal{I}(r(b)) \end{cases}$

that is, $\mathcal{I}$ fulfills $\begin{cases} \mathcal{I}(p(a)) \geq \gamma \dot{\vee} \bot = \gamma \\ \mathcal{I}(p(b)) \geq \bot \dot{\vee} \delta = \delta \\ \mathcal{I}(p(a')) \geq \alpha \dot{\wedge} \gamma = \alpha \\ \mathcal{I}(p(b')) \geq \beta \dot{\wedge} \delta = \beta \end{cases}$

Note that this process allows us to calculate the least Herbrand model $\mathcal{I}_\mathcal{P}$ and also suggests how to obtain all Herbrand models $\mathcal{I}$ of $\mathcal{P}$.

	$\mathcal{I}_\mathcal{P}$
vanguardist(hydropolis)	0.9
vanguardist(ritz)	0.6
elegant(hydropolis)	0.6
elegant(ritz)	0.8
close(hydropolis, taxi)	0.7
close(hydropolis, metro)	0.4
close(hydropolis, bus)	0.5
good_hotel(hydropolis)	0.38
good_hotel(ritz)	0.4

Following the same methodology explained so far, the interested reader can easily check that the least Herbrand model for the program illustrated in Sect. 2 is the one given in the adjoint table (where the interpretations for all atoms not included on it are assumed to be 0).

4 Conclusions and Future Work

FASILL is a fuzzy logic programming language with implicit/explicit truth degree annotations, a great variety of connectives and unification by similarity. In [7] we have recently provided the syntax, operational semantics, and implementation issues[11] of this language which in essence integrates and extends features coming from MALP (*Multi-Adjoint Logic Programming*, a fuzzy logic language with explicitly annotated rules) and Bousi~Prolog (which uses a weak unification algorithm and is well suited for flexible query answering). Hence, it properly manages similarity and truth degrees in a single framework combining the expressive benefits of both languages. In this work we have focused on the formulation of a least model declarative semantics for FASILL, being this action a mandatory task in the development of the design of this framework. Obviously, a pending task for the immediate future consists in establishing the connections between our new fuzzy version of the least Herbrand model and the operational semantics of FASILL programs, in order to prove the correctness of the whole framework.

References

1. Arcelli, F.: Likelog for flexible query answering. Soft Comput. **7**(2), 107–114 (2002)
2. Arcelli, F., Formato, F.: Likelog: a logic programming language for flexible data retrieval. In: Proceedings of the ACM Symposium on Applied Computing, SAC 1999, San Antonio, Texas, pp. 260–267. ACM, Artificial Intelligence and Computational Logic (1999)
3. Caballero, R., Rodríguez-Artalejo, M., Romero-Díaz, C.A.: Similarity-based reasoning in qualified logic programming. In: Proceedings of the 10th International ACM SIGPLAN Conference on Principles and Practice of Declarative Programming, PPDP 2008, pp. 185–194. ACM, New York (2008)
4. Caballero, R., Rodríguez-Artalejo, M., Romero-Díaz, C.A.: A transformation-based implementation for CLP with qualification and proximity. Theory Pract. Logic Program. **14**(1), 1–63 (2014)
5. Dubois, D., Prade, H.: Fuzzy Sets and Systems: Theory and Applications. Academic Press, New York (1980)
6. Formato, F., Gerla, G., Sessa, M.I.: Similarity-based unification. Fundamenta Informaticae **41**(4), 393–414 (2000)
7. Julián Iranzo, P., Moreno, G., Penabad, J., Vázquez, C.: A fuzzy logic programming environment for managing similarity and truth degrees. In: Escobar, S. (ed.) Proceedings of XIV Jornadas sobre Programación y Lenguajes, PROLE 2014, Cádiz, Spain. EPTCS, vol. 173, pp. 71–86 (2015). http://dx.doi.org/10.4204/EPTCS.173.6
8. Julián, P., Moreno, G., Penabad, J.: On fuzzy unfolding. A multi-adjoint approach. Fuzzy Sets Syst. **154**, 16–33 (2005)
9. Julián, P., Moreno, G., Penabad, J.: On the declarative semantics of multi-adjoint logic programs. In: Cabestany, J., Sandoval, F., Prieto, A., Corchado, J.M. (eds.) IWANN 2009, Part I. LNCS, vol. 5517, pp. 253–260. Springer, Heidelberg (2009)

---

[11] The last version of the FLOPER system which copes with similarity relations can be freely downloaded from http://dectau.uclm.es/floper/?q=sim and it can be tested on-line through http://dectau.uclm.es/floper/?q=sim/test.

10. Julián-Iranzo, P., Moreno, G., Vázquez, C.: Similarity-based strict equality in a fully integrated fuzzy logic language. In: Bassiliades, N., Gottlob, G., Sadri, F., Paschke, A., Roman, D. (eds.) RuleML 2015. LNCS, vol. 9202, pp. 193–207. Springer, Heidelberg (2015)
11. Julián-Iranzo, P., Rubio-Manzano, C.: A declarative semantics for Bousi~Prolog. In: Proceedings of 11th International ACM SIGPLAN Conference on Principles and Practice of Declarative Programming, PPDP 2009, Coimbra, Portugal, pp. 149–160. ACM (2009)
12. Julián-Iranzo, P., Rubio-Manzano, C.: An efficient fuzzy unification method and its implementation into the Bousi~Prolog system. In: Proceedings of the 2010 IEEE International Conference on Fuzzy Systems, Barcelona, Spain, pp. 1–8 (2010). http://dx.doi.org/10.1109/FUZZY.2010.5584193
13. Kifer, M., Subrahmanian, V.S.: Theory of generalized annotated logic programming and its applications. J. Logic Program. **12**, 335–367 (1992)
14. Lloyd, J.W.: Foundations of Logic Programming. Springer, Berlin (1987)
15. Medina, J., Ojeda-Aciego, M., Vojtáš, P.: Similarity-based unification: a multi-adjoint approach. Fuzzy Sets Syst. **146**, 43–62 (2004)
16. Morcillo, P.J., Moreno, G., Penabad, J., Vázquez, C.: A practical management of fuzzy truth-degrees using FLOPER. In: Dean, M., Hall, J., Rotolo, A., Tabet, S. (eds.) RuleML 2010. LNCS, vol. 6403, pp. 20–34. Springer, Heidelberg (2010)
17. Moreno, G., Penabad, J., Vázquez, C.: Beyond multi-adjoint logic programming. Int. J. Comput. Math. **92**(9), 1956–1975 (2014)
18. Moreno, G., Vázquez, C.: Fuzzy logic programming in action with FLOPER. J. Softw. Eng. Appl. **7**, 237–298 (2014)
19. Muñoz-Hernández, S., Ceruelo, V.P., Strass, H.: RFuzzy: Syntax, semantics and implementation details of a simple and expressive fuzzy tool over Prolog. Inform. Sci. **181**(10), 1951–1970 (2011)
20. Nguyen, H.T., Walker, E.A.: A First Course in Fuzzy Logic. Chapman & Hall, Boca Ratón (2006)
21. Rodríguez-Artalejo, M., Romero-Díaz, C.A.: Quantitative logic programming revisited. In: Garrigue, J., Hermenegildo, M.V. (eds.) FLOPS 2008. LNCS, vol. 4989, pp. 272–288. Springer, Heidelberg (2008)
22. Rubio-Manzano, C., Julián-Iranzo, P.: A fuzzy linguistic prolog and its applications. J. Intell. Fuzzy Syst. **26**(3), 1503–1516 (2014)
23. Sessa, M.I.: Translations and similarity-based logic programming. Soft Comput. **5**(2), 160–170 (2001). http://dx.doi.org/10.1007/PL00009891
24. Sessa, M.I.: Approximate reasoning by similarity-based SLD resolution. Theoret. Comput. Sci. **275**(1–2), 389–426 (2002)
25. van Emden, M.H.: Quantitative deduction and its fixpoint theory. J. Logic Program. **3**(1), 37–53 (1986)

Controlling the Average Behavior of Business Rules Programs

Olivier Wang[1,2], Leo Liberti[2(✉)], Claudia D'Ambrosio[2],
Christian de Sainte Marie[1], and Changhai Ke[1]

[1] IBM France, 9 Rue de Verdun, 94250 Gentilly, France
[2] CNRS LIX, Ecole Polytechnique, 91128 Palaiseau, France
olivier.wang@polytechnique.edu, liberti@lix.polytechnique.fr

Abstract. Business Rules are a programming paradigm for non-programmer business users. They are designed to encode empirical knowledge of a business unit by means of "if-then" constructs. The classic example is that of a bank deciding whether to open a line of credit to a customer, depending on how the customer answers a list of questions. These questions are formulated by bank managers on the basis of the bank strategy and their own experience. Banks often have goals about target percentages of allowed loans. A natural question then arises: can the Business Rules be changed so as to meet that target *on average*? We tackle the question using "machine learning constrained" mathematical programs, which we solve using standard off-the-shelf solvers. We then generalize this to arbitrary decision problems.

1 Introduction

For the purpose of this work, a *Business Rule* (BR) program is an ordered list of sentences of the form:

    if cond(p, x) then
        x ← act(p, x)
    end if

where p is a *control parameter* symbol vector which encodes a possible "tuning" of the program (e.g. thresholds which can be adjusted by the user), $x \in X \subseteq \mathbb{R}^d$ is a *variable* symbol vector of dimension d representing intermediate and final stages of computation, cond is a boolean function, and act a function with values in X. We call rule such a sentence, condition an expression cond(p, x) and action an instruction $x \leftarrow$ act(p, x), which indicates a modification of the value of x. If P is the BR program, we write the final value of the variable x as $x^f = P(p, q)$, where q is an *input parameter* symbol vector representing a problem instance and equal to the initial value of x. Although in general BR programs may have any type of output, many BR programs encode decision problems, in which case the part of the output that matters can be represented by a single bit (one component of x is a binary variable).

BR programs are executed in an external loop construct which is transparent to the user. Without getting into the details of BR semantics, the loop executes

© Springer International Publishing Switzerland 2016
J.J. Alferes et al. (Eds.): RuleML 2016, LNCS 9718, pp. 83–96, 2016.
DOI: 10.1007/978-3-319-42019-6_6

a single action from a BR whose condition is True at each iteration. Which BR is executed depends on a conflict resolution strategy with varying complexity. De Sainte Marie et al. [22] describe typical operational semantics, including conflict resolution strategy, for industrial BR management systems. In this paper, the list of rules is ordered and the loop executes the first BR of the list with a condition evaluating to True at each iteration. The loop only terminates once it satisfies a termination condition, which we assume to be that none of the conditions of the BRs is True at the last iteration (as is usual). We proved in [27] that there is a universal BR program which can simulate any Turing Machine (TM), which makes the BR language Turing-complete.

The BR language is useful as a "programming tool for non-programmers", since it hides the two aspects of imperative computer programming which most non-programmers find confusing: loops and function calls. As mentioned above, BR programs only have a single loop, which is part of the interpreter, and external to the language itself. The BR language replaces function calls (up to a point) by factorizing many code fragments into a single 'rule'. The BR interpreter instantiates each rule into as many code fragments as possible by matching all consistent variable types at compile time.

The BR language is often used in medium-to-large sized corporations to encode their policies and empirical knowledge – often easily representable as "if-then" type statements. Such business processes are often embedded in a database of BRs representing a mix of regulations, organizational policies and operational knowledge. The latter can be collected from multiple employees over a possibly long period of time. BR interpreters are implemented by all BR management systems, e.g. [14].

The aim of this paper is to describe a method for changing the control parameters of BR programs as little as possible so that they approximately meet a given "average behavior" goal. This issue arises in the following setting:

- the BR program $P(p, q)$ encoding the business process has a (non-empty) control parameter symbol vector p;
- the BR program is run using the parameter vector p^0;
- the corporation owning the business process has an average goal to meet on a function f, with values in $\mathbb{R}$, of the outcomes of the BR program;
- the average of $P(p^0, q)$ where q ranges over a (possibly large but finite) set Q of instances is different from the goal.

We discuss the concrete example of a bank using a BR program in order to decide whether to grant a loan to a customer or not. The BR program depends on a variable vector x and initializes its parameter vector (a component of which is the minimum income level) to p^0. The BR program is used to decide whether the bank will reject the loan request, and therefore has a binary return value. Assume that the bank high-level strategy requires that no more than 40 % of loans should be rejected automatically, and that the BR program currently rejects about 60 %. Our aim is to adjust p, e.g. modifying the income level, so that the BR program satisfies the bank's goal regarding automatic loan rejection. This adjustment of parameters could be required after a change of internal or external conditions, for example.

Let $g \in \mathbb{R}$ be the desired goal. Then the problem can be formalized as:

$$\left.\begin{array}{c} \min_{p,x} \|p - p^0\| \\ |\mathbb{E}_{q \in Q}[f(P(p,q))] - g| \leq \varepsilon, \end{array}\right\} \tag{1}$$

where $\| \cdot \|$ is a given norm, p, q must satisfy the semantics of the BR program $P(p,q)$ when executed within the loop of a BR interpreter, $\mathbb{E}$ is the usual notation for the expected value and ε is a given tolerance. This formalization is closer to the reality of BR users than the reverse (minimizing $\mathbb{E}(P) - g$ while constraining $p - p^0$), as corporations will often consider goals more rigidly than changes to the business process, and the value of the objective will speak to them more as a kind of quantification of the changes to be made. The form this quantification takes, from minimizing the variation of each parameter in p to minimizing the number of parameters whose value is modified, depends on the definition of the norm $\| \cdot \|$. By using a linearizable norm, such as $\| \cdot \|_1$ or $\| \cdot \|_\infty$, we can solve Eq. (1) for linear BR programs using MILP solvers, through a pre-processing reformulation. While this problem looks like a supervised learning problem at first glance, standard supervised learning algorithms cannot help here as there is no 'correct' answer for each separate instance q. Rather, a global approach is necessary as, in the general case, the correct classifier is defined as a frequency distribution over the set of all instances Q. In this paper we consider the simplified case where the expected value serves as the classifier, which is equivalent to having the frequency distribution in the common case of a binary output.

Traditionally, this problem would be solved heuristically by treating P as a black-box, or by replacing it by means of a simplified model, such as e.g. a low-degree polynomial. Our approach is different: we model the algorithmic dynamics of P by means of Mixed-Integer Programming (MIP) constraints, in view to solving Eq. (1) with an off-the-shelf solver. That this is at all possible in full generality follows because Mathematical Programming (MP) is itself Turing-complete [16].

We make a number of simplifying assumptions in order to obtain a practically useful methodology, based on solving a Mixed-Integer Linear Programming (MILP) reformulation of Eq. (1) using a solver such as CPLEX [13] or BonMin [3]:

1. We replace Q by a smaller "training set" S for which we know the BR outcome. We choose S small enough that solving the MILP is (relatively) computationally cheap.
2. We assume a finite BR program with a known bound $(n-1)$ on the number of iterations of the loop for any input q (industrial BR programs often have a low value of n relative to the number of rules). This in turn implies that the values taken by x during the execution of the BR program are bounded. We assume that $M \gg 1$ is an upper bound of all absolute values of all p, q, and x, as well as any other values appearing in the BR program. It serves as a "big M" for the MP described in the rest of the paper.

3. We assume that the conditions and actions of the BR program give rise to constraints for which an exact MILP reformulation is possible. In order to have a linear model, each BR must thus be "linear", i.e. have the form:

if $L \leq x \leq G$ then
$\qquad x \leftarrow Ax + B$
end if

with $L, G, B \in \mathbb{R}^d$ and $A \in \mathbb{R}^{d \times d}$. We see in Sect. 3 that an actual MILP actually requires $A \in \{0, 1\}^{d \times d}$ in some cases.

We shall attempt to relax some or all of these assumptions in later works.

We also remark that this setting easily generalizes to any class of decision problems depending on a "tuning" parameter p, for which an average behavior is prescribed.

For the rest of the paper, we make the following simplifying assumptions (all of which afford no loss of generality).

1. We assume that the dimension of p is one, making it a scalar. Consequently, we choose the norm in Eq. 1 to be the absolute value for the rest of the paper. Additional parameters correspond to additional constraints that mirror the ones used for the first parameter.
2. We assume that the relevant function of the outcome f is the projection on the first dimension: $f(x) = x_1$. Any linear f can be used instead with no difference in the constraints, but BR programs usually have a projection of the variable x as their output.

1.1   Related Works

Business Rules (also known as *Production Rules*) are well studied as a knowledge representation system [8,10,18], originating as a psychological model of human behavior [19,20]. They have further been used to encode expert systems, such as MYCIN [6,25], EMYCIN [6,23], OPS5 [5,11], or more recently ODM [14] or OpenRules. On the business side of things, they have been defined broadly and narrowly in many different ways [12,15,21]. We consider Business Rules as a computational tool, which to the best of our knowledge has not been explored in depth before.

Supervised Learning is also a well studied field of Machine Learning, with many different formulations [2,17,24,26]. There exist many algorithms for this problem, from simple linear regression to neural networks [1] and support vector machines [9]. When the learner does not have as many known output values as it has items in the training set, the problem is known as Semi-Supervised Learning [7]. Similarly, there has been research into machine learning when the matching of the known outputs values to the inputs is not certain [4]. However, the fact that each known value corresponds to a single input item has not been questioned before, to the best of our knowledge.

2   MIP Constraints for the BR Program Dynamics

We study a BR program with a rule set $\{\mathcal{R}_r \mid r \leq \rho\}$ containing rules of the form:

    if $L_r \leq x \leq G_r$ **then**
        $x \leftarrow A_r x + B_r$
    end if

with rule $\mathcal{R}_1$ being instead:

    if $L_1 \leq x \leq G_1$ **then**
        $x \leftarrow A_1^p x + B_1$
    end if

where A_1^p is a $d \times d$ matrix satisfying:

$$\begin{cases} \forall k_1, k_2 \in D, k_1 \neq 1 \vee k_2 \neq 1 \Rightarrow (A_1^p)_{k_1,k_2} = (A_1)_{k_1,k_2} \\ \qquad\qquad\qquad (A_1^p)_{1,1} = p \end{cases}$$

with $D = \{1, \ldots, d\}$.

In the rest of this paper, we concatenate indices so that $(L_r)_k = L_{r,k}$, $(G_r)_k = G_{r,k}$, $(A_r)_{k_1,k_2} = A_{r,k_1,k_2}$ and $(B_r)_k = B_{r,k}$. We assume that rules are meaningful, such that $L_k \leq G_k$.

2.1   Modeling a BR Program

We exhibit a set of MIP constraints (Fig. 1) modeling the execution of the BR program. The iterations of the execution loop are indexed by $i \in I = \{1, \ldots, n\}$ where $n - 1$ is the upper bound on the number of iterations, the final value of x corresponds to iteration n. The rules are indexed by $r \in R = \{1, \ldots, \rho\}$. We use an auxiliary binary variable $y_{i,r}$ with the property: $y_{i,r} = 1$ iff the rule $\mathcal{R}_r$ is executed at iteration i. The vectors of binary variables $y_{i,r}^g$ and $y_{i,r}^l$ are used to enforce this property. In the rest of this section, the parameter is assumed to take the place of $A_{1,1,1}$, so we note a an additional variable initialized to $a = A$ except for $a_{1,1,1} = p$. Similar sets of constraints exists for when the parameter p takes the place of a scalar in B_r, L_r or G_r.

We note (C1), (C2), etc. the constraints related to the evolution of the execution and (IC1), (IC2), etc. the constraints related to the initial conditions of the BR program:

- (C1) represents the evolution of the value of the variable x
- (C2) represents the property that at most one rule is executed per iteration
- (C3) represents the fact that a rule whose condition is False cannot be executed
- (C4) through (C6) represent the fact that only the first rule whose condition is True can be executed
- (IC1) through (IC3) represent the initial value of a
- (IC4) represents the initial value of x

$$\forall i \in I \setminus \{n\} \qquad x^{i+1} = \sum_{r \in R} (a_r x^i + B_r) y_{i,r} + (1 - \sum_{r \in R} y_{i,r}) x^i \qquad (C1)$$

$$\forall i \in I \qquad \sum_{r \in R} y_{i,r} \le 1 \qquad (C2)$$

$$\forall (i,r) \in I \times R \qquad L_r - M(1 - y_{i,r})e \le x^i \le G_r + M(1 - y_{i,r})e \qquad (C3)$$

$$\forall (i,r,k) \in I \times R \times D \qquad x_k^i \ge G_{r,k} - M y_{i,r,k}^g - M \sum_{r'<r} y_{i,r'} \qquad (C4)$$

$$\forall (i,r,k) \in I \times R \times D \qquad x_k^i \le L_{r,k} + M y_{i,r,k}^l + M \sum_{r'<r} y_{i,r'} \qquad (C5)$$

$$\forall (i,r) \in I \times R \qquad 2d - 1 + y_{i,r} \ge \sum_{k \in D} (y_{i,r,k}^g + y_{i,r,k}^l) \qquad (C6)$$

$$\forall r \in \{2, \dots, \rho\} \qquad a_r = A_r \qquad (IC1)$$

$$a_{1,1,1} = p \qquad (IC2)$$

$$\forall (k_1, k_2) \in D^2 \setminus \{1,1\} \qquad a_{1,k_1,k_2} = A_{1,k_1,k_2} \qquad (IC3)$$

$$x^1 = q \qquad (IC4)$$

$$\forall i \in I \qquad x^i \in X$$

$$\forall r \in R \qquad a_r \in \mathbb{R}^{d \times d}$$

$$\forall (i,r) \in I \times R \qquad y_{i,r}, y_{i,r,k}^g, y_{i,r,k}^l \in \{0,1\}$$

Fig. 1. Set of constraints modeling the execution of a BR program with $e = (1, \dots, 1) \in \mathbb{R}^d$ a vector of all ones

Theorem 1. *The MIP constraints from Fig. 1 correctly model the execution of the BR program with input (p, q). The value of x^n after applying the constraints is then the output of the BR program: $x^n = P(p, q)$.*

Proof. We begin by proving that for a given $i \in I$, it is true that $y_{i,r} = 1$ iff x^i fulfills the condition for rule $\mathcal{R}_r$ and does not fulfill the condition for any rule $\mathcal{R}_{r'}$ where $r' < r$. Suppose $y_{i,r} = 1$. (C3) $\Rightarrow L_r \le x^i \le G_r$ implies that x^i fulfills the condition for rule $\mathcal{R}_r$. Let us now set $r' < r$.

$$C2 \Rightarrow y_{i,r'} = 0 \wedge \sum_{r''<r'} y_{i,r''} = 0$$

$$C6 \Rightarrow \exists k \in D : y_{i,r',k}^g = 0 \vee y_{i,r',k}^l = 0$$

As we also have:

$$y_{i,r',k}^g = 0 \wedge C4 \Rightarrow x_k^i \ge G_{r',k}$$

$$y_{i,r',k}^l = 0 \wedge C5 \Rightarrow x_k^i \le L_{r',k}$$

We have one of $x_k^i \ge G_{r',k}$ or $x_k^i \le L_{r',k}$. Either of those means that x^i does not fulfill the condition for rule $\mathcal{R}_{r'}$.

Conversely, suppose that x^i fulfills the condition for rule $\mathcal{R}_r$ and does not fulfill the condition for any rule $\mathcal{R}_{r'}$ where $r' < r$. Reasoning by induction over r', we see that assuming $\sum_{r''<r'} y_{i,r''} = 0$ (which is true for $r' = 1$) we have:

$$C4 \wedge C5 \wedge C6 \Rightarrow y_{i,r'} = 0$$

because the condition for $\mathcal{R}_{r'}$ is not fulfilled. We thus have $\sum_{r'<r} y_{i,r'} = 0$. This and the fact that the condition for $\mathcal{R}_r$ is fulfilled means that $y_{i,r} = 1$.

A simple inductive proof over the $i \in I$ then proves that the x^i are the successive values taken by x during the execution of the BR program as long as $\sum_{r \in R} y_{i,r} = 1$ and that the value of x^i does not change as long as $\sum_{r \in R} y_{i,r} = 0$, which corresponds to the stopped execution of the BR program. This also proves $x^n = P(p,q)$. □

2.2 A MIP Formulation

Having modeled the dynamics of a single execution of the BR program by means of the constraints of the previous section, we now come back to our original purpose: we exhibit a MIP that finds a value of p satisfying Eq. 1 in Fig. 2.

We index the instances in S with $j \in J = \{1, \ldots, m\}$, where $m = |S|$ is the number of instances in the training set S. The parameter p is now one of the variables. We note $e = (1, \ldots, 1) \in \mathbb{R}^d$ the vector of all ones.

As modifying the parameter means modifying the BR program, the assumptions made regarding the finiteness of the program might not be verified when optimizing over p. One of those which might lead to unusable solutions is the assumption that the computations terminate in less than $n-1$ iterations. In the case where the MIP finds a value of p for which the BR program is stopped by this limit on the loop rather than by the proper termination condition, the MIP

$$\begin{array}{ll}
\underset{p,a,x,y,y^g,y^l}{\text{minimize}} & |p^0 - p| \\
\text{subject to} & \\
& \text{(C1), (C2), (C3), (C4), (C5), (C6), (IC1), (IC2), (IC3)} \\
\forall j \in J & \sum_{r \in R} y_{n,j,r} = 0 \qquad\qquad\qquad \text{(C7)} \\
& \left| \frac{1}{m} \sum_{j \in J} x_1^{n,j} - g \right| \le \epsilon \qquad\qquad \text{(C8)} \\
\forall j \in J & x^{1,j} = q^j \qquad\qquad\qquad\qquad \text{(IC4')} \\
\forall (i,j) \in I \times J & x^{i,j} \in X \\
\forall k \in R & a_k \in \mathbb{R}^{d \times d} \\
& p \in \mathbb{R} \\
\forall (i,j,r,k) \in I \times J \times R \times D & y_{i,j,r}, y_{i,j,r,k}^g, y_{i,j,r,k}^l \in \{0,1\}
\end{array}$$

Fig. 2. MIP Formulation for Solving Eq. 1 with $e = (1, \ldots, 1) \in \mathbb{R}^d$ a vector of all ones

would not actually solve Eq. 1. We therefore limit ourselves to solutions which result in computations that terminate in less than $n - 1$ rule executions.

Any constraints numbered as before fulfills the same role. The additional constraints are:

- (C7) represents the need for the computation to have terminated after $n - 1$ executions
- (C8) represents the goal from Eq. 1, that is a constraint over the average of the final values of x.

Theorem 2. *The MIP from Fig. 2 finds a value of p that satisfies Eq. 1.*

The proof derives directly from Theorem 1.

3   A MILP Reformulation

The problem as written in Eq. 2 is not linear. A linear reformulation exists for when the parameter p takes the place of a scalar in B_r, L_r or G_r. Figure 3 describes such a MILP when p takes the place of $B_{1,1}$. We linearize the products of $A_r x^{i,j} + b_r$ by $y_{i,j,r}$ and $x^{i,j}$ by $y_{i,j,r}$ in (C1) using factorization and an auxiliary variable $w \in \mathbb{R}^{I \times J \times R}$. We arrange to have $w_{i,j,r} = (A_r x^{i,j} + b_r - x^{i,j}) y_{i,j,r}$, i.e. $w_{i,j,r} = A_r x^{i,j} + b_r - x^{i,j}$ (the difference between the new and the old values of x^j) iff rule r is executed, and 0 otherwise.

Theorem 3. *This MILP finds a value of p that satisfies Eq. 1, when p takes the place of $B_{1,1}$. A similar MILP exists for when p takes the place of another scalar in $B_{r,k}$, $L_{r,k}$ and $G_{r,k}$.*

The proof derives directly from Theorem 2, by factoring constraint (C1) in Fig. 2 and studying the possible values of $y_{i,j,k}$.

When the parameter takes the place of $A_{1,1,1}$, a linear formulation is only possible if $A_{1,1,1}$ is a discrete variable. For the purpose of this article, we only use the case where A_{1,k_1,k_2} are binary variables. The associated MILP is in Fig. 4. In that case, we have the additional product of ax to linearize, so we use another auxiliary variable $z \in \mathbb{R}^{I \times J \times R \times D^2}$ such that $z_{i,j,r,k_1,k_2} = a_{r,k_1,k_2} x_{i,j,k_2}$.

Theorem 4. *The MILP in Fig. 4 finds a value of p that satisfies Eq. 1, when p takes the place of $A_{1,1,1}$ and A_{1,k_1,k_2} are binary variables.*

The proof derives from Theorem 3 and a study of the possible values of A_{1,k_1,k_2} and $y_{i,j,r}$. We can trivially expand the MILP to optimize over more than one parameter, adding constraints similar to constraints (IC1), (IC2) and (IC3) or (IC1"), (IC2") and (IC3") in Fig. 1 or Fig. 3 as necessary and having an objective of $\sum_p \|p^0 - p\|$.

$$\underset{p,b,x,y,y^g,y^l,w}{\text{minimize}} \qquad |p^0 - p|$$

subject to

$$(\text{C2}), (\text{C3}), (\text{C4}), (\text{C5}), (\text{C6}), (\text{C7}), (\text{IC4'})$$

$$\forall (i,j) \in I \backslash \{n\} \times J \qquad x^{i+1,j} = \sum_{r \in R} w_{i,j,r} + x^{i,j} \qquad (\text{C1''}_1)$$

$$\forall (i,j) \in I \times J \times R \qquad -M y_{i,j,r} e \le w_{i,j,r} \le M y_{i,j,r} e \qquad (\text{C1''}_2)$$

$$\forall (i,j,r) \in I \times J \times R \qquad A_r x^{i,j} + b_r - x^{i,j} - M(1 - y_{i,j,r}) e$$

$$\le w_{i,j,r} \le A_r x^{i,j} + b_r - x^{i,j} \qquad (\text{C1''}_3)$$

$$-\varepsilon \le \frac{1}{m} \sum_{j \in J} x_1^{n,j} - g \le \varepsilon \qquad (\text{C8''})$$

$$\forall r \in \{2, \dots, \rho\} \qquad b_r = B_r \qquad (\text{IC1''})$$

$$b_{1,1} = p \qquad (\text{IC2''})$$

$$\forall k \in \{2, \dots, d\} \qquad b_{1,k} = B_{1,k} \qquad (\text{IC3''})$$

$$\forall (i,j) \in I \times J \qquad x^{i,j} \in X$$

$$\forall (i,j,r) \in I \times J \times R \qquad b_r, w_{i,j,r} \in \mathbb{R}^d$$

$$p \in \mathbb{R}$$

$$\forall (i,j,r,k) \in I \times J \times R \times D \quad y_{i,j,r}, y_{i,j,r,k}^g, y_{i,j,r,k}^l \in \{0,1\}$$

Fig. 3. MILP Formulation with p Taking the Place of $B_{1,1}$ with $e = (1, \dots, 1) \in \mathbb{R}^d$ a vector of all ones

$$\underset{p,a,x,y,y^g,y^l,w,z}{\text{minimize}} \qquad |p^0 - p|$$

subject to

$$(\text{C1''}_1), (\text{C1''}_2), (\text{C2}), (\text{C3}), (\text{C4}), (\text{C5}), (\text{C6})$$
$$(\text{C7}), (\text{C8''}), (\text{IC1}), (\text{IC2}), (\text{IC3}), (\text{IC4'})$$

$$\forall (i,j,r,k_1) \in I \times J \times R \times D \qquad \sum_{k_2 \in D} z_{i,j,r,k_1,k_2} + B_r - x^{i,j} - M(1 - y_{i,j,r}) e$$

$$\le w_{i,j,r} \le \sum_{k_2 \in D} z_{i,j,r,k_1,k_2} + B_r \qquad (\text{C1}_3^{(3)})$$

$$- x^{i,j} + M(1 - y_{i,j,r}) e$$

$$\forall (i,j,r) \in I \times J \times R \qquad -M a_r \le z_{i,j,r} \le M a_r \qquad (\text{C1}_4^{(3)})$$

$$\forall (i,j,r,k_1,k_2) \in I \times J \times R \times D^2 \qquad x_{i,j,k_2} - M(1 - a_{r,k_1,k_2})$$

$$\le z_{i,j,k_1,k_2} \le x_{i,j,k_2} \qquad (\text{C1}_5^{(3)})$$

$$\forall (i,j,r,k_1,k_2) \in I \times J \times R \times D^2 \qquad x^{i,j}, z_{i,j,r,k_1,k_2} \in X$$

$$\forall (i,j,r) \in I \times J \times R \qquad w_{i,j,r} \in \mathbb{R}^d$$

$$\forall r \in R \qquad a_r \in \{0,1\}^{d \times d}$$

$$p \in \{0,1\}$$

$$\forall (i,j,r,k) \in I \times J \times R \times D \quad y_{i,j,r}, y_{i,j,r,k}^g, y_{i,j,r,k}^l \in \{0,1\}$$

Fig. 4. MILP Formulation with p Taking the Place of $A_{1,1,1}$ with $e = (1, \dots, 1) \in \mathbb{R}^d$ a vector of all ones

Table 1. Experimental values for the scalability of the MILP method

Value of ρ	Proportion of instances solvable in an hour	Average solver times over solvable instances	Average objective values over solvable instances
1	1.0	2.0877	0.9772
2	0.98	22.9848	2.1363
3	0.96	265.3536	4.0421
4	0.89	737.6687	6.9834
5	0.66	929.3174	7.771

4 Implementation and Experiments

We use a Python script to randomly generate samples of 100 BR programs and corresponding sets of instances with $d = 3$, $n = 10$ and $m = 100$. We define the space X as $X \subseteq \mathbb{R} \times \mathbb{R} \times \mathbb{Z}$. The BR programs are sets of a variable number ρ of rules of the type:

if $L_r \leq x \leq G_r$ **then**
$\quad x \leftarrow A_r x + B_r$
end if

where L_r, G_r, B_r are vectors of scalars in $[-5, 5]$; $L_r \leq G_r$ and A_r are $d \times d$ matrices of binary variables. The instances are vectors q_j with values in $[-5, 5]$. All values are generated using a uniform distribution. We use a variable value of ε. For each BR program, we try to obtain a goal $g = 0$ by optimizing over $\phi = 5\rho$ randomly chosen parameters.

We use these BR programs to study the computational properties of the MILP. The value of M used is customized according to each constraint, and is ultimately bounded by 51 (strictly greater than five times the range of possible values for x). We write the MILP as an AMPL model, and solve it using the CPLEX solver on a Dell PowerEdge 860 running CentOS Linux.

4.1 Scalability

We set a fixed ε value of 1. This corresponds to a very high tolerance (20 % of the range of possible values). We observe the average solving time and optimal objective for different values of ρ (Table 1) among the solvable MILP instances. An instance is considered unsolvable if it is infeasible or it has no integer solution after 1 h (3600 s) of solver time.

While it could be argued that the increase in the number of parameters has an obvious effect over the difficulty of the problem, the study of an increase in ρ without the proportional increase in ϕ leads to a drastic and predictable increase in infeasible instances. Even with our setup, the proportion of solvable instances is lower as ρ increases, although that is mostly due to the solver exceeding the time limit. As a high value of ρ is the main issue when scaling up to industrial BR programs, it still seems worth studying.

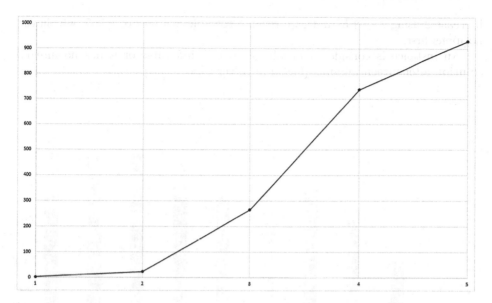

Fig. 5. Variation of computational time (in seconds) with ρ (the number of rules in the BR program)

Unfortunately, we observe that the direct solving of the MILP described in Sect. 3 is not practical for learning parameters in industrial-sized BR programs. Furthermore, the increase in computational time is not linear with the number of ρ, but rather exponential as seen on Fig. 5. The increase in the optimal objective value is intuitive and does not seem drastic, which indicates that the experimental setup is somewhat realistic. A reformulation of the MILP to improve the solving time of the MILP is a possible follow-up area of research.

Another possibility we plan on researching is to check whether using sparse matrices for L, G, A and B significantly improves the computational experience: most industrial business processes do not use complex rules, but rather many rules each applying to one or two components of the variable x. This does not immediately imply a better performance as the value of n would realistically need to be increased to compensate.

4.2   Accuracy

We fix the number of rules to $\rho = 4$ and so the number of parameters is 20. This is much lower than the number of rules used by BR programs destined to industrial usage. We observe the average solving time and the proportion of solvable MILP instances among all instances for different values of ε. In this case, it means we have only generated one hundred BR programs, on which we test the accuracy of our method.

For each BR program, we start with $\varepsilon = 1$. If the instance is solvable, we decrease ε using $\varepsilon \leftarrow \varepsilon - 0.2$ until we reach an unsolvable instance; otherwise we increase ε using $\varepsilon \leftarrow 1.5\varepsilon$ until we reach a solvable instance or $\varepsilon \geq 5$, whichever happens first.

An instance is considered unsolvable if it is infeasible or it has no integer solution after fifteen minutes (900 s) of solver time.

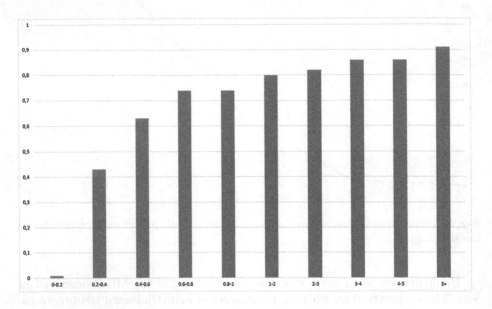

Fig. 6. Proportion of solvable instances for varying values of ε

Figure 6 shows the proportion of solvable instances as a function of ε. Being careful of the nonlinear scale of the figure, ε seems to have a greater influence on solvability when small and a reduced influence as it grows. In other words, our method will relatively easily find the best parameter in most cases, but difficult problems remain difficult even when allowing for a greater distance to the desired average f.

Furthermore, with random BR problems that include both unsolvable and already optimal situations, we solve 50 percent of problems with $\varepsilon = 0.4$ which means allowing $\mathbb{E}(f) \in [-0.4, 0.4]$. This is too low for industrial applications, but approaching the desired average by 8 percent of the possible range in half the cases is a promising start. Our method as it is described cannot currently be used as a general tool as too many BR programs cannot be solved accurately.

The restriction to $n = 10$ for those orders of ρ accurately models real business processes where BRs rarely loop. The sample size of $m = 100$ is also somewhat realistic. The dimension $d = 3$ is arbitrary and much lower than can be expected in actual business processes, where dimensionality can be over an order of magnitude higher.

5   Conclusion, Discussion and Future Work

We have presented a way to use mathematical programming to model learning problems of an unusual type: learning the parameters of a BR program so that its average output over a set of instances Q meets a target g. This can be extended to learning the parameters of any program where the semantics of an execution are well-defined, to reach a targeted average output. In such a program, the semantics lead directly to mathematical constraints defining a MIP, with the execution being modeled by indexing the variables over the steps of the computation. Depending on the program, solving can then be easy, if the program is linear like in our case, or lead to more complex optimization methods. Where standard supervised learning algorithms are difficult to apply with a target defined on average, our method can help fill the blanks.

While the computational performance indicates that directly solving the MILP formulation described in this article is impractical, it does hold promise. In particular, the optimal values obtained when scaling up prove that if the computational cost can be reduced, the methodology has possible industrial implications. The potential avenues of research in this direction are working on the MILP itself (e.g. through reformulations) and experimenting on BR programs closer to the reality of business processes (e.g. through sparse matrices).

A better methodology for choosing the best possible ε might also be needed, as the current one only yields a broad estimate. A possible avenue of research pertaining to the accuracy of our method is evaluating the risk of over-fitting, through the generation of additional samples $q \in Q \backslash S$ and using a parameter-less version of the MILP in Fig. 3 to evaluate the average $\frac{1}{m} \sum_{j \in J} x_1^{n,j}$.

As many real-life applications use rules with a linear structure, our model has direct applications in many industries that rely on BR programs to automate decisions, some of which might not even need additional refinements depending on the size of the BR programs they use.

Acknowledgments. The first author (OW) is supported by an IBM France/ANRT CIFRE Ph.D. thesis award.

References

1. Atiya, A.: Learning algorithms for neural networks. Ph.D. thesis, California Institute of Technology, Pasadena, CA (1991)
2. Bakir, G., Hofmann, T., Schölkopf, B., Smola, A., Taskar, B., Vishwanathan, S.: Predicting Structured Data (Neural Information Processing). The MIT Press, Cambridge (2007)
3. Bonami, P., Lee, J.: BONMIN user's manual. Technical report, IBM Corporation, June, 2007
4. Brodley, C., Friedl, M.: Identifying mislabeled training data. J. Artif. Intell. Res. **11**, 131–167 (1999)

5. Brownston, L., Farrell, R., Kant, E., Martin, N.: Programming Expert Systems in OPS5: An Introduction to Rule-based Programming. Addison-Wesley Longman Publishing Co., Boston (1985)
6. Buchanan, B., Shortliffe, E. (eds.): Rule Based Expert Systems: The Mycin Experiments of the Stanford Heuristic Programming Project. (The Addison-Wesley Series in Artificial Intelligence). Addison-Wesley Longman Publishing Co., Boston (1984)
7. Chapelle, O., Schlkopf, B., Zien, A.: Semi-Supervised Learning. The MIT Press, Cambridge (2010)
8. Clancey, W.: The epistemology of a rule-based expert system: a framework for explanation. Artif. Intell. **20**(3), 215–251 (1983)
9. Cortes, C., Vapnik, V.: Support-vector networks. Mach. Learn. **20**(3), 273–297 (1995)
10. Davis, R., Buchanan, B., Shortliffe, E.: Production rules as a representation for a knowledge-based consultation program. Artif. Intell. **8**(1), 15–45 (1977)
11. Forgy, C.: OPS5 User's Manual. Department of Computer Science, Carnegie-Mellon University, Pittsburgh (1981)
12. Knolmayer, G., Herbst, H.: Business rules. Wirtschaftsinformatik **35**(4), 386–390 (1993)
13. IBM: ILOG CPLEX 12.2 User's Manual. IBM, New York (2010)
14. IBM: Operational Decision Manager 8.8 (2015)
15. Kolber, A., et al.: Defining business rules - what are they really? Project report 3, The Business Rules Group (2000)
16. Liberti, L., Marinelli, F.: Mathematical programming: turing completeness and applications to software analysis. J. Comb. Optim. **28**(1), 82–104 (2014)
17. Liu, T.Y.: Learning to rank for information retrieval. Found. Trends Inf. Retr. **3**(3), 225–331 (2009)
18. Lucas, P., Gaag, L.V.D.: Principles of Expert Systems. Addison-Wesley Longman Publishing Co., Boston (1991)
19. Newell, A.: Production systems: models of control structures. In: Chase, W. (ed.) Visual Information Processing, pp. 463–526. Academic Press, New York (1973)
20. Newell, A., Simon, H.: Human Problem Solving. Prentice-Hall, Upper Saddle River (1972)
21. Ross, R.: Principles of the Business Rule Approach. Addison-Wesley Longman Publishing Co., Boston (2003)
22. de Sainte Marie, C., Hallmark, G., Paschke, A.: RIF Production Rule Dialect. 2nd edn. Recommendation, W3C (2013)
23. Scott, A., Bennett, J., Peairs, M.: The EMYCIN Manual. Department of Computer Science, Stanford University, Stanford (1981)
24. Settles, B.: Active learning literature survey. Computer Sciences Technical report 1648, University of Wisconsin-Madison (2009)
25. Shortcliffe, E.: Computer-Based Medical Consultations: MYCIN. Elsevier, New York (1976)
26. Vapnik, V.: The Nature of Statistical Learning Theory. Springer, New York (1995)
27. Wang, O., Ke, C., Liberti, L., de Sainte Marie, C.: The learnability of business rules. In: International Workshop on Machine Learning, Optimization, and Big Data (MOD 2016) (2016)

Bridge Rules for Reasoning in Component-Based Heterogeneous Environments

Stefania Costantini[(✉)] and Giovanni De Gasperis

Dipartimento di Ingegneria e Scienze dell'Informazione e Matematica,
Università degli Studi dell'Aquila, Via Vetoio snc, L'Aquila, Italy
{stefania.costantini,giovanni.degasperis}@univaq.it

Abstract. Multi-Context Systems (MCS) model in Computational Logic distributed systems composed of heterogeneous sources, or "contexts", interacting via special rules called "bridge rules". In this paper we consider how to enhance flexibility and generality of such systems; in particular, we discuss aspects that might be improved to increase practical applicability.

1 Introduction

Multi-Context Systems (MCSs) have been proposed in Artificial Intelligence and Knowledge Representation to model information exchange among several diverse sources [1–3]. MCSs are designed so as to deal with heterogeneous sources: in fact, the approach explicitly considers their different representation languages and semantics. Heterogeneous sources are called "contexts" (or, equivalently, we will call them "sources", or "modules"), and interact through special inter-context rules called *bridge rules*, similar in format to datalog rules with negation[1].

The reason why MCSs are particularly interesting is that they aim at modeling in a formal way real applications requiring access to sources distributed on the web. Among the relevant domains where the adoption of MCSs can bring real advances is for instance health care (see, e.g., the running example in [6]). In view of such practical applications it is important to notice that, being logic-based, contexts may encompass logical agents, to which MCSs have in fact already been extended (cf. [7,8]).

Despite the importance of MCSs for practical knowledge representation and reasoning, their definition is under some aspects too abstract, and the functioning modalities of such systems are considered under ideal circumstances. In this paper we try to tackle in a formal way the practical aspects related to these systems, and attempt at a systematization that should also provide guidelines for implementations. The paper proposes some substantial technical improvements concerning bridge rules, also in relation to the evolution of an MCS over time.

The paper is organized as follows. In Sect. 2 we introduce Multi-Context Systems. In Sect. 3 we propose a motivating application scenario, and with respect

---

[1] Cf. [4,5] for standard datalog, logic programming and prolog terminology.

© Springer International Publishing Switzerland 2016
J.J. Alferes et al. (Eds.): RuleML 2016, LNCS 9718, pp. 97–112, 2016.
DOI: 10.1007/978-3-319-42019-6_7

to such scenario we outline some aspects where the original MCS definition is not fully adequate in practice. In Sect. 4 we propose some variations, enhancements and extensions to the basic approach, that introduce improvements concerning these aspects. Finally, in Sect. 5 we conclude.

2   Bridge Rules and Multi-Context Systems: Background

Heterogeneous Multi-Context systems have been introduced in the seminal work of [9] in order to integrate different inference systems without resorting to non-classical logical systems.

Later, the idea has been further developed and generalized to non-monotonic reasoning domains in [1–3,6] and other related papers. There, (managed) Multi-Context systems aim at making it possible to build systems that need to access multiple possibly heterogeneous data sources, called "contexts", by modeling the necessary information flow via "bridge rules", whose form is similar to datalog rules with negation (cf., e.g., [5]). Bridge rules allow for inter-context interaction: in fact, each element in their "body" explicitly includes the indication of the context from which information is to be obtained.

In order to account for heterogeneity, each context is supposed to be based on its own *logic*. Reporting from [2], a logic L is a triple $(KB_L; Cn_L; ACC_L)$, where KB_L is the set of admissible knowledge bases of L, that are sets of KB-elements ("formulas"); underlying (though here implicitly) there is a signature Σ_L including sets of constants, predicate and function symbols, and a set of variables; KB_L elements are thus specified over this signature and involve terms that can be either variables or constants or compound terms built out of function symbols and other terms; atoms are defined as the application of a predicate over a set of terms, according to the predicate's arity; a term/atom/formula is "ground" if there are no variables occurring therein; a logic is *relational* if in its signature the set of function symbols is empty, so its terms are variables and constants only. Cn_L is the set of possible sets of consequences of knowledge bases in KB_L; sets in Cn_L can be called "belief sets" or "data sets", as their elements are data items or "beliefs" or "facts", that we assume to be ground. The function $ACC_L : KB_L \rightarrow 2^{Cn_L}$ defines the semantics of L by assigning to each knowledge base "acceptable" sets of consequences; so, only some (or possibly none) of the possible sets of consequences in Cn_L are acceptable.

A multi-context system (MCS) $M = (C_1, \ldots, C_n)$ is a collection of contexts $C_i = (L_i; kb_i; br_i)$ where L_i is a logic, $kb_i \in KB_{L_i}$ is a knowledge base and br_i is a set of bridge rules. Each such rule ρ is of the following form, where the left-hand side s is called the *head*, denoted as $hd(\rho)$, the right-hand side is called the *body*, also denoted as $body(\rho)$, and the comma stand for conjunction.

$$s \leftarrow (c_1 : p_1), \ldots, (c_j : p_j), not\,(c_{j+1} : p_{j+1}), \ldots, not\,(c_m : p_m).$$

For each bridge rule included in context C_i the head s can be any formula in L_i. It is required that $kb_i \cup s$ belongs to KB_{L_i} and, for every $k \le m$, c_k is a constant denoting a context included in M (in the original definitions c_k is simply be an integer number $i \le n$, though more expressive "names" can be used), and each p_k belongs to some set in Cn_{L_k}, i.e., it is a possible consequence of context c_k's knowledge base according to the logic in which c_k is defined. The head s is any formula in L_i, where however $kb_i \cup \{s\} \in KB_{L_i}$. A *relational* MCS [10] is a variant where all the involved logics are relational, and aggregate operators in database style are admitted in bridge-rule bodies.

A data state of MCS M is a tuple $S = (S_1, \ldots, S_n)$ such that for $1 \leq i \leq n$, $S_i \in Cn_{L_i}$. Thus, a data state associates to each context a possible set of consequences.

Given data state S, $app(S)$ is the set composed of the heads of those bridge rules which are *applicable* in S as their body is entailed by S; i.e., those such that for every positive literal $(c_i : p_i)$ in the body, $1 \leq i \leq j$, $p_i \in S_i$ and for every negative literal $not\,(c_k : p_k)$ in the body, $j + 1 \leq k \leq m$, $p_k \notin S_k$.

In managed MCSs (mMCSs)[2] the conclusion s, which represents the "bare" bridge-rule result, becomes $o(s)$ where o is a special operator. The meaning is that the result computed by a bridge rule is not blindly incorporated into the "destination" context's knowledge base: rather, it is processed by operator o, that can possibly perform any elaboration, such as format conversion, belief revision, etc.

More precisely, for given logic L, $F_L = \{s \in kb \,|\, kb \in KB_L\}$ is the set of formulas occurring in its knowledge bases. A *management base* is a set of operation names (briefly, operations) OP, defining elaborations that can be performed on formulas, e.g., addition of, revision with, etc. For a logic L and a management base OP, the set of operational statements that can be built from OP and F_L is $F_L^{OP} = \{o(s) \,|\, o \in OP, s \in F_L\}$. The semantics of such statements is given by a *management function*, which maps a set of operational statements and a knowledge base into a modified knowledge base. In particular, a management function over a logic L and a management base OP is a function $mng : 2^{F_L^{OP}} \times KB^L \to 2^{KB_L} \setminus \emptyset$. We assume a management function to be deterministic, i.e., to produce a unique new knowledge base. Each context in an mMCS has its specific management function mng_i, which is crucial for knowledge incorporation from external sources. Notice that each mng_i can be non-monotonic, i.e., it may imply deletion of formulas. Now, we can see a context as $C_i = (c_i; L_i; kb_i; br_i; OP_i; mng_i)$ where c_i is a constant acting as the context "name" that, if omitted, is assumed to be integer number i.

Desirable data states, called *equilibria*, are those which encompass bridge-rules application. In fact in (m)MCSs equilibria are those data states S where each S_i is acceptable according to function ACC_i associated to L_i, given that every applicable bridge rule has indeed been applied. Formally, a data state S is an equilibrium for an MCS iff, for $1 \leq i \leq n$,

$$S_i \in ACC_i(mng_i(app(S), kb_i)) \tag{1}$$

---

[2] We introduce mMCSs in a simplified form with respect to [5]: in fact, they generalize from a logic to a "logic suite", where one can select the desired semantics among a set of possibilities, while we define mMCS simply over logics.

I.e., one (i) applies all C_i's bridge rules which are applicable in data state S; (ii) applies the management function which, by incorporating bridge-rule results into C_i's knowledge base kb_i, computes a new knowledge base kb'_i; (iii) determines via ACC_i the set of acceptable sets of consequences of kb'_i. In an equilibrium such set includes S_i, i.e., an equilibrium is "stable" w.r.t. bridge-rule application.

Conditions for existence of equilibria have been studied [1], and basically require cyclic application of bridge rules to be avoided. The complexity of deciding whether some equilibrium exists depends upon composing contexts' complexity, basically upon the complexity of computing formula (1).

Algorithms for computing equilibria have recently been proposed [2,11,12]. Methods also exist [6] to detect and enforce MCS's consistency, i.e., to ensure that an equilibrium does not include inconsistent data sets (*local consistency*) and that the composing data sets are mutually consistent (*global consistency*). It has been proved that *local consistency* is achieved whenever all management functions are (lc-) preserving, i.e., if they always determine a kb' which is consistent.

Bridge rules as defined in mMCSs are basically a *reactive* device, as a bridge rule is applied whenever applicable. In dynamic environments, a bridge rule in general will not be applied only once, and it does not hold that an equilibrium, once reached, lasts forever. In fact, contexts may be able to incorporate new data items, e.g., as discussed in [3] for Reactive MCSs (rMCSs), the input provided by sensors ("observations"). Therefore, a bridge rule can be in principle re-evaluated upon new observations, thus leading to evolving equilibria and to the notion of a "run" of an rMCS.

3   Motivating Scenario and Discussion

Some of the reasons of our interest in (m)MCSs and bridge-rules stem from a project where we are among the proponents [13], concerning smart Cyber Physical Systems with particular attention (though without restriction) to applications in the e-Health field. The general scenario of such "F&K" ("Friendly-and-Kind") systems is depicted in Fig. 1.

We have a set of computational entities, of knowledge bases and of sensors, all immersed in the "Fog" of the Internet of Everything. All components can, in time, join or leave the system. Some computational components will be agents. In the envisaged e-Health application for instance, an agent will be in charge of each patient. The System's engine will keep track of the present system's configuration, and will enable the various classes of rules to work properly. Terminological rules will allow for more flexible knowledge exchange via Ontologies. Pattern Rules will have the role of defining and checking coherence/correctness of system's behavior. Bridge rules are the vital element, as they allow knowledge to flow among components in a clearly-specified principled way: referring to Fig. 1, devices for bridge-rule functioning can be considered as a part of the System's engine. Therefore, F&Ks are "knowledge-intensive" systems, providing

ENVISAGED SMART CPS GENERAL ARCHITECTURE

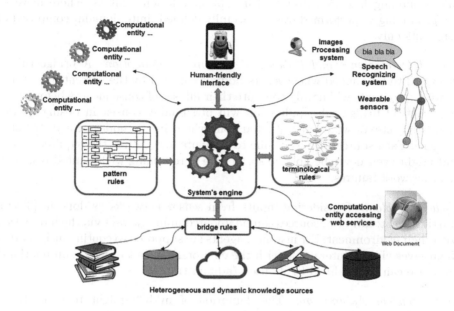

Fig. 1. Motivating scenario

flexible access to dynamic, heterogeneous, and distributed sources of knowledge and reasoning, within a highly dynamic computational environment. We basically consider such systems to be (enhanced) mMCSs: as mentioned in fact, suitable extensions to include agents and sensors in such systems already exist.

In the perspective of such kind of systems, the definition of (m)MCS recalled in Sect. 2 is, though neat, quite abstract. Some limitations can be identified, that we list below.

Grounded Knowledge Assumption. Bridge rules are by definition ground, i.e., they do not contain variables. In [6] it is literally stated that [in their examples] they *"use for readability and succinctness schematic bridge rules with variables (upper case letters and '_' [the 'anonymous' variable]) which range over associated sets of constants; they stand for all respective instances (obtainable by value substitution)"*. Basic definition of mMCS do not require either contexts' knowledge bases or bridge rules to be finite sets. Though contexts' knowledge bases will in practice be finite, they cannot be assumed to necessarily admit a finite grounding, and thus a finite number of bridge-rules' ground instances. This assumption can be reasonable, e.g., for standard relational databases and logic programming under the answer set semantics [14]. In other kinds of logics, for instance simply "plain" general logic programs, it is no longer realistic. In practical applications however, there should either be a finite number of applicable (ground instances of) bridge-rules, or some suitable device for run-time dynamic bridge-rule instantiation and application should be provided. The issue of bridge-rule grounding has been discussed in [15] for relational MCSs, where however the grounding is performed over a carefully defined finite domain, composed of constants only.

Logical Omniscience and Unbounded Resources Assumption. A bridge rule is supposed to be applied whenever its body is entailed by the current data state. However, contexts will hardly compute their full set of consequences beforehand. So, practical bridge rule application will presumably consist in posing queries to other contexts which are situated somewhere in the nodes of a distributed systems. Each source will need time to compute and deliver the required result, and might even never be able do so, in case of reasoning with limited resources or of network failures.

Update Problem. Considering inputs from sensor networks as done in [3] is a starting point: however, sources can be updated in many ways via the interaction with their environment. For instance, agents are supposed to continuously modify themselves via the interaction with the environment, but even a plain relational database can be modified by its users/administrators.

Static System Assumption. The definition of mMCS might realistically be extended to a setting where the set of contexts changes over time, maybe because some context gets momentarily disconnected, or because components may freely either join or abandon the system. Moreover inter-context reachability might be limited, e.g., via authorizations of some kind.

Full System Knowledge Assumption. A context might know the *role* of another context it wants to query (e.g., a diagnostic knowledge base) but not its "name", that could be, for instance, its URI or anyway some kind of reference that allows for actually posing a query.

Unique Source Assumption. In the body of bridge rules, each literal mentions a specific context. In practice, that context might not be able to return a result while another context with the same role instead might.

Uniform Knowledge Representation Format Assumption. Different contexts might represent similar concepts in different ways: this aspect is taken into account in [8], where ontological definitions can be exchanged among contexts, and a possible global ontology is also considered.

Equilibria Computation and Consistency Check Assumption. Algorithms for computing equilibria are practically applicable only if open access to contexts' contents is granted. The same holds for local and global consistency checking. However, the potential of MCSs is in our view that of modeling real distributed systems where contexts in general keep their knowledge bases private. Therefore, in practice one will often just assume the existence of consistent equilibria.

4 Proposed Extensions

Below we consider the points raised in previous section and provide, whenever not already existing, related extensions/enhancements to the basic mMCS paradigm.

4.1 Grounded Knowledge Assumption

To the best of our knowledge, the problem of loosening the constraint of bridge-rules groundedness has not been so far extensively treated in the literature. The issue has been discussed in [15] for relational MCSs, where however the grounding of bridge rules is performed over a carefully defined finite domain, composed of constants only. Instead, we intend to consider any, even infinite, domain.

The procedure for computing equilibria that we propose for the case of non-ground bridge rules is, informally, the following. (i) We consider an initial data state S_0 composed of finite sets; this is without loss of generality because, as seen below, it does not actually limit the grounding to finite domains. (ii) We instantiate bridge rules over the finite number of (ground) terms occurring in S_0; we thus obtain an initial finite grounding relative to S_0; (iii) we evaluate whether S_0 is an equilibrium, i.e., if S_0 coincides with the data state S_1 resulting from applicable bridge rules. (iv) In case S_0 is not an equilibrium, bridge rules can now be grounded w.r.t. terms occurring in S_1, and so on, until either an equilibrium is reached, or no more applicable bridge rules are generated.

It is reasonable to start the procedure from a basic data state consisting of finite ground instances of the initial contexts' knowledge bases, obtained by substituting variables with constants. By definition, a ground instance of a context's C_i knowledge base is in fact in Cn_i, i.e., it is indeed a set of possible consequences, though in general it is not acceptable. Notice that starting from a finite data state does not guarantee however neither the existence of a finite equilibrium, nor that an equilibrium can be reached in a finite number of steps.

Consider as an example an MCS composed of two contexts C_1 and C_2, both based upon plain logic programming and concerning the representation of natural numbers. Assume such contexts to be characterized respectively by the following knowledge bases and bridge rules (where C_1 has no bridge rule).

%kb_1
  $nat(0).$
%kb_2
  $nat(suc(X)) \leftarrow nat(X).$
%br_2
  $nat(X) \leftarrow (c1 : nat(X)).$

The unique equilibrium is reached in one step from basic data state $S_0 = (\{nat(0)\}, \emptyset)$ via the application of br_2 which "communicates" fact $nat(0)$ to C_2. In fact, due to the the recursive rule, we have the equilibrium (S_1, S_2) where $S_1 = \{nat(0)\}$ and $S_2 = \{nat(0), nat(suc(0)), nat(suc(suc(0))), \ldots\}$
I.e., S_2 is an infinite set representing all natural numbers. If we assume to add a third context C_3 with empty knowledge base and a bridge rule br_3 defined

as $nat(X) \leftarrow (c2 : nat(X))$, then the equilibrium would be (S_1, S_2, S_3) with $S_3 = S_2$. There in fact, br_3 would be grounded on the infinite domain of the terms occurring in S_2, thus admitting an infinite number of instances.

The next example is a variation of the former one where C_1 "produces" the even natural numbers (starting from 0) and C_2 the odd ones. There is clearly a unique equilibrium, that cannot however be reached in finite time.

$\%kb_1$
    $nat(0)$.
$\%br_1$
    $nat(suc(X)) \leftarrow (c2 : nat(X))$.
$\%kb_2$
    $\emptyset$
$\%br_2$
    $nat(suc(X)) \leftarrow (c1 : nat(X))$.

We may notice that the contexts in the above example enlarge their knowledge by means of mutual "cooperation". Let us consider, according to our proposed method, again the basic data state $S_0 = (\{nat(0)\}, \emptyset)$.

As stated above, we ground bridge rules on the terms occurring therein. S_0 is not an equilibrium for the given MCS: in fact, the bridge rule in kb_2, once grounded on constant 0, is applicable but not applied. The data set resulting from the application, i.e., $S' = (\{nat(0)\}, \{nat(suc(o))\})$ is not an equilibrium either, because now the bridge rule in kb_1 (grounded on $suc(0)$) is in turn applicable but not applied.

We may go on, as $S'' = (\{nat(0), nat(suc(suc(0)))\}, \{nat(suc(o))\})$ leaves the bridge rule in kb_2 to be applied (grounded on $suc(suc(0))$), and so on. The unique equilibrium, that cannot be reached in finite time, is composed of two infinite sets, the former one representing the even natural numbers (including zero) and the latter representing the odd natural number. The equilibrium may be represented as:

$$E = (\{nat(0), nat(suc^k(0)))\}, \ k \bmod 2 \ = 0\}, \{nat(suc^k(o)), \ k \bmod 2 \ = 1\})$$

We have actually devised and applied an adaptation to non-ground bridge rules of the operational characterization introduced in [1] for the grounded equilibrium of a *definite* MCS, as in fact (according to the conditions stated therein) C_1 and C_2 are monotonic and admit at each step a unique set of consequences, and bridge-rule application is not unfounded (cyclic). In our more general setting the set of ground bridge rules associated to given knowledge bases cannot be computed beforehand, and the step-by-step computation must take contexts interactions into account.

Since reaching equilibria finitely may have advantages in practical cases, we show below a suitable reformulation of the above example. We require a minor modification in bridge-rule syntax: we assume in particular that whenever in some element the body of a bridge rule the context is omitted, i.e., we have just p_j instead of $(c_j : p_j)$, then we assume that p_j is proved locally from the present context's knowledge base. Previous example can be reformulated as follows, where we assume the customary prolog's syntax, and prolog's procedural semantics where elements in the body of a rule are proved/executed left-to-right. The knowledge bases and bridge rules now are:

$\%kb_1$
  $nat(0).$
  $count(0).$
  $threshold(t).$
$\%br_1$
  $new(nat(suc(X))) : - count(C), threshold(T), C < T, (c2 : nat(X))).$
$\%kb_2$
  $count(0).$
  $threshold(t).$
$\%br_2$
  $new(nat(suc(X))) : - count(C), threshold(T), C < T, (c1 : nat(X)).$

In the new definition there is a counter (initialized to zero) and some threshold, say t. We will exploit a management function that suitably defines the operator new which is now applied to bridge-rule results. A logic programming definition of such management function might be the following, where the counter is incremented and the new natural number asserted. Notice that such definition is by no means not logical, as we can shift to the "evolving logic programming" extension [16].

$new(nat(Z)) : - assert(nat(Z)), increment(C).$
$increment(C) : - retract(count(C)),$
$\qquad\qquad\quad C1\ is\ C + 1, assert(count(C1)).$

Consequently, bridge rules will now produce a result only until the counter reaches the threshold, which guarantees the existence of a finite equilibrium.

Below we formalize the procedure that we have empirically illustrated via the examples, so as to generalize to mMCS with non-ground bridge rules the operational characterization of [1] for monotonic MCSs (i.e., those where each context's knowledge base admits a single set of consequences, which grows monotonically when information is added to the context's knowledge base). Following [1], for simplicity we assume bridge-rules bodies to include only positive literals, and the formula s in its head $o(s)$ to be an atom. So, we will be able to introduce the definition of *grounded equilibrium of grade* κ. Preliminarily, in order to admit non-ground bridge rules we have to specify how we obtain their ground instances, and how to establish applicability.

Definition 1. *Let $r \in br_i$ be a non-ground bridge rule occurring in context C_i of a given mMCS M with belief state S. A ground instance ρ of r w.r.t. S is obtained by substituting every variable occurring in r (i.e., occurring either in the elements $(c_j : p_j)$ in the body of r or in its head $o(s)$ or in both) via (ground) terms occurring in S.*

For mMCS M, data state S and ground bridge rule ρ, let $app^\vDash_g(\rho, S)$ be a Boolean function which checks, in the ground case, bridge-rule body entailment w.r.t. S. Let thus redefine bridge-rule applicability.

Definition 2. *The set $app(S)$ relative to ground bridge rules which are applicable in a data state S of a given mMCS $M = (C_1, \ldots, C_n)$ is now defined as follows.*

$$app(S) = \{hd(\rho) \mid \rho \text{ is a ground instance w.r.t. } S \text{ of some}$$
$$\text{bridge rule } r \in br_i, 1 \leq i \leq n,$$
$$\text{and } app\models_g(\rho, S) = \text{true}\}$$

We assume, analogously to [1], that given mMCS is *monotonic*, which here means that for each C_i: (i) ACC_i is monotonic w.r.t. additions to the context's knowledge base, and (ii) mng_i is monotonic, i.e., it allows to only add formulas to C_i's knowledge base. Let, for context C_i, function ACC_i' be a variation of ACC_i which selects one single set E_i among those generated by ACC_i. I.e., given context C_i and knowledge base $\hat{kb} \in KB_{L_i}$, $ACC_i'(\hat{kb}) = E_i$ where $E_i \in ACC_i(\hat{kb})$. Let ∞ be the first infinite ordinal number isomorphic to the natural numbers.

Definition 3. *Consider mMCS $M = (C_1, \ldots, C_n)$ with no negative literals in bridge-rule bodies, and assume arbitrary choice of function ACC_i' for each composing context C_i. Let, for $1 \leq i \leq n$, $gr(kb_i)$ be the grounding of kb_i w.r.t. the constants occurring in any kb_j, $1 \leq j \leq n$. A data state of grade κ is obtained as follows.*

For $i \leq n$ and $\alpha = 0$, we let $kb_i^0 = gr(kb_i)$, and we let $S^\alpha = S^0 = (kb_1^0, \ldots, kb_n^0)$
For each $\alpha > 0$, we let $S^\alpha = (S_1^\alpha, \ldots, S_n^\alpha)$ and $S_i^\alpha = ACC_i'(kb_i^\alpha)$
where for finite κ and $\alpha \geq 0$ we have
$$kb_i^{\alpha+1} = mng_i(app(S^\alpha), kb_i^\alpha) \text{ if } \alpha < \kappa,$$
$$kb_i^{\alpha+1} = kb_i^\alpha \text{ otherwise}$$
while if $\kappa = \infty$ we have $kb_i^\infty = \bigcup_{\alpha \geq 0} kb_i^\alpha$

Differently from [1], the computation of a new data state element is provided here according to mMCSs, and thus involves the application of the management function to the present knowledge base so as to obtain a new one. Such data state element is then the unique set of consequences of the new knowledge base, as computed by the ACC_i' function.

The result can be an equilibrium only if the specified grade is sufficient to account for all potential bridge-rules applications. In the terminology of [1] it would then be a *grounded equilibrium*, as it is computed iteratively and deterministically from the contexts' initial knowledge bases. We have the following.

Definition 4. *Let $M = (C_1, \ldots, C_n)$ be a monotonic mMCS with no negative literals in bridge-rule bodies. A belief state $S = (S_1, \ldots, S_n)$ is a grounded equilibrium of grade κ of M iff $ACC_i'(mng_i(app(S), kb_i^\kappa)) = S_i$, for $1 \leq i \leq n$.*

Several grounded equilibria may exist, depending upon the choice of ACC_i'. The required grade for obtaining an equilibrium would be $\kappa = \infty$ in the former version of the example, where in the latter version if setting threshold t we would have $\kappa = t$. We can state the following relationship with [1]:

Proposition 1. *Let $M = (C_1, \ldots, C_n)$ be a definite MCS (in the sense of [1]), and let $S = (S_1, \ldots, S_n)$ be a grounded equilibrium for M, reachable in δ steps. Then, there exists a choice of function ACC'_i for each context C_i of M such that S is a grounded equilibrium of grade δ for the mMCS M' obtained from M by choosing, for $i \leq n$, a management function mng_i that just adds to kb_i every s such that $o(s) \in app(S)$.*

In an implemented mMCS, as remarked in [15], "...computing equilibria and answering queries on top is not a viable solution." So, they assume a given MCS to admit an equilibrium, and define a query-answering procedure based upon some syntactic restriction on bridge-rule form, and involving the application and a concept of "unfolding" of positive atoms in bridge-rule bodies w.r.t. their definition in the "destination" context. Still, they assume an open system, where every context's contents are visible to others (save some possible restrictions). We assume instead contexts to be *opaque*, i.e., that contexts' contents are accessible from the outside only via queries.

Also, we assume that bridge-rule application is not necessarily reactive but that, according to a context's own logic, other modalities of application may exist; for instance, the modalities introduced in [7, 8] cope with "Logical Omniscience and Unbounded Resources Assumption" by detaching (proactive) bridge-rule application from the processing of the management function. Thus, in our case the grounding of literals in bridge rule bodies w.r.t. the present data state will most presumably be performed at run-time, whenever a bridge rule is actually applied. Such grounding, and thus the bridge-rule result, can be obtained for instance by "executing" or "invoking" literals in the body (i.e., querying contexts) left-to-right in prolog style. In practice, we can allow bridge rules to have negative literals in their body. To this aim, we introduce a syntactic limitation in the form of non-ground bridge rules very common in logic programming approaches, i.e., we assume that *(i) every variable occurring in the head of a non-ground bridge rule r also occurs in some positive literal of its body; and (ii) in the body of such rule, positive literals occur (in a left-to-right order) before negative literals.*

So, at run-time variables in a bridge rule will be incrementally and coherently instantiated via results returned by contexts. Each positive literal $(c_i : p_i)$ in the body may fail (i.e., c_i will return a negative answer), if none of the instances of p_i given the partial instantiation computed so far is entailed by c_i's present data state. Otherwise, the literal succeeds and subsequent ones are instantiated to its results. Negative literals $not\,(c_j : p_j)$ make sense only if p_j is ground at the time of invocation, and succeed if p_j is *not* entailed by c_j's present data state. In case either some literal fails or a non-ground negative literal is encountered, the overall bridge rule evaluation fails without returning results. Otherwise the evaluation succeeds, and the result can be elaborated by the management function of the "destination" context. It is easy to prove that the invocation of a bridge rule leads to success if and only if, given its ground instance obtained via the above-specified evaluation pattern, the body is entailed by the present system's data state (which is hopefully an equilibrium) and thus the rule is applicable (according to the previously-reported notions of applicability). We omit formal definitions and proofs for lack of space. However, we may notice that asynchronous application of bridge rules determine evolving equilibria.

4.2   Update Problem

In dynamic environments, contexts are in general able to incorporate new data items, e.g., as discussed in [3], the input provided by sensors. We intend to explicitly take into account not only sensor input, but more generally the interaction of contexts with an external environment. As a premise we assume, similarly to what is done in Linear Time Logic (LTL), a discrete, linear model of time where each state/time instant can be represented by an integer number. States $t_0, t_1, \ldots$ can be seen as time instants (or 'time points') in abstract terms, though in practice we have $t_{i+1} - t_i = \delta$, where δ is the actual interval of time after which we assume a given system to have evolved.

We assume then that each context is subjected at each time point to a (possibly empty) finite update. Thus, for mMCS $M = (C_1, \ldots, C_n)$ let $\Pi_T = \langle \Pi_T^1, \ldots \Pi_T^n \rangle$ be a tuple composed of the finite updates performed to each module at time T, where for $1 \leq i \leq n$ Π_T^i is the update to C_i. Let $\Pi = \Pi_1, \Pi_2, \ldots$ be a sequence of such updates performed at time instants $t_1, t_2, \ldots$. Let us assume that each context copes with updates in its own particular way, so let $\mathcal{U}_i$, $1 \leq i \leq n$ be the *update operator* that module C_i employs for incorporating the new information, and let $\mathcal{U} = \{\mathcal{U}_1, \ldots, \mathcal{U}_n\}$ be the tuple composed of all these operators. We assume $\mathcal{U}_i$ to encompass all possible updated performed to a module, included sensor input. So (analogously to the management function) let the *update base uops_i* be a set of update operations which are admitted on context C_i. Then we have: $\mathcal{U}_i : 2^{uops} \times KB^L \to 2^{KB_L} \setminus \emptyset$. Notice that updates can be non-monotonic.

Consequently, we allow contexts' knowledge bases and data states to evolve in time: a *timed* data state at time T is a tuple $S^T = (S_1^T, \ldots, S_n^T)$ such that each S_i^T is an element of Cn_i at time T. We assume the timed data state S^0 to be an equilibrium according previous definitions. Later on however, transition from a timed data state to the next one, and consequently the definition of an equilibrium, is determined both by the update operators and by the application of bridge rules. An mMCS at time 0 is as defined previously, while at time $T+1$ its knowledge base, and thus its data states and equilibria, will have evolved, where also the notion of bridge-rule applicability is now performed according to Definitions 1 and 2, but relatively to a timed data state S^T.

Therefore, by letting, for each C_i $i \leq n$, $kb_i^0 = kb_i$ we have that

Definition 5. *A timed data state of mMCS M at time $T+1$ is an equilibrium iff, for $1 \leq i \leq n$,*
$$S_i^{T+1} \in ACC_i(mng_i(app(S^T), kb_i^{T+1}))$$
where $kb_i^{T+1} = \mathcal{U}_i(kb_i^T, \Pi_T^i)$.

The meaning is that an equilibrium is now a data state which encompasses bridge rules applicability on the updated contexts' knowledge bases. Notice that, in practice, for each bridge rule applicable at time T the state when its result will actually affect the destination context is in general unpredictable. In fact, contexts occurring in bridge-rule bodies will require some amount of time for returning their results.

4.3   Static System and Full System Knowledge Assumption

A heterogeneous collection of distributed sources will not necessarily remain static in time. New contexts can be added to the system, or can be removed, or can be momentarily unavailable due to network problems. Moreover, a context may be known by the others only via the role(s) that it assumes or the services which it provides within the system. Although not explicitly specified in the original MCS definition, context *names* occurring in bridge-rule bodies must represent all the necessary information for reaching and querying a context, e.g., names might be URIs. It is however useful for a context to be able to refer to other contexts via their roles, without necessarily being explicitly aware of their names. Also, a context which joins an MCS will not necessarily make itself visible to every other context: rather, there might be specific authorizations involved. These aspects may be modeled by means the following extensions:

Definition 6. *A* dynamic *managed Multi-Context System (dmMCS) at time T is a set $M^T = (C_1, \dots, C_n, Dir, Reach)$ of contexts where $M = (C_1, \dots, C_n,)$ is an mMCS and Dir and Reach are special contexts without associated bridge rules where:*

- *Dir is a* directory *which contains the list of the contexts, namely $C_1, \dots, C_n$, participating in the system at time T where, for each C_i, its name is associated with its* roles. *We assume Dir to admit queries of the form 'role@Dir', returning the name of some context with role 'role', where 'role' is assumed to be a constant.*
- *Reach contains a directed graph determining which other contexts are* reachable *from each context C_i. For simplicity, we may see Reach as composed of couples of the form (C_r, C_s) meaning that context C_s is (directly or indirectly) reachable from context C_r.*

For now, let us assume that a query $role@Dir = c$ where $c \in \{C_1, \dots, C_n\}$, i.e., returns a unique result. The definition of timed data state remains unchanged. Bridge rule syntax must instead be extended accordingly:

Definition 7. *Given a dmMCS (at time T) M^T, each (non-ground) bridge rule r in the composing contexts $C_1, \dots, C_n$ has the form:*
$$s \leftarrow (\mathcal{C}_1 : p_1), \dots, (\mathcal{C}_j : p_j),$$
$$not\,(\mathcal{C}_{j+1} : p_{j+1}), \dots, not\,(\mathcal{C}_m : p_m).$$
where for $1 \le k \le m$ the expression $\mathcal{C}_k$ is either a context name, or an expression $role_k@Dir$.

Bridge-rule grounding and applicability must also be revised. In fact, for checking bridge rule applicability: (i) each expressions $role_k@Dir$ must be substituted by its result and (ii) every context occurring in bridge rule body must be reachable from the context where the bridge rule occurs.

Definition 8. *Let M^T be a dmMCS (at time T) and S^T be a timed data state for M^T. Let r be a bridge rule in the form specified in Definition 7. The pre-ground version r' of r is obtained by substituting each expression $role_k@Dir$ occurring in the body of r with its result c_k obtained from Dir.*

Notice that r' is a bridge rule in "standard" form, and that r and r' have the same head, where their body differ since in r' all context names are specified explicitly.

Definition 9. *Let r' be a pre-ground version of a bridge rule r occurring in context $\hat{C}$ of dmMCS M^T (at time T) with timed data state S^T. Let ρ be a ground instance w.r.t. S^T of r'. We have now $hd(\rho) \in app(S^T)$ if ρ fulfills the conditions for applicability w.r.t. S^T and, in addition, for each context $\tilde{C}$ occurring in the body of ρ we have that $(\hat{C}, \tilde{C}) \in Reach$.*

The definition of equilibria is basically unchanged, save the extended bridge-rule applicability. However, suitable update operators (that we do not discuss here) will be defined for both Dir and $Reach$, to keep both the directory and the reachability graph up-to-date with respect to the actual system state. The question may arise of where such updates might come from. This will in general depend upon the application at hand: the contexts might themselves generate an update when joining/leaving a system, or some kind of monitor (that might be one of the composing contexts, presumably however equipped with reactive, proactive and reasoning capabilities) might take care of such task.

4.4   Unique Source Assumption

There might sometimes be the case where a specific context is not able to return a required answer, while another context with the same role instead would. More generally, we may admit a query $role@Dir$ to return not just one, but possibly several results, representing the set of contexts which, in the given dmMCS, have the specified role. So, the extension that we propose in this section can be called a *multi-source option*. In particular, for dmMCS M^T, composed at time T of contexts $C_1, \ldots, C_n$, the expression $role_k@Dir$ occurring in bridge rule $r \in br_s$ will now denote some nonempty set $SC_k \subseteq (\{C_1, \ldots, C_n\} \setminus \{C_s\})$, indicating the contexts with the required role (where C_s is excluded as a context would not look for itself). Technically, there will be now several pre-ground versions of a bridge rule, which differ relative to the contexts occurring in their body.

Definition 10. *Let M^T be a dmMCS (at time T) and S^T be a timed data state for M^T. Let $r \in br_s$ be a bridge rule in the form specified in Definition 7 occurring in context C_s. A pre-ground version r' of r is obtained by substituting each expression $role_k@Dir$ occurring in the body of r with $c \in SC_k$.*

Bridge-rule applicability is still as specified in Definition 9, and the definition of equilibria is also basically unchanged.

In practice, one may consider to implement the multi-source option in bridge-rule run-time application by choosing an order for querying the contexts with a certain role as returned by the directory. The evaluation would proceed to the next one in case the answer is not returned within a time-out, or if the answer is under some respect unsatisfactory (according to the management function).

A further refinement might consist in considering, among the contexts returned by *role@Dir*, only the *preferred* ones.

Definition 11 (Preferred Source Selection). *Given a query role@Dir with result SC, a preference criterion $\mathcal{P}$ returns a (nonempty) ordered subset $SC^{\mathcal{P}} \subseteq SC$.*

Different preference criteria can be defined according to several factors such as trust, reliability, fast answer, and others. Approaches to preferences in logic programming might be adapted to the present setting: cf., among many, [3] and the references therein, [17–19]). The definition of a context will now be as follows.

Definition 12. *A context C_i included in a dmMCS (except for Dir and Reach) is defined as $C_i = (L_i; kb_i; br_i; \mathcal{P}_i)$ where L_i, kb_i and br_i are as defined before, and $\mathcal{P}_i$ is a preference criterion as specified in Definition 11.*

5 Concluding Remarks

In this paper we have discussed and extended mMCSs, which are a general and powerful framework for modeling systems composed by several heterogeneous and possibly distributed sources (contexts), that interact via so-called bridge rules. The proposed extensions improve practical applicability of mMCSs by: making bridge rules more general and flexible; introducing explicit time so as to model contexts' updates and consequent system's evolution; introducing concepts of inter-context reachability and contexts' role, and preferences among reachable contexts with desired role. We believe that implementations of mMCSs might profit from the enhancements that we have introduced here.

Future work involves in fact the implementation as an mMCS of a smart Cyber-Physical System in the e-Health domain for intelligent monitoring of patients with comorbidities [13]. This will allow us to experiment, refine and further develop the new features.

References

1. Brewka, G., Eiter, T.: Equilibria in heterogeneous nonmonotonic multi-context systems. In: Proceedings of 22nd AAAI Conference on Artificial Intelligence, pp. 385–390. AAAI Press (2007)
2. Brewka, G., Eiter, T., Fink, M.: Nonmonotonic multi-context systems: a flexible approach for integrating heterogeneous knowledge sources. In: Balduccini, M., Son, T.C. (eds.) Logic Programming, Knowledge Representation, and Nonmonotonic Reasoning: Essays Dedicated to Michael Gelfond on the Occasion of His 65th Birthday. LNCS, vol. 6565, pp. 233–258. Springer, Heidelberg (2011)

3. Brewka, G., Ellmauthaler, S., Pührer, J.: Multi-context systems for reactive reasoning in dynamic environments. In: Schaub, T. (ed.) Proceedings of 21st European Conference on Artificial Intelligence, ECAI 2014. IJCAI/AAAI (2014)
4. Lloyd, J.W.: Foundations of Logic Programming. Springer, Heidelberg (1987)
5. Apt, K.R., Bol, R.N.: Logic programming and negation: a survey. J. Log. Program. **19–20**, 9–71 (1994)
6. Brewka, G., Eiter, T., Fink, M., Weinzierl, A.: Managed multi-context systems. In: Walsh, T. (ed.) Proceedings of 22nd International Joint Conference on Artificial Intelligence, IJCAI 2011, pp. 786–791. IJCAI/AAAI (2011)
7. Costantini, S.: Knowledge acquisition via non-monotonic reasoning in distributed heterogeneous environments. In: Calimeri, F., Ianni, G., Truszczynski, M. (eds.) LPNMR 2015. LNCS, vol. 9345, pp. 228–241. Springer, Heidelberg (2015)
8. Costantini, S., De Gasperis, G.: Exchanging data and ontological definitions in multi-agent-contexts systems. In: Paschke, A., Fodor, P., Giurca, A., Kliegr, T. (eds.) Proceedings of RuleMLChallenge Track, CEUR Workshop Proceedings. CEUR-WS.org (2015)
9. Giunchiglia, F., Serafini, L.: Multilanguage hierarchical logics or: how we can do without modal logics. Artif. Intell. **65**(1), 29–70 (1994)
10. Fink, M., Ghionna, L., Weinzierl, A.: Relational information exchange and aggregation in multi-context systems. In: Delgrande, J.P., Faber, W. (eds.) LPNMR 2011. LNCS, vol. 6645, pp. 120–133. Springer, Heidelberg (2011)
11. Dao-Tran, M., Eiter, T., Fink, M., Krennwallner, T.: Distributed evaluation of nonmonotonic multi-context systems. J. Artif. Int. Res. (JAIR) **52**, 543–600 (2015)
12. Eiter, T., Šimkus, M.: Linking open-world knowledge bases using nonmonotonic rules. In: Calimeri, F., Ianni, G., Truszczynski, M. (eds.) LPNMR 2015. LNCS, vol. 9345, pp. 294–308. Springer, Heidelberg (2015)
13. Aielli, F., Ancona, D., Caianiello, P., Costantini, S., De Gasperis, G., Di Marco, A., Ferrando, A., Mascardi, V.: FRIENDLY & KIND with your health: human-friendly knowledge-INtensive dynamic systems for the e-Health domain. In: Hallenborg, K., Giroux, S. (eds.) International Workshop on Agents and Multi-agent Systems for AAL and e-HEALTH (A-HEALTH) at PAAMS 2016, Proceedings of Communications in Computer and Information Science. Springer (2016)
14. Gelfond, M.: Answer sets. In: Handbook of Knowledge Representation. Elsevier, Amsterdam (2007)
15. Barilaro, R., Fink, M., Ricca, F., Terracina, G.: Towards query answering in relational multi-context systems. In: Cabalar, P., Son, T.C. (eds.) LPNMR 2013. LNCS, vol. 8148, pp. 168–173. Springer, Heidelberg (2013)
16. Alferes, J.J., Brogi, A., Leite, J., Moniz Pereira, L.: Evolving logic programs. In: Flesca, S., Greco, S., Leone, N., Ianni, G. (eds.) JELIA 2002. LNCS (LNAI), vol. 2424, pp. 50–61. Springer, Heidelberg (2002)
17. Bienvenu, M., Lang, J., Wilson, N.: From preference logics to preference languages, and back. In: Proceedings of 12th International Conference on the Principles of Knowledge Representation and Reasoning (KR 2010), pp. 414–424 (2010)
18. Brewka, G., Niemelä, I., Truszczyński, M.: Preferences and nonmonotonic reasoning. AI Mag. **29**(4), 69 (2008)
19. Costantini, S., Formisano, A.: Modeling preferences and conditional preferences on resource consumption and production in ASP. J. Algorithms Cogn. Inform. Log. **64**(1), 3–15 (2009)

Choreographic Compilation of Decentralized Comprehension Patterns

Iliano Cervesato$^{(\boxtimes)}$, Edmund Soon Lee Lam, and Ali Elgazar

Carnegie Mellon University, Doha, Qatar
{iliano,aee}@cmu.edu, sllam@andrew.cmu.edu

Abstract. We develop an approach to compiling high-level specifications of distributed applications into code that is executable on individual computing nodes. The high-level language is a form of multiset rewriting augmented with comprehension patterns. It enables a programmer to describe the behavior of a distributed system as a whole rather than from the perspective of the individual nodes, thus dramatically reducing opportunities for programmer errors. It abstracts away the mechanics of communication and synchronization, resulting in concise and declarative specifications. Compilation generates low-level code in a syntactic fragment of this same formalism. This code forces the point of view of each node, and standard state-of-the-art execution techniques are applicable. It is relatively simple to show the correctness of this compilation scheme.

1 Introduction

Rule-based programming, a model of computation by which rules modify a global state by concurrently rewriting disjoint portions of it, is emerging as an effective paradigm for implementing complex distributed applications [1,4,8,12]. Rule-based languages are declarative, which promises simpler reasoning than conventional languages, and even a safeguard against many of the pitfalls of concurrency [2]. Their main benefit, however, is that they can capture the behavior of a distributed application as a single entity [8], giving the programmer a bird's-eye view that abstracts away the tedium of explicitly managing communication and the intricacies of implementing synchronization. The resulting *system-centric specifications* are concise, high-level, and again declarative. Now, because a distributed application ultimately runs on an ensemble of communicating devices, such system-centric specifications need to be compiled into code that runs on the individual devices, *node-centric code*. The translation from high-level system-centric specifications to lower level node-centric code is called *choreographic compilation* [9]. It automatically weaves in the code that handles messaging and synchronization, which are notorious sources of concurrency bugs

---

This paper was made possible by grants NPRP 4-341-1-059, NPRP 4-1593-1-260, and JSREP 4-003-2-001, from the Qatar National Research Fund (a member of the Qatar Foundation). The statements made herein are solely the responsibility of the authors.

© Springer International Publishing Switzerland 2016
J.J. Alferes et al. (Eds.): RuleML 2016, LNCS 9718, pp. 113–129, 2016.
DOI: 10.1007/978-3-319-42019-6_8

(especially in the hands of novice programmers). Choreographic compilation is especially effective when the resulting code is in a fragment of the source, rule-based, language, as their declarative nature enables simple proofs of correctness, verifiable complexity bounds, and other forms of assurance.

In this paper, we develop a choreographic compilation scheme for a specific class of rule-based languages, namely multiset rewriting languages with support for multiset comprehension patterns. *Multiset rewriting languages* represent the state of an ensemble as a multiset of located facts, each describing information held by a participating node. Computation happens by applying rules that rewrite a fixed number of facts into new facts. *Comprehension patterns* allow a programmer to write rules that operate not only on a fixed multiset of facts, but on all the facts that match a given pattern, ensemble-wide. This yields more readable, concise and declarative programs that coordinate large amounts of data or use aggregate operations. We implemented this idea into Comingle [8], a rule-based language for programming mobile distributed applications.

Compiling comprehension patterns in a distributed setting requires addressing the compounded effects of two challenges. The first is that multiset rewriting rules are executed *atomically*. This entails that a high-level rule, which may involve multiple locations, needs to be compiled into a set of node-centric rules, each taking the point of view of a single location, plus coordination rules that provide the illusion of atomicity [9]. The second challenge is that comprehension patterns operate *maximally* [6]: they identify *all* facts that match them in the ensemble.

We limit the discussion to the common rule format where one node has a direct connection to all other nodes participating in the rule, thereby ruling out multi-hop communications. At its core, atomicity is achieved by running a two-phase commit protocol centered on this primary node. A naive way to achieve maximality is to lock all nodes involved, so that no concurrently executing code can consume or add facts while this rule is undergoing piecemeal execution. We mitigate the obvious adverse effect on performance by locking only facts that appear in relevant comprehension patterns. This already gives all Comingle programs we have developed an acceptable running time.

Altogether, this paper makes the following main contributions:

– We identify a practical class of system-centric rules with comprehensions that enable effective choreographic compilation.
– We give a mathematical description of this transformation for a large fragment.
– We prove that the node-centric code produced by this compilation scheme retains the behavior of the source system-centric program.

Section 2 of this paper introduces our language through an example, with Sect. 3 formally defining it. We discuss rule topology in Sect. 4 and give selected details of our choreographic compilation scheme in Sect. 5. Correctness results are presented in Sect. 6. We review related work in Sect. 7 and outline further developments in Sect. 8. Omitted details can be found in a companion technical report [7].

2   A Motivating Example

Consider the problem of computing the average temperature from the readings of an ensemble of networked sensors. Traditionally, this involves writing at least three programs: one that probes each sensor, computes the average temperature and reports the result; the second is a sensor-side program that returns a reading when probed; the last expects the result.

Comingle takes a different approach. The information held by each device is stored as a series of *facts*. For example, a temperature reading of 16.3 degrees could be expressed as the fact $temp(16.3)$. We visualize the node where a fact is held as a *located fact*, writing for example $[\ell_{23}]temp(16.3)$ to express that the reading at node ℓ_{23} is 16.3 degrees. Located facts are used for all kinds of information. Here, the topology of the sensor network could be given as located facts of the form $[\ell]neighbor(\ell')$, expressing that ℓ' is directly connected to ℓ. Similarly, the request for node ℓ to compute the temperature average A of its neighbors and report it to node ℓ' would be written as located facts $[\ell]getAvg(\ell')$ and $[\ell']report(A)$, respectively.

Programs in Comingle take the form of a collection of rules that consume some of the facts held in the ensemble and replace them with other facts, possibly at different nodes. For our example, a single rule suffices. A buggy solution that always reports 25.0 degrees without consulting the sensors would have the form

$$\forall X, Y. [X]getAvg(Y) \multimap [Y]report(25.0) \tag{1}$$

This rule is parametric in the locations involved: X is the node computing the average and Y is the location where to deliver the result. Whenever the ensemble contains an instance, say $[\ell_{12}]getAvg(\ell_9)$, of the left-hand side, this rule can be applied with the effect of replacing this fact with $[\ell_9]report(25.0)$. Observe that this effect is global: it consumes a fact from one node and creates a related fact in a different node. This reading makes rule (1) *system-centric* as it describes a computation that views the ensemble as a single entity.

But of course this rule comes short of correctly solving our problem. Node X, which does the polling, needs to collect the temperature of all its neighbors. Comingle provides *multiset comprehension patterns* as a convenient primitive for this kind of actions. The comprehension pattern $\wr[X]neighbor(N)\wr_{N \to Ns}$ collects all the neighbors N of X into a multiset Ns. While this is a local computation occurring at X, comprehension patterns do not need to be local: the comprehension $\wr[N]temp(T) \mid N \in Ns\wr_{T \to Ts}$ collects the temperature reading $[N]temp(T)$ held at each node N among Ns into a multiset Ts. At this point, the average is simply computed by adding up the values in Ts and dividing by the number of such values, all primitive operations in Comingle. The overall computation is captured by the rule

$$\forall \begin{bmatrix} \wr[X]neighbor(N)\wr_{N \to Ns}, \\ \wr[N]temp(T) \mid N \in Ns\wr_{T \to Ts} \end{bmatrix} \setminus [X]getAvg(Y) \multimap [Y]report(A) \tag{2}$$
$$\text{where } A = sum(Ts)/size(Ts)$$

where the facts matched by the expressions before "\" are consulted but not deleted by the rule application, while the fact after it is consumed. The "where" clause denotes a side computation, something we will generalize into the notion of a guard. Both are convenience syntax that are not part of the core language.

Rule (2) is system-centric too, even more so than our first example. Its application is atomic and maximal: from the point of view of the programmer, the matching of facts on the left-hand side of $\multimap$ and the rewriting on its right-hand side happen in one go, moreover *all* facts matching $[X]neighbor(N)$ are collected in Ns, and similarly for Ts.

While rule (2) captures exactly the process of solving our example problem, and in a most concise way, it is impossibly abstract from the point of view of the nodes in a distributed system: such nodes are only able to send and receive messages, and perform local computation. We bridge this abstraction gap by transforming rule (2) into a set of rules that look much more like rule (1). This rule has, in fact, a simple operational interpretation in a decentralized ensemble of computing nodes: its left-hand side, $[X]getAvg(Y)$, performs some local computation at node X (here retrieving the value of a stored fact), while its right-hand side can be understood as sending the message $report(25.0)$ to node Y — the underlying networking middleware will take care of delivering it to Y as a fact that it can then use. Rule (1) has therefore also a *node-centric* interpretation, that can be used operationally. The main challenges of designing a choreographic compilation scheme for Comingle — i.e., a transformation of each abstract, system-centric, rule into an equivalent set of operational, node-centric, rules — is to maintain the illusion of atomicity and maximality at the operational level. This is the subject of the remainder of this paper and of the technical report [7].

3   Core Comingle

In this section, we formalize the core syntax and semantics of Comingle — the full language is described in [7,8]. We begin by introducing some notation. We write $\bar{o}$ for a multiset of syntactic objects o. We denote the extension of a multiset $\bar{o}$ with an object o as "$\bar{o}, o$", with $\varnothing$ indicating the empty multiset. We also write "$\bar{o}_1, \bar{o}_2$" for the union of multisets $\bar{o}_1$ and $\bar{o}_2$. The literal multiset containing $o_1, \ldots, o_n$ is denoted $\wr o_1, \ldots, o_n \wr$. Given a multiset of labels $\mathcal{I}$, the multiset of objects o_i for $i \in \mathcal{I}$ is denoted $\bigcup_{i \in \mathcal{I}} o_i$. We write $\vec{o}$ for a tuple of o's and $[\vec{t}/\vec{x}]o$ for the simultaneous substitution within object o of all free occurrences of variable x_i in $\vec{x}$ with the corresponding term t_i in $\vec{t}$. A generic substitution is denoted θ. Substitution implicitly α-renames bound variables as needed to avoid capture. We write $FV(o)$ for the set of free variables in o.

Syntax. Figure 1 defines the abstract syntax of Comingle. *Locations* ℓ are names that uniquely identify computing nodes, and the set $\mathcal{L}$ of all nodes participating in a Comingle computation is called an *ensemble*. At the Comingle level, computation happens by rewriting *located facts* F of the form $[\ell]p(\vec{t})$ where p

Variables: x Locations: ℓ Terms: t Guards: g Predicates: p

Base Facts	$f ::= p(\vec{t})$	Located Facts	$F ::= [\ell]f$
Expressions	$E ::= F \mid \wr F \mid g\int_{\vec{x} \rightleftarrows t}$	Rules	$R ::= \forall \vec{x}.\, H \mid g \multimap B$
Heads, Bodies	$H, B ::= \overline{E}$	Programs	$\mathcal{P} ::= \overline{R}$

Fig. 1. Abstract syntax of core Comingle

is a predicate symbol and $\vec{t}$ is a tuple of *terms*. We will simply refer to them as facts. The semantics of Comingle is largely agnostic to the specific language of terms — in this paper, we assume a first-order term language extended with primitive multisets. We write $[\ell]f$ for a generic fact f located at node ℓ.

Computation in Comingle happens by applying *rules* of the form $\forall \vec{x}.\, H \mid g \multimap B$. We refer to H as the *head* of the rule, to g as its *guard* and to B as its *body*. The head of a rule consists of *atoms* F and of *comprehension patterns* of the form $\wr F \mid g \int_{\vec{x} \rightarrow ts}$ (written $\wr F \mid g \int_{\vec{x} \leftarrow ts}$ in the body — the direction of the arrow is suggestive of the flow of information). An atom F is a located fact $[\ell]p(\vec{t})$ that may contain variables in the terms $\vec{t}$ or even as the location ℓ. Guards in rules and comprehensions are Boolean-valued expressions constructed from terms and are used to constrain the values that the variables can assume. Just like for terms we keep guards abstract, writing $\models g$ to express that ground guard g is satisfiable. Two types of guards used pervasively in this paper are term equality $t = t'$ and multiset membership $t \in ts$. We drop the guard from rules and comprehensions when it is the always-satisfiable constant $\top$. A comprehension pattern $\wr F \mid g\int_{\vec{x} \rightleftarrows ts}$ represents a multiset of facts that match the atom F and satisfy guard g under the bindings of variables $\vec{x}$ that range over ts, a multiset of tuples called the *comprehension range*. We call F the *subject* of the comprehension. The scope of $\vec{x}$ is the atom F and the guard g. We implicitly α-rename bound variables to avoid capture. A comprehension pattern $\wr [x]p(\vec{t}) \mid g\int_{\vec{x} \rightleftarrows ts}$ is *system-centric* whenever x appears in $\vec{x}$. The body B of a rule is also a multiset of atoms and comprehension patterns.

The universal variables $\vec{x}$ in a rule $\forall \vec{x}.\, H \mid g \multimap B$ account for all the free variables in H, g and B, and we often write $\forall (H \mid g \multimap B)$ for succinctness. Moreover, we only consider *safe* rules where $FV(B) \subseteq FV(H, g)$. We will occasionally use rules of the form $\forall \vec{x}.\, H_r \backslash H_c \mid g \multimap B$, viewed as an abbreviation for $\forall \vec{x}.\, (H_c, H_r) \mid g \multimap (B, H_r)$; we then refer to H_r and H_c as the retained and consumed heads of the rule.

A Comingle *program* is a collection of rules.

Semantics. We describe the computation of a Comingle system by means of a small-step transition semantics. Its basic judgment has the form $\mathcal{P} \triangleright St \longmapsto St'$ where $\mathcal{P}$ is a program, St is a store and St' is a store that can be reached in one (abstract) step of computation. A *store* St is a multiset of ground located facts $[\ell]p(\vec{t})$.

Rule (rw) in Fig. 2 describes a step of computation that applies a rule $\forall (H \mid g \multimap B)$. This involves identifying a closed instance of the rule obtained

Comingle transitions: $\mathcal{P} \triangleright St \longmapsto St'$

$$\frac{\forall (H \mid g \multimap B) \in \mathcal{P} \quad \models \theta g \quad \theta H \triangleq_{\text{head}} St_H \quad \theta H \triangleq^{\neg}_{\text{head}} St \quad \theta B \ggg_{\text{body}} St_B}{\mathcal{P} \triangleright St_H, St \longmapsto St_B, St} \text{ (rw)}$$

where $H \triangleq_{\text{head}} St$ *iff* store St matches ground head H
        $\models g$ *iff* ground guard g is satisfiable
        $H \triangleq^{\neg}_{\text{head}} St$ *iff* store St matches no comprehension patterns in ground head H
        $B \ggg_{\text{body}} St$ *iff* ground body B unfolds to store St

Fig. 2. Abstract semantics of Comingle

by means of a substitution θ. The instantiated guard must be satisfiable ($\models \theta g$) and we must be able to partition the store into two parts St_H and St. The instance of the head must match St_H ($\theta H \triangleq_{\text{head}} St_H$), while the remaining fragment St must not match any comprehension in it ($\theta H \triangleq^{\neg}_{\text{head}} St$). The rule body instance θB is then unfolded ($\theta B \ggg_{\text{body}} St_B$) into St_B which replaces St_H in the store. A reading of these auxiliary judgments is given in Fig. 2. A formal description can be found in [7,8].

Rule (rw) embodies a system-centric abstraction of the rewriting semantics of Comingle as it atomically accesses facts at arbitrary locations. Indeed, it views the facts of all participating locations in the ensemble as one virtual collection. This abstract notion of rule application needs to be compiled into a concurrent, node-centric model of computation, where each node manipulates its local facts and sends messages to other nodes.

4   Neighbor Restriction

In this section, we identify a syntactic class of Comingle rules that support efficient node-level execution. Characteristic of these *1-neighbor restricted rules* is that, in any instance, there is one node that has every other location participating in the rule as a *neighbor*. Operationally, the execution of the rule can use this *primary location* as a communication hub to all the other participating nodes, called *forwarding locations*. For brevity, we provide only the intuition behind most definitions. See [7] for full details.

To start with, consider a rule $R = \forall (H \multimap B)$ with an empty guard and without comprehension patterns in its head. A node X has Y as a its *neighbor* in R if the head H contains a fact $[X]p(\vec{t})$ such that Y occurs in $\vec{t}$. For simplicity, we take this as a proxy for a direct communication link — in actuality only certain facts may be used to describe point-to-point messaging.

Guards somewhat complicate this definition as they are often used to calculate new values, including locations, on the basis of existing values. Let g be a guard with free variables $\vec{x}$ and $\vec{y}$. We say that $\vec{x}$ *determines* $\vec{y}$ in g, written $\vec{x} \xrightarrow{g} \vec{y}$, if for every ground substitution $\vec{t}/\vec{x}$ there is at most one substitution $\vec{s}/\vec{y}$ that makes g satisfiable, i.e., such that $\models [\vec{t}/\vec{x}, \vec{s}/\vec{y}]g$. We write $\vec{x} \xrightarrow{g} y$ if

y is among such $\vec{y}$. Then, Y is a neighbor of X in rule $\forall (H \mid g \multimap B)$ if the set of variables occurring in facts located at X in H determines Y. In symbols, $\{x \in FV(E) : E = [X]f \text{ in } H\} \overset{g}{\Rightarrow} Y$.

Comprehension patterns further complicate this definition as they may identify participating locations indirectly through their comprehension range — for example N in $\wr[N]temp(T) \mid N \in Ns\wr_{T \to Ts}$ but also Ns in $\wr[X]neighbor(N)\wr_{N \to Ns}$. Thus, a (possibly bound) variable Y in $\wr[Y]f \mid g_Y \wr_{\vec{y} \to ts}$ is a neighbor of X in rule $\forall (H \mid g \multimap B)$ if $\{x \in FV(E) : E = [X]f' \text{ or } E = \wr[X]f' \mid g'\wr_{\vec{x} \to ts'} \text{ in } H\} \overset{g,g_Y}{\Longrightarrow} Y$.

Given this definition of neighbor, a location X_n is n hops away from X_0 in rule R if n is the smallest number such that there are nodes $X_1, \ldots X_{n-1}$ such that X_i has X_{i+1} as its neighbor for each i from 0 to $n-1$. Rule R is n-neighbor restricted with primary location X, something we denote $\vdash^n_{\mathsf{NB}} R \gg X$, if every location Y such that $[Y]f$ appears in R is at most n hops away from X. Each such Y other than X is called a forwarding location. A Comingle rule that is not n-neighbor for any n has mutually unreachable nodes and therefore cannot be concretely executed on a distributed collection of nodes as it would require out-of-band synchronization that bypasses the underlying communication infrastructure. We are particularly interested in rules where $n = 1$. In fact, 1-neighbor restricted rules are such that the primary location has a direct communication link to every other location participating in the rule, which entails that device-level code that implements it only needs to use point-to-point messaging primitives to and from the primary location, thereby avoiding complex routing. Furthermore, 1-neighbor restricted rules where all head facts are at the primary location are such that local computation is sufficient to determine applicability, i.e., if there is a match for their head in the computing state — their body may however locate facts at other nodes. We call such rules node-centric. Rule (1) from Sect. 2 is node centric with primary location X as its head contains a single atom located at X. Rule (2) is 1-neighbor restricted with primary location X (but not node-centric) as the comprehension $\wr[X]neighbor(N)\wr_{N \to Ns}$ (locally) determines the contents of the multiset Ns from which the value of every location N in $\wr[N]temp(T) \mid N \in Ns\wr_{T \to Ts}$ is drawn. Thus each value T held in $[N]temp(T)$ can be accessed in one hop from X.

A Comingle program is 1-neighbor restricted if all its constituent rules are such. All applications we have developed using Comingle have naturally been 1-neighbor restricted [8], and therefore we will limit our discussion to this class of programs. We will use programs consisting solely of node-centric rules (node-centric programs) as the target of the compilation of 1-neighbor restricted programs. See [9] for a generalization in the absence of comprehensions.

5   Choreographic Transformation

Choreographic compilation elaborates each system-centric rewrite rule R into a set $\llbracket R \rrbracket$ of node-centric rewrite rules that execute portions of R at the participating locations. The challenge is to design $\llbracket R \rrbracket$ so that it behaves exactly like R, i.e., that it is applicable whenever R is and eventually achieves its effects (completeness), and that it does not introduce any new effects (soundness), especially partial execution. In Sect. 6, we spell out these requirements and outline proofs that our compilation satisfies them.

In the absence of comprehension patterns, Comingle is *monotonic*:

Property 1 (Monotonicity).

$$\text{If } \mathcal{P} \triangleright St \longmapsto St', \text{then } \mathcal{P} \triangleright St, St'' \longmapsto St', St'' \text{ for any } St''.$$

This property, typical of traditional multiset rewriting, allows processing head atoms incrementally, both in a centralized [3] and in a distributed [9] setting. Incremental processing is precisely what is done by the node-centric rules $[\![R]\!]$ a system-centric rule R is compiled into: a primary location combines data incrementally from the forwarding locations.

However, because comprehension patterns have a maximal semantics, monotonicity does not hold for full Comingle [6]. A naive approach to incrementally matching the head of a system-centric rule, as adapted from [9] for example, would be unsound. Consider the rule head $[X]p(Y_1, Y_2), \{[Y_1]q(\vec{x})\int_{\vec{x} \to ts_1}, \{[Y_2]q(\vec{x})\int_{\vec{x} \to ts_2}$ where incremental execution proceeds from left to right, say. By the time X has received the facts collected at Y_2, new facts matching $[Y_1]q(\vec{x})$ may have arrived at Y_1, violating maximality. We recover soundness by locking all facts that can thus compromise incremental processing. In general, these are facts headed by a predicate p such that the atom $[\ell]p(\vec{x})$ occurs as the subject F of a comprehension $\{F \mid g\int_{\vec{x} \to ts}$ anywhere in the program. We call them *non-monotonic predicates*. Predicates that never appear within a comprehension pattern are *monotonic*, and we do not need to take special precautions for them.

5.1   An Example

As an example, consider the following Comingle rule, which we call *swp*:

$$\forall \begin{bmatrix} [X]swap(Y, P), \ [Y]okSwap \\ \{[X]data(N) \mid N \leq P \int_{N \to Ns} \\ \{[Y]data(M) \mid M \geq P \int_{M \to Ms} \end{bmatrix} \multimap \begin{bmatrix} \{[X]data(M)\int_{M \leftarrow Ms} \\ \{[Y]data(N)\int_{N \leftarrow Ns} \end{bmatrix}$$

This rule lets two parties X and Y atomically swap values up to a threshold P. It is triggered when node X holds a fact $swap(Y, P)$ while node Y holds $okSwap$. It retrieves all the facts $data(N)$ held at X such that $N \leq P$ (that is $\{[X]data(N) \mid N \leq P\int_{N \to Ns})$ and sends them to Y (with body expression $\{[Y]data(N)\int_{N \leftarrow Ns})$. At the same time, it transfers all $data(M)$ such that $M \geq P$ from Y (i.e., $\{[Y]data(M) \mid M \geq P\int_{M \to Ms})$ to X (as $\{[X]data(M)\int_{M \leftarrow Ms})$. The mention of Y as an argument of $swap$ makes this rule 1-neighbor restricted with X as its primary location and Y the only forwarding location.

This rule is compiled into the six node-centric rules (exec_X^{swp} to abort_X^{swp}) discussed next. Each of these rules executes an aspect of the overall system-centric rewriting embodied by rule *swp*. It makes use of various auxiliary predicates, which we capitalize for ease of identification, and it introduces new variables, which we write in lower case. We write the auxiliary predicates as a root possibly superscripted by a rule or predicate name, and possibly subscripted by a relevant location variable, for example Req_Y^{swp} below. We further highlight them using various background colors, that the reader may safely ignore. The new facts are categorized as follows.

- *Locking facts* have the form $[X]Free^p$. For emphasis, we will highlight locking facts with a light-blue background . Such facts are a means to lock non-monotonic predicates p in order to guarantee maximality: a rule that makes use of such a predicate at some location X, either in its head or in its body, will be compiled into a rule that acquires $[X]Free^p$, thereby inhibiting the execution of other rules that make use of p at X. This fact is put back into X's local state once the rule execution has completed successfully, or if it gets aborted.
- *Transaction facts* are of the form $[X]Next(n)$, $[X]Trans(e)$, $[X]Done(e)$ or $[X]Abort(e)$. We highlight them in pale orange . Their purpose is to keep track of and manage ongoing system-centric rule execution attempts, which we call *transactions*. The variable n is a counter incremented each time node X initiates a transaction, while e is another number computed from n and the location name X to act as a global transaction identifier. The fact $[X]Next(n)$ holds the current value of X's counter n, the fact $[X]Trans(e)$ indicate that transaction e is ongoing at X, while $[X]Done(e)$ and $[X]Abort(e)$ signal that e has either completed successfully or is being aborted.
- There are three types of *staging facts* for each rule R (identified by some unique name r), all highlighted in a pale green background for ease of identification. With the fact $[Y]Req_Y^r(e, X, \vec{x})$, primary location X issues a request to Y to gather relevant local facts in the head of R as part of transaction e. The parameters $\vec{x}$ list the information that X was able to secure and that may be useful to Y. The answer $\vec{y}$ is returned to X by means of the fact $[X]Ans_Y^r(e, Y, \vec{y})$. Finally, X can remember information $\vec{z}$ for its own records by means of the fact $[X]Wait^r(\vec{z})$. They are used to implement the various stages of a two-phase commit among the parties involved.

The first compiled node-centric rule is to be executed at the primary location, X:

$$\forall \begin{bmatrix} [X]swap(Y,P), \\ \wr[X]data(N) \mid N \leq P \wr_{N \to Ns}, \\ [X]Free^{data}, [X]Next(n) \end{bmatrix} \multimap \begin{bmatrix} [Y]Req_Y^{swp}(e, X, Ns, P), \\ [X]Wait^{swp}(e, Y, Ns, P), \\ [X]Trans(e), [X]Next(n') \end{bmatrix} (\text{exec}_X^{swp})$$

where $e = H(X, n)$ and $n' = n + 1$.

The head of this rule contains all the expressions that our original rule could match locally, namely $[X]swap(Y, P)$ and $\wr[X]data(N) \mid N \leq P \wr_{N \to Ns}$. Because predicate *data* occurs within a comprehension — it is non-monotonic — this rule also acquires a lock on it ($[X]Free^{data}$). Finally, it increments the local counter

n (retrieved as $[X]Next(n)$ and reasserted as $[X]Next(n')$ with $n' = n+1$). The function $H(X,n)$ combines the value of this counter and the primary location's identity into a globally unique value e which will act as a transaction identifier, recorded as fact $[X]Trans(e)$. The body of this rule also includes the staging fact $[Y]Req_Y^{swp}(e, X, Ns, P)$ to request the matching data values from node Y. Note that the arguments mention the transaction identifier e, who to return the results to (X), and the variables corresponding to data that X could compute locally (a more refined compilation scheme could optimize Ns away as it is not needed by Y). Node X also asserts the staging fact $[X]Wait^{swp}(e, Y, Ns, P)$ for its own records, so that it can continue execution once it receives a response from Y.

The forwarding location Y can respond to X in one of two ways: by returning the requested data, or by aborting the transaction. A successful response begins with the following rule:

$$\forall \left[\begin{array}{l} [Y]okSwap, \; \{[Y]data(M) \mid M \geq P\}_{M \rightarrow Ms}, \\ [Y]Free^{data}, \; [Y]Req_Y^{swp}(e, X, Ns, P) \end{array} \right] \multimap \left[\begin{array}{l} [Y]Trans(e), \\ [X]Ans_Y^{swp}(e, Y, Ms) \end{array} \right] \; (\text{exec}_Y^{swp})$$

Here, Y retrieves its part of the original rule head, $\{[Y]data(M) \mid M \geq P\}_{M \rightarrow Ms}$ and $[Y]okSwap$, and locks the non-monotonic predicate $data$ (with $[Y]Free^{data}$). It notes that it is engaged in transaction e with the fact $[Y]Trans(e)$ and sends X the expected answer, $[X]Ans_Y^{swp}(e, Y, Ms)$. Observe that, at this point, it is still in the transaction.

Next, X resumes execution by asserting the body of swp:

$$\forall \left[\begin{array}{l} [X]Wait^{swp}(e, Y, Ns, P), \\ [X]Ans_Y^{swp}(e, Y, Ms) \end{array} \right] \multimap \left[\begin{array}{l} \{[X]data(M)\}_{M \leftarrow Ms}, \; \{[Y]data(N)\}_{N \leftarrow Ns}, \\ \{[l]Free^{data}\}_{l \leftarrow \{X,Y\}}, \; \{[l]Done(e)\}_{l \leftarrow \{X,Y\}} \end{array} \right] \; (\text{succ}_X^{swp})$$

With it, X combines the values it had computed locally ($[X]Wait^{swp}(e, Y, Ns, P)$) and the values obtained from Y (as $[X]Ans_Y^{swp}(e, Y, Ms)$) and asserts the body of the original rule ($\{[X]data(M)\}_{M \leftarrow Ms}, \{[Y]data(N)\}_{N \leftarrow Ns}$). It also releases all locks ($\{[l]Free^{data}\}_{l \leftarrow \{X,Y\}}$) and signals that the transaction has completed successfully ($\{[l]Done(e)\}_{l \leftarrow \{X,Y\}}$).

One last clean-up rule is needed to remove all facts associated with a completed transaction e, namely $\{[Z]Trans(e)\}$, $[Z]Done(e)$. It does this at every participating node Z.

$$\forall \left(\{[Z]Trans(e)\}, \; [Z]Done(e) \multimap \varnothing \right) \; (\text{done})$$

The transaction started by rule (exec_X^{swp}) can fail for one of two reasons: either because the forwarding node Y does not have the requested data (e.g., if there is no $okSwap$ at Y), or because Y is already engaged in possibly conflicting transactions. Although comprehension patterns are able to express the absence of a fact (or class of facts) in the state, we will approximate the first option by non-deterministically aborting the transaction (see the note below). Transaction failure is then captured by the following rule, executed at Y:

$$\forall \left(\, \mathopen{?}[Y]\,Trans(e')\,\mathopen{\}}_{e'\to es} \setminus [Y]\,Req_Y^{swp}(e, X, Ns, P) \mid e \not\ll es \multimap [X]\,Abort(e) \right) \quad (\text{fail}_Y^{swp})$$
where $e \not\ll es$ iff $es = \varnothing$ or for some $e' \in es$ and $e < e'$

Upon receiving the staging fact $[Y]\,Req_Y^{swp}(e, X, Ns, P)$, node Y collects all of its active transactions in the multiset es. The guard $e \not\ll es$ succeeds in one of two circumstances. The first is when there is no other ongoing transaction (which approximates an unsuccessful match). The second is when some other ongoing transaction e' has a larger identifier ($e < e'$). This guarantees that at least one transaction (the "strongest") will delay its decision to abort, until all others at the same location have terminated (with either success or failure). This avoids livelocks between transactions attempting to acquire the same facts. Conversely, the uniqueness of transaction identifiers guarantees that only one such transaction at a location delays its abort — otherwise we risk inducing deadlocks. Because rules (exec_X^{swp}) and (fail_Y^{swp}) are competing for the same staging fact $[Y]\,Req_Y^{swp}(e, X, Ns, P)$, exactly one of them is applicable in general, and only the latter is enabled when Y does not have the data requested by X.[1]

Rule (fail_Y^{swp}) is followed by rule (abort_Y^{swp}), examined next. It is executed at X:

$$\forall \left[\begin{array}{l} [X]\,Trans(e)\,,\; [X]\,Abort(e)\,, \\ [X]\,Wait^{swp}(e, Y, Ns, P) \end{array} \right] \multimap \left[\begin{array}{l} [X]\,swap(Y, P), \mathopen{?}[X]\,data(N)\,\mathopen{\}}_{N\leftarrow Ns}, \\ [X]\,Free^{data} \end{array} \right] \quad (\text{abort}_Y^{swp})$$

It aborts transaction e by consuming the fact $[X]\,Trans(e)$ and reverting X's local computation, recorded in $[X]\,Wait^{swp}(e, Y, Ns, P)$), back into the state.

5.2 Choreographic Compilation

We now describe Comingle's choreographic compilation scheme on the basis of this intuition for one form of rules — see [7] for the general case. We write $NM(\mathcal{P})$ for the set of all non-monotonic predicate names in program $\mathcal{P}$ and $NM_\mathcal{P}(\overline{E})$ for the subset of $NM(\mathcal{P})$ that occur in expressions $\overline{E}$ (see [7] for a formal definition).

The choreographic compilation $\llbracket \mathcal{P} \rrbracket$ of a 1-neighbor restricted program $\mathcal{P}$ is a node-centric program equivalent to $\mathcal{P}$, a program that consists only of node-centric rules. The compiled program $\llbracket \mathcal{P} \rrbracket$ is comprised of the compilation $\llbracket R \rrbracket^\mathcal{P}$

---

[1] A version of rule (fail_Y^{swp}) that is mutually exclusive with rule (exec_X^{swp}) is as follows:

$$\forall \left(\, \mathopen{?}[Y]\,Trans(e')\,\mathopen{\}}_{e'\to es} \setminus [Y]\,Req_Y^{swp}(e, X, Ns, P)\,, \underline{\mathopen{?}[Y]\,okSwap\,\mathopen{\}}_{()\to os}} \mid e \not\ll es \;\&\; \underline{os = \varnothing} \multimap [X]\,Abort(e) \right)$$

where the underlined components check that Y does not hold a fact $okSwap$. A general treatment of *negation as absence*, as this feature is known, is beyond the scope of this paper.

$$\forall \left[\begin{array}{l} [x]H_x, \\ [x]Free, \\ [x]Next(n) \end{array}\right] \Big| g_x \multimap \left[\begin{array}{l} [x]Next(n'), [x]Trans(e), \\ [x]Wait^r(e, FV(H_x)), \\ \bigcup_{j\in\mathcal{I}\cup\mathcal{K}}[j]Req_j^r(e, FV(H_x)) \end{array}\right] \quad \begin{array}{l} \text{where } e = H(x,n) \\ \text{and } n' = n + 1 \end{array} \quad (\text{exec}_x^r)$$

$$\bigcup_{j\in\mathcal{I}\cup\mathcal{K}} \forall \Big([j]H_j, [j]Free, [j]Req_j^r(e, FV(H_x)) \mid g_j \multimap [j]Trans(e), [x]Ans_j^r(e, j, FV(H_j))\Big) \quad (\text{exec}_j^r)$$

$$\bigcup_{j\in\mathcal{I}\cup\mathcal{K}} \forall \Big(\{[j]Trans(e')\}_{e'\in es} \setminus [j]Req_j^r(e, \text{-}) \mid e \ll es \multimap [x]Abort(e)\Big) \quad (\text{fail}_j^r)$$

$$\forall \left[\begin{array}{l} [x]Trans(e), [x]Wait^r(e, FV(H_x)), \\ \bigcup_{j\in\mathcal{I}\cup\mathcal{K}}[x]Ans_j^r(e, j, FV(H_j)) \end{array}\right] \Big| g \multimap \left[\begin{array}{l} [x]B_x, [\mathcal{I}]B_\mathcal{I}, [\mathcal{K}]B_\mathcal{K}, \\ [x,\mathcal{I},\mathcal{K}]Free, [\mathcal{I},\mathcal{K}]Done(e) \end{array}\right] \quad (\text{succ}_x^r)$$

$$\forall \Big([x]Wait^r(e, \text{-}), \bigcup_{j\in\mathcal{I}\cup\mathcal{K}}[x]Ans_j^r(e, j, \text{-}) \setminus \varnothing \mid \neg g \multimap [x]Abort(e)\Big) \quad (\text{fail}_x^r)$$

$$\bigcup_{j\in\mathcal{I}\cup\mathcal{K}} \forall \Big([x]Abort(e) \setminus [x]Ans_j^r(e, j, \text{-}) \multimap [j]H_j, [j]Free, [j]Done(e)\Big) \quad (\text{abort}_j^r)$$

$$\forall \Big([x]Abort(e) \setminus [x]Wait^r(e, \text{-}) \multimap [x]H_x, [x]Free, [x]Done(e)\Big) \quad (\text{abort}_x^r)$$

Fig. 3. Compilation of simple rule $\forall ([x]H_x, [\mathcal{I}]H_\mathcal{I} \mid g_x \wedge g_\mathcal{I} \wedge g \multimap [x]B_x, [\mathcal{I}]B_\mathcal{I}, [\mathcal{K}]B_\mathcal{K})$

of each source rule R in $\mathcal{P}$, plus rule (done) above — this rule is "global" in that it is shared by the encoding of all rules in $\mathcal{P}$.

$$\llbracket \mathcal{P} \rrbracket = \begin{cases} \bigcup_{R\in\mathcal{P}} \llbracket R \rrbracket^\mathcal{P} & \text{(rule names given below)} \\ \forall j, e. \, \{[j]Trans(e)\}, [j]Done(e) \multimap \varnothing & \text{(done)} \end{cases}$$

Simple 1-Neighbor Restricted Rules. We consider *simple* 1-neighbor restricted rules, that contain only *localized comprehension patterns*. The location of the subject of such patterns is bound outside the comprehension itself. Thus, in rule (2), the comprehension $\{[X]neighbor(N)\}_{N\to Ns}$ was localized, but $\{[N]temp(T) \mid N \in Ns\}_{T\to Ts}$ is not. The case study in Sect. 5.1 consisted of a simple rule.

Using some abbreviations of convenience (explained next), a source rule R with such characteristics can be written as follows:

$$\forall x, \mathcal{I}, \mathcal{K}. \, [x]H_x, [\mathcal{I}]H_\mathcal{I} \mid g_x \wedge g_\mathcal{I} \wedge g \multimap [x]B_x, [\mathcal{I}]B_\mathcal{I}, [\mathcal{K}]B_\mathcal{K}$$

Here, x is the primary location of R and H_x collates all the facts in R's head located at x. These can be either atoms $[x]f$ or localized comprehensions $\{[x]f \mid g\}_{z\to zs}$. Similarly, B_x refers to the body expressions located at x. The set $\mathcal{I}$ contains all forwarding nodes that locate facts in the head of R. We write $[\mathcal{I}]H_\mathcal{I}$ for $\bigcup_{i\in\mathcal{I}} H_i$ where each H_i follows the same conventions as H_x, and similarly for body expressions $B_\mathcal{I}$. The set $\mathcal{K}$, disjoint from x and $\mathcal{I}$, lists all forwarding nodes that locate expressions only in the body of R — we call them *receiving locations*. The guard of R is partitioned into fragment g_x whose satisfiability can be determined locally by x, i.e., such that $FV(H_x) \overset{g_x}{\Longmapsto} \vec{y}$ for some $\vec{y}$, into similar fragments g_i for each $i \in \mathcal{I}$ which we abbreviate as $g_\mathcal{I}$, and into a final fragment g which cannot be determined locally by any of these nodes.

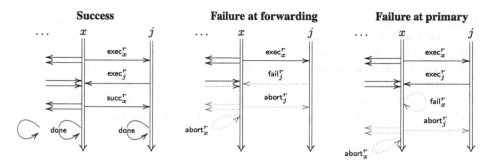

Fig. 4. Possible execution sequences of a compiled system-centric rule

Figure 3 defines the compilation $[\![\mathcal{P}]\!]^R$ of a simple system-centric rule R named r. The constituent node-centric rules implement a two-phase commit with the same behavior as R. The possible executions patterns are sketched in Fig. 4. The encoding $[\![\mathcal{P}]\!]^R$ relies on further abbreviations: given a location j among $x, \mathcal{I}, \mathcal{K}$, we write $[j]\,Free$ for $\bigcup_{p \in NM_\mathcal{P}(H_j, B_j)} [j]\,Free^p$, the locks of all non-monotonic predicates mentioned by j. Furthermore, we write $[\mathcal{J}]\,Free$ for $\bigcup_{j \in \mathcal{J}} [j]\,Free$, the locks of any location j in set $\mathcal{J}$. We also write "_" for irrelevant terms, realized in a rule as an appropriate number of single-occurrence variables.

Rule (exec_x^r) initiates execution at the primary location x by matching local facts ($[x]H_x$), locking non-monotonic predicates ($[x]\,Free$) and setting up a new transaction e as discussed in Sect. 5.1. It sends a request to each forwarding location ($\bigcup_{j \in \mathcal{I} \cup \mathcal{K}} [j]\,Req_j^r(e, FV(H_x))$) and prepares for their response with $[x]\,Wait^r(e, FV(H_x))$. Rule (exec_j^r) implements a successful reply by a forwarding location j: it locks its non-monotonic predicates ($[j]\,Free$), records the transaction ($[j]\,Trans(e)$) and returns a response ($[x]\,Ans_j^r(e, j, FV(H_j))$) — in the case of a receiving location in $\mathcal{K}$ this amounts to just locking non-monotonic predicates. Execution then continues at x with rule (succ_x^r) which collates all the responses ($\bigcup_{j \in \mathcal{I} \cup \mathcal{K}} [x]\,Ans_j^r(e, j, FV(H_j))$), checks the remaining guards g, rolls out the body of R, frees all non-monotonic predicates and prepares for clean-up using rule (done). This execution sequence is shown on the left of Fig. 4.

As described in Sect. 5.1, rule (fail_j^r) aborts execution at a forwarding node j in response to a match failure or to preempt livelock. This is followed by rules (abort_j^r) and (abort_x^r) with which primary location x rolls back all head facts that had been consumed and frees the locks. This possibility is sketched in the central portion of Fig. 4.

One more behavior, which was not possible in the example in Sect. 5.1, is depicted on the right-hand side of Fig. 4. Here, primary x has collected responses from all forwarding locations, but they cannot be combined as prescribed by R because the guard g is not satisfiable. In this case, rule ($\mathsf{fail}_x''^r$) is applicable and triggers the abort rules just described.

Generic 1-Neighbor Restricted Rules. The techniques deployed for simple rules form the core of the compilation of generic 1-neighbor restricted rules whose full treatment can be found in [7], for space reasons. The treatment of system-centric comprehension patterns, whose subject $[z]f$ is located at a bound variable z, requires some care as such z may be among $\mathcal{I}$ or $\mathcal{K}$, or could be x itself above. Naively sending separate requests for different predicates would stall execution as the first request would lock the non-monotonic predicates, thereby preventing the others from making progress. We address this issue by having each node involved acquire all information it needs in one go.

Store. The node-centric encoding of a store St, denoted $\llbracket St \rrbracket_{\vec{c}}^{\mathcal{P}}$, extends St with, for each location ℓ in an ensemble $\mathcal{L}$, (a) a locking fact $[\ell]Free^p$ for each non-monotonic predicate p of $\mathcal{P}$ and (b) a local transaction counter c_ℓ in $\vec{c}$ for ℓ. It is defined as follows:

$$\llbracket St \rrbracket_{\vec{c}}^{\mathcal{P}} = \begin{cases} St, \\ \bigcup_{\ell \in \mathcal{L}} \bigcup_{p \in NM(\mathcal{P})} [\ell]Free^p, \\ \bigcup_{\ell \in \mathcal{L}} [\ell]Next(c_\ell) \end{cases}$$

6   Formal Results

In this section, we present some properties of the transformation in the previous section, and give sketches of their proof. Details can be found in [7]. Specifically, we show that choreographic compilation is sound and complete: it transforms a system-centric program into node-centric rules with what amounts to the same behavior. We also note that the computation carried out by a compiled rule can never get stuck midway.

For the convenience of the reader, we distinguish between source and encoded rewrite states by denoting the former St and the latter Et. The operation $\lVert Et \rVert^{\mathcal{P}}$ that *decodes* a compiled state Et back into a corresponding source state St, relative to a 1-neighbor restricted program $\mathcal{P}$ is defined in [7]. It does so by discarding all locking and transaction facts, by keeping source facts, and by reverting request and waiting facts to the source fact they had replaced. Other staging facts are ignored. We write *obligations*$(\mathcal{P}, E)$ for the result of this extraction on a staging fact E.

To begin with, the following property shows that for every reachable encoded state Et, we can always derive another state Et' such that it does not contain "stuck" transactions. Specifically, there are no encoded matching obligations in Et'.

Theorem 1 (Progress). *If $\llbracket \mathcal{P} \rrbracket \triangleright \llbracket St \rrbracket_{\vec{c}}^{\mathcal{P}} \longmapsto^* Et$, then $\llbracket \mathcal{P} \rrbracket \triangleright Et \longmapsto^* Et'$ for some Et' such that obligations$(\mathcal{P}, Et') = \varnothing$.*

Proof. By structural induction on our choreographic transformation schemes, we first show that any individual transaction e can always be concluded as an abort or a successful application of a system-centric rewriting. In either case, encoded matching obligations are consumed. This result is extended to an arbitrary number of transactions, which the antecedent of the theorem may be executing concurrently.

Next, we show that every derivation of a compiled program $[\![\mathcal{P}]\!]$ is derivable in its source states. Hence the choreographic transformation is sound.

Theorem 2 (Soundness). *If* $[\![\mathcal{P}]\!] \triangleright [\![St]\!]_{\bar{c}}^{\mathcal{P}} \longmapsto^* Et$, *then* $\mathcal{P} \triangleright St \longmapsto^* [\![Et]\!]^{\mathcal{P}}$.

Proof. The proof starts by considering a single step, where it induces the definition of our choreographic transformation. Specifically, we show that every encoded derivation step corresponds to either a source derivation step or a stuttering step (i.e., zero step $\mathcal{P} \triangleright St \longmapsto^* St$). This involves showing that for derivable states of each choreographic transformation, every removal of a matching obligation (i.e., $[j]H_j$) is accompanied by an addition of a corresponding encoded matching obligation (e.g., $[j]Wait^r(e, j, \vec{v})$), hence via the decoding operation, source facts are never wrongfully omitted. A simple induction lifts this result to the multiple step case.

Theorem 3 states that every derivation of a source program $\mathcal{P}$ can be simulated by $[\![\mathcal{P}]\!]$. Hence the choreographic transformation is complete.

Theorem 3 (Completeness). *If* $\mathcal{P} \triangleright St \longmapsto^* St'$, *then* $[\![\mathcal{P}]\!] \triangleright [\![St]\!]_{\bar{c}}^{\mathcal{P}} \longmapsto^* Et'$ *for some* Et' *such that* $[\![Et']\!]^{\mathcal{P}} = St'$.

Proof. The proof proceeds by structural induction on our transformation. Specifically, we show that, using Theorem 1, we can always simulate each source derivation step with a series of encoded derivation steps that applies a transaction of the corresponding source derivation. Therefore, Et' exists. A further induction is used to stretch this result to multiple derivation steps.

7 Related Works

An extension of Datalog for implementing network protocols is explored in [12]. This paper defines *link-restricted* Datalog rules and *rule localizing* encodings which are specific instances of neighbor restriction and choreographic transformation discussed here.

Our work draws inspiration from research on choreographic programming (e.g., [10]). An example of a coordination language in this domain is Jolie [11], which is targeted at service-oriented web applications. By and large, these works focus on choreographic projections of lower-level imperative-style programming languages, our transformation share the same goals and intuition, at a higher level of abstraction, though.

The execution model underlying Comingle is inspired by the run-time architecture of Constraint Handling Rules [3] (CHR). Also based on rule-based multiset rewriting, the CHR language can be viewed as an ancestor of Comingle. There is abundant research on exploiting CHR as a parallel execution model, of example as an extension of the actor model [13] and for programming FGPAs [14].

Comingle is a logic programming framework aimed at simplifying the development of applications distributed over multiple mobile devices. The original prototype [5,8] targeted the Android SDK, and has recently been extended to x86 devices running Java, thereby supporting mobile applications over heterogeneous platforms.

8   Conclusions

In this paper, we develop a choreographic compilation scheme for multiset rewriting languages with support for multiset comprehension patterns. This choreographic compilation scheme preserves soundness: it transforms a system-centric Comingle program into a node-centric encoding that ensures both atomicity of the rule application and maximality of comprehension patterns. Node-centric encodings have a straightforward node-centric operational interpretations (message passing), and thus are immediately executable by individual computing nodes. In all, our work here provides a foundational bridge between high-level system-centric specifications of decentralized multiset rewriting with comprehension patterns, and their lower-level node-centric operational interpretations.

References

1. Ashley-Rollman, M.P., Lee, P., Goldstein, S.C., Pillai, P., Campbell, J.D.: A language for large ensembles of independently executing nodes. In: Hill, P.M., Warren, D.S. (eds.) ICLP 2009. LNCS, vol. 5649, pp. 265–280. Springer, Heidelberg (2009)
2. Caires, L., Pfenning, F.: Session types as intuitionistic linear propositions. In: Gastin, P., Laroussinie, F. (eds.) CONCUR 2010. LNCS, vol. 6269, pp. 222–236. Springer, Heidelberg (2010)
3. Frühwirth, T.: Constraint Handling Rules. Cambridge University Press, Cambridge (2009)
4. Grumbach, S., Wang, F.: Netlog, a rule-based language for distributed programming. In: Carro, M., Peña, R. (eds.) PADL 2010. LNCS, vol. 5937, pp. 88–103. Springer, Heidelberg (2010)
5. Lam, E.S.L.: Comingle: Distributed Logic Programming Language for Android Mobile Ensembles (2014). https://github.com/sllam/comingle
6. Lam, E.S.L., Cervesato, I.: Optimized compilation of multiset rewriting with comprehensions. In: Garrigue, J. (ed.) APLAS 2014. LNCS, vol. 8858, pp. 19–38. Springer, Heidelberg (2014)
7. Lam, E.S.L., Cervesato, I.: Decentralized compilation of multiset comprehensions. Technical report CMU-CS-16-101, Carnegie Mellon University (2016)
8. Lam, E.S.L., Cervesato, I., Fatima, N.: Comingle: distributed logic programming for decentralized mobile ensembles. In: Holvoet, T., Viroli, M. (eds.) COORDINATION 2015. LNCS, vol. 9037, pp. 51–66. Springer, Heidelberg (2015)
9. Lam, E.S.L., Cervesato, I.: Decentralized execution of constraint handling rules for ensembles. In: PPDP 2013, Madrid, Spain, pp. 205–216 (2013)

10. Lanese, I., Guidi, C., Montesi, F., Zavattaro, G.: Bridging the gap between interaction- and process-oriented choreographies. In: SEFM 2008, pp. 323–332 (2008)
11. Lanese, I., Montesi, F., Zavattaro, G.: The evolution of Jolie. In: De Nicola, R., Hennicker, R. (eds.) Software, Services, and Systems. LNCS, vol. 8950, pp. 506–521. Springer, Heidelberg (2015)
12. Loo, B.T., Condie, T., Garofalakis, M., Gay, D.E., Hellerstein, J.M., Maniatis, P., Ramakrishnan, R., Roscoe, T., Stoica, I.: Declarative networking: language, execution and optimization. In: SIGMOD 2006, pp. 97–108 (2006)
13. Sulzmann, M., Lam, E.S.L., Van Weert, P.: Actors with multi-headed message receive patterns. In: Lea, D., Zavattaro, G. (eds.) COORDINATION 2008. LNCS, vol. 5052, pp. 315–330. Springer, Heidelberg (2008)
14. Triossi, A., Orlando, S., Raffaetà, A., Frühwirth, T.: Compiling CHR to parallel hardware. In: PPDP 2012, New York, NY, USA, pp. 173–184 (2012)

Minimal Objectification and Maximal Unnesting in PSOA RuleML

Gen Zou[(✉)] and Harold Boley[(✉)]

Faculty of Computer Science, University of New Brunswick, Fredericton, Canada
{gen.zou,harold.boley}@unb.ca

Abstract. The paper introduces two connected advancements of Positional-Slotted, Object-Applicative RuleML: (1) a model-theoretic semantics, realized transformationally, that directly handles atoms (i.e., predicate applications) without object identifiers (e.g., relationships as in Prolog) and (2) a transformational semantics that handles nested atomic formulas (e.g., nested frames as in Flora-2/F-logic). For (1), the model theory is extended to atoms with optional OIDs, the transformation is developed from static to dynamic objectification, and the correctness of the realization is proved. For (2), the unnesting transformation is defined to decompose nested atomic formulas into equivalent conjunctions.

1 Introduction

The relational and graph (object-centered) modeling paradigms have been widely used for knowledge representation in AI and the Semantic Web. The relational paradigm (e.g., classical logic and logic programming) is built on top of *relationships* with positional arguments, while the object-centered paradigm (e.g., RDF, N3, and F-logic) is built on top of *frames* with a globally unique Object IDentifier (OID), usually typed by a class, and an unordered collection of slotted (attribute-value) arguments. To facilitate interoperation between the two paradigms, e.g. for expressing mappings between frames and relational databases in rule-based data access, combined object-relational paradigms have been studied. F-logic [1,2] and RIF-BLD [3] employ a heterogeneous approach to allow the combined use of relationships and frames. In contrast, the Web rule language PSOA RuleML [4] employs a homogeneous approach by generalizing relationships and frames to positional-slotted object-applicative (psoa) terms[1], which permit the application of a predicate (acting as a relation) to be [in an *oidless/oidful* dimension] without or with an OID – typed by the predicate (acting as a class) – and the predicate's arguments to be [in an orthogonal dimension] *positional, slotted, or combined*.

PSOA RuleML allows the interchangeable use of oidless and oidful *atoms* (i.e., predicate applications) through the *objectification* transformation, which

---

[1] We use the upper-cased "PSOA" as a qualifier for the language and the lower-cased "psoa" for its terms.

© Springer International Publishing Switzerland 2016
J.J. Alferes et al. (Eds.): RuleML 2016, LNCS 9718, pp. 130–147, 2016.
DOI: 10.1007/978-3-319-42019-6_9

creates an OID for each oidless atom. Earlier, OIDs needed to be statically generated for each oidless psoa term before applying the model-theoretic semantics [4,5]. This is inappropriate for *expressions* (i.e., function applications) since their functions cannot act as classes. It also causes overhead for an atom whose predicate in the clauses of the Knowledge Base (KB) is used only as a Prolog-like relation, in particular does not occur with an OID or slots (the latter also requires an OID for slotribution, explained in Sect. 2). To address these issues, the model theory is extended so that atoms and expressions can be interpreted without the need for an explicit OID, and an equivalence between an oidless atom and its existential oidful form is guaranteed. A novel static/dynamic objectification transformation – which is minimal by performing as little as possible in a static manner – is introduced to realize this semantics while leaving unchanged as many of the oidless atoms as possible, allowing better use of the underlying Prolog engine in our PSOATransRun [6] implementation since version 1.0, and better interoperation with ground facts in relational databases.

Frames are often nested. PSOA RuleML's presentation syntax (PSOA/PS) generally permits embedded atoms almost everywhere. However, the semantics of embedded atoms has not been clearly defined in the earlier version of the language. In this paper, the unnesting transformation is formally defined to decompose nested atomic formulas into equivalent conjunctions, augmenting our implementation in the PSOATransRun 1.1 release.[2] It recursively extracts oidful atoms from an atomic formula, e.g. another atom, leaving behind their OIDs in the "trimmed" version. Unnesting is maximal by extracting atoms not only from other atoms but also from expressions. This transformational semantics is applied to every atomic formula before the model-theoretic semantics is applied.

The rest of the paper is organized as follows. Section 2 reviews the PSOA RuleML language. Section 3 gives the new semantics with minimal objectification and discusses different objectification transformations. Section 4 discusses the syntax of embedded atoms as well as the unnesting transformation. Section 5 concludes the paper.

2   PSOA RuleML

In this section we introduce the basics of the object-relational Web rule language PSOA RuleML [4], which generalizes RIF-BLD [3] and POSL [7] by introducing psoa terms of the following general forms:

$$\textbf{Oidless:} \quad f([t_{1,1} \ldots t_{1,n_1}] \ldots [t_{m,1} \ldots t_{m,n_m}] \; p_1\text{->}v_1 \ldots p_k\text{->}v_k) \quad (1)$$

$$\textbf{Oidful:} \; o\#f([t_{1,1} \ldots t_{1,n_1}] \ldots [t_{m,1} \ldots t_{m,n_m}] \; p_1\text{->}v_1 \ldots p_k\text{->}v_k) \quad (2)$$

Both (1) and (2) apply a function or predicate f, possibly identified by an OID o through a membership $o\#f$ of o in f (acting as a class), to a bag of tupled

---

[2] Available from http://psoa.ruleml.org/transrun/1.1/local/.

arguments $[t_{i,1} \ldots t_{i,n_i}]$, $i = 1, \ldots, m$, and to a bag of slotted arguments $p_j \rightarrow v_j$, $j = 1, \ldots, k$, representing attribute-value pairs. For the most often used special case of single-tuple psoa terms (m=1), the square brackets enclosing the tuple may be omitted.

A psoa term can be interpreted as a psoa expression or a psoa atom, depending on whether f is a function or predicate. The interpretation as an expression was earlier allowed for both oidless and oidful psoa terms (i.e., (1) and (2) above) but will be restricted to oidless psoa terms here, as explained in Sect. 4. The interpretation as an atom is permitted for both (1) and (2) on the top-level, while restricted to (2) when embedded, as explained in Sect. 4.

The OID, tuples, and slots in a psoa atom are all optional. For an oidless psoa atom, without a 'user' OID, *objectification* can introduce a 'system' OID to make it oidful, as detailed in Sect. 3. Untyped objects are notated by using the root class Top as their type f. An oidful psoa atom of the form (2) is equivalent to a conjunction

$$\text{And}(o\#f\ o\#\,\text{Top}(t_{1,1} \ldots t_{1,n_1}) \ldots o\#\,\text{Top}(t_{m,1} \ldots t_{m,n_m})$$
$$o\#\,\text{Top}(p_1\rightarrow v_1) \ldots o\#\,\text{Top}(p_k\rightarrow v_k))$$

of its class membership, its bag of object-centered tuples (*tupribution*), and its bag of object-centered slots (*slotribution*). This *distribution* (tupribution and/or slotribution) could be physically implemented on the Web. A systematics of special kinds of psoa atoms, including (oidless) *relationships* $f(t_1 \ldots t_n)$ and (oidful) *frames* $o\#f(p_1\rightarrow v_1 \ldots p_k\rightarrow v_k)$, is elaborated in [5] with many examples.

The alphabet of PSOA RuleML includes a single set Const of individual, function, and predicate constants – to prepare functional-logic integration as, e.g., in Relfun, Hilog, and RIF – as well as a set Var of variables. Constants include Top, denoting the root class, and '_'-prefixed *local constants* (e.g., _a). Variables are '?'-prefixed (e.g., ?X).

The syntax of PSOA RuleML is built on *terms*. A *simple term* is a constant or a variable. An *atomic formula* is a psoa atom in the form of terms (1) or (2), a subclass term c1##c2, an equality term t1=t2, or an external term External(f(...)). Complex formulas can be constructed using the Horn-like subset of first-order logic (FOL), including conjunctions $\text{And}(\tau_1 \ldots \tau_n)$, disjunctions $\text{Or}(\tau_1 \ldots \tau_n)$ in the rule body, top-level rule implications $\tau_1 \text{ :- } \tau_2$, existential quantification $\text{Exists }?X_1 \ldots ?X_n\ (\tau_1)$, and top-level universal quantification $\text{Forall }?X_1 \ldots ?X_n\ (\tau_1)$. A *group formula* $\text{Group}(\tau_1 \ldots \tau_n)$ wraps a set of facts and rules into a KB.

The model-theoretic semantics of PSOA RuleML is defined through semantic structures [4]. A semantic structure $\mathcal{I}$ is a tuple $<\boldsymbol{TV}, \boldsymbol{DTS}, \boldsymbol{D}, \boldsymbol{D}_{\text{ind}}, \boldsymbol{D}_{\text{func}}, \boldsymbol{I}_C, \boldsymbol{I}_V, \boldsymbol{I}_{\text{psoa}}, \boldsymbol{I}_{\text{sub}}, \boldsymbol{I}_=, \boldsymbol{I}_{\text{external}}, \boldsymbol{I}_{\text{truth}}>$. Here $\boldsymbol{D}$ is a non-empty set called the domain of $\mathcal{I}$. $\boldsymbol{D}_{\text{ind}}$ and $\boldsymbol{D}_{\text{func}}$ are subsets of $\boldsymbol{D}$ for individual and function interpretations. $\boldsymbol{I}_C$ and $\boldsymbol{I}_V$ interpret constants and variables. $\boldsymbol{I}_{\text{psoa}}$ interprets predicates/functions of psoa terms as semantic functions, which will be shown in Sect. 3.1. $\boldsymbol{I}_{\text{sub}}$, $\boldsymbol{I}_=$, and $\boldsymbol{I}_{\text{external}}$ interpret subclass, equality, and external terms. A generic mapping $\boldsymbol{I}$ from terms to $\boldsymbol{D}$ can be defined using the above interpretation mappings. $\boldsymbol{I}_{\text{truth}}$ maps domain elements to the set of truth values $\boldsymbol{TV} = \{\mathbf{t}, \mathbf{f}\}$. We will write $\mathcal{I}.\boldsymbol{D}$, $\mathcal{I}.\boldsymbol{I}_{\text{V}}$, etc.,. for the components of $\mathcal{I}$ in the rest of the paper.

Truth evaluation for formulas is determined by a recursive evaluation function $TVal_{\mathcal{I}}$ defined in [4]. A semantic structure $\mathcal{I}$ is called a *model* of a KB ϕ if $TVal_{\mathcal{I}}(\phi) = \mathbf{t}$ and $\mathcal{I}$ conforms to all semantic restrictions (e.g., subclass and slotribution/tupribution restrictions), denoted by $\mathcal{I} \models \phi$. A PSOA KB ϕ is said to *entail* a formula ψ, denoted by $\phi \models \psi$, if for every model $\mathcal{I}$ of ϕ, $\mathcal{I} \models \psi$ holds.

We illustrate the syntax and semantics through an example, previewing key concepts, e.g. *non-relational* and *virtual OID*.

Example 1. Consider the following KB:

```
Group (
  Forall ?Pers ?JobTitle ?Comp1 ?Comp2 (
    _transfer(?Pers ?Comp1 ?Comp2) :-
       And(_work(?Pers ?Comp1 ?JobTitle)
            _acquire(_buyer->?Comp2 _seller->?Comp1)))
  _e1#_transfer(_Tony _Rho4biz _Chi4corp _bonus->20000)
  _work(_Kate _Rho4biz "Director")
  _a1#_acquire(_buyer->_Chi4corp _seller->_Rho4biz)
)
```

We will query this KB as follows, without (left) and with (right) an OID:

```
_work(?P ?C ?J)          ?O#_work(?P ?C ?J)
_transfer(?P ?C1 ?C2)    ?O#_transfer(?P ?C1 ?C2)
```

The _work fact is relational while the _acquire fact has two slots centered on the object _a1. The _transfer rule uses premises satisfied by these facts. Its _acquire premise needs to be objectified to ?1#_acquire(_buyer->?Comp2 _seller->?Comp1), so that the generated fresh OID variable ?1 unifies with _a1. The _transfer fact is non-relational, centered on the graph-node-like object _e1 – typed by _transfer acting as a class – and having one tuple of arguments as well as a slot for an optional _bonus. Since _transfer acts as a non-relational predicate in this KB atom, it is a non-relational predicate in the entire KB (although it acts as a relation in the rule).

Let us query the KB: The query _work(?P ?C ?J) uses the relational KB predicate _work in a relationship, while the query ?O#_work(?P ?C ?J) uses _work non-relationally with an OID variable ?O, which can be bound to a virtual OID created by objectification. The _transfer(?P ?C1 ?C2) query uses the non-relational KB predicate _transfer without an OID. The _transfer rule is invoked, binding ?P to _Kate, ?C1 to _Rho4biz, and ?C2 to _Chi4corp. The second solution is dependent on query objectification, introducing the existential OID variable ?1, yielding Exists ?1 (?1#_transfer(?P ?C1 ?C2)); the _transfer fact is retrieved with the _bonus slot ignored, binding ?P to _Tony, ?C1 to _Rho4biz, and ?C2 to _Chi4corp (the ?1 binding to _e1 is not shown because of its `Exists` encapsulation). In the query `?O#_transfer(?P ?C1 ?C2)`, `_transfer` acts as a class – i.e., as a non-relational predicate – with an explicit OID variable `?O`. For successful query answering, the `_transfer` rule (e.g., its conclusion) requires objectification while the fact can be used directly.   □

More (e.g., geospatial) examples and the open-source implementation of PSOA are available online,[3] for explorations in its operational semantics.

3 Minimal Objectification

In PSOA RuleML, each oidless psoa atom σ is understood as having an implicit OID, which allows the interchangeable use of oidless and oidful atoms of the respective term forms (1) and (2) in Sect. 2. The earlier semantics can only interpret an oidless psoa term after *static objectification*, which generates OIDs for all of the KB's oidless terms. This causes reasoning overhead for an atom whose predicate in the KB clauses is used only as a Prolog-like relation, e.g. does not occur with an OID or slots. Moreover, since it will turn out that it is inappropriate to give OIDs to expressions, the earlier semantics cannot deal with expression terms. In this section, we will thus first introduce a modified model-theoretic semantics to allow the direct interpretation of oidless psoa terms. Then we will discuss an objectification systematics for oidless atoms, including undifferentiated and differentiated static objectification transformations, as well as a novel static/dynamic transformation. Static/dynamic objectification is minimal in the sense that it generates as few explicit OIDs as possible, instead constructing virtual OIDs as query variable bindings. The current section assumes that the only allowed embedded complex terms are expressions, which can be achieved by maximal unnesting of embedded atoms – the central theme of Sect. 4.

3.1 New Semantics for Oidless Psoa Terms

The earlier semantics of PSOA RuleML [4] defined the interpretation of a psoa term as follows, where I is a generic mapping for interpreting any term:

$$I(\texttt{o\#f}([\texttt{t}_{1,1} \ldots \texttt{t}_{1,n_1}] \ldots [\texttt{t}_{m,1} \ldots \texttt{t}_{m,n_m}] \texttt{p}_1\texttt{->v}_1 \ldots \texttt{p}_k\texttt{->v}_k) =$$
$$I_{\text{psoa}}(I(\texttt{f}))(I(\texttt{o}),$$
$$\{\langle I(\texttt{t}_{1,1}), \ldots, I(\texttt{t}_{1,n_1})\rangle, \ldots, \langle I(\texttt{t}_{m,1}), \ldots, I(\texttt{t}_{1,n_m})\rangle\}, \quad (3)$$
$$\{\langle I(\texttt{p}_1), I(\texttt{v}_1)\rangle, \ldots, \langle I(\texttt{p}_k), I(\texttt{v}_k)\rangle\})$$

I first gives a domain element interpretation in D to each component of the psoa term, including: the OID o; the predicate/function f; each positional argument $\texttt{t}_{i,j}$, $1 \leq i \leq m$, $1 \leq j \leq n_i$; each slot name $\texttt{p}_h$ and filler $\texttt{v}_h$, $1 \leq h \leq k$. Then I_{psoa} maps $I(\texttt{f}) \in D$ to a semantic function of the general form $D_{\text{ind}} \times \texttt{SetOfFiniteBags}(D^*_{\text{ind}}) \times \texttt{SetOfFiniteBags}(D_{\text{ind}} \times D_{\text{ind}}) \rightarrow D$, which takes the following three arguments and returns an element $\texttt{d} \in D$:

---

[3] See PSOA's entry to the RuleML website: http://psoa.ruleml.org.

- The interpreted OID $I(o) \in D_{ind}$;
- The bag of interpreted tuples $\{\langle I(t_{i,1}), \ldots, I(t_{i,n_i}) \rangle \mid 1 \leq i \leq m\}$ $\in$ SetOfFiniteBags(D^*_{ind}), where D^*_{ind} denotes the set of all finite-length tuples over D.
- The bag of interpreted slots $\{\langle I(p_h), I(v_h) \rangle \mid 1 \leq h \leq k\}$ $\in$ SetOfFiniteBags$(D_{ind} \times D_{ind})$.

I_{psoa} can be applied to $I(f)$ no matter f is a predicate or function symbol, where $I_{psoa}(I(f))$ must be a D_{ind}-valued semantic function if f is a function. Notice that in the above definitions, the mappings I and I_{psoa} are only defined for oidful psoa terms and their predicates/functions, hence all psoa terms need to be objectified before applying the semantics. This has several shortcomings:

- Expressions should not have OIDs, which will be explained in Sect. 4.
- Atoms are required to have OIDs before they can be semantically evaluated, which creates overhead for each atom whose predicate in the KB clauses is used only as a Prolog-like relation.

In order to resolve these problems, we will redefine I and I_{psoa} to allow a direct interpretation of oidless psoa terms, and also incorporate the objectification virtually into the semantics using a logical equivalence. Specifically, the following changes are introduced:

1. The definition of I for **oidful** psoa terms is changed to

$$I(o\#f([t_{1,1} \ldots t_{1,n_1}] \ldots [t_{m,1} \ldots t_{m,n_m}] p_1\text{->}v_1 \ldots p_k\text{->}v_k)) =$$
$$I_{psoa}(I(f))(\{I(o)\},$$
$$\{\langle I(t_{1,1}), \ldots, I(t_{1,n_1}) \rangle, \ldots, \langle I(t_{m,1}), \ldots, I(t_{1,n_m}) \rangle\}, \quad (4)$$
$$\{\langle I(p_1), I(v_1) \rangle, \ldots, \langle I(p_k), I(v_k) \rangle\})$$

where the first argument of the semantic function $I_{psoa}(I(f))$ is wrapped into a singleton set $\{I(o)\}$. This allows defining I for **oidless** psoa terms separately, by using the empty set $\{\}$ as the first argument:

$$I(f([t_{1,1} \ldots t_{1,n_1}] \ldots [t_{m,1} \ldots t_{m,n_m}] p_1\text{->}v_1 \ldots p_k\text{->}v_k)) =$$
$$I_{psoa}(I(f))(\{\},$$
$$\{\langle I(t_{1,1}), \ldots, I(t_{1,n_1}) \rangle, \ldots, \langle I(t_{m,1}), \ldots, I(t_{1,n_m}) \rangle\}, \quad (5)$$
$$\{\langle I(p_1), I(v_1) \rangle, \ldots, \langle I(p_k), I(v_k) \rangle\})$$

2. The definition of I_{psoa} is changed to map D to semantic functions of the form SetOfPhiSingletons$(D_{ind}) \times$ SetOfFiniteBags$(D^*_{ind}) \times$ SetOfFiniteBags$(D_{ind} \times D_{ind}) \to D$, where SetOfPhiSingletons(D_{ind}) is defined as $\{\{\}\} \cup \{\{o\} \mid o \in D_{ind}\}$, whose elements contains the empty set $\{\}$ and a singleton set $\{o\}$ for each $o \in D_{ind}$. With this definition, the semantic function $I_{psoa}(I(f))$ can be correctly applied to the arguments in Eqs. (4) and (5).

3. Define truth evaluation for oidless psoa terms used as atoms as follows.

$$TVal_{\mathcal{I}}(\texttt{f}(\texttt{[}t_{1,1} \ldots t_{1,n_1}\texttt{]} \ldots \texttt{[}t_{m,1} \ldots t_{m,n_m}\texttt{]} \ \texttt{p}_1\texttt{->}\texttt{v}_1 \ldots \texttt{p}_k\texttt{->}\texttt{v}_k)) =$$
$$\boldsymbol{I}_{\text{truth}}(\boldsymbol{I}(\texttt{f}(\texttt{[}t_{1,1} \ldots t_{1,n_1}\texttt{]} \ldots \texttt{[}t_{m,1} \ldots t_{m,n_m}\texttt{]} \ \texttt{p}_1\texttt{->}\texttt{v}_1 \ldots \texttt{p}_k\texttt{->}\texttt{v}_k)) \quad (6)$$

Here, the following *objectification restriction* is required to capture the logical equivalence between an oidless atom (notice the absence of "o#" in front of "f(...)") and its existentially objectified form:

$$TVal_{\mathcal{I}}(\texttt{f}(\texttt{[}t_{1,1} \ldots t_{1,n_1}\texttt{]} \ldots \texttt{[}t_{m,1} \ldots t_{m,n_m}\texttt{]} \ \texttt{p}_1\texttt{->}\texttt{v}_1 \ldots \texttt{p}_k\texttt{->}\texttt{v}_k)) = \texttt{t}$$

if and only if

$$TVal_{\mathcal{I}}(\texttt{Exists ?O (?O\#f(}\texttt{[}t_{1,1} \ldots t_{1,n_1}\texttt{]} \ldots \texttt{[}t_{m,1} \ldots t_{m,n_m}\texttt{]} \ \texttt{p}_1\texttt{->}\texttt{v}_1 \ldots \texttt{p}_k\texttt{->}\texttt{v}_k))) = \texttt{t}$$

where ?O is a fresh variable representing the postulated virtual OID of the atom. Notice that the restriction applies only to atoms – after unnesting (cf. Sect. 4) occurring only the top-level – but not to – embedded – expressions, which do not have a truth value. In the rest of the paper, we will call the semantics with and without objectification restriction *objectification-including* and *objectification-excluding* semantics, respectively.

Next we define the objectification transformation, which realizes the objectification-including semantics by transforming KBs and queries such that entailment can be established under the objectification-excluding semantics.

Definition 1. *(Entailment under objectification-excluding/-including semantics) An interpretation $\mathcal{I}$ is an objectification-excluding (resp., objectification-including) model of ϕ, written as $\mathcal{I} \models_{-o} \phi$ (resp., $\mathcal{I} \models_{+o} \phi$), iff $TVal_{\mathcal{I}}(\phi) = \texttt{t}$ and $TVal_{\mathcal{I}}$ conforms to all other semantic restrictions [4] (e.g., slotribution/tupribution), while it does not (resp., does) guarantee the objectification restriction. A KB ϕ entails a query q under the objectification-excluding (resp. objectification-including) semantics, written as $\phi \models_{-o} q$ (resp., $\phi \models_{+o} q$), iff for every $\mathcal{I}$ such that $\mathcal{I} \models_{-o} \phi$ (resp. $\mathcal{I} \models_{+o} \phi$), $\mathcal{I} \models_{-o} q$ (resp. $\mathcal{I} \models_{+o} q$) holds.*

Since the default semantics is objectification-including, we will use the short notation $\models$ for $\models_{+o}$ in the rest of the paper.

Definition 2. *(Objectification Transformation) An objectification transformation obj with respect to a set of KBs Φ and a set of queries Q is a transformation $\Phi \times \Gamma \to \Gamma$, where Φ and Q are subsets of Γ, such that for every KB $\phi \in \Phi$ and query $q \in Q$, $\phi \models q$ iff $\mathsf{obj}(\phi, \phi) \models_{-o} \mathsf{obj}(\phi, q)$. For convenience, we write $\mathsf{obj}(q)$ for $\mathsf{obj}(\phi, q)$ if $\mathsf{obj}(\phi, q)$ is independent of ϕ, and $\mathsf{obj}(\phi)$ for $\mathsf{obj}(\phi, \phi)$.*

The second argument of obj is the input formula to be transformed, while the first argument is the corresponding KB of the formula providing necessary context information. Next, we define a schema for constructing such a transformation obj for KBs and queries from a transformation defined only for atoms.

Definition 3. *Given a set of KBs Φ and a set of queries Q, for any $\phi \in \Phi$, if $\mathsf{obj}(\phi, \tau)$ has been defined, with τ being any atom, then $\mathsf{obj}(\phi, \tau)$ can be extended for τ being a formula other than an atom, where (1) for a subclass or an equality, $\mathsf{obj}(\phi, \tau) = \tau$ is just a projection; (2) for other formulas, $\mathsf{obj}(\phi, \tau)$ is obtained by recursively applying obj to each subformula of τ, while keeping the surrounding formula structure unchanged.*

Note that $\mathsf{obj}(\phi, \tau)$ is the same as the formula obtained by replacing every atom ω in τ with $\mathsf{obj}(\phi, \omega)$; for some ω's, this is just a projection $\mathsf{obj}(\phi, \omega) = \omega$. In the rest of the paper we assume every obj is constructed using Definition 3.

In order to prove $\phi \models q$ iff $\mathsf{obj}(\phi) \models_{-o} \mathsf{obj}(\phi, q)$, as required by Definition 2 for any particular obj, one can prove $\phi \models q$ iff $\mathsf{obj}(\phi) \models \mathsf{obj}(\phi, q)$ and $\mathsf{obj}(\phi) \models \mathsf{obj}(\phi, q)$ iff $\mathsf{obj}(\phi) \models_{-o} \mathsf{obj}(\phi, q)$. The next lemma gives a sufficient condition for $\phi \models q$ iff $\mathsf{obj}(\phi) \models \mathsf{obj}(\phi, q)$, where we write $\mathsf{Var}(\tau)$ for the set of all free variables in a formula τ, $\mathsf{M}(\mathsf{Var}(\tau), \boldsymbol{D})$ for the set of all mappings from $\mathsf{Var}(\tau)$ to $\boldsymbol{D}$, and $\mathsf{v}(\mathcal{I}, \boldsymbol{I}_V)$ for an interpretation that coincides with $\boldsymbol{I}_V$ on all variables it interprets, and with $\mathcal{I}$ on everything else.

We say that a formula has a *positive* occurrence if it is in a fact or a rule conclusion, and a *negative* occurrence if in a query or a rule premise. A semantic structure $\mathcal{I}$ is called a *counter-model* for $\phi \models q$ if $\mathcal{I} \models \phi$ and $\mathcal{I} \not\models q$.

Lemma 1. *Given a KB ϕ, a query q, and a transformation obj, $\phi \models q$ iff $\mathsf{obj}(\phi) \models \mathsf{obj}(\phi, q)$ holds if obj has the following properties:*

(1) For every counter-model $\mathcal{I}$ for $\phi \models q$, there exists $\mathcal{I}'$ s.t. for every KB/query atom ω, $\boldsymbol{I}_V \in \mathsf{M}(\mathsf{Var}(\omega), \mathcal{I}.\boldsymbol{D})$,
  (1.a) if ω is positive and $\mathsf{v}(\mathcal{I}, \boldsymbol{I}_V) \models \omega$, then $\mathsf{v}(\mathcal{I}', \boldsymbol{I}_V) \models \mathsf{obj}(\phi, \omega)$;
  (1.b) if ω is negative and $\mathsf{v}(\mathcal{I}', \boldsymbol{I}_V) \models \mathsf{obj}(\phi, \omega)$, then $\mathsf{v}(\mathcal{I}, \boldsymbol{I}_V) \models \omega$.
(2) For every counter-model $\mathcal{I}'$ for $\mathsf{obj}(\phi) \models \mathsf{obj}(\phi, q)$, there exists $\mathcal{I}$ s.t. for every KB/query atom ω, $\boldsymbol{I}_V \in \mathsf{M}(\mathsf{Var}(\omega), \mathcal{I}'.\boldsymbol{D})$,
  (2.a) if ω is positive and $\mathsf{v}(\mathcal{I}', \boldsymbol{I}_V) \models \mathsf{obj}(\phi, \omega)$, then $\mathsf{v}(\mathcal{I}, \boldsymbol{I}_V) \models \omega$,
  (2.b) if ω is negative and $\mathsf{v}(\mathcal{I}, \boldsymbol{I}_V) \models \omega$, then $\mathsf{v}(\mathcal{I}', \boldsymbol{I}_V) \models \mathsf{obj}(\phi, \omega)$.

Proof. (Sketch) Proving $\phi \models q$ iff $\mathsf{obj}(\phi) \models \mathsf{obj}(\phi, q)$ is equivalent to proving $\phi \not\models q$ iff $\mathsf{obj}(\phi) \not\models \mathsf{obj}(\phi, q)$. We first prove the 'if' part. If $\mathsf{obj}(\phi) \not\models \mathsf{obj}(\phi, q)$, then there exists a counter-model $\mathcal{I}'$ for $\mathsf{obj}(\phi) \models \mathsf{obj}(\phi, q)$. Using condition (2.a), we can prove by induction that for every positive formula τ and $\boldsymbol{I}_V \in \mathsf{M}(\mathsf{Var}(\tau), \mathcal{I}.\boldsymbol{D})$, if $TVal_{\mathsf{v}(\mathcal{I}', \boldsymbol{I}_V)}(\mathsf{obj}(\phi, \tau)) = \mathbf{t}$ then $TVal_{\mathsf{v}(\mathcal{I}, \boldsymbol{I}_V)}(\tau) = \mathbf{t}$. Using condition (2.b), we can also prove by induction that for every negative formula τ, if $TVal_{\mathsf{v}(\mathcal{I}, \boldsymbol{I}_V)}(\tau) = \mathbf{t}$ then $TVal_{\mathsf{v}(\mathcal{I}', \boldsymbol{I}_V)}(\mathsf{obj}(\phi, \tau)) = \mathbf{t}$.

Then we can prove that for each top-level formula τ in ϕ, $TVal_{\mathcal{I}}(\mathsf{obj}(\phi, \tau)) = \mathbf{t}$.

- If τ is a ground fact, τ is a positive formula so $TVal_{\mathcal{I}}(\mathsf{obj}(\phi, \tau)) = \mathbf{t}$.
- If τ is a rule of the form Forall $?X_1 \ldots ?X_n$ $(\tau_1 \mathbin{:-} \tau_2)$, $TVal_{\mathcal{I}'}(\tau) = \mathbf{t}$ means for every $\boldsymbol{I}_{V*} \subseteq \mathsf{M}(\{?X_1, \ldots, ?X_n\}, \mathcal{I}.\boldsymbol{D})$, $TVal_{\mathsf{v}(\mathcal{I}', \boldsymbol{I}_{V*})}(\tau_1) = \mathbf{t}$ or $TVal_{\mathsf{v}(\mathcal{I}', \boldsymbol{I}_{V*})}(\tau_2) = \mathbf{f}$ holds. Since τ_1 is positive and τ_2 is negative, either $TVal_{\mathsf{v}(\mathcal{I}, \boldsymbol{I}_{V*})}(\tau_1) = \mathbf{t}$ or $TVal_{\mathsf{v}(\mathcal{I}, \boldsymbol{I}_{V*})}(\tau_2) = \mathbf{f}$ holds for every $\boldsymbol{I}_{V*}$. So $TVal_{\mathcal{I}}(\tau) = \mathbf{t}$.

– If τ is a non-ground fact, it can be seen as a rule with an empty premise, so that the above proof for general rules still apply.

Hence $\mathcal{I} \models \phi$. Also since the query q is negative, hence $\mathcal{I} \not\models q$. Thus $\phi \not\models q$.

The 'only if' part can be proved using a similar approach based on the existence of a counter-model $\mathcal{I}'$ for $\mathsf{obj}(\phi) \models \mathsf{obj}(\phi, q)$. □

Corollary 1. *Given a KB ϕ, a query q, and a transformation* obj*, $\phi \models q$ iff* $\mathsf{obj}(\phi) \models \mathsf{obj}(\phi, q)$ *holds if for every KB/query atom ω and semantic structure* $\mathcal{I}^*$*, $\mathcal{I}^* \models \omega$ iff $\mathcal{I}^* \models \mathsf{obj}(\phi, \omega)$ holds.*

Proof. We will show that obj has the properties (1) and (2) in Lemma 1. For property (1), if $\mathcal{I}$ is a counter-model for $\phi \models q$, then we can choose $\mathcal{I}' = \mathcal{I}$. For every $\boldsymbol{I}_{\mathrm{V}} \in \mathsf{M}(\mathsf{Var}(\omega), \mathcal{I}.\boldsymbol{D})$, according to the assumption where $\mathcal{I}^*$ becomes $\mathsf{v}(\mathcal{I}, \boldsymbol{I}_{\mathrm{V}})$, we have $\mathsf{v}(\mathcal{I}, \boldsymbol{I}_{\mathrm{V}}) \models \omega$ iff $\mathsf{v}(\mathcal{I}, \boldsymbol{I}_{\mathrm{V}}) \models \mathsf{obj}(\phi, \omega)$. Hence (1.a) and (1.b) are satisfied and obj has property (1).

That obj has property (2) can be proved similarly by choosing $\mathcal{I} = \mathcal{I}'$. □

Lemma 2 gives a sufficient condition for $\mathsf{obj}(\phi) \models \mathsf{obj}(\phi, q)$ iff $\mathsf{obj}(\phi) \models_{\text{-}o} \mathsf{obj}(\phi, q)$.

Lemma 2. *Given a KB ϕ' and a query q', $\phi' \models q'$ iff $\phi' \models_{\text{-}o} q'$ holds if for each counter-model $\mathcal{I}''$ for $\phi' \models_{\text{-}o} q'$ there exists a counter-model $\mathcal{I}'$ for $\phi' \models q'$.*

Proof. We first prove the 'if' part. For every $\mathcal{I}'$ s.t. $\mathcal{I}' \models \phi'$, $\mathcal{I}' \models_{\text{-}o} \phi'$ since $\models$ more restricted than $\models_{\text{-}o}$. Also since $\phi' \models_{\text{-}o} q'$, $\mathcal{I}' \models_{\text{-}o} q'$. Because $\mathcal{I}' \models \phi'$, $\mathcal{I}'$ guarantees the objectification restriction. Hence $\mathcal{I}' \models q'$ always holds and $\phi' \models q'$ is proved.

Next we prove the 'only if' part, which is equivalent to $\phi' \not\models q'$ if $\phi' \not\models_{\text{-}o} q'$. If $\phi' \not\models_{\text{-}o} q'$, there exists a counter-model $\mathcal{I}''$ for $\phi' \models_{\text{-}o} q'$. According to the assumption of the lemma, there exists a counter-model $\mathcal{I}'$ for $\phi' \models q'$, hence $\phi' \not\models q'$ is proved. □

The next subsections will discuss different objectification transformations.

3.2 Static Objectification Transformations

The static objectification $\mathsf{obj}_s(\alpha)$ of a KB/query α is obtained by replacing each oidless atom σ with its objectified form $\mathsf{obj}_s(\sigma)$ having a generated OID. The generation can adopt either an undifferentiated method $\mathsf{obj}_{s=}$, which uniformly transforms σ everywhere, or a differentiated method $\mathsf{obj}_{s\neq}$ [6], which transforms σ differently based on its occurrence.

Definition 4. *(Undifferentiated static objectification) The undifferentiated static objectification* $\mathsf{obj}_{s=}(\omega)$ *of atom is* **(a)** ω *if ω is oidful;* **(b)** Exists ?i (?i#f(...)) *if ω is oidless, where ?i is a fresh variable in the clause chosen from* ?1, ?2, ...

$\mathsf{obj}_{s=}$ *is extended for other formulas according to Definition 3.*

In Example 1, $obj_{s=}$ of the KB and the queries replaces all oidless _transfer, _work, and _acquire atoms with their existential forms.

The following theorem shows the correctness of $obj_{s=}$.

Theorem 1. $obj_{s=}$ *is an objectification transformation for any KB and query.*

Proof. We first show that for every KB / query atom ω and semantic structure $\mathcal{I}^*$, $\mathcal{I}^* \models \omega$ iff $\mathcal{I}^* \models obj_{s=}(\omega)$ holds. If ω is oidful, then $obj_{s=}(\omega) = \omega$, and the statement holds trivially. Otherwise ω is oidless. If $\mathcal{I}^* \models \omega$, then $\mathcal{I}^*$ guarantees the objectification restriction. So $TVal_{\mathcal{I}^*}(obj_{s=}(\omega)) = TVal_{\mathcal{I}^*}(\omega) = \mathbf{t}$, and $\mathcal{I}^* \models obj_{s=}(\omega)$ holds. Similarly, if $\mathcal{I}^* \models obj_{s=}(\omega)$, $\mathcal{I}^* \models \omega$ also holds. Hence $\mathcal{I}^* \models \omega$ iff $\mathcal{I}^* \models obj_{s=}(\omega)$ holds also for oidless atoms. Thus the condition of Corollary 1 is fulfilled and $\phi \models q$ iff $obj_{s=}(\phi) \models obj_{s=}(q)$.

Next we will show that for each $obj_{s=}(\phi)$ and $obj_{s=}(q)$, the condition of Lemma 2 is fulfilled. If there exists a counter-model $\mathcal{I}''$ for $\phi \models q$, then it can be made into a model $\mathcal{I}'$ that guarantees the objectification restriction, by redefining $TVal_{\mathcal{I}'}(\omega)$ for every atom ω that is oidless to be the same as $TVal_{\mathcal{I}''}(obj_{s=}(\omega))$. Since the change only affect oidless atoms, which neither exist in $obj_{s=}(\phi)$ nor in $obj_{s=}(q)$, $TVal_{\mathcal{I}'}(\phi) = TVal_{\mathcal{I}''}(\phi) = \mathbf{t}$ and $TVal_{\mathcal{I}'}(q) = TVal_{\mathcal{I}''}(q) = \mathbf{f}$. Hence $\mathcal{I}'$ is a counter-model for $\phi \models q$ and the condition of Lemma 2 is fulfilled. Thus $obj_{s=}(\phi) \models obj_{s=}(q)$ iff $obj_{s=}(\phi) \models_{-o} obj_{s=}(q)$.

So $\phi \models q$ iff $obj_{s=}(\phi) \models_{-o} obj_{s=}(q)$ and the theorem is proved. $\qquad\square$

Definition 5. *(Differentiated static objectification) For an atom ω, the differentiated static objectification $obj_{s\neq}(\omega)$ is defined as ω if ω is oidful, or as follows if ω is oidless:*

Case 1: If ω is a ground fact, $obj_{s\neq}(\omega) = \_i\,\#f(...)$, where $\_i$ is a fresh local constant symbol chosen from $\_1, \_2, ...$, which neither occurs elsewhere in the KB nor is used for the objectification of other atoms.

Case 2: If ω is a non-ground fact, a rule conclusion atom, or a query atom, $obj_{s\neq}(\omega) = $ Exists $?j\,(?j\,\#f(...))$.

Case 3: If ω is a rule premise atom, $obj_{s\neq}(\omega) = ?j\,\#f(...)$, where $?j$ is a fresh variable scoped universally by the enclosing rule.

$obj_{s\neq}$ *is extended for other formulas according to Definition 3.*

In Example 1, differentiated static objectification generates a fresh OID constant for the _work ground fact according to Case 1, replaces the oidless _work and _transfer atoms in the rule conclusion and in the queries with existentials according to Case 2, and generates fresh universal OID variables for the _work and _acquire atoms in the rule premise according to Case 3.

It is easy to prove the correctness of $obj_{s\neq}$ by showing that it leads to the same set of entailed queries as $obj_{s=}$.

Lemma 3. *Given a KB ϕ and a query q, if q does not use a generated OID constant symbol $\_1, \_2, ...$, then $obj_{s=}(\phi) \models_{-o} obj_{s=}(q)$ iff $obj_{s\neq}(\phi) \models_{-o} obj_{s\neq}(q)$.*

Proof. According to their definitions, both methods transform oidless query atoms into the same existential form, hence $\mathsf{obj}_{s=}(q) = \mathsf{obj}_{s\neq}(q)$ for any query q. Thus $\mathsf{obj}_{s\neq}(\phi) \models_{-o} \mathsf{obj}_{s=}(q)$ iff $\mathsf{obj}_{s\neq}(\phi) \models_{-o} \mathsf{obj}_{s\neq}(q)$.

For KB atoms, the two methods are identical in Case 2 and differ in Case 1 and 3. The transformation of a rule premise atom in Case 3 using a universal OID variable on the top-level is equivalent to using an embedded existentially quantified formula with an existential OID variable in the rule premise. For a ground fact ω handled by Case 1, $\mathsf{obj}_{s\neq}(\omega)$ can be seen as a Skolemized version of $\mathsf{obj}_{s=}(\omega)$ using Skolem constants $\_1, \_2, \dots$, hence they entail the same set of queries as long as these queries do not use the Skolem constants, thus avoiding a clash of constant symbols. Hence we have $\mathsf{obj}_{s=}(\phi) \models_{-o} \mathsf{obj}_{s=}(q)$ iff $\mathsf{obj}_{s\neq}(\phi) \models_{-o} \mathsf{obj}_{s=}(q)$. So $\mathsf{obj}_{s=}(\phi) \models_{-o} \mathsf{obj}_{s=}(q)$ iff $\mathsf{obj}_{s\neq}(\phi) \models_{-o} \mathsf{obj}_{s=}(q)$, and the lemma holds.   □

Theorem 2. $\mathsf{obj}_{s=}$ *is an objectification transformation with respect to a set of KBs Φ and to a set of queries Q that do not use constants $\_1, \_2, \dots$*

Proof. For any $\phi \in \Phi$ and $q \in Q$, by Theorem 1 we have $\phi \models q$ iff $\mathsf{obj}_{s=}(\phi) \models_{-o} \mathsf{obj}_{s=}(q)$. By Lemma 3, $\mathsf{obj}_{s=}(\phi) \models_{-o} \mathsf{obj}_{s=}(q)$ iff $\mathsf{obj}_{s\neq}(\phi) \models_{-o} \mathsf{obj}_{s\neq}(q)$. Hence $\phi \models q$ iff $\mathsf{obj}_{s\neq}(\phi) \models_{-o} \mathsf{obj}_{s\neq}(q)$. So the statement holds by Definition 2.   □

3.3 Static/Dynamic Objectification Transformation

For KBs in which most or all of the predicates are Prolog-like relations, it is often not necessary to generate OIDs for their oidless atoms explicitly. In this subsection, a novel static/dynamic objectification approach is introduced to keep unchanged as many of the KB's oidless atoms as possible, instead constructing virtual OIDs at query time when bindings for OID variables are being queried.

In order to apply static/dynamic objectification to a KB ϕ and its queries, the set of KB predicates $\mathsf{PredKB}(\phi)$ will be partitioned into two disjoint subsets. $\mathsf{PredKB}(\phi)$ is defined as $\{\mathsf{Pred}(\lambda) \mid \lambda$ is an atom in $\phi\}$, where $\mathsf{Pred}(\lambda)$ denotes the predicate symbol of λ. The partitioning of $\mathsf{PredKB}(\phi)$ is defined next.

Definition 6. *(Non-relational and relational predicates) Given a KB ϕ, a predicate $\mathtt{f} \in \mathsf{PredKB}(\phi)$ is **non-relational** in ϕ if $\mathtt{f}$ occurs at least once in a multituple, oidful, or slotted atom of ϕ, or in a subclass formula of ϕ. Conversely, $\mathtt{f}$ is **relational** in ϕ if it has no such occurrence. The sets of non-relational and relational predicates of ϕ are written as $\mathsf{PredKB}_{NR}(\phi)$ and $\mathsf{PredKB}_R(\phi)$, respectively.*

For atoms using a relational predicate in $\mathsf{PredKB}_R(\phi)$, their OIDs can be virtualized by dynamic objectification:

Definition 7. *(Dynamic objectification) The dynamic objectification $\mathsf{obj}_d(\phi, \omega)$ of an atom ω with respect to a KB ϕ, where $\mathsf{Pred}(\omega) \in \mathsf{PredKB}_R(\phi)$, is defined as ω if ω is a KB atom in ϕ, or as the following rewriting if ω is a query atom:*

Case 1: If ω is a relationship, $\mathsf{obj}_d(\phi, \omega) = \omega$.

Case 2: If ω has a non-variable (e.g., constant or expression) OID or a slot, $\mathrm{obj}_d(\phi, \omega) = \mathrm{Or}()$, where $\mathrm{Or}()$ is an encoding of explicit falsity.

Case 3: If ω has an OID variable and $m > 0$ tuples, being of the form $?0\#f([t_{1,1} \ldots t_{1,n_1}] \ldots [t_{m,1} \ldots t_{m,n_m}])$, equivalent (via 'class-reproducing' tupribution) to a conjunction separately applying $?0\#f$ to all tuples,

$$\mathrm{And}(?0\#f([t_{1,1} \ldots t_{1,n_1}]) \ldots ?0\#f([t_{m,1} \ldots t_{m,n_m}])),$$

abbreviated to

$$\mathrm{And}(?0\#f(t_{1,1} \ldots t_{1,n_1}) \ldots ?0\#f(t_{m,1} \ldots t_{m,n_m})),$$

then $\mathrm{obj}_d(\phi, \omega)$ is a relational conjunction querying the oidless versions of these applications while using explicit equalities between the OID variable $?0$ and an OID-constructor function _oidcons applied to the predicate and the elements of each tuple (where the $?0$ equalities also enforce tuple unification, so that the m single-tuple f relationships can be satisfied by a single KB clause, thus realizing special 'virtual multi-tuple' psoa atoms as queries):

$$\mathrm{And}(f(t_{1,1} \ldots t_{1,n_1}) \ ?0 = \_oidcons(f \ t_{1,1} \ldots t_{1,n_1})$$

$$\ldots$$

$$f(t_{m,1} \ldots t_{m,n_m}) \ ?0 = \_oidcons(f \ t_{m,1} \ldots t_{m,n_m}))$$

In the special case of $m = 1$, the query atom $?0\#f(t_1 \ldots t_n)$ becomes

$$\mathrm{And}(f(t_1 \ldots t_n) \ ?0 = \_oidcons(f \ t_1 \ldots t_n))$$

The function _oidcons is employed to universally construct OIDs for all relationships so that it needs to take the predicate symbol as the first argument to distinguish between relationships with different predicates.

Case 4: If ω is a membership of the form $?0\#f$, $\mathrm{obj}_d(\phi, \omega)$ is a disjunction of k formulas $\mathrm{obj}_d(?0\#f(?X_1 \ldots ?X_{n_i}))$, where $n_1, \ldots, n_k$ are the k different arities of f in the KB:

$$\mathrm{Or}(\mathrm{obj}_d(?0\#f(?X_1 \ldots ?X_{n_i})) \ldots \mathrm{obj}_d(?0\#f(?X_1 \ldots ?X_{n_k})))$$

Case 5: If ω of the form $f(\ldots)$ has no OID but m tuples, $m > 1$, $\mathrm{obj}_d(\phi, \omega) = \mathrm{Exists} \ ?0 \ (\mathrm{obj}_d(?0\#f(\ldots)))$, where $?0$ is a fresh variable in the query.

Definition 8. *(Static/dynamic objectification) Let obj_s be a transformation chosen from $\{\mathrm{obj}_{s\neq}, \mathrm{obj}_{s=}\}$ and ϕ be a KB. The static/dynamic objectification $\mathrm{obj}_{s+d}(\phi, \omega)$ of an atom is $\mathrm{obj}_s(\phi, \omega)$ if $\mathrm{Pred}(\omega) \in \mathrm{PredKB}_{NR}(\phi)$, or $\mathrm{obj}_d(\phi, \omega)$ if $\mathrm{Pred}(\omega) \in \mathrm{PredKB}_R(\phi)$. obj_{s+d} is extended for the KB ϕ and other formulas, using Definition 3, if the following conditions are satisfied:*

(i) For every KB clause, universal variables occurring in its conclusion must also occur in its premise (e.g., prohibiting non-ground facts).

*(ii) There does not exist a predicate variable or an untyped (Top-typed) atom with
positional arguments in the premise of a rule or in the top-level query.*

In Example 1, conditions (i) and (ii) are satisfied so that static/dynamic
objectification can be applied. In the KB, the predicate _work is relational while
the others are non-relational. Thus, all oidless _work atoms are kept unchanged
while for the other oidless atoms OIDs are introduced via one of the two static methods. The query `?O#_work(?P ?C ?J)` is rewritten into the conjunction
`And(_work(?P ?C ?J) ?O=_oidcons(_work ?P ?C ?J))` according to Case 3 of
Definition 7.

In the following we will show the correctness of $\mathsf{obj}_{s=+d}$ and $\mathsf{obj}_{s\neq+d}$, which
correspond to the two obj_{s+d} versions using $\mathsf{obj}_{s=}$ and $\mathsf{obj}_{s\neq}$ for the static part.

Lemma 4. *Let ϕ be a KB and q be a query without _oidcons and let ϕ and q
comply to the above conditions (i) and (ii). Then $\mathsf{obj}_{s=+d}$ has the properties (1)
and (2) of Lemma 1 with respect to ϕ and q.*

Proof. (Sketch) If $\mathcal{I}$ is a counter-model for $\phi \models q$, we can define $\mathcal{I}'$ to be
modified from $\mathcal{I}$ by adding interpretation of _oidcons so that for every rela-
tionship ω where $\mathsf{Pred}(\omega) \in \mathsf{PredKB}_R(\phi)$, being of the form $\mathtt{f(t_1 \ldots t_n)}$,
$TVal_{\mathcal{I}'}(\_oidcons(\mathtt{f\ t_1 \ldots t_n})\#\mathtt{f(t_1 \ldots t_n)}) = t$. This is done by making
$\mathbf{I}(\_oidcons(\mathtt{f\ t_1 \ldots t_n}))$ the domain element that represents the OID of ω.
We can prove that $\mathcal{I}'$ fulfills the conditions (1.a) and (1.b) for every KB/query
atom ω and $\mathbf{I}_V \in \mathsf{M}(\mathsf{Var}(\omega), \mathcal{I}.\mathbf{D})$ performing a case-by-case analysis for ω. We
can also prove that $\mathsf{obj}_{s=+d}$ satisfies conditions (2) by choosing $\mathcal{I} = \mathcal{I}'$ and doing
a case-by-case analysis. □

Lemma 5. *Let ϕ be a KB and q be a query without _oidcons, let ϕ and q
comply to the above conditions (i) and (ii), and let $\phi' = \mathsf{obj}_{s=+d}(\phi)$ and $q' =
\mathsf{obj}_{s=+d}(\phi, q)$. Then ϕ' and q' fulfill the conditions of Lemma 2.*

Proof. (Sketch) If $\mathcal{I}''$ is a counter-model for $\phi' \models_{-o} q'$, then $\mathcal{I}'' \models_{-o} \phi'$ and $\mathcal{I}'' \not\models_{-o}
q'$. We modify $\mathcal{I}''$ into a semantic structure $\mathcal{I}'$ that guarantees the objectification
restriction using the following redefinitions:

(a) For every oidful atom ω' in ϕ' and q', we redefine $TVal_{\mathcal{I}'}(\omega)$ for its oidless
form ω to be the same as $TVal_{\mathcal{I}''}(\omega')$.
(b) For every oidless atom ω' in ϕ' and q' of the form $\mathtt{f(t_1 \ldots t_n)}$,
let $\mathsf{o}(\omega')$ be the virtual OID _oidcons($\mathtt{f\ t_1 \ldots t_n}$); we redefine
$TVal_{\mathcal{I}'}(\mathsf{o}(\omega')\#\mathtt{f(t_1 \ldots t_n)})$, $TVal_{\mathcal{I}'}(\mathsf{o}(\omega')\#\mathtt{f})$, and $TVal_{\mathcal{I}'}(\mathsf{o}(\omega')\#\mathtt{Top(t_1 \ldots t_n)})$
to be the same as $TVal_{\mathcal{I}''}(\omega')$. All other atoms that have a component $\mathsf{o}(\omega')$
are required to evaluate to false.

If $\mathsf{Pred}(\omega') \in \mathsf{PredKB}_{NR}(\phi')$, definition (a) applies, and the redefinition would
not affect the truth evaluation for formulas in ϕ' and q' since ω does not occur
in ϕ'.

If $\mathsf{Pred}(\omega') \in \mathsf{PredKB}_R(\phi')$, definition (b) applies, and the objectification
restriction is guaranteed. We will show that the redefinition would not affect the

truth evaluation for top-level formulas in ϕ' and q'. Since $\mathtt{f} \in \mathsf{PredKB}_R(\phi')$, it does not occur in an oidful or multi-tuple atom. So $\mathcal{I}'$ preserves the truth evaluation of all atoms with the predicate $\mathtt{f}$. We discuss different top-level formulas τ in ϕ':

- For τ being a ground fact, if $\mathsf{Pred}(\tau) \in \mathsf{PredKB}_R(\phi')$ then $TVal_{\mathcal{I}'}(\tau) = TVal_{\mathcal{I}''}(\tau) = \mathbf{t}$. Otherwise, its components cannot be interpreted to any $o(\omega')$ so $TVal_{\mathcal{I}'}(\tau) = TVal_{\mathcal{I}''}(\tau) = \mathbf{t}$ still holds.
- τ being a non-ground fact is disallowed by condition (i).
- For τ being a rule $\mathtt{Forall}\ ?X_1 \ldots ?X_n\ (\tau_1 :- \tau_2)$, for every $\boldsymbol{I}_V \in M(\{?X_1, \ldots, ?X_n\}, \mathcal{I}''.\boldsymbol{D})$, if for some i, $\boldsymbol{I}_V(?X_i)$ interprets to any $o(\omega')$, then it can be shown that $TVal_{\vee(\mathcal{I}', \boldsymbol{I}_V)}(\tau_2) = \mathbf{f}$ always holds based on Conditions (i) and (ii). So $TVal_{\vee(\mathcal{I}', \boldsymbol{I}_V)}(\tau_1 :- \tau_2) = \mathbf{t}$. Otherwise, $TVal_{\vee(\mathcal{I}', \boldsymbol{I}_V)}(\tau_1 :- \tau_2) = TVal_{\vee(\mathcal{I}'', \boldsymbol{I}_V)}(\tau_1 :- \tau_2) = \mathbf{t}$. Hence $TVal_{\mathcal{I}'}(\tau) = \mathbf{t}$.

$\mathcal{I}'$ can also be verified to conform to the subclass and slotribution/tupribution restrictions. So $\mathcal{I}'$ is a counter-model for $\phi' \models q'$, and the lemma holds. □

Theorem 3. $\mathsf{obj}_{s=+d}$ *is an objectification transformation with respect to a set of KBs Φ and a set of queries Q that do not use _oidcons and satisfy conditions (i) and (ii).*

Proof. By Lemmas 4, $\phi \models q$ iff $\mathsf{obj}_{s=+d}(\phi) \models \mathsf{obj}_{s=+d}(\phi, q)$. By Lemmas 5 and 5, $\mathsf{obj}_{s=+d}(\phi) \models \mathsf{obj}_{s=+d}(\phi, q)$ iff $\mathsf{obj}_{s=+d}(\phi) \models_{-o} \mathsf{obj}_{s=+d}(\phi, q)$. Hence $\phi \models q$ iff $\mathsf{obj}_{s=+d}(\phi) \models_{-o} \mathsf{obj}_{s=+d}(\phi, q)$ and the theorem is proved. □

Theorem 4. $\mathsf{obj}_{s\neq+d}$ *is an objectification transformation with respect to KBs Φ and queries Q that do not use constants _oidcons, _1, _2, ... and satisfy conditions (i) and (ii).*

Proof. (Sketch) This can be proved similarly to Theorem 2 by first proving a corresponding version of Lemma 3 for $\mathsf{obj}_{s\neq+d}$ and $\mathsf{obj}_{s=+d}$. □

4   Maximal Unnesting

In this section we first discuss the syntax and semantics of embedded psoa terms and then formally define the unnesting transformation of nested atomic formulas. Unnesting is maximal in the sense that it can extract atoms not only from other atoms but also from expressions, which may themselves be embedded at any level.

4.1   Syntax and Semantics of Embedded Psoa Terms

In PSOA RuleML, embedded psoa terms can be semantically classified into expressions or atoms, and syntactically classified into oidful or oidless terms. We will discuss different combinations of the two dimensions in the following.

Expressions. A psoa expression is a psoa term interpreted as a function application. Like in classical logic and logic programming languages, we require a (psoa) expression to be oidless, having the form $f(...)$, with f acting as a function, hence leading to an arbitrary value. The expression cannot be given an OID and have the form $o\#f(...)$, because this would make f act the class of o, hence lead to a truth value.

The semantics for expressions uses the I and I_{psoa} mappings defined in Sect. 3.1. However, because these expressions must be oidless, I_{psoa} interprets $I(f)$ into a semantic function that takes the empty set for oidless psoa terms, besides a bag of tuples and a bag of slots, and returns an arbitrary domain element. The lack of an OID for an expression also prevents its slotribution/tupribution, thus avoiding that its arbitrary value gets 'distributed over' the resulting conjunction of single-slot/tuple expressions or 'absorbed by' its truth value.[4]

Atoms. A psoa atom is a psoa term interpreted as a predicate application. Embedded atoms have been widely used in object-centered languages such as RDF, N3 [8], and Flora-2/F-logic [9] as a shorthand notation. An atomic formula containing an embedded atom can be unnested into a conjunction of trimmed formulas, which will be illustrated in Sect. 4.2.

In RDF and N3, embedded atoms are oidless and are 'objectified-while-embedded' using blank nodes, while in Flora-2/F-logic they are oidful. Because in PSOA/PS the set Const of constants contains both functions and predicates (cf. Sect. 2), an oidless embedded atom cannot be distinguished from an expression through the alphabet, hence we use the syntactic distinction between an embedded oidless term for an expression and an embedded oidful term for an atom. The distinction applies only to embedded psoa terms but not to top-level terms, where both oidful and oidless forms are interpreted as atoms. To indicate an RDF/N3-like embedded blank node, the atom can use an explicit OID, thus: (1) _#f(...) in ground facts, where '_' is the fresh-constant generator; (2) Exists ?O (... ?O#f(...) ...) in non-ground facts and rule conclusions; and (3) ?#f(...) in queries/rule premises, where '?' is the anonymous variable.

4.2   Unnesting Transformation for Embedded Psoa Atoms

In this section we will define the unnesting transformation Unnest(α) for a given atomic formula α, which is extended from the definition in [10]. Before performing Unnest(α), anonymous OID constants and variables in α need to be eliminated, because they cannot be used as co-references for the same constant/variable in two separate formulas. The elimination can be done by replacing '_' with a fresh constant and '?' with a fresh variable.

---

[4] Relfun's *valued conjunctions* of functional-logic expressions only retain the value of the right-most, '&'-prefixed conjunct: http://www.relfun.org.

In the following we give the definition of $\mathsf{Unnest}(\alpha)$ based on the recursive Atoms. Here, $\mathsf{Oid}(t)$ denotes the OID of an oidful term t. Also, $\mathsf{Parts}(t)$ denotes the set of top-level components of an atomic formula or a term t, including, optionally, $\mathsf{Oid}(t)$, its positional arguments, slot names, slot fillers, as well as its predicate/function.

$$\mathsf{Unnest}(\alpha) ::= \mathtt{And}(\sigma_1 \ldots \sigma_n) \quad \text{s.t. } \{\sigma_1, \ldots, \sigma_n\} = \cup_{t \in \mathsf{Parts}(\alpha)} \mathsf{Atoms}(t) \bigcup \{\mathsf{Trim}(\alpha)\}$$

$$\mathsf{Atoms}(t) ::= \begin{cases} \emptyset & t \text{ is a simple term} \\ \cup_{s \in \mathsf{Parts}(t)} \mathsf{Atoms}(s) & t \text{ is oidless (expression)} \\ \cup_{s \in \mathsf{Parts}(t)} \mathsf{Atoms}(s) \bigcup \{\mathsf{Trim}(t)\} & t \text{ is oidful (atom)} \end{cases}$$

$\mathsf{Trim}(t) ::= \text{Term/Formula obtained by replacing every } s \in \mathsf{Parts}(t) \text{ in } t \text{ with } \mathsf{Retain}(s)$

$$\mathsf{Retain}(t) ::= \begin{cases} t & t \text{ is a simple term} \\ \mathsf{Trim}(t) & t \text{ is oidless (expression)} \\ \mathsf{Retain}(\mathsf{Oid}(t)) & t \text{ is oidful (atom)} \end{cases}$$

$\mathsf{Unnest}(\alpha)$ is a conjunction of formulas σ_i without embedded atoms. Each σ_i is a trimmed version of the top-level formula α or of some embedded psoa atom. The set $\mathsf{Atoms}(t)$ contains each σ_i trimmed from an atom embedded in t or t itself. It is constructed by recursively traversing through each component $s \in \mathsf{Parts}(t)$, collecting $\mathsf{Atoms}(s)$ into $\mathsf{Atoms}(t)$, and then adding $\mathsf{Trim}(t)$ to $\mathsf{Atoms}(t)$ if t is oidful, which indicates that t is an atom. The transformation $\mathsf{Trim}(t)$ splits off all embedded atoms from t and leaves behind its 'ultimate' OID for each of them. It is constructed by replacing each $s \in \mathsf{Parts}(t)$ with $\mathsf{Retain}(s)$, which defines the left-behind term for each embedded term s.

In the following we use an example to explain the unnesting transformation. Let the input formula α be `o1#c(p->f(o2#c#d))`. Note that '#' is left-associative, hence the embedded atom `o2#c#d` is interpreted to have the OID `o2#c` and the class `d`. The conjuncts of $\mathsf{Unnest}(\alpha)$ are constructed as follows:

$$\{\sigma_1, \ldots, \sigma_n\} = \cup_{t \in \mathsf{Parts}(\alpha)} \mathsf{Atoms}(t) \bigcup \{\mathsf{Trim}(\alpha)\}$$

$$= (\mathsf{Atoms}(\mathtt{o1}) \cup \mathsf{Atoms}(\mathtt{c}) \cup \mathsf{Atoms}(\mathtt{p}) \cup \mathsf{Atoms}(\mathtt{f(o2\#c\#d)})) \bigcup \{\mathsf{Trim}(\alpha)\}$$

$$= \mathsf{Atoms}(\mathtt{f(o2\#c\#d)}) \bigcup \{\mathsf{Trim}(\alpha)\}$$

$$= (\mathsf{Atoms}(\mathtt{f}) \cup \mathsf{Atoms}(\mathtt{o2\#c\#d})) \bigcup \{\mathsf{Trim}(\alpha)\}$$

$$= \mathsf{Atoms}(\mathtt{o2\#c\#d}) \bigcup \{\mathsf{Trim}(\alpha)\}$$

$$= (\mathsf{Atoms}(\mathtt{o2\#c}) \cup \mathsf{Atoms}(\mathtt{d}) \cup \{\mathsf{Trim}(\mathtt{o2\#c\#d})\}) \bigcup \{\mathsf{Trim}(\alpha)\}$$

$$= \mathsf{Atoms}(\mathtt{o2\#c}) \bigcup \{\mathsf{Trim}(\mathtt{o2\#c\#d})\} \bigcup \{\mathsf{Trim}(\alpha)\}$$

$$= (\mathsf{Atoms}(\mathtt{o2}) \cup \mathsf{Atoms}(\mathtt{c}) \cup \{\mathsf{Trim}(\mathtt{o2\#c})\}) \bigcup \{\mathsf{Trim}(\mathtt{o2\#c\#d})\} \bigcup \{\mathsf{Trim}(\alpha)\}$$

$$= \{\mathsf{Trim}(\mathtt{o2\#c}), \mathsf{Trim}(\mathtt{o2\#c\#d}), \mathsf{Trim}(\alpha)\}$$

The Trim transformations work as follows, using the recursive Retain transformation:

$$\mathsf{Trim(o2\#c)} = \mathsf{Retain(o2)\#Retain(c)} = \mathsf{o2\#c}$$
$$\mathsf{Trim(o2\#c\#d)} = \mathsf{Retain(o2\#c)\#Retain(d)}$$
$$= \mathsf{Retain(Oid(o2\#c))\#d} = \mathsf{Retain(o2)\#d} = \mathsf{o2\#d}$$
$$\mathsf{Trim(\alpha)} = \mathsf{Trim(o1\#c(p\text{->}f(o2\#c\#d)))}$$
$$= \mathsf{Retain(o1)\#Retain(c)(Retain(p)\text{->}Retain(f(o2\#c\#d)))}$$
$$= \mathsf{o1\#c(p\text{->}Retain(f)(Retain(o2\#c\#d)))}$$
$$= \mathsf{o1\#c(p\text{->}f(Retain(Oid(o2\#c\#d))))}$$
$$= \mathsf{o1\#c(p\text{->}f(Retain(o2\#c)))}$$
$$= \mathsf{o1\#d(p\text{->}f(o2))}$$

Hence, the unnesting $\mathsf{Unnest(\alpha)}$ results in $\mathsf{And(o2\#c\ o2\#d\ o1\#c(p\text{->}f(o2)))}$.

The unnesting transformation has been implemented in the latest release of PSOATransRun 1.1 using a separate ANTLR tree walker.

5 Conclusions

This paper discusses advanced objectification and unnesting transformations for the PSOA RuleML language as well as a novel model-theoretic semantics.

The refined semantics is introduced to allow a direct interpretation of oidless psoa terms. It includes the objectification restriction to establish the equivalence between an oidless atom and its existentially objectified form. Based on the new semantics, a systematics of three objectification transformations is defined, whose correctness is proved. A novel static/dynamic objectification approach for oidless atoms is introduced, which is minimal in that it generates as few explicit OIDs as possible, instead constructing virtual OIDs as query variable bindings. This approach provides better efficiency for the PSOATransRun implementation by allowing direct use of the underlying Prolog engine.

The unnesting transformation is formalized to decompose nested atomic formulas into equivalent conjunctions before applying the model-theoretic semantics. Unnesting is maximal in that it can recursively extract oidful atoms – leaving behind their OIDs – not only from other atoms but also from expressions, which may themselves be embedded at any level. Since embedded oidless terms are interpreted as expressions (usable, e.g., as 'passive' data constructors), rather than as atoms to be 'objectified-while-embedded', for embedded atoms OIDs need to be explicitly provided to enable unnesting. The unnesting transformation has been implemented in PSOATransRun 1.1.

Future work includes exploring further optimizations for objectification and complementing the unnesting transformation with a flattening transformation for extracting 'active' expressions from both atoms and expressions. For this, PSOATransRun's flattening of expressions calling built-in functions can be easily transferred to expressions with equality-defined functions.

References

1. Kifer, M., Lausen, G., Wu, J.: Logical foundations of object-oriented and frame-based languages. J. ACM **42**(4), 741–843 (1995)
2. Yang, G., Kifer, M.: Reasoning about anonymous resources and meta statements on the Semantic Web. In: Spaccapietra, S., March, S., Aberer, K. (eds.) Journal on Data Semantics I. LNCS, vol. 2800, pp. 69–97. Springer, Heidelberg (2003)
3. Boley, H., Kifer, M.: RIF Basic Logic Dialect, 2nd edn. W3C Recommendation. http://www.w3.org/TR/rif-bld
4. Boley, H.: A RIF-Style semantics for RuleML-integrated positional-slotted, object-applicative rules. In: Bassiliades, N., Governatori, G., Paschke, A. (eds.) RuleML 2011 - Europe. LNCS, vol. 6826, pp. 194–211. Springer, Heidelberg (2011)
5. Boley, H.: PSOA RuleML: Integrated object-relational data and rules. In: Faber, W., Paschke, A. (eds.) Reasoning Web 2015. LNCS, vol. 9203, pp. 114–150. Springer, Heidelberg (2015)
6. Zou, G., Boley, H.: PSOA2Prolog: Object-relational rule interoperation and implementation by translation from PSOA RuleML to ISO prolog. In: Bassiliades, N., Gottlob, G., Sadri, F., Paschke, A., Roman, D. (eds.) RuleML 2015. LNCS, vol. 9202, pp. 176–192. Springer, Heidelberg (2015)
7. Boley, H.: Integrating positional and slotted knowledge on the Semantic Web. J. Emerg. Technol. Web Intell. **4**(2), 343–353 (2010)
8. Berners-Lee, T., Connolly, D., Kagal, L., Scharf, Y., Hendler, J.: N3Logic: A logical framework for the World Wide Web. Theor. Pract. Logic Program. (TPLP) **8**(3), 249–269 (2008)
9. Kifer, M., Yang, G., Wan, H., Zhao, C.: $\mathcal{E}RGO^{Lite}$ (a.k.a.$\mathcal{F}$lora-2): User's Manual, v1.1 (2015). http://flora.sourceforge.net/docs/floraManual.pdf
10. Boley, H., Kifer, M.: RIF Basic Logic Dialect (Working Draft) W3C Working Draft. https://www.w3.org/TR/2007/WD-rif-bld-20071030/

Smart Contracts, Blockchain and Rules

Setting Standards for Altering
and Undoing Smart Contracts

Bill Marino[1](✉) and Ari Juels[2]

[1] Cornell Tech, New York, USA
wlm67@cornell.edu
[2] Cornell Tech (Jacobs Institute), New York, USA
juels@cornell.edu

Abstract. Often, we wish to let parties alter or undo a contract that has been made. Toward this end, contract law has developed a set of traditional tools for altering and undoing contracts. Unfortunately, these tools often fail when applied to smart contracts. It is therefore necessary to define a new set of standards for the altering and undoing of smart contracts. These standards might ensure that the tools we use to alter and undo smart contracts achieve their original (contract law) goals when applied to this new technology. This paper develops such a set of standards and, then, to prove their worth as a framework, applies to them to an existing smart contract platform (Ethereum).

Keywords: Smart contracts · Contract law · Blockchain · Ethereum

1 Introduction

If a covenant be made wherein neither of the parties perform presently, but trust one another, in the condition of mere nature ... upon any reasonable suspicion, it is void: but if there be a common power set over them both, with right and force sufficient to compel performance, it is not void.

— Thomas Hobbes, *Leviathan* (1651)

The purpose of contracts is to solve a game-theoretic problem: it is to our mutual benefit to cooperate in some way. But if we cooperate, then one of us can do even better by defecting.

— sirclueless [psued.], comment on *What is Ethereum?*, Hacker News (2015)

Tyrell Corporation, manufacturer of replicant humans in Philip K. Dick's *Do Androids Dream of Electric Sheep?*, famously touted their wares as "more human than human". Riffing on that motto, we might say that smart contracts are able to beat analog contracts at their own game and are therefore "more contract than contract".

This is because the "fundamental function of contract law (and recognized as such at least since Hobbes's day) is to deter people from behaving opportunistically toward their contracting parties" [1]. And that is something a smart contract — at least, in its paradigmatic form — does better than any analog contract ever could. In fact, a

© Springer International Publishing Switzerland 2016
J.J. Alferes et al. (Eds.): RuleML 2016, LNCS 9718, pp. 151–166, 2016.
DOI: 10.1007/978-3-319-42019-6_10

well-designed smart contract drives the probability of opportunistic breach toward zero as such behavior becomes impossible or, at least, "expensive (if desired, sometimes prohibitively so) for the breacher" [2].

Mind you, this feat is not possible for a contract that is merely "a set of promises, specified in digital form" [2] — i.e., a digital contract. Breaching a contract recorded in binary is no harder than breaching one recorded in ink. What lets smart contracts rise above their brethren is that they additionally include "protocols within which the parties perform on ... promises" [2]. These protocols beget smart contracts' hallmark ability to "automatically enforce" [2] themselves, a quality that, in turn, eliminates the need for "trusted intermediaries" [3] and, of course, court enforcement [4].

Smart contracts' performance protocols take many forms, as there are countless ways to embed promises in technology so as to make breach infeasible or unduly expensive. They include the controller and motors of the "humble vending machine" [5], embedding, as they do, the promise of the vendor to deliver a Mr. Pibb to anyone inserting a dollar. They include the blockchain-dwelling bytecode of an evergreen loan contract on Ethereum, embedding, as it does, a creditor's promise to issue a new cryptocurrency loan to the debtor who repays a prior one [6].

Observe what these examples share: security. When promises are embedded in technology, one (perhaps the only) way to breach them is to disrupt that technology. Most smart contracts include security measures aimed at deterring this type of breach. To breach the vending machine's smart contract, you must break into its lockbox. To breach the blockchain loan contract, you must compromise the blockchain's consensus protocol. In this manner, security mechanisms form the archstone in the promise of smart contracts to transcend analog contracts. The problem, however, is that securing contracts against disruption for the purpose of breach often means securing them against disruption of any sort. And that is not always a desirable result.

The fact is, as "performance unfolds, circumstances change, often unforeseeably" [7]. External events like price shifts may degrade a contract's value in the eyes of the parties. It may come to light that there is a typo in the contract, or that one party was defrauded during its creation. When such events arise, the parties — and sometimes courts and or even the public — may find themselves wanting the contract to be performed differently (or not at all). This is why contract law has a well-honed set of tools for undoing and altering contracts, including termination and rescission (for undoing contracts) as well as modification and reformation (for altering contracts).

Unfortunately, these traditional tools often fail when applied to smart contracts. True, they successfully undo the legal agreement that a smart contract manifests. If these tools are exercised, no court will enforce the agreement. The problem, of course, is that technology still might. What is needed, then, is to define new standards for these tools as applied to smart contracts, making sure they remain robust for this new medium. That is the goal of this paper.

2 Termination and Rescission of Smart Contracts

2.1 Termination and Rescission Generally

"Rescission", the 1912 edition of *Black's Law Dictionary* tells us, "is where a contract is canceled, annulled, or abrogated by the parties, or one of them" [8]. Importantly, this definition turns out to be somewhat half-baked, with another corner of Henry Campbell Black's own oeuvre — 1916's *A Treatise On the Rescission of Contracts and Cancellation of Written Instruments* — cautioning that "[t]o rescind a contract is not merely to terminate it" and "release the parties from further obligation" but to "restore the parties to the relative positions which they would have occupied if no such contract had ever been made" [9]. After highlighting this restorative aspect of rescission, the latter text outlines three situations in which rescission may be implemented. These, like the definition that precedes them, have endured:

First, rescission may be implemented when "a right to take this action [is] reserved to either or both of the parties in the contract itself [9]. If reserved, such a right "may then be exercised without other grounds for it than the mere will of the party rescinding" [9]. Today, this is called "termination by right" ("Termination by Right").

Second, there may be a "rescission by the mutual agreement of the parties to the contract" [9]. This is, "in effect the discharge of both parties from the legal obligations admittedly existing thereunder, by a subsequent agreement made before the complete performance of the original contract" [9]. In modern times, this is called "mutual rescission" or "rescission by agreement" ("Rescission by Agreement").

Third, "one of the parties may declare a rescission of the contract, without the constant of the other … if a legally sufficient ground therefor exists, such, for instance, as fraud, false representations, [unilateral] mistake, duress, or infancy" [9]. The rescinding party may then ask a court to "set aside" the contract "by the equity decree" [10]. The modern label for this is simply "rescission" ("Rescission by Court").

Let us examine each of these three versions of rescission as applied to smart contracts, sketching new standards for each as we proceed:

2.2 Termination by Right

At law, Termination by Right is implemented passively: it bars future breach of contract actions [11]. For smart contracts, unfortunately, this approach often fails. If a smart contract is terminated at law, and nothing more is done, the smart contract will still automatically perform ("auto-perform") the parties' promises (as it is designed to do), negating the termination. Accordingly, the first standard we will set for smart contract Termination by Right is that, when the right is exercised, auto-performance indeed ceases. To permit otherwise means the termination is an empty gesture.

A second standard is this: the smart contract must ensure that Termination by Right is implemented if and only if the party holding the right exercises it. No other party may initiate termination. To permit otherwise, again, undermines the goals of contract law by rewarding opportunistic breach by non-right holding parties.

A third standard is this: echoing Black's emphasis on restoration, before implementing a Termination by Right, the smart contract's machinery must ensure that all partial performance that has occurred is compensated. For example, partial payments sent by either party must be returned. If this is not done, then parties will resort to courts to enforce restitution of that partial performance, undoing one of the primary efficiency benefits of smart contracts.

A fourth standard is this: the smart contract's machinery must ensure that all conditions placed on the termination right are met before termination is implemented. For example, if payment of a termination fee is a condition of the right, the contract must pay such a fee to the appropriate party (or otherwise ensure that it is paid) before initiating termination. To permit otherwise undermines the aim of contract law by rewarding opportunistic breach by the right holder. To summarize:

- Smart contract Termination by Right halts all auto-performance;
- Smart contract Termination by Right is enabled if and only if the party holding that right exercises it;
- Smart contract Termination by Right automatically compensates partial performance;
- Smart contract Termination by Right is enabled if and only if any termination conditions are satisfied.

2.3   Rescission by Agreement

Rescission, like termination, is implemented passively at law: when there has been a valid rescission, there is "no longer a cause of action for breach" [12]. Again, for smart contracts, this passive approach fails. Accordingly, our first standard for smart contract Rescission by Agreement is the same as our first standard for smart contract Termination by Right: automated performance must be halted.

Our second stand is unique to Rescission by Agreement: unlike with Termination by Right, the power to rescind a smart contract by mutual agreement may not lie with one party. An agreement to rescind, like the initial contract, takes the "form of an offer by one and an acceptance by the other" [13]. So this brand of smart contract rescission must be conditioned, by the smart contract, on mutual agreement: an offer to rescind by one party and acceptance of that offer by all other parties. To allow otherwise contravenes the goals of contract law by encouraging opportunistic breach.

Our final standard for smart contract rescission is this: smart contract Rescission by Agreement, like smart contract Termination by Right, should include restoration of any partial performance. To summarize:

- Smart contract Rescission by Agreement halts all auto-performance;
- Smart contract Rescission by Agreement is enabled and if all parties mutually agree to it;
- Smart contract Rescission by Agreement automatically compensates partial performance.

2.4   Rescission by Court

Of the grounds for rescission, unilateral mistake (when one party *thinks* the smart contract does one thing, while the other party *knows* it does another) is of particular interest to smart contracts. Due to the introduction of code to the agreement-making process, unilateral mistake may be a greater danger than ever before. Few feel confident reading "legalese"; even fewer feel confident reading code.

In light of this, our first standard is a familiar one: when there is a unilateral mistake — or when any of the other bases for Rescission by Court exist — and a court orders a smart contract rescinded, auto-performance must cease.

Our second standard is more unique: the power to order Rescission by Court may only lie with and be exercised by the appropriate court. Neither party may have the power to jeopardize that right. Naturally, that would undermine the goals of contract law (by encouraging opportunistic breach).

Our third demand is this: upon rescission by a court, restoration must occur, just as it would in the case of Termination by Right or Rescission by Agreement. If partial performance is not automatically compensated, parties may petition the court to enforce restitution of that performance, erasing one of the primary efficiency benefits of smart contracts. To summarize:

- Smart contract Rescission by Court halts all auto-performance;
- Smart contract Rescission by Court is enabled if and only if triggered by an appropriate court;
- Smart contract Rescission by Court automatically compensates partial performance.

3   Modification and Reformation of Smart Contracts

3.1   Modification and Reformation of Smart Contracts

Sometimes, we do not wish to wholly discard an agreement, but merely wish to alter *some* of its terms. Such alteration provides an "efficient mechanism for changing agreements in response to altered circumstances ... saving a deal that would otherwise have ended in an inefficient breach" [14]. Like the undoing of a contract, the alteration of a contracts comes in three flavors:

The first is where "[u]nilateral-modification clauses give one party the unfettered right to amend … the underlying contract, often with neither notice to, nor consent from, the other party [15]. This is called "modification by right" ("Modification by Right"). (Note that some courts will uphold this right, while others will not [16]).

Second, contracting parties have a well-established right "to modify their original contract by mutual agreement" [17]. Such a modification is itself a contract [18] and must be based on mutual assent and supported by its own consideration [19]. This is referred to as "modification by agreement" ("Modification by Agreement").

Third, a court may, in some cases, order a modification of a contract even over the objections of one or more parties. It may do so based on three grounds: mistakes mutual to all parties [20], fraud [21], and "unconscionable" terms — i.e., terms born out of "an absence of meaningful choice" for one party and "unreasonably favorable to the other" [22]. This is type of modification is called "reformation" ("Reformation").

3.2 Modification by Right

If undoing a smart contract calls for an axe — a blanket action turning the entire contract off all at once — modifying it calls for a scalpel. Specifically, modification must halt auto-performance of only the terms that are intended to be modified while simultaneously initiating auto-performance of the new versions intended to replace them.

With that said, our first standard is this: upon Modification by Right of a smart contract term, auto-performance of that term's original iteration must cease, while auto-performance of its new iteration must, concurrently, initialize.

Our second standard is a familiar one: modification of a term can be initiated if and only if a party holding the right to modify that term wills it.

Our third standard is also a familiar one: if the modification is conditioned on the occurrence of events, such as the payment of a modification fee, those events must occur before modification can take place.

Our final standard is a twist on a standard previously forth for the ways of undoing smart contracts: a smart contract must automatically compensate for any partial performance that has occurred and which is tied to obligations embedded in the terms being removed during modification. (It need not compensate for partial performance of any terms that, though modified, remain active; those terms will be compensated through the performance of the contract.) To summarize:

- Smart contract Modification by Right simultaneously halts auto-performance of original, modified terms and instantiate auto-performance of new ones;
- Smart contract Modification by Right is enabled if and only if the party holding the right exercises it;

- Smart contract Modification by Right automatically compensates partial performance *of deleted terms*;
- Smart contract Modification by Right is enabled if and only if any modification conditions are satisfied.

3.3 Modification by Agreement

The issues faced when implementing Modification by Agreement resemble those faced during Modification by Right. So our standards are similar. The key difference is that a Modification by Agreement must be approved by all parties. To summarize:

- Smart contract Modification by Agreement simultaneously halts auto-performance of original, modified terms and instantiate auto-performance of new ones;
- Smart contract Modification by Agreement is enabled if and only if all parties mutually agree to it;
- Smart contract Modification by Agreement automatically compensates partial performance *of deleted terms*.

3.4 Reformation

Some grounds for reformation are of special interest to smart contracts. That includes mutual mistake, which covers the so-called "scrivener's error", an "accidental deviation from the parties' agreement" made while recording the agreement in writing [19]. In smart contracts, the risk of this error is high because of, again, the introduction of code to contracting. Fraud and unconscionability are high risks for the same reason: code-savvy parties are in a position to defraud or force unconscionable terms on code-naive parties. For these reasons, Reformation of smart contracts is likely to occur.

Our first standard for Reformation is familiar: it must halt auto-performance of the original versions of modified terms and instantiates auto-performance of the new version of modified terms.

Second, the power to reform the contract, like the power for Rescission by Court, must lie strictly with the court. And our third standard is a familiar one as well: once triggered, the Reformation must compensate for the partial performance of any terms that are being deleted. To summarize:

- Smart contract Reformation simultaneously halts auto-performance of original, reformed terms and instantiate auto-performance of new ones;
- Smart contract Reformation is enabled if and only if triggered by an appropriate court;
- Smart contract Reformation automatically compensates partial performance *of deleted terms*.

4 Testing Our New Standards on Ethereum

4.1 Ethereum Generally

Let's put our new standards for altering and undoing smart contracts to the test on an existing smart contract platform: Ethereum. Can smart contract alteration and undoing on this platform meet our standards? How?

Ethereum, "arguably the most ambitious crypto-ledger project," [25] is built on a blockchain. Ethereum blockchain stores both transaction data (concerning its native cryptocurrency, Ether) and the code of computer programs called, for better or for worse [26], "contracts." The code for these contracts is injected onto the blockchain when a personal account sends contract code in the data field of an unaddressed transaction. After this, the contract is added to a block and assigned an address, at which point its code becomes immutable [27]. Importantly, what is not immutable is the contract's state. Specifically, the nodes in the Ethereum network, besides being able to add transactions to the ledger, also run contract code and maintain and adjust contract states in a virtual machine they all host, the Ethereum Virtual Machine.

Contracts on Ethereum can hold balances of Ether. Like objects in object oriented programming, they can also have variables and functions that, if called, adjust those variables or do other nifty things, like send Ether to other contracts or accounts on Ethereum. Note that these functions cannot "wake" on their own and, in order to execute, must be called (by parties to the contract, third parties, or other contracts).

One of Ethereum's high level languages, Solidity, is a cross "between JavaScript and C++ but with a number of syntactic additions to make it suitable for writing contracts within Ethereum" [28] and is what we will use to prototype below.

4.2 Undoing Contracts on Ethereum

There are at least two ways to *undo* contracts (i.e., implement Termination by Right, Rescission by Agreement, or Rescission by Court) on Ethereum. The first, the global selfdestruct function, is easy to implement and effective. That said, it is also a blunt instrument, lacking the nuance of the second way, which is to turn the entire contract "off" at the function level using a combination of Solidity's modifiers and enums.

Undoing Contracts on Ethereum Using Selfdestruct. As stated, Ethereum contract code, once on the blockchain, cannot be altered. But it can be deleted. The global selfdestruct function, if called from inside a contract, sends the contract's Ether balance to the address this function takes as its sole argument, then deletes the contract's code from the blockchain going forward. This means the contract's functions cannot be called. Since Ethereum contract functions cannot self-wake, this halts auto-performance and thus satisfies the first (shared) standard we set for smart contract Termination by Right, Rescission by Agreement, and Rescission by Court.

It is also easy, on Ethereum, to satisfy the second (shared) standard for each of these tools by granting the power to selfdestruct a contract only to those entities that should have it. If that is a single party (which is the case for Termination by Right and Rescission by Court), this can be done by wrapping selfdestruct function inside a conditional statement that checks if the address calling it belongs to the rightful exerciser:

```
function terminate() {
if (partyWithTerminationRightOrCourt == msg.sender) {
selfdestruct( partyReceivingContractBalance ); }}
```

If multiple parties must approve the undoing, as in Rescission by Agreement, there are a few ways to achieve this. One is to use Solidity's modifiers and enums (user defined types) to create states that log the consent of parties and then to throw exceptions when selfdestruct is called and those states do not reflect the necessary values:

```
contract Undoable {
address partyWithTerminationRight;
address partyWithoutTerminationRight;

enum State {RescissionByAgreementSuggested}
State public state;

modifier inState(State _state) {
if (state != _state) throw;
    _ }

function suggestRescissionByAgreement() {
   if ( partyWithoutTerminationRight == msg.sender) {
state = State.RescissionByAgreementSuggested; }}

function approveRescissionByAgreement()
inState(State.RescissionByAgreementSuggested) {
   if (partyWithTerminationRight == msg.sender) {
selfdestruct(partyWithoutTerminationRight); }}}
```

Next is the third standard, shared by each of these tools, that demands that any partial performance that has occurred be compensated automatically before the contract is undone. With selfdestruct, this is easy to engineer. All that is needed is a variable that tracks the level of performance, a function that lets one party suggest a new value for that variable, and a second function that lets the counterparty approve the new value. When the contract is undone, the latest value for the variable will be paid out.

Termination by Right is the only version of contract undoing with a fourth standard. It comes in many shapes, but we can address the simplest here. This is where the right is conditioned on the payment of a termination fee. To satisfy this standard, we can use a much more streamlined version of this approach used to satisfy the third standard.

Here is contract code that ties together all of the above, satisfying the conditions for our three methods of undoing contracts by creating functions for Termination by Right, Rescission by Agreement, and Rescission by Court, giving the power over those functions to the right parties, and paying out termination and partial performance fees when required. To simplify things, let us assume partial performance is only possible for one party (e.g., it is a labor contract that the hirer has endowed with the full payment, such that partial performance is only an issue for the laborer):

```
contract Undoable {
address partyWithTerminationRight;
address partyWithoutTerminationRight;
address partialPerformanceApprover;
address court;
uint terminationFee;
uint suggestedPartialPerformanceCompensation;

enum State {RescissionByAgreementSuggested,
PartialPerformanceCompensationSuggested,
PartialPerformanceCompensationApproved}
State public state;

modifier inState(State _state) {
if (state != _state) throw;
    _ }

function terminateOrRescind(uint _terminationFee, address
_partyWithTerminationRight, address
_partyWithoutTerminationRight, address _court, address
_partialPerformanceApprover) {
terminationFee = _terminationFee;
partyWithTerminationRight = _partyWithTerminationRight;
partyWithoutTerminationRight =
_partyWithoutTerminationRight;
partialPerformanceApprover = _partialPerformanceApprover;
court = _court;}

function suggestPartialPerformanceCompensation(uint
_suggestedPartialPerformanceCompensation) {
if ( partyWithoutTerminationRight == msg.sender) {
suggestedPartialPerformanceCompensation =
_suggestedPartialPerformanceCompensation;
state = State.PartialPerformanceCompensationSuggested;}}

function approvePartialPerformanceCompensation()
inState( State.PartialPerformanceCompensationSuggested){
if (partyWithTerminationRight == msg.sender) {
state = State.PartialPerformanceCompensationApproved ;}}
```

```
function terminate()
inState(State.PartialPerformanceCompensationApproved){
if (partyWithTerminationRight == msg.sender) {
    partyWithoutTerminationRight.send(terminationFee);
    partyWithoutTerminationRight.send(
suggestedPartialPerformanceCompensation);
selfdestruct(partyWithoutTerminationRight);}}

function rescindByCourt()
inState(State.PartialPerformanceCompensationApproved){
if (court == msg.sender) {
    partyWithoutTerminationRight.send(
suggestedPartialPerformanceCompensation);
selfdestruct(partyWithoutTerminationRight); }}

function suggestRescissionByAgreement()
inState(State.PartialPerformanceCompensationApproved){
if (partyWithoutTerminationRight == msg.sender) {
state = State.RescissionByAgreementSuggested; }}

function approveRescissionByAgreement()
inState(State.RescissionByAgreementSuggested){
if (partyWithTerminationRight == msg.sender) {
    partyWithoutTerminationRight.send(
    suggestedPartialPerformanceCompensation);
selfdestruct(partyWithoutTerminationRight); }}}
```

While this code does not cover edge cases (such as the situation where conditions placed upon Termination by Right represent the occurrence of real world events), we have shown that our standards can reasonably be applied — and to some extent, satisifed — using one of the methods for undoing smart contracts (selfdestruct) on Ethereum. Now let us repeat the process for a second (and arguably superior) method for undoing smart contracts on the same platform:

Undoing Contracts on Ethereum Using Modifiers and Enums. The selfdestruct function is a convenient "one-stop" solution for undoing contracts. But Solidity's modifiers and enums are a more nuanced tool for this — one that, as we will see later, meshes well with existing tools for altering contracts.

We used modifiers and enums above, in conjunction with selfdestruct. We can extend the same strategy to implement Termination by Right, Rescission by Agreement, and Rescission by Court without selfdestruct. Specifically, we can create two states: one for a contract that has been undone — let's call it ContractUndone — and one for a contract that is not undone — let's call it ContractNotUndone. Upon instantiation, we can set the state as ContractNotUndone. Then, we can create a function that enables the state to be toggled to ContractUndone (but not toggled in the other direction). Lastly, we can can cause all other functions to throw if the ContractUndone state exists. This will halt performance of the contract, satisfying the first standard for our three methods of undoing contracts. Then we can also satisfy the other standards for undoing smart contracts in the same ways we set forth above for selfdestruct.

4.3   Modifying Contracts on Ethereum

Modifying contracts (i.e., implementing Modification by Right, Modification by Agreement, and Reformation) on Ethereum is more nuanced than undoing contracts on Ethereum. Roughly speaking, there are three ways to achieve modification on Ethereum: modification of *variable*-captured terms, deletion of *function*-captured terms, and addition or alteration of *function*-captured terms.

Modifying Variable-Captured Terms. Contract terms like price (or labor hours, etc.) will often be captured as variables in smart contract code. When this is the case, modifying these terms is simple as assigning a new value to the variable using a set-type function. If such a function exists, this method of modification satisfies the first (shared) standard of our three flavors of modifying contracts: it halts performance of the old term and instantiates performance of the new one. If the set function is narrowly tailored to this variable, then this method of modification also satisfies the second standard of Termination by Right: that the scope must be hard-coded into the smart contract during formation. Satisfying the remaining standards for Modification by Right, Modification by Agreement, and Reformation can all be accomplished in much the same way there were accomplished above, for Termination by Right, Rescission by Agreement, and Rescission by Court.

Modifying Function-Captured Terms. Sometimes, contract terms are captured by functions and not variables. In that case, modification means deleting, adding, or swapping the relevant function(s). This must be handled differently than variable-level modification because, while variables can be changed freely, the functions in an Ethereum contract code are immutable once it is issued to the blockchain.

Deleting Function-Captured Terms. Of the types of function-level changes, the easiest to implement is deletion: i.e., subtraction of terms. For that, we can recycle the approach taken for Termination by Right, Rescission by Agreement, and Rescission by

Court: using modifiers and enums to create and toggle states, then causing functions to throw exceptions if the states do not exist. Using this method, we can build functions that can be turned off, on demand, if the parties agree to a deletion-style modification. This will halt performance much as it did above, satisfying the first standard for our three ways of undoing a contract. Beyond that, the remaining standards can be satisfied much as they were above for variable-captured functions.

Adding or Modifying Function-Captured Terms. Adding wholly new functions and replacing existing functions is accomplished in a similar fashion. The difference between the two that, if a function is being replaced, the initial version of it must also be turned off. (This can be accomplished using the methods described above for deletion of functions.) On Ethereum, there are at least two ways to add or swap functions in a contract. Both demand a bit of prognostication.

The first is to use modifiers and enums can be used to turn functions "off", they can be used to turn functions "on". Of course, in order to be turned on, those functions must be in the contract to begin with. Since contract code is immutable after initialization, this means functions that the parties suspect they may later wish to turn "on" during a modification must be included in the initial contract *in an "off" state*. That said, if this can be accomplished, then the standards for all three flavors of contract modification can be satisfied much as they would be for variable-captured functions.

A second way to add or modify function-captured terms — and, seemingly, the one endorsed by Ethereum's architects [6] — is to create, at the outset, satellite contracts that capture certain function-terms. The addresses of these satellite contracts can be stored in address variables or an arrays of address variables in the central contract. Using these pointers, the central contract can to call out to the satellite contracts when it needs to reference certain terms. If this is architected properly, modifying function-terms is as simply as changing the pointers.

As an example, suppose the parties wish to build flexibility into their price term. They can initialize a central contract with pointers to a satellite price calculation contract. Changing the price calculation method (e.g., swapping price datafeeds or formulas) is as simple as changing the pointers in the central contract. The code for such a contract might look like the code below, which contains a pair of functions that let one party suggest a new satellite contract and let the other approve the suggestion before making the change (note that, in order to call an outside contract's functions on Ethereum, the code for the outside contract must appear in the code for your present contract):

```
contract Satellite {
function returnPrice() returns (uint _price){
//calculate price
}}
contract Modifiable {
uint price;
address party1;
address party2;
address satelliteAddress;
address suggestedSatelliteAddress;

function setPrice(){
Satellite m = Satellite(satelliteAddress);
price = m.returnPrice();}

enum State {ModificationSuggested,ModificationApproved}
State public state;

modifier inState(State _state) {
if (state != _state) throw;
    _}

function suggestModification(address
_suggestedSatelliteAddress){
if (party1 ==  msg.sender){
suggestedSatelliteAddress = _suggestedSatelliteAddress;
state = State.ModificationSuggested;}}

function approveModification()
inState(State.ModificationSuggested){
if (party2 == msg.sender){
satelliteAddress = suggestedSatelliteAddress;}}}
```

As is, this contract satisfies the first standard for all three flavors of modifying contracts; by de-linking the original satellite contract and linking the new one, it simultaneously halts auto-performance of the original versions of modified terms and instantiates auto-performance of the new versions. If it contains code to ensures that the party initiating the pointer swap is the correct one and additionally contains code that tracks and compensates partial performance in the event of a modification, then it can satisfy the second and third conditions of all three flavors of modification as well. Finally, it can satisfy the fourth condition of Modification by Right by additionally including code that prohibits modification unless certain conditions have been met.

5 Conclusion and Future Work

Contract law has developed a well-honed and necessary set of tools for altering and undoing contracts. Unfortunately, these tools often fail when applied to smart contracts. It is therefore crucial to define a new set of standards against which we can create a similar set of tools for altering and undoing smart contracts. These standards should be drawn from the principals of contract law but work for the new technology. We have sketched such standards. Further, by applying these standards to the present methods for altering and undoing smart contracts on Ethereum, we have proven that there is value to such a framework. Let the smart contract community take note. It is essential that the architects of this new technology, like the architects of contracts, create viable ways to alter and undo them.

References

1. Posner, R.: Economic Analysis of Law. Little Brown and Co., Boston (1986)
2. Szabo, N.: Smart Contracts: Building Blocks for Digital Markets (1996)
3. Juels, A., Kosba, A., Shi, E.: The Ring of Gyges: Investigating the Future of Criminal Smart Contracts (2015)
4. Szabo, N.: Smart Contracts (1994)
5. Szabo, N.: The Idea of Smart Contracts (1997)
6. Buterin, V.: Ethereum White Paper (2014)
7. Posner, R.: Let us never blame a contract breaker. Mich. Law Rev. **107**, 1360 (2009)
8. Black, H.C.: Black's Law Dictionary, p. 1025 (1910)
9. Black, H.C.: A Treatise on the Rescission of Contracts and Cancellation of Written Instruments, vol. 1 (1916)
10. Koford, H.S.: Recessions at law and in equity. Calif. Law Rev. **36**, 608 (1948)
11. Atlas Trucking v. City of Lompoc, S224878, 2015 Cal. LEXIS 2165 (Sup. Ct. Cal., 15 April 2015)
12. Great American Ins. v. General Builders, 934 p. 2d 257, 262 n. 6 (Nev. 1997)
13. Corbin, A.L.: Corbin on Contracts, vol. 5A (1964)
14. Russell, I.S.: Reinventing the deal: a sequential approach to analyzing claims for enforcement of modified sales contracts. Fla. Law Rev. **53**, 51 (2001)
15. DeMichele, M.L., Bales, R.A.: Unilateral-modification provisions in employment arbitration agreements. Hofstra Employ. Law J. **24**, 64 (2006)
16. Carey v. 24 Hour Fitness, USA, Inc., 669 F.3d 202 (5th Cir. 2012)
17. Christine, C.: Contracts as bilateral commitments: a new perspective on contract modification. J. Legal Stud. **26**, 204 (1997)
18. Hillman, R.A.: A study of uniform commercial code methodology: contract modification under article two. N. C. Law Rev. **59**, 339 (1981)
19. Williston, S., Lord, R.: Williston on Contracts (1992)
20. Moffett, Hodgkins & Clarke Co. v. Rochester, 178 U.S. 373, 385 (1900)
21. Link v. Kroenke, 909 S.W.2d 740, 745 (Mo. App. W.D. 1995)
22. Williams v. Walker-Thomas Furniture Co., 350 F.2d 445, 449 (D.C. Cir. 1965)
23. The Great Chain of Being Sure About Things. The Economist (2015)

166   B. Marino and A. Juels

24. Marino, B.: https://medium.com/@ConsenSys/unpacking-the-term-smart-contract-e63238f7db65
25. Delmolino, K., Arnett, M., Kosba, A., Miller, A., Shi, E.: Step by Step Towards Creating a Safe Smart Contract: Lessons and Insights from a Cryptocurrency Lab (2015)
26. Wood, G.: https://github.com/ethereum/wiki/wiki/Solidity,-Docs-and-ABI

Evaluation of Logic-Based Smart Contracts for Blockchain Systems

Florian Idelberger[1]([✉]), Guido Governatori[2]([✉]),
Régis Riveret[2]([✉]), and Giovanni Sartor[1]([✉])

[1] European University Institute, Fiesole, Italy
{florian.idelberger,Giovanni.Sartor}@eui.eu
[2] Data61 - CSIRO - NICTA, Brisbane, Australia
{guido.governatori,regis.riveret}@data61.csiro.au

Abstract. While procedural languages are commonly used to program smart contracts in blockchain systems, logic-based languages may be interesting alternatives. In this paper, we inspect what are the possible legal and technical (dis)advantages of logic-based smart contracts in light of common activities featuring ordinary contracts, then we provide insights on how to use such logic-based smart contracts in combination with blockchain systems. These insights lead us to emphasize a fundamental challenge - algorithms for logic approaches have to be efficient, but they also need to be literally cheap as measured within the environment where they are deployed and according to its economic rules. We illustrate this with different algorithms from defeasible logic-based frameworks.

Keywords: Smart contract · Blockchain · Programming paradigm · Logic

1 Introduction

A smart contract is a computer program that both expresses the contents of a contractual agreement and operates the implementation of that content, on the basis of triggers provided by the users or extracted from the environment. Smart contracts are currently promoted as means to leverage efficiency, security and impartiality in the execution of an agreement, thereby reducing the costs in implementing contracts and increasing trust between parties.

While imperative languages, especially procedural languages, are mostly used to code smart contracts in current blockchain platforms, declarative languages for such contracts, and in particular logic-based rule languages, should also be considered to better represent and reason upon them, towards a concept that we may call *declarative smart contracts*, in particular the concept of *logic-based smart contracts*.

Combinations of logic frameworks and blockchain systems may lead to smart contracts that are easier to work with for jurists and developers and have technical advantages over procedural coding of the contracts. These combinations may also lead to new opportunities for applications for these logic frameworks.

© Springer International Publishing Switzerland 2016
J.J. Alferes et al. (Eds.): RuleML 2016, LNCS 9718, pp. 167–183, 2016.
DOI: 10.1007/978-3-319-42019-6_11

In this paper, we investigate the utility of logic-based smart contracts and possible ways to use them in combination with blockchain systems:

- to understand what legal and technical (dis)advantages logic-based smart contracts can provide w.r.t. their procedural counterparts, we structure this investigation in light of a common contract lifecycle;
- to show how logic-based smart contracts can be used in combination of blockchain systems, we inspect different combinations for leveraging logic-based languages to operate smart contracts in combination with such systems.

These insights will lead us to emphasize a foundational challenge to fully take advantage of logic-based smart contracts with blockchain systems: algorithms for logic approaches have to be efficient, but they also need to be literally cheap in execution. Since logic models of defeasible reasoning are often advocated to capture legal knowledge and reasoning (see e.g. [16]), we will illustrate our discourse with defeasible rules and associated logic frameworks.

This paper is organised as follows. In Sect. 2, we outline some basic elements and mechanisms of blockchain systems. In Sect. 3, we define and illustrate logic-based smart contracts and in Sect. 4 we examine the possible legal and technical utility of such logic-based smart contracts compared to procedural smart contracts, and we do so in light of common legal activities. In Sect. 5, we investigate different options for the operation of smart contracts in combination with blockchain systems, before concluding.

2   Blockchain Systems

A blockchain system consists of a network of computing nodes, sharing a common data structure (the blockchain) with consensus about the state of this structure.

The most prominent example of such a system is Bitcoin [13], which established a distributed network of accounts and transactions (a ledger), where revisions or tampering is made prohibitively difficult due to the algorithm used in conjunction with economic consensus. Since Bitcoin is the most prominent example, most explanations regarding blockchain systems below will be based on this system; the functioning of different blockchains may differ in detail but such differences fall outside of the scope of this paper.

The data structure backing a blockchain system is distributed because it is replicated amongst the nodes (i.e. computers) of the system. As new blocks of recent transactions are added to the distributed data structure, they include a reference back to the previous blocks, so that any node can consequentially verify the integrity of the data structure. This chain of blocks of transactions is called a blockchain.

Transactions on the blockchain are not cost-free. Miners have to spend computing power (tied to hardware) and energy to integrate blocks of transactions into the blockchain. As incentives, if a miner 'discovers' the solution of the problem to include a block, such miner receives economic incentives in the form of new Bitcoins (block reward) and transaction fees. It is presently unclear how this system will function once the algorithmically predetermined number of Bitcoins has been reached.

The transaction fee is an incentive for a miner to include this transaction in their block. For advanced blockchain systems, the fee *may* also cover the cost of the computational steps required to operate the transaction, in particular when the transactions are associated with extra instructions. The computation of the amount of the fee is outside of the scope of this paper, but as rule of thumb, the simpler a transaction in terms of computational complexity, the less it costs.

Since transactions can be costly, it is often advanced that heavy computation should occur 'off-chain' instead of 'on-chain'. In off-chain scenarios, computation is performed outside the blockchain-based system, e.g. on the server of an intermediation service, while, in on-chain scenarios, computation is performed and validated in the blockchain-based system by the miners. Of course, off-chain computation results can be recorded in a blockchain, however parties may prefer to avoid off-chain intermediation services that can be performed on-chain, for example to increase trust.

While blockchain technology was initially used as a distributed ledger of crypto-currency transactions (namely Bitcoin transactions), such a technology can also be used to manage smart contracts and associated transactions.

3   Logic-Based Smart Contracts

The term *smart contract* was originally introduced in the 90s by Szabo [17], stemming from the idea that a more technological legal framework would help commerce and cut down on disputes. Lately the idea came to popularity again with the rise and expanding capabilities of blockchain based systems. Parts of a *smart contract* can correspond to a legal contract or a clause in a legal contract, but they do not have to.

When there is a condition to which certain legal consequences are attached, the *smart contract* executes the corresponding statements and any potential contractual consequences. Examples for applying *smart contracts* are programmatic banking functions (see e.g. Automated Escrow, Savings), decentralized markets (e.g. OpenBazaar, EtherMarket), prediction markets (Augur, Gnosis), distribution of music royalties (Ujo) and encoding of virtual property (Ascribe).

Smart contracts in blockchains are typically programmed in a *procedural* language. On the platform Ethereum [5,18], developers can encode smart contracts in a procedural language called Solidity[1]. When programming in a procedural language, the programmer writes an explicit sequences of steps that are executed to produce what has to be done. The programmer has to write *what* has to be done and *how* to achieve it.

Example 1. This example is based on the structure of the example provided in [7] to illustrate some intricacies of the logical formalisation of legal reasoning

---

[1] Solidity. Available at https://ethereum.github.io/solidity.

Let us consider the following licensing contractual clauses for the evaluation of a product.

Article 1. The Licensor grants the Licensee a licence to evaluate the Product.
Article 2. The Licensee must not publish the results of the evaluation of the Product without the approval of the Licensor; the approval must be obtained before the publication. If the Licensee publishes results of the evaluation of the Product without approval from the Licensor, the Licensee has 24 h to remove the material.
Article 3. The Licensee must not publish comments on the evaluation of the Product, unless the Licensee is permitted to publish the results of the evaluation.
Article 4. If the Licensee is commissioned to perform an independent evaluation of the Product, then the Licensee has the obligation to publish the evaluation results.
Article 5. This license will terminate automatically if Licensee breaches this Agreement.

Suppose that the licensee evaluates the product and publishes on their website the results of the evaluation without having received an authorisation from the licensor. The licensee realises that they were not allowed to publish the results of the evaluation, and they remove the published results from their website within 24 h from the publication. Is the licensee still able to legally use the product? Since the contract contains a compensatory clause, it is possible to argue that the license to use the product still holds. Suppose now that the licensee, right after publishing the results, posted a tweet about the evaluation of the product and that the tweet counts as commenting on the evaluation. In this case, we have a violation of Article 3, since, even if the results were published, according to Article 2 the publication was not permitted. Thus, they are no longer able to legally use the product under the term of the license. The final situation we want to analyse is when the publication and the tweet actions take place after the licensee was commissioned to perform an independent evaluation from the licensor. In this case, the licensee has the obligation to publish the result, which then means that they were also permitted to publish the result, and thus they were free to post the tweet. Accordingly, they can continue to use the product under the terms of the licence.   □

Algorithm 1 gives a pseudo-code example of how a procedural smart contract can implement the contractual clause of Example 1. The smart contract includes a sequence of instructions updating the normative states (obligations, prohibitions and permissions in force) depending on what actions have been done and then the current state. The program has to set the initial state for the contract, then the procedure EVALUATIONLICENSECONTRACT has to be invoked every time there is a trigger for the program. Notice that the order of the instructions in the procedure does not reflect the natural order of the contract clauses expressed in natural language. The programmer has to come up with such an order, and also the programmer has to manually determine how a trigger changes

---

Algorithm 1. Pseudo-code of the licensing contractual clauses.

1: Initialise getLicence, getApproval, getCommission, use, publish, comment, remove
2: [Forb$_{licensee}$] use ← true
3: [Forb$_{licensee}$] publish ← true
4: [Forb$_{licensee}$] comment ← true
5: violation ← false
6:
7: **procedure** EVALUATIONLICENSECONTRACT
8:     **if** getLicence = true **then**
9:         [Forb$_{licensee}$] use ← false
10:         [Perm$_{licensee}$] use ← true   ▷ Article 1
11:
12:     **if** getLicence = true and (getApproval = true or getCommission = true) **then**
13:         [Forb$_{licensee}$] publish ← false
14:         [Perm$_{licensee}$] publish ← true   ▷ Article 2, 4
15:
16:     **if** getLicence = true and
17:        getApproval = false and
18:        getCommission = false and
19:        publish = true **then**
20:         [Obl$_{licensee}$] remove ← true   ▷ Article 2
21:
22:     **if** [Perm$_{licensee}$] publish = true **then**
23:         [Forb$_{licensee}$] comment ← false
24:         [Perm$_{licensee}$] comment ← true   ▷ Article 3
25:
26:     **if** getLicence = true and getCommission = true **then**
27:         [Forb$_{licensee}$] publish ← false
28:         [Obl$_{licensee}$] publish ← true
29:         [Perm$_{licensee}$] publish ← true   ▷ Article 4
30:
31:     **if** ([Forb$_{licensee}$] use = true and use = true) or
32:        ([Forb$_{licensee}$] publish = true and publish = true) or
33:        ([Obl$_{licensee}$] publish = true and publish = false) or
34:        ([Forb$_{licensee}$] comment = true and comment = true) or
35:        ([Obl$_{licensee}$] remove = true and remove = false) **then**
36:         violation ← true
37:     **if** violation = true **then**
38:         [Forb$_{licensee}$] use ← true
39:         [Forb$_{licensee}$] publish ← true
40:         [Forb$_{licensee}$] comment ← true
41:         [Perm$_{licensee}$] use ← false
42:         [Perm$_{licensee}$] publish ← false
43:         [Perm$_{licensee}$] comment ← false
44:         [Obl$_{licensee}$] publish ← false   ▷ Article 5

---

the state of the normative provisions (i.e., obligations, permissions and prohibitions), and to propagate the changes according to the meaning. This means that the programmer is responsible to perform the legal reasoning implied by the contract clauses. For example, when a permission becomes true, the corresponding prohibition should be set to false; similarly, when we set an obligation as true, the corresponding permission should be set to true as well. For large and complex smart contracts, an alternative is to set an auxiliary procedure to be invoked, when the state of a normative provision has to be changed, and propagate the changes to all related normative provisions.

The process of writing a procedural program corresponding to a contract can be cumbersome and error prone since the order of instruction affects the correctness of the resulting smart contract. A possible solution to alleviate this problem is to create a state machine for the contract (Fig. 1 shows a state machine for the contract in Example 1). Then, the programmer can use the state machine as a guide to derive the procedural code. Alternatively, the state machine could be represented directly in the program and a state machine engine could then be used to execute the resulting smart contract. This approach can grow exponentially large in the number of states and transitions for non-trivial contracts, and the programmer still remains in charge of the legal reasoning implied by the contract.

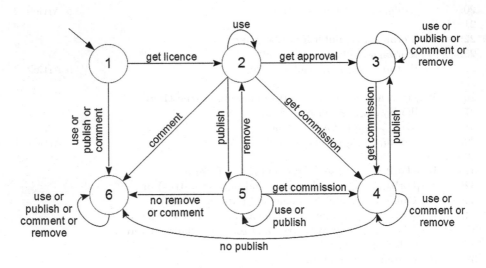

Fig. 1. State machine of the licensing contractual clauses.

Besides imperative languages for smart contracts, one may consider *declarative* languages (in particular logic-based languages). When programming in a declarative language, the programmer does not have to explicitly write the sequence of steps to produce what has to be done. Instead the programmer describes what has to be done, but not how to do it. In particular, languages for logic programming can be used to represent and reason upon the rules represented by smart contracts. With the logic approach, contractual clauses are rephrased into explicit formal statements which are separated from the embedding program, and the program has inferential functionalities to reason upon these statements. In practice, the contractual clauses would be encoded into logic rules, and a rule-based engine would reason upon the rules.

Example 2. Since logic-based models of defeasible reasoning are often advocated to capture legal knowledge and reasoning (see e.g. [16]), let us consider the representation of the contract given in Example 1 provided by the (deontic) defeasible logic (Formal Contract Logic, FCL) of [6] and implemented by the defeasible logic engine SPINdle [10].

```
Article1.0: => [Forb_licensee] use
Article1.1: getLicense => [Perm_licensee] use
Article2.1: => [Forb_licensee] publish [Compensated] [Obl_licensee]remove
Article2.2: getApproval => [Perm_licensee] publish
Article3.1: => [Forb_licensee] comment
Article3.2: [Perm_licensee] publish => [Perm_licensee] comment
Article4.1: getCommission => [Obl_licensee] publish
Article4.2: getCommission => getLicense
Article5: violation => [Forb_licensee] use
% Superiority relation
Article1.1 > Article1.0,   Article5 > Article1.1,
Article2.2 > Article2.1,   Article3.2 > Article3.1
```

The order of the rules is irrelevant, and as should be visible, the declarative rules are shorter than procedural code and easier to use, they would later then be evaluated by a rule engine on the blockchain or deployed in conjunction with a rule engine.

If there are no triggers, then `Article1.0`. `Article2.1` and `Article3.1` fire and we conclude the prohibitions of `use`, `publish` and `comment`. When, `getLicense` and `publish` hold, then `Article1.1` overrides `Article1.0` thus we have the permission of `use`, but we continue to have the prohibition to `publish`, thus the publication contravenes Article 2, and we can use rule `Article2.1` to derive the mandated compensation, that is the obligation of removing the material is now in force, i.e., we conclude `[Obl_licensee] remove`. See [6] for the details of FCL.   □

4   Utility of Logic-Based Smart Contracts

The successes of blockchain-based systems for smart contracts, or at least the amounts of investments in such systems suggest the viability of 'procedural smart contracts', while the utility of logic-based smart contracts has been hardly investigated.

In this section, we consider the utility of the logic approach w.r.t. its procedural counterpart. Too bridge the gap between smart contracts and legal contracts, this is done in the light of the lifecycle of a contract.

Formation and Negotiation. Based on the 'freedom to contract', any legal entities are free to form contracts, within the limits of the law. Necessary conditions for the formation are the 'meeting of the minds' (i.e. the parties have the intentions to form the contract) and the 'Offer and Acceptance' (i.e. the expression of an offer to contract on certain terms by one person to another person, and its acceptance of those terms). In practice, parties often negotiate the terms until they reach an agreement.

As any ordinary contracts, a smart contract can be negotiated i.e. the smart contract program is coded, and this creation can occur through a negotiation. In a blockchain system, agreement about what a contract should perform is defined before deploying the contract in the blockchain system. After creation and giving assent by calling the contract in the required way, the contract establishes legal relations between the parties. Often, a contract is first created in a natural language (as in the case of the creation using a template), and then this contract is translated into a smart contract. However, a smart contract program can be created without a natural language counterpart, the same as normal computer programs.

Using procedural languages, fairly sophisticated smart contracts can be formed already. However, the procedural coding of a smart contract may appear difficult to apprehend, slowing down its negotiation and formation. As the procedural code may appear difficult to understand, one can wonder whether the contractual clauses are properly coded. In this regard, the procedural code can be 'validated' (unit testing etc.) to determine whether this smart contract is fit for use, but testing procedural code is well-known to be time consuming and error prone. In logic-based smart contracts, as logic statements can be understood as high-level specifications, they constitute executable specifications of smart contracts, i.e. specifications that can be directly executed by the smart contracts, thereby decreasing the risks of errors in the implementation. Moreover, a logic representation can ease validation by taking advantage of logic-based techniques, such as formal verification, to detect if certain properties hold. This can be automated, but since such techniques are often heavy in terms of computation, they will most likely occur off-chain. Furthermore, a logic representation may ease the formation of a smart contract resulting from a negotiation between parties. When the formation and negotiation are delegated by humans to artificial agents, the logic approach may particularly facilitate these activities (w.r.t. a procedural counterpart) since in this case such activities require, presumably, some artificial intelligence to represent and reason upon contractual terms.

Contract Storage/Notarizing. A contract can be binding in many forms, such as by oral agreement, hand shake or intangible agreement. Thus, in principle there are little formalities required (though exceptions apply). The real problem arises when there is contention on whether there was a contract or not, and what its contents were. In those cases, it helps to have a written record of what was agreed stored and certified. To be extra certain, contracts can be certified by a trusted third party, a notary. For non-digital contracts, the content has to be described in natural language and a date manually inserted.

Contract storage can be straightforwardly related to the storage of smart contracts using file systems or database systems. Instead of storing the smart contract into the machine(s) of particular entities (such as the parties and intermediaries), one can use a blockchain system to store it (its bytecode) with a relatively accurate timestamp.

There are no particular restrictions on the types of data that can be stored in blockchains, and therefore smart contracts with logic statements can be stored in them. As logic statements (e.g. the set of rules stored within a procedural smart contract and meant to be passed to a rule engine) are generally more compact than its procedural counterpart, the logic approach may decrease the cost of storage, in particular when there is an explosion of possible states on which rules can be applied.

Enforcement and Monitoring. Once a contract is formed, it has to be performed; the parties have to take appropriate actions to fulfil the contractual clauses. If parties are encouraged or forced to perform their required actions, this is called enforcement for the purposes of this paper.[2] Monitoring is the activity of checking whether the appropriate actions are taken. Enforcement and monitoring can be described as the deployment and the execution of a program, which can to some degree be automated by the blockchain consensus code.

The efficient execution and monitoring of a smart contract is a necessary condition for the use of such a contract, in particular in regard to the worst-case scenarios. While the computational complexity of the execution of a procedural smart contract can be quite easily controlled, the complexity of a logic-based smart contract relies on the complexity of the underlying inference mechanisms (we will further instigate this point in the next section). Concerning monitoring, 'controls' can be typically integrated in the procedural code of a smart contract, while in logic contracts, monitoring can take advantage of more formal run-time compliance techniques. Furthermore, the execution and monitoring of a contract is not necessarily meant to occur in isolation. On the contrary, when executing smart contracts, contractual clauses may have to be considered w.r.t. exogenous (legal) information, such as rules from other contracts or the embedding normative environments (the law in particular). While procedural smart contracts can interact with each other rudimentarily, a logic approach would take advantage of efforts in rule interchange languages (such as LegalRuleML [2]) to express rules and ease interoperability amongst the contracts and other rule systems.

Modification. If all parties perform their contractual duties, then a contract may in principle not be unilaterally modified. If a party fails to perform or if a predetermined condition in the contract is activated, then a change in the contractual relationship can be invoked. If all parties to a contract agree to a change, the contract can be amended accordingly.

These considerations for non-smart contracts also hold for smart contracts. In current blockchain systems, a contract cannot be modified but the data stored in it can be updated. As such, one model to enable flexible solutions is the 'hub

---

[2] While encouragement is not enforcement in all meanings of the word, it is either a precursor or a part of it.

and spoke' model where one main smart contract holds addresses/pointers to all other necessary contracts that contain the specific clauses and functionality.

The hub and spoke model allows the modification of smart contracts, but it may appear quite coarse. In logic-based smart contracts, the statements of the knowledge base can be coded as 'public' variables, thus allowing more fine-grained updates. A modified knowledge base can also be passed to an existing contract, which then acts accordingly, similar to how in the hub and spoke model addresses of subcontracts are exchanged. Moreover, the order of instructions and procedures is fundamental in the procedural approach (as illustrated in Algorithm 1), and thus the hub and spoke model may cause some issues in that regard. As the order of the statement in a knowledge base does not matter w.r.t. the conclusions that can be derived from it, a logic-based language can greatly help to tackle modifications.

Dispute Resolution. A dispute regarding a contract may occur, and thus such a dispute has to be resolved. Two major types of dispute resolution exist: (i) adjudicative resolution, such as litigation or arbitration, where a judge, jury or arbitrator determines the outcome, and (ii) consensual resolution, such as collaborative law, mediation, conciliation, or negotiation, where the parties attempt to reach agreement.

Smart contracts can be disputed too, and adjudicative resolution as well as consensual resolution can be attempted. The final arbiter of legal technological innovation is always acceptance by the courts. At the moment there is no useful case law on this for smart contracts, but this would also depend strongly on the nature of the smart contract, i.e. whether it is linked to a contract in natural language as well as other factors. In principle, based on Bitcoin case law and the freedom to contract, it can be said that smart contracts are binding [19, pp. 11–24].

With regard to a consensual resolution, a smart contract could specify a committee of human or computational arbitrators that should be consulted first. It is unclear at present how a court would interpret such a choice of law or arbitration clause in a smart contract.

In principle smart contracts can be considered to be legally valid (exceptions notwithstanding); to this end, it likely does not matter if the smart contract is programmed using an imperative or a declarative language. Nevertheless, one may argue that, as some imperative code (and, to a lesser extent, some procedural code), may be difficult to comprehend, it may be the case that the control structures of these smart contracts rebut jurists and hamper their interpretation of the contract (this would lead to the emergence of case law setting precedent on how to interpret smart contracts; however so far this does not exist). On the contrary, as logic rules are meant to reflect contractual clauses, their logic representation will ease the work of jurists, in particular to structure, evaluate, and compare legal arguments constructed from formal statements. However, if there are legal rules that a human has to be told to what he agrees to, there has to be a natural language equivalent anyway. Then the logic rules might make the implementation or the interpretation of the contract easier, but they may not be close enough to natural language to be a substitute, particularly to people who might not be technical experts.

In summary, the logic approach has the potential to advantageously complement its procedural counterpart for each activity thereof. Whilst advantages are clearly backed by technical considerations, it is less evident whether a logic approach provides a stronger legal foundation to smart contracts. As previously alluded to, one may argue that a full representation of a smart contract has to explicitly establish and link the normative effects (rights, obligation, transfers of entitlement) resulting from the contract, and the procedure for implementing these rights and obligations though the computational actions performed by the contract, in the given infrastructure. Thus, a hybrid approach combining logic and procedural components may help to bridge the gap between smart contracts and their legal counterparts.

5 Use of Logic-Based Smart Contracts with Blockchain Systems

In this section, we investigate different technical options to use logic-based smart contracts in combination with blockchain systems, and we will discuss these options w.r.t. the legal activities we previously identified.

Given a set of statements, inferences can be performed in different manners. Every inferential mechanism has its own characteristics, and the adoption of a particular mechanism to execute logic contractual clauses should be based on these characteristics.

Example 3. Considering a defeasible logic framework for the representation of the contractual clauses; conclusions can be derived by using dialectic proofs (DPs) [14] or an algorithm based on the fixed-point of the characteristic function of the grounded semantics [4] (FP), see e.g. [12], more efficient algorithms stemming from Defeasible Logic (DL) [1,11] or even equation-based approaches (EB), see e.g. [15] and neuro-symbolic systems (NS), see e.g. [3]. In most cases, it is preferable to use the algorithm with the lowest computational complexity, but for some reasons, one may prefer other algorithms to provide, for example, more intelligible inferences. How to use these mechanisms to deal with smart contracts in blockchain-based systems?   □

Beside the characteristics of the inferential mechanisms, it is important to notice that inferences can occur on-chain or off-chain.

1. On-chain: inferences are made within the blockchain platform;
2. Off-chain: inferences are made outside the blockchain system, e.g. on a third party server.

The distinction of on-chain and off-chain inferences leads us to distinguish off-chain options for logic-based smart contracts and on-chain options.

5.1   Off-Chain Options

When miners are processing transactions into blocks to append to the blockchain, the security model of the virtual machine in which smart contracts on existing blockchain platforms operate and the co-processing by nodes does not allow to call outside resources. Thus, we must discard the option where an off-chain inferential mechanism is called by the smart contract.

Though an off-chain inferential mechanism cannot be called from a smart contract, another off-chain option simply consists in recording the smart contract (i.e. knowledge base and the reference to the semantics) and the inferential conclusions in the blockchain. On the basis of the inferential conclusions, procedural code of the contract can then execute particular transactions. Activities that we identified in the previous section are accommodated as follows.

Formation and negotiation. The contract can be formed and negotiated off-chain or on-chain.

Contract storage/notarizing. A contract is stored off-chain (so that it can be executed off-chain) and in the blockchain.

Enforcement and monitoring. Enforcement and monitoring are achieved off-chain, the conclusions can be stored in the blockchain.

Modification. If a contract is modified, then the off-chain smart contract will be updated, and stored in the blockchain. If the knowledge base can be updated, then the smart contract can be updated without interrupting associated processes.

Dispute resolution. One can check whether an off-chain contract matches a blockchain code (bytecode). Thus in case of a dispute, the parties can check whether the recorded conclusions are proper conclusions of the smart contract (w.r.t. the given semantics).

The main advantage of this off-chain option is the lower cost of associated transactions, since the inferences are performed off-chain. The disadvantage is that such an off-chain inferential mechanism may be simply seen as an intermediary service, while the parties may prefer to avoid such intermediation and associated costs or trust issues.

5.2   On-Chain Options

Instead of an off-chain inferential mechanism, one may prefer an on-chain mechanism. The availability of a logic-based language to program smart contracts shall facilitate such options, but a procedural language can also be used to write meta-programs (i.e. programs with the ability to treat programs as their data). For example, a rule-engine can be integrated in a smart contract to derive some conclusions given a particular knowledge base. Based on the results, some procedural code can execute the transactions. The rule-engine can also be a smart contract script of its own, so that smart contracts can always refer to this smart contract. Having the inference engine as an immutable contract on the blockchain

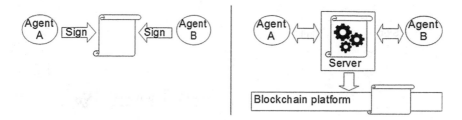

Fig. 2. Off-chain option. Agents A and B form a (smart) contract which is stored on a blockchain. The contract is executed in a server external to the blockchain system, and transactions can be recorded in the blockchain.

allows participants' confidence into the smart contract engine to increase over time (test once, utilize n-fold).

Formation and negotiation. The contract can be formed and negotiated off-chain or on-chain.

Contract storage/notarizing. A contract can be stored off-line, but it has to be stored in the blokchain (so that it can be executed on-chain).

Enforcement and monitoring. Enforcement and monitoring is achieved on-chain, the conclusions can be stored in the blockchain.

Modification. If the knowledge base can be updated, then the contract can be updated without interrupting associated processes.

Dispute resolution. One can check whether an off-chain contract matches a blockchain code. Thus in case of a dispute, the parties can check whether the recorded conclusions are proper conclusions of the smart contract (w.r.t. the given semantics).

The major advantages of on-chain solutions is that some off-chain intermediation services are eliminated, and the inferential mechanisms (e.g. the rule engine) are themselves recorded in the blockchain, resulting into more scrutinizable and trustful inferences.

The main disadvantage of on-chain solutions may regard the costs. To address the costs of on-chain inferences, algorithms with low computational complexity shall be favoured. If the selected algorithm provides inferences which appears sufficiently efficient but insufficiently intelligible for human operators, then more intelligible inferences can be used to explain the results off-chain.

Example 4. Considering DPs, FP or DL algorithms for the on-chain option, DPs have higher complexity than FP algorithms, which have higher complexity than algorithms from DL [8]. Consequently, one shall prefer DL algorithms to derive conclusions on-chain.   □

Interestingly, it is also possible to propose an on-chain option, that we may call the 'on-off' option where, given a knowledge base, this knowledge is converted (let's say 'compiled') into a lower-level representation to increase the speed of

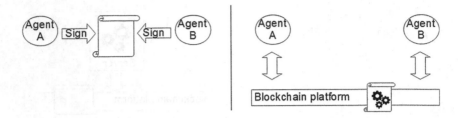

Fig. 3. On-chain option. Here, agents A and B form a (smart) contract which is stored and executed in a blockchain platform.

inferential computation, and this compiled code is part of the smart contract (this smart contract is eventually recompiled to run on the virtual machines of the blockchain network).

Formation and negotiation. The contract can be formed and negotiated off-chain or on-chain. The compiled code can be generated off-chain or on-chain. If compilation occurs off-chain then third party services may again appear, along with the associated disadvantages. If compilation is done on-chain then the compiler may be scrutinised and gain trust from the parties, at the expense of extra costs for compilation.

Contract storage/notarizing. A contract and its compiled code can be stored off-chain, but the compiled code has to be stored in the blockchain (so that it can be executed on-chain).

Enforcement and monitoring. Enforcement and monitoring is achieved on-chain, the conclusions can be stored in the blockchain.

Modification. If a contract is modified, then the logic statements have to be recompiled. If the compiled knowledge base can be updated, then the contract can be updated without interrupting associated processes.

Dispute resolution. One can check whether the compiled off-chain contract matches a blockchain code. Thus in case of a dispute, the parties can check whether the recorded conclusions are proper conclusions of the smart contract (w.r.t. the given semantics).

Compared to the off-chain option, the need for intermediation services is mitigated since inferences are achieved on-chain. Compared to the on-chain option, the costs of transactions may be decreased because the compiled knowledge base is meant to lower the computational complexity. The costs will be presumably higher than the off-chain option, therefore, such on-off approaches shall have a cost intermediate between off-chain and on-chain solutions.

Example 5. EB and NS approaches can be considered for 'on-off' solutions. In the EB approach, the considered knowledge base is 'compiled' into a set of equations, and these equations are stored into the smart contract to compute conclusions given a set of facts. In the NS approach, the knowledge base is 'compiled' into a neural network instead. While such approaches are interesting,

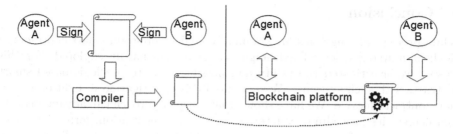

Fig. 4. On-off option. Agents A and B form a (smart) contract which is compiled. The compiled contract is stored and executed in a blockchain platform.

they may be quite limited in terms of expressiveness; for example we know neither EB nor NS approaches able to deal with temporal aspects for any defeasible rule-based framework, whereas there are works introducing temporal extensions to DL, see e.g. [9].   □

Whatever the option, and as previously mentioned, verification of the conclusions should be possible, and understandable by humans. In this regard, given some semantics, the conclusions of efficient but unintelligible approaches can be verified off-chain by more comprehensible proof systems.

Example 6. DPs clearly provide more intelligible proof systems for human operators w.r.t. other solutions. Hence, one may use efficient algorithms such as DL algorithms for routine operations, and human operators can rely on DPs to verify results if necessary.   □

So, if comprehensible proof systems are available for the considered logic-based system, then the choice of the option to execute a logic-based smart contract in combination with a blokchain system largely depends on the costs of such execution. As revealing experiment, we compared the cost of the procedural code (PC) for a modus ponens inference (from the premises 'a' and 'if a then b', then we derive b) with a rule reduction as used in a reasonably efficient algorithm for DL, and with an EB approach. The estimated cost for PC was 1480, 11859 for DL and 1418 for an EB approach.[3] For a simple modus ponens inference, the reduction rule was thus approximately 8 times more costly than the two other approaches. This result suggests that blockchain systems bring a new important technical challenge which is hardly addressed by the community: algorithms for a logic approach will not only be required to be efficient, but they also are required to be cheap as measured within the environment where they are deployed and according to its economic rules.

---

[3] This comparison was conducted by writing the basic solidity code for the requisite modus ponens inference and then comparing the 'gas' cost as estimated by the official solidity compiler.

6   Conclusion

While procedural languages are commonly used to program smart contracts in blockchain systems, logic-baed languages have been hardly explored. For this reason, we investigated the utility and possible ways to use logic-based smart contracts with such systems. We structured this investigation in light of a common contract lifecycle. We have shown that a logic approach can advantageously complement its procedural counterpart w.r.t. the negotiation, formation, storage/notarizing, enforcement, monitoring and activities related to dispute resolution.

To show how logic-based smart contracts could be used, we inspected different combinations for leveraging logic programming languages to operate smart contracts with such blockchain systems, and we illustrated our discourse with different algorithms from defeasible logic frameworks. This led us to emphasize a fundamental challenge to fully take advantage of a combination of logic-based smart contracts and blockchain systems: algorithms for logic-based approaches have to be efficient and cheap as measured within the environment where they are deployed and according to its economic rules, to ensure feasability in an environment where economic governance and consensus is used to ensure a working system and abuse prevention.

Finally, we have to emphasize that the logic and procedural approaches are not incompatible, on the contrary, they have the potential to advantageously complement each other. By providing a declarative specification of the content of the contract, to be complemented with a procedural definition of the steps needed to perform the obligations in the contract — either automatically or through specification introduced by the parties — more clarity is established, and a criterion is provided for matching automatic execution and shared intention of the parties, as expressed in the declarative specification.

Acknowledgements. NICTA is funded by the Australian Government through the Dept of Communications and the Australian Research Council through the ICT Centre for Excellence Program.

References

1. Antoniou, G., Billington, D., Governatori, G., Maher, M.J.: Representation results for defeasible logic. ACM Trans. Comput. Log. **2**(2), 255–287 (2001)
2. Athan, T., Governatori, G., Palmirani, M., Paschke, A., Wyner, A.: LegalRuleML: design principles and foundations. In: Faber, W., Paschke, A. (eds.) Reasoning Web 2015. LNCS, vol. 9203, pp. 151–188. Springer, Heidelberg (2015)
3. d'Avila Garcez, A.S., Gabbay, D.M., Lamb, L.C.: A neural cognitive model of argumentation with application to legal inference and decision making. J. Appl. Log. **12**(2), 109–127 (2014)
4. Dung, P.M.: On the acceptability of arguments and its fundamental role in non-monotonic reasoning, logic programming and n-person games. Artif. Intell. **77**(2), 321–358 (1995)

5. Ethereum Foundation. Ethereum's white paper
6. Governatori, G.: Representing business contracts in RuleML. Int. J. Coop. Inf. Syst. **14**(2–3), 181–216 (2005)
7. Governatori, G.: Thou shalt is not you will. In: Atkinson, K., (ed.) Proceedings of the Fifteenth International Conference on Artificial Intelligence and Law, pp. 63–68. ACM, New York (2015)
8. Governatori, G., Pham, D.H.: DR-CONTRACT: an architecture for e-contracts in defeasible logic. Inter. J. Bus. Process Integr. Manag. **5**(3), 187–199 (2009)
9. Governatori, G., Rotolo, A., Riveret, R., Palmirani, M., Sartor, G.: Variants of temporal defeasible logics for modelling norm modifications. In: Proceedings of the 11th International Conference on Artificial Intelligence and Law, Stanford, California, USA, pp. 155–159. ACM (2007)
10. Lam, H.-P., Governatori, G.: The making of SPINdle. In: Governatori, G., Hall, J., Paschke, A. (eds.) RuleML 2009. LNCS, vol. 5858, pp. 315–322. Springer, Heidelberg (2009)
11. Maher, M.J.: Propositional defeasible logic has linear complexity. Theor. Pract. Log. Program. **1**(6), 691–711 (2001)
12. Modgil, S., Caminada, M.: Proof theories and algorithms for abstract argumentation frameworks. In: Simari, G., Rahwan, I. (eds.) Argumentation in Artificial Intelligence, pp. 105–129. Springer, Heidelberg (2009)
13. Nakamoto, S.: Bitcoin: A Peer-to-Peer Electronic Cash System (2008). (The Nakamoto paper)
14. Prakken, H., Sartor, G.: A dialectical model of assessing conflicting arguments in legal reasoning. Artif. Intell. Law **4**(3–4), 331–368 (1996)
15. Riveret, R., Rotolo, A., Sartor, G.: Probabilistic rule-based argumentation for norm-governed learning agents. Artif. Intell. Law **20**(4), 383–420 (2012)
16. Sartor, G.: Legal Reasoning: A Cognitive Approach to the Law. Springer, Heidelberg (2005)
17. Szabo, N.: The idea of smart contracts (1997)
18. Wood, G.: Ethereum: a secure decentralised generalised transaction ledger (2014)
19. Wright, A., De Filippi, P.: Decentralized Blockchain Technology and the Rise of Lex Cryptographia. SSRN Scholarly Paper ID 2580664, Social Science Research Network, Rochester, NY, March 2015

Blockchain Temporality: Smart Contract Time Specifiability with Blocktime

Melanie Swan[⊠]

Philosophy and Economic Theory,
New School for Social Research, New York, NY, USA
m@melanieswan.com
http://www.BlockchainStudies.org

Abstract. The aims of this paper are to (1) provide a conceptual context for smart contracts, (2) argue that blockchains are a next-generation technology enabling much larger-scale and more complex computing projects, and (3) posit blocktime as a new mode of conceiving time. Blockchains are the distributed ledger technology underlying Bitcoin and other cryptocurrencies; the payments layer the Internet never had; a mechanism for updating truth states in distributed network computing through consensus trust; and overall, a new form of general computational substrate. Blocktime is the time over which a certain number of blocks will have confirmed; and this creates an alternative event trajectory in time which can be offset against human-time or other computing clocktime regimes for arbitrage or complementary purposes. The result of this effort is to show that blocktime allows the contingency of future events to be more robustly orchestrated through temporality as a selectable smart contract feature.

Keywords: Bitcoin · Cryptocurrency · Blockchain · Temporality · Algorithmic trust · Information theory · Distributed computing · Decentralization · Network computing · Byzantine agreement

1 Introduction

1.1 Background Context

I have divided the paper into three sections toward the aims of providing a conceptual context for smart contracts, arguing that blockchains are a next-generation technology enabling much larger-scale and more complex computing projects, and positing blocktime as a new mode of conceiving time. First, I discuss computational substrates. I argue that current computational models may be limited in scope and unable to scale to address the next tiers of computing challenges. Some of these computing projects could include genome and microbiome research banks with billions of files, national property registries, searchable government records databases, astronomical data management, unified Electronic Medical Record systems, and Internet of Things (IoT) connected sensor and device coordination. I suggest that blockchain technology could be one solution for creating a next-generation computational architecture to address these kinds of larger-scale computational projects that have been impossible before. The payments layer installs a valuable functionality that allows remuneration,

© Springer International Publishing Switzerland 2016
J.J. Alferes et al. (Eds.): RuleML 2016, LNCS 9718, pp. 184–196, 2016.
DOI: 10.1007/978-3-319-42019-6_12

which could support an accelerated move to the automation economy in enabling a more sophisticated level of secure automated payments. For example, eventually the entire mortgage servicing industry could be outsourced to a package of smart contracts. Second, I discuss the properties of blockchain computing such as Byzantine Agreement and consensus algorithms, and new classes of blockchain applications. I suggest that blockchains comprise a new and unique form of computing system wherein trust, transparency, and entropy are reliably produced and persist over time. Third, I discuss Turing completeness and blocktime. Blockchains, and particularly smart contract platforms, are a general universal computing substrate in the Turing-complete sense, a generic computational infrastructure. I posit the idea of blocktime that makes time more malleable as a specifiable parameter of smart contracts, and offers a tool for managing the contingency of future events. Previously, the available time selections were generally restricted to human time and computing event time. Now however, there is blocktime (the time over which a certain number of blocks will have confirmed), which is a separate time regime unto itself that can be played off and against other time trajectories, and allow processes to be configured internally within the realm of blocktime. I conjecture that there is a sense of the possibility of creating "more time" by being able to access events in alternative time trajectories, like blocktime. A practical example is that I can be earning cryptocurrency with my numerous and parallel blockchain DACs (distributed autonomous corporations) that I can swap out to fiat currency to pay my physical-world obligations. The key point is starting to conceive of time in this unprecedented way as a malleable resource that can be specified in different ways as a contract feature.

1.2 Computational Substrates

A general computational substrate may be conceived as a platform upon which calculations related to information processing may be performed. Numerous computation substrates have been proposed and developed to different degrees. The most obvious and familiar in existence is the worldwide silicon chip-based computing infrastructure. Other platforms are in development such as quantum computing. In biology, there are suggestions for computational models using molecular nanotechnology, positional assembly, social network graphs, and ant colonies and other swarm-coordinated behaviors. DNA has been proposed as a miniaturized and durable means of storage and computation [1]. Organic-inorganic hybrid computational substrates have been outlined, for example Brainets (linking organic computing units (brains) to silicon computing networks) [2], and Neural Dust (thousands of 10–100 micron-sized in-brain sensor nodes providing neural recording and interface support) [3].

While the existing silicon-chip based computational infrastructure is ubiquitous in some sense, it has some challenges. First, it is not a general computational substrate upon which any program can run fungibly. There are many different kinds of machines, operating systems, languages, software versions, and installed configurations which can prevent even seemingly interoperable software programs from running in a new environment. One recent strategy designed to address this is executing software applications inside Docker containers which do not require underlying machine configurations to be a certain way. Second, there is an ongoing explosion in the number and species of Internet-connected devices. 20–30 billion Internet-connected devices are estimated to be online worldwide by 2020 [4]. At the same time, there are more different kinds of computing devices. The computing world is no longer just servers and PCs; it includes drones, robots, self-driving vehicles, IoT (Internet of Things) sensors, smart phones, wearables, smart roads, and other devices. Each new species has its own processing requirements and protocols, and a different kind of infrastructure might be required to manage the traffic of all of the communication and coordination for these platforms. A third factor is the need to accommodate a higher magnitude of very large data files, for example nation-wide EMRs (electronic medical records) or million-member genome banks. In order to progress to a new era of computing that incorporates the IoT explosion, very-large data files, and interoperability, a more universal computing schema is needed, a truly general computational substrate that can handle the magnitude of IoT device messaging, that includes a remunerative payments layer, that is a truly next-generation global infrastructure, and this could be blockchain technology.

Blockchain technology is a new arrival in computational substrates. A blockchain is a software protocol and decentralized ledger for recording transactions, but more fundamentally blockchains are a global-scale computational substrate for the processing of any kind of digitized activity. Blockchains are a general base for computation [5, 6]. The first application of blockchain technology is cryptocurrencies, where the key property is being able to securely update truth states in a distributed computing network. This has been a known challenge called the Byzantine Generals Problem; e.g.; how to communicate effectively across a distributed war field of generals, not knowing which generals might be compromised [7]. One way of reaching Byzantine Agreement or Byzantine Consensus in computing systems has been needed. Several solutions have been proposed in the previous decades, and finally blockchains have a number of checks and balances such that reaching secure and accurate consensus across networks despite any failing nodes (malicious or otherwise) might be more reliably achieved. Blockchains are a software technology for updating every node in a distributed computing system with the current state of the world; a means of conferring a shared truth state in a distributed system. Blockchains are an important innovation for large-scale activity in both computing and social cohesion, where some of the social layers created are economic remuneration and distribution, and societal shared trust that is simultaneously global and local, and can facilitate human and machine interaction and collaboration.

A blockchain is like a giant interactive Google doc spreadsheet that anyone can view on-demand, where independent administrators (miners) continually verify and update the ledger to confirm that each transaction is valid. It is called a blockchain because blocks or batches of transactions are posted sequentially to a ledger, and each new block starts by referencing the prior block, so a chain of blocks is created. The result is that a secure network is created where any transaction can be independently confirmed as unique and valid without a centralized intermediary like a bank, government, or other institution. Creating trust in a distributed computing system without an intermediary (Byzantine Consensus) had been an unsolved computing problem with many other attempts at producing a workable digital cash solution failing. Blockchain technology is called *trustless* in the sense of not needing to trust the counterparty but instead trusting the blockchain software system. Trust is created by using the software system, as opposed to the old model of trust, which was the need to know and trust the counterparty of the transaction. Some of the implications of trusting the software system instead of having to find and trust counterparties is that not only is there more freedom with whom one can transact (essentially any human or machine agent across the global Internet), but also there is a much larger scale of transactions that can occur. There is a worry that the extreme openness of transactability on blockchain networks enables illegal criminal activity, most notably operations like Silk Road, but more fundamentally blockchains are a technology like the Internet, which too was initially used for illicit activity (some thought it would not progress beyond pornography), but quickly became an indispensable infrastructural element for coordinating and expanding all human and machine activity. The same could be true for blockchains.

Cryptocurrencies like Bitcoin are one of the first applications using blockchain technology. Bitcoin is like 'Skype for money;' [8] performing the same transformation that Skype did for phone calls in the context of digital cash, or what email did for post office mail, which is move physical world processes with plant and materials into more efficient digital network models. Bitcoin is the first robust demonstration of blockchain technology and decentralized models more generally. Since the middle ages, hierarchical models have been the primary means of organizing large-scale activity and they work up to a point, however now decentralized models are a striking new entrant in the possibility space of the models for large-scale coordination. Further, decentralized models suggest particular traction in coordinating truly global-scale activity at a larger and more complicated level than has been previously possible. Decentralized technologies could mark the next node in the evolution of humans and computing, and are required in the contemporary big data era to orchestrate projects such as effectively-sized health data commons for research involving thousands or millions of whole human genome files beyond the mere 3,751 that have been amassed so far [5]. It is not that centralized hierarchical models would be replaced overnight; the longer-term future could be one of a coexistence of many different kinds of organizational models: centralized, decentralized, and hybrid structures, and other new forms of models (for example based on complexity), where the important dynamic becomes tuning the orchestration system to the requirements of the underlying situation.

2 Properties of Blockchain Computing

Blockchains are a universal, large-scale, global, detailed, distributed, permanent transaction record available for on-demand look-up at any future moment. It is a system wherein trust, transparency, and entropy are reliably produced and persist over time. Computation takes place in the blockchain model in different ways. The first computational area is mining, the process by which independent third parties (miners) validate and record transactions. The blockchain software system automatically packages submitted transactions (on the order of thousands) into blocks, creates a random number specific to the block, and publishes metadata about the block parameters (cryptographic difficulty, service string, nonce (32-bit number), and counter (https://en.bitcoin.it/wiki/Block_hashing_algorithm)). Then anyone running the mining software performs computations and submits cryptographic guesses as to the specific parameters and nonce of the block. The mining machine with the correct guess wins the right to actually record the transactions, and receives the block rewards (transaction fee) for doing so.

2.1   Byzantine Agreement

One of the reasons that blockchain technology is such an advance is that it provides Byzantine agreement, a long-sought means of truth-state updating and trust generation in distributed computing networks. In the general space variously labeled as Byzantine fault tolerance, Byzantine consensus, and Byzantine agreement, a number of solutions have been proposed [9]. These consensus protocols are all some form of Byzantine agreement about how to arrive at secure trustable truth state updating in a consensus model in a distributed computing network. Consensus protocols can be seen in different modes of development. First there were Byzantine Agreement Protocols (BAPs) for the synchronous updating of network nodes. Beginning in the 1980s, these protocols include the Paxis algorithm for state machine replication from Lamport and Microsoft. Then Google's Chubby algorithm is a next-generation of Paxos, focused on the ability to serve strongly consistent files. Since it is not feasible to update very-large network systems of worldwide distributed nodes synchronously, more recently asynchronous models have been proposed.

Thus in the second moment of evolution, there are the different asynchronous updating algorithms proposed by blockchain technology. These include 'Nakamoto Consensus,' the proof-of-work model used with the Bitcoin blockchain, which is effective, but expensive and high latency. The proof-of-stake model is also here, which requires resource ownership, but has the risk of 'nothing-at-stake' attacks per escrow-revoking by malicious agents. There is now a third class of asynchronous Byzantine agreement consensus protocols under development for the longer-term future of cryptographic blockchain models. Some proposed models here include ARBC (Asynchronous Randomized Byzantine Consensus) from Pebble which combines traditional Byzantine Agreement Protocols with Nakamoto chains as a randomness source for faster and more-scalable decentralized networks. Other proposals are the BAR (Byzantine, altruistic, rational) protocol from the University of Texas at Austin, and the Stellar Consensus Protocol based on Quorum Slicing (trusting and updating via next-neighbor nodes, not the network as a whole). Prediction markets have been suggested as a longer-term alternative for reaching trustable truth-state consensus in distributed computing networks.

2.2   Blockchain Supercomputing

In the last two years, Bitcoin has arrived rapidly out of nowhere and created what is noted by some as being by far the world's largest and fastest computing network. While the Bitcoin blockchain is currently used to conduct necessarily wasteful cryptographic trail-and-error guessing for transaction recording, it might be more widely conceived as a computational resource and deployed in applications well beyond proof-of-work mining. Some projects seeking to harness otherwise wasted mining cycles into wider computational use include Primecoin (prime number factoring) [10], GreenCoin (carbon credit offsets) [11], and Gridcoin [12] and FoldingCoin (rewarding and facilitating community computing projects) [13].

All of the worldwide computers running the Bitcoin mining operation collectively comprise the world's biggest and fastest supercomputer. Bitcoin reached 1 PetaHash per second (PH/s) of computing power/speed on September 15th, 2013. In 2015, the Bitcoin network has been routinely operating at over 350 PH/s, or over 350,000,000 GH/s [14], specifically at 380 PH/s as of August 2015 (http://www.bitcoinwatch.com/). Bitcoin's hash-rate is the total computing power of the network, defined as the number of SHA-256 cryptographic hashes (or guesses) it can compute per second. Comparisons could be made with Google, who is estimated to have 10 million servers comprising one PetaHash (Smart 2015), and the estimated 2 billion worldwide personal computers thought to comprise 20 PetaHash [15]. Another comparison is vis-à-vis supercomputers, where the world's largest supercomputer, China's Tianhe-2 (MilkyWay-2) at the National University of Defense Technology has a performance of 33.86 PetaFLOPS (quadrillions of calculations per second) [16], compared to Bitcoin's network hash rate of 4,858,117.28 PetaFLOPS.

2.3 Blockchain Consensus Algorithms

A crucial part of blockchain computing is the consensus protocol by which transactions are confirmed. The Bitcoin blockchain runs on *proof of work*, where there is a high cost to demonstrate a proof of work; the mining operation has to spend the cost and energy of doing 'real work' to make guesses at the cryptographic nonce. This is the model to deter malicious players and produce a distributed system that is trustworthy. Since cryptocurrencies involve money and financial assets, there is incentive to game the system and crypto-security must be high. However, proof-of-work mining is expensive and may not be a long-term sustainable model for consensus derivation. Therefore other less-intense mining protocols might be employed as the transaction confirmation mechanism. Another familiar proposed model is *proof of stake*, where mining participation is determined by asset ownership in the mining system (thus possibly better aligning incentives to maintain a correct and orderly system). The proof of stake miners would own a stake in the mining operation, but not necessarily be the transaction parties or otherwise connected to the transactions, so the mining operation would still be a separate and independent function from the transactions. As an example of these protocols in practice, the smart-contract platform Ethereum has launched with a proof of work model, and then envisions shifting to a proof of stake model for the system to mature into a steady-state model. Several other consensus protocols for Byzantine Agreement are in development and discussion for other means of arriving at trustable truth states in decentralized networks. For example, there is proof of existence (time-date-stamped proof of a certain document or digital asset existing in a certain state at a certain time), and proof of truth (proof of a truth state having occurred, such as an automobile being damaged in a collision). Other more abstract models for proving agent ability to participate in consensus validation and confirmation processes could include *proof of entropy*, *proof of intelligence*, *proof of reputation*, and *proof of capability*; all as a means of demonstrating some sort of trustable proof of ability to do something as a means of access-granting to systems platforms, resources, or activities. *Proof of n* as an access mechanism to digital smartnetwork assets is a futuretech concept that could be quite extensible.

2.4   New Classes of Blockchain Applications

Blockchains are a computational model in how they themselves operate, and also in the new classes of computing operations that they enable. By analogy, there are the layers of computation that facilitate the Internet's own operations as a network, and the numerous additional layers of computational applications for which the Internet is an input and infrastructure; and this could be similarly true with blockchains. The bigger endgame with blockchains is their use as a basis for many new classes of applications in areas ranging from economics and finance to legal services and governance to health and science to literacy and art. Some practical applications could be decentralized credit bureaus, open-source FICO scores, and literacy smart contracts. Another example is health data analysis, where blockchains could be used as the infrastructure and permissioning mechanism for coordinating secure access to various big health data streams from millions of persons, using blockchain pointers to secure off-chain stored files. A firm in this space is DNA.bits, offering a blockchain-based solution for the de-identified continuous sharing of genetic and correlated clinical data. A vast global-scale health commons database could be created that is decentralized and unassembled, queryable on demand. Deep-learning algorithms could then be run over this massive decentralized datastore, possibly creating the crucial large data corpora which have been established as a necessary condition for advance in artificial intelligence [17, 18], and could lead to significant medical discovery.

New theories, modes, and means of computation may be required to work with the new kinds of vastly-larger datasets that could become available and workable for worldwide processing with blockchains. Right now the epitome of computing is large centralized datastores like Google's estimated 10 million servers continually crawling the web. Now, however, blockchains invite a completely new conceptual paradigm in computing systems, one that is a completely distributed decentralized blanket of available resources that can be called upon as needed. Computing as a ubiquitous reliably-available flexible resource creates a new reality, one based on certainty, trust, and assurity; one of abundance as opposed to scarcity and constraint. This resource can be seen and experienced at different levels, from a universal computational substrate, to its higher-level applications such as a distribution mechanism for GBI (guaranteed basic income) initiatives and in the farther future, for the safely orchestrated participation in collaborative cloudminds. Philosophically, blockchains thus contribute to the constitution of a conceptually different reality, one where computing as a paradigm is pushed farther into the position of being a seamlessly available background resource like air.

2.5 Blockchains and Complexity

An argument can be made that blockchains are systems of general complexity, as set forth by Morin [19]. General complexity systems are those that are non-linear, emergent, open, unknowable at the outset, interdependent, and self-organizing; an accurate descriptor of blockchains in their current early evolutionary moments. What is important in systems of general complexity is the relationality between the components as opposed to the parts or the whole, or the beginnings, endpoints, and boundaries of the system. Morin's *general complexity* is distinct from *restricted complexity*, where restricted complexity the position that despite the intricate and complicated nature of complex systems, the underlying rules may become known and enumerated through scientific study. The other position, general complexity, is that an approach that is itself complexity-congruent is potentially a more accurate investigatory stance towards complex systems, especially in the case of blockchains as complex systems, including since they themselves are still evolving. Blockchains are complex systems and also generators of complexity. They reliably create randomness, indeterminacy, and entropy as it is not known or predictable ahead of time which node will 'win' the right to confirm the next block by correctly guessing the cryptographic nonce. This feature of blockchains as a robust, reliable, persistent, global source of entropy generation is being proposed for use in a number of applications.

The reason that complexity is important is that complex systems are a new kind of technology which might accommodate precisely the next phase of larger global scale projects like million-member genome banks that traditional linear hierarchical models are unable to address. One example is the idea of Blockchain Supercomputing. One of the biggest evolutionary needs in supercomputing is to address new tiers of more sophisticated computational problems, expanding beyond simple linearized parallel processing methods into situations of greater computational complexity, including with currently contemplated desktop and peer-to-peer grid computing, and beyond. Blockchains, particularly with their complexity properties, could be a model to configure new forms of non-linear supercomputing problems. The Bitcoin mining network is the biggest supercomputer we have ever built, and what does this mean? It is used for transaction confirmation and shifting balances between wallet addresses but could be used more broadly for anything.

3 Turing Completeness and Blocktime

While initial blockchain projects like Bitcoin-based cryptocurrencies are specifically not Turing-complete [20] and focus computationally on unspent transaction balances, the second generation of projects, smart contract platforms like Ethereum (launched July 2015) [21] and Eris Industries [22] are designed to be Turing-complete in the sense of running any program. Smart contract platforms accommodate more complicated validation and confirmation functionality including vast value-chain ecologies with independent truth oracles, escrow services, and multi-signature contract co-signing parties. Having Turing-complete platforms could allow a full and portable class of computing problems to be addressed, including orchestrating uncertain future events. Digital cryptocurrencies could be conceived as blockchain computing 1.0, and smart contract platforms, essentially Turing-complete state-change machines as blockchain computing 2.0, and connote a completely different tier of computational complexity. Smart contracts have a number of important features related to computational complexity.

Definitionally, smart contracts are as any contract, agreements between parties, but in this case, posted to the blockchain for some sort of automated execution. Smart contracts may be (1) compliant, in accord with current legal regimes as legal contracts with the four required features of mutual assent, consideration, capacity, and legality, or (2) a-compliant, operating in a-legality outside of current regulatory mechanisms. Smart contracts are state-change machines; they are launched and await events or changes in conditions to update their states. These code-contracts (as opposed to discretionarily-enforced human contracts) will execute inexorably. They can call each other in a near-infinite complexity and be used as the architecture for autonomous entities, DAOs, Dapps, DACs, DASs, and DCOs (distributed autonomous organizations, applications, corporations, societies; distributed collaborative organizations), propelling the automation economy forward.

3.1   Temporality as a Feature

Blockchains are an important reality-making technology, a mode and means of implementing many different flavors of "crypto-enlightenment." This includes newer, flatter, more autonomous economic, political, ethical, scientific, and community systems. But not just in the familiar human social constructs like economics and politics, possibly in physical realities too like time. Blocktime's temporal multiplicity and malleability suggest a reality feature we have never had access to before – a way of possibly making more time. Blocktime as blockchains' own temporality allows the tantalizing possibility of rejiggering time and making it a malleable property of blockchains. The in-built time clock in blockchains is blocktime, the chain of time by which a certain number of blocks will have been confirmed. Time is specified in units of transaction block confirmation times, not minutes or hours like in a human time system. Block confirmation times are convertible to minutes, but these conversion metrics might change over time (for example with block confirms being of the scale and frequency to convert to micro-minutes or nano-minutes).

3.2   Blocktime Arbitrage

One key point is that the notion of blocktime, as an extension of computing clocktime more generally, creates a differential. Blocktime and human time already exist as different time schemas. A differential suggests that the two different systems might be used to reinforce each other, or that the differential could be exploited, arbitraging the two time frameworks. Through the differential too is the way to 'make more time,' by accessing events in another time trajectory. The conceptualization of time in computer science is already different than in human time. Computing clocktime has more dimensions (discrete time, no time, asynchronous time, etc.) than human physical and biological time, which is continuous. Clocktime has always been different than human time. What is different with blocktime is that it builds in even more variability, and the future assignability of time through dapps and smart contracts. For example, MTL (machine trust language) time primitives might be assigned to a micropayment channel dapp as a time arbiter. Time has not been future-specifiable before, in the way that it can be assigned in blocktime smart contracts.

Temporality could be a standard smart contract feature. Time speed-ups, slow-downs, event-waiting, and event-positing (a true futures-class technology) could become *de rigueur* blocktime specifications. Even the blocktime regime itself could be a contract-specifiable parameter per drop-down menu, just like legal regime. Temporality becomes a feature as smart contracts are launched and await events or changes in conditions to update contract states. Time malleability could itself be a feature, arbitraging blocktime with real time. An example of a time schema differential arising could be for example, a decentralized peer-to-peer loan that is coming due in blocktime, but where there have not been enough physical-world time cycles available for generating the 'fiat resources' to repay the loan.

In blocktime, the time interval at which things are done is by block. This is the time that it takes blocks to confirm, so blockchain system processes like those involving smart contracts are ordered around the conception of blocktime quanta or units. This is a different temporal paradigm than human lived time. The human time paradigm is one that is more variable and contingent. Human time is divided and unitized by the vagaries of human experience, by parameters such as day and night; week, weekend, and holiday; seasons; and more contingently, crises, eras, and historical events. Since blocktime is an inherent blockchain feature, one of the easiest ways to programmatically specify future time intervals for event conditions and state changes in blockchain-based events is via blocktime. Arguably, it is easier, and more congruent and efficient, to call a time measure from within a system rather than from outside. It could be prohibitively costly for example, to specify an external programmatic call to NIST or another time oracle. Possibly the emerging convention could be to call NIST, including as a backup, confirmation, or comparison for blocktime. Currently, blockchain systems do not necessarily synchronize their internal clocktime with NIST, but the possibility of a vast web of worldwide smart contracts suggests the value and necessity of external time oracles, and raises new issues about global time measurement more generally. Especially since each different blockchain might have its own blocktime, there could be some standard means of coordinating blocktime synchronizations for interoperability, maybe via a time sidechain for example. The key point is starting to conceive of time in a mode which has been unprecedented; time is not a fixed given, time is a malleable resource that can be specified in different ways as a contract feature. In fact, I conjecture that the malleability of time engenders a sense of the possibility of creating "more time" by being able to access events in alternative time trajectories such as blocktime [23].

3.3   Computing Creates Novel Temporalities of Discontinuity and Prediction

First computing clocktime made time malleable through its different discontinuous forms. Then machine learning and big data facilitated a new temporality, one oriented to the present and future, instead of responding to just the past. There was a shift from only being able to react to events retrospectively after they had passed, to now being able to model, simulate, plan, and act in real-time as events occur, and proactively structure future events. The current change is that blockchains and particularly smart contracts add exponential power to this; they are in some sense a future reality-making technology on steroids. Whole classes of industries (like mortgage servicing) might be outsourced to the seamless orchestration of blockchain dapps and DACs in the next phases of the automation economy. While Bitcoin is the spot market for transactions in the present moment, smart contracts are a robust futures market for locking in the automated orchestration of vast areas of digital activity.

3.4   Blockchain Historicity: Computer Memory of Human Events

Blockchain logs are in a sense a human event memory server. Blockchains are already event history keepers, and now with blocktime could have even more responsibility as the memory computer of human events. It is now possible to think in terms of blockchain time sequences, in the anticipation and scoping of future events and activities, as blockchain reality unfolds, as opposed to human time scales and events. For example, there are normal human time sequences, like a one-year lease agreement. Other sequentiality is based on human-experienced conditions like 'the park is open until dark,' which makes little sense in a blocktime schema. There are time guidelines that vary per lived experience in human realities. Likewise, there could be analogs in lived experience in blockchain realities. Different events could mark the historicity of blockchains, for example, the time elapsed since the genesis block, and other metrics regarding number, amount, and the speed of transactions. Gesturing towards a crypto-philosophy, Hegel, Benjamin, Hölderlin, and Heidegger already have more malleable conceptions of historicity and temporality that might be instantiated in the blocktime paradigm. There is much more linkage and portability between past, present, and future (all arguably human constructions), for example, in ecstatic temporality, where the event from the future reaches back to inform the present now moment, as extended from the past [24].

4   Conclusion

In this paper, my contribution is to (1) provide a conceptual context for smart contracts, (2) argue that blockchains are a next-generation technology enabling much larger-scale and more complex computing projects, and (3) posit blocktime as a new mode of conceiving time. Blockchains are a universal general computing substrate in the Turing-complete sense: any computing problem can be formulated and run on blockchains as a universal computing platform. Not only can blockchains run any program, they are an improved computational substrate because of their universality, accessibility, availability, scalability (both vertical (Merkle rooting) and horizontal (distributed network nodes)), always-on connection to the Internet, permanent record-maintaining, and auditable record-keeping. More broadly, blockchains are a new form of cryptographic software protocol and a programming paradigm for secure distributed computing. They could have a wide variety of uses in the implementation of digital currencies, financial and economic transfers; the administration, registration, and exchange of all forms of tangible and intangible assets as smart property; and the coordination of governance, legal, health, and scientific activity via smart contracts and distributed autonomous entities, ushering in a productive and trust-building era of human-machine collaboration. Computationally, blockchains provide an unprecedented fully-scalable universal worldwide computing infrastructure with built-in security and a remunerative payments layer. Blockchains could be the next evolutionary addition to the Internet by enabling a new degree of sophistication and resolution in computing. Thus there could be the start of a universal computing substrate, an always-on ubiquitous background resource, a blanket of secure processing that supports greater possibilities for human endeavor. Blockchains as a new core infrastructural tier of computational resource could prompt a reconception of computing: philosophically, mathematically, and practically. As a general computational substrate, blockchains expand the reach of computing, and this in turn expands the reach of our thinking and realizing in terms of what is possible in computing.

References

1. Connor, S.: Single DNA molecule could store information for a million years following scientific breakthrough. Independent (2015)
2. Pais-Vieira, M., Chiuffa, G., Lebedev, M., Yadav, A., Nicolelis, M.A.L.: Building an organic computing device with multiple interconnected brains. Nat. Sci. Rep. **5**, 11869 (2015)
3. Seo, D., Carmena, J.M., Rabaey, J.M., Alon, E., Maharbiz, M.M.: Neural dust: an ultrasonic, low power solution for chronic brain-machine interfaces (2013). arXiv:1307.2196 [q-bio NC]
4. Bauer, H., Patel, M., Veira, J.: The Internet of Things: Sizing up the Opportunity. McKinsey and Co., New York (2014)
5. Swan, M.: Blockchain: Blueprint for a New Economy. O'Reilly Media, Sebastopol (2015)
6. Merkle, R.: DAOs, Democracy and Governance. Version 1.2 (2015)
7. Lamport, L., Shostak, R., Pease, M.: The Byzantine generals problem. ACM Trans. Program. Lang. Syst. **4**(3), 382–401 (1982)
8. Antonopoulos, A.M.: Mastering Bitcoin: Unlocking Digital Cryptocurrencies. O'Reilly Media, Sebastopol (2014)
9. Swan, M.: Blockchain Consensus Protocols. Bitcoin Meetup (2015). http://www.slideshare.net/lablogga/blockchain-consensus-protocols
10. Buterin, V.: Primecoin: The cryptocurrency whose mining is actually useful. Bitcoin Mag. (2013). http://primecoin.io
11. Dollentas, N.: Greencoin: carbon emissions coin. Bitcoinist (2014). http://www.grcoin.com

196   M. Swan

12. Cawrey, D.: 5 Global problems Bitcoin's proof of work can help solve. CoinDesk (2014). http://www.gridcoin.us
13. Menezes, N.: Interview with the Foldingcoin team. Bitcoinist (2014). http://foldingcoin.net
14. Smart, E.: Bitcoin is 100 times more powerful than Google. Cryptocoin News (2015)
15. Gill, T.: Bitcoin hash-rate exceeds total computing power of all the world's computers! Taran Gill Blog (2014)
16. Top 500: The List - June 2015. http://www.top500.org/lists/2015/06
17. Halevy, A., Norvig, P., Pereira, F.: The unreasonable effectiveness of data. IEEE Intell. Syst. 24(2), 8–12 (2009)
18. Le, Q.V., Ranzato, M., Monga, R., Devin, M., Chen, K., Corrado, G.S., Dean, J., Ng, A.Y.: Building high-level features using large scale unsupervised learning (2011). arXiv:1112.6209 [cs.LG]
19. Morin, E.: Restricted complexity, general complexity. In: Gershenson, C., Aerts, D., Edmonds, B. (eds.) Worldviews, Science and Us: Philosophy and Complexity, pp. 5–29. World Scientific, Singapore (2007). Trans. by, Gershenson, C.
20. Nakamoto, S.: Bitcoin: a peer-to-peer electronic cash system (2008)
21. Liang, C.C.: A next-generation smart contract and decentralized application platform. Ethereum White paper (2016). https://github.com/ethereum/wiki/wiki/White-Paper
22. Lewis, A.: In a nutshell: Eris (Epicenter Bitcoin Interview – January 2016). Bits on Blocks Blog (2016)
23. Swan. M.: Temporality of the Future: A New Theory of Time: X-tention is Simultaneously Discrete and Continuous. Institute for Ethics and Emerging Technologies (2016). http://www.slideshare.net/lablogga/temporality-of-the-future
24. Heidegger, M.: Being and Time, pp. 1–474. Harper Perennial Modern Classics, New York (2008)

Constraint Handling Rules

A Numerical Optimisation Based Characterisation of Spatial Reasoning

Carl Schultz[1,3](✉) and Mehul Bhatt[2,3]

[1] University of Münster, Münster, Germany
schultzc@uni-muenster.de
[2] University of Bremen, Bremen, Germany
[3] The DesignSpace Group, Bremen, Germany
http://www.design-space.org,
http://www.spatial-reasoning.com

Abstract. We present a novel *numerical optimisation* based characterisation of spatial reasoning in the context of constraint logic programming (CLP). The approach —formalised and implemented within CLP— is developed as an extension to CLP(QS), a declarative spatial reasoning framework providing a range of mixed quantitative-qualitative spatial representation and reasoning capabilities. We demonstrate the manner in which the numerical optimisation based extensions further enhance the declarative spatial reasoning capabilities of CLP(QS).

Keywords: Numerical optimisation · Declarative spatial reasoning · Constraint logic programming · Geometric and spatial reasoning

1 Introduction

Declarative spatial reasoning is a paradigm that aims to integrate spatial representation and reasoning natively within general Knowledge Representation and Reasoning (KR) frameworks to support seamless high-level reasoning about both domain-specific knowledge and spatial constraints [4]. For instance, we would like to employ logic programming for Question/Answering in application domains where *space* plays a central role (product design, geographic information systems, histopathology, etc.) by posing *queries* over a knowledge base of facts and rules that can also involve *spatial* constraints.

Consider an example: let p be a 2D point defined by real coordinates x_p, y_p, and let c be a circle defined by a 2D centre point x_c, y_c and a real-valued radius r_c. We pose the following query in the Prolog logic programming language that the point p is both in the interior of c (inside) and exterior to c (outside):

```
?- point(P), circle(C),
|  incidence(interior, P, C),
|  incidence(exterior, P, C).
```

As it is impossible for a point to be both inside and outside of a circle simultaneously the correct answer is:

```
false.
```

© Springer International Publishing Switzerland 2016
J.J. Alferes et al. (Eds.): RuleML 2016, LNCS 9718, pp. 199–207, 2016.
DOI: 10.1007/978-3-319-42019-6_13

Notice that no numerical coordinates for p nor c were given. The interpretation of the query result is that: there does not exist *any* 2D point p that is both inside and outside of some circle c. Thus, to fully support spatial reasoning we require that Prolog can handle variables that range over *infinite* domains of possible spatial objects.

We have pursued various approaches for declarative spatial reasoning in KR [4,16,18,19] in an attempt to balance expressiveness against the prohibitive computational complexity of spatial reasoning in the absence of a complete numerical description of the objects involved (we provide further details in Sect. 2). In addition to CLP, most recently we have also explored the integration of spatial reasoning with Answer Set Programming (Modulo Theories) [19] in order to handle non-monotonic spatial reasoning in a *dynamic spatial systems* setting. In this paper, we further extend the foundations of declarative spatial reasoning in the context of CLP. We target a specific class of *qualitative* spatial constraints that we formulate in the framework of *numerical optimisation* (Sect. 2), including: *contact, incidence, orientation, relative size*. By the use of *attributed variables*, we show that our approach fully adheres to the semantics of CLP. Furthermore, we also deomontrate that spatial solving in our framework is *incremental*, and thus avoids costly re-solving of subproblems.

2   Spatial Representation and Reasoning

Constraint Logic Programming [9] extends standard Logic Programming unification by allowing certain goals to be sent to a *constraint store* handled by a specialised constraint solver for determining satisfiability. This greatly expands the domains that can be reasoned about, such as linear constraints over the *reals* $CLP(\mathbb{R})$ [9], qualitative spatial relations [4] etc.

Spatial Entities in $\mathcal{QS}$. Domain entities in $\mathcal{QS}$ include *points*, *line segments*, *circles*, *simple polygons*, and *egg-yolk regions*. Our method is applicable to a wide range of 2D and 3D spatial objects, e.g. [4,13].

- a *point* is a pair of reals x, y,
- a *line segment* is a pair of end points p_1, p_2 ($p_1 \neq p_2$),
- a *circle* is a centre point p and a real radius r ($0 < r$),
- an *egg yolk* region[1] is defined by a circular upper and lower approximation c^+, c^- such that c^- is a *proper part* of c^+,
- a *simple polygon* is defined by a list of n vertices (points) $p_1, \ldots, p_n$ (spatially ordered counter-clockwise) such that the boundary is non-self-intersecting, i.e., there does not exist a polygon boundary edge between vertices p_i, p_{i+1} that intersects some other edge p_j, p_{j+1} for all $1 \leq i < j < n$ and $i + 1 < j$.

---

[1] We employ the egg-yolk method of modelling regions with indeterminante boundaries [6] to characterise a class of regions (including polygons) that satisfies topological and relative orientation relations [17]. Each egg-yolk region is an equivalence class for all regions that are contained within the upper approximation (the *egg white*), and completely contain the lower approximations (the *egg yolk*).

A spatial *object* in a spatial reasoning problem is a variable associated with a spatial domain (e.g. the domain of $2D$ points). An *instance* of an object is an element from the domain, e.g. the point $(0,1)$ is an instance of a *point* object. A *configuration* of objects is a set of instances such that each object corresponds to exactly one instance.

Spatial Relations in QS. We define the following spatial relations in QS (see Fig. 2) as they have been studied extensively within AI and demonstrate a range of spatial aspects.

Mereotopology. Part-whole and *contact* relations between regions [15]: *disconnected (dc), externally connected (ec), partially overlapping (po), tangential proper-part (tpp), non-tangential proper part (ntpp), equal (eq), discrete from (dr)* defined as *dc* or *ec*, and *proper part (pp)* defined as *tpp* or *ntpp*.

Relative Orientation. Left, right, collinear, in front, behind orientation relations of *points* and *regions* with respect to *line segments*, and *parallel, perpendicular* relations between *line segments* [4].

Incidence. Interior, on boundary, exterior incidence relations between *points* and *regions*.

Size. Smaller, equisized, larger size relations between *regions*.

Spatial Reasoning Tasks. In the following tasks the input is a set of objects and a set of qualitative spatial relations between those objects.

Consistency. Determine whether the relations are satisfiable, i.e., whether there exists at least one configuration of the objects that satisfies all spatial relations.

Generating Configurations. Find a configuration of objects that satisfies the given relations.

Interactive Geometry. Intuitively, allow a user to "move", "resize" or otherwise manipulate object instances in a configuration. The spatial solver automatically updates the other object instances so that the given spatial relations are maintained at all times. More formally, given a set of objects O, a set of relations, a configuration C_1, and an object $o \in O$ (that the user manipulated) find a new consistent configuration C_2 such that the instance of o is the same in C_1 and C_2.

2.1 Formulating Spatial Semantics as Numerical Optimisation

One approach for formalising the semantics of spatial reasoning is by *analytic geometry*, i.e. to encode qualitative spatial relations as systems of polynomial equations and inequalities. The task of determining whether a set of spatial relations is consistent is then equivalent to determining whether the set of polynomial constraints are satisfiable. Iterative methods for solving systems of polynomial constraints generate sequences of approximate solutions that aim to converge on a solution, and include Newton- and Quasi-Newton-based methods [11]. Let $X = (x_1, \dots, x_n)$ be a vector of n real variables (encoding the object parameters) over m polynomial equation constraints (encoding the qualitative spatial relations): $f_i(x_1, \ldots, x_n) = 0$ for $1 \leq i \leq m$. Numerical optimisation solves the system of constraints by minimising the sum of squares [8]:

$$\sigma(X) = \sum_{i=1}^{m} f_i(X)^2$$

Many specialised global and local optimisation algorithms have been developed e.g. low storage BFGS [5].

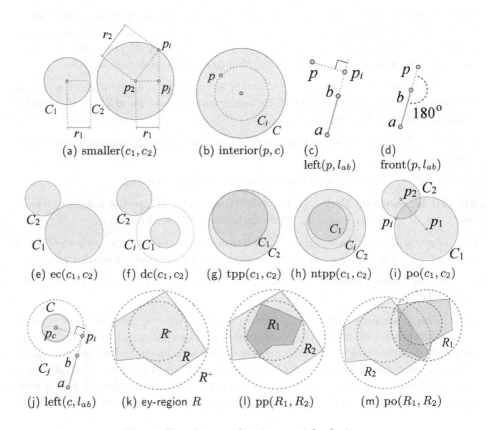

(a) smaller(c_1, c_2)   (b) interior(p, c)   (c) left(p, l_{ab})   (d) front(p, l_{ab})

(e) ec(c_1, c_2)   (f) dc(c_1, c_2)   (g) tpp(c_1, c_2)   (h) ntpp(c_1, c_2)   (i) po(c_1, c_2)

(j) left(c, l_{ab})   (k) ey-region R (l) pp(R_1, R_2)   (m) po(R_1, R_2)

Fig. 1. Encoding qualitative spatial relations.

Table 1 presents our set of primitive geometric functions that we use to encode qualitative spatial relations (Fig. 1). Each function f_i is satisfied by the given arguments X when $f_i(X) = 0$, and thus can be robustly solved for by standard numerical optimisation algorithms. For example, we make circle c_1 *smaller* than circle c_2 by introducing points p_i, p_j such that the points p_i, p_j and p_2 (the centre of c_2) make a right-angled triangle. The distance $|p_2 p_j|$ between p_2, p_j equals the radius r_1 of c_1. The distance $|p_2 p_i|$ between points p_2, p_i equals the radius r_2 of

Table 1. Primitive geometric functions.

Function	Polynomial expression	Description
$\mathrm{coll}(x_p, y_p, x_a, y_a, x_b, y_b)$	$(x_b - x_a)(y_p - y_a) - (x_b - y_a)(x_p - x_a)$	point p collinear to line l_{ab}
$\mathrm{coin}(x_p, y_p, x_c, y_c, r_c)$	$(x_p - x_c)^2 + (y_p - y_c)^2 - r_c^2$	point p coincident to boundary of circle c
$\mathrm{perp}(x_a, y_a, x_b, y_b, x_c, y_c, x_d, y_d)$	$(y_b - y_a)(y_d - y_c) + (x_b - x_a)(x_d - x_c)$	lines l_{ab}, l_{cd} are perpendicular
$\mathrm{para}(x_a, y_a, x_b, y_b, x_c, y_c, x_d, y_d)$	$(y_b - y_a)(x_d - x_c) - (x_b - x_a)(y_d - y_c)$	lines l_{ab}, l_{cd} are parallel
$\mathrm{angl}(x_a, y_a, x_b, y_b, x_c, y_c, x_d, y_d, \theta)$	$\theta - \mathrm{atan2}((y_a - y_b), (x_a - x_b))$ $+ \mathrm{atan2}((y_c - y_d), (x_c - x_d))$	angle θ between lines l_{ab}, l_{cd}
$\mathrm{diff}(v_a, v_b, v_c)$	$v_c - (v_a - v_b)$	value v_c equals values v_a minus v_b
$\mathrm{tang\_int}(x_a, y_a, r_a, x_b, y_b, r_b)$	$(x_a - x_b)^2 + (y_a - y_b)^2 - (r_a - r_b)^2$	circle c_a is inside circle c_b, touching the boundary (tangent internal)
$\mathrm{tang\_ext}(x_a, y_a, r_a, x_b, y_b, r_b)$	$(x_a - x_b)^2 + (y_a - y_b)^2 - (r_a + r_b)^2$	circles c_a, c_b have external contact (tangent external)

c_2. By Pythogoras' Theorem, $|p_2 p_j|$ must be less than $|p_2 p_i|$. Therefore $r_1 < r_2$. This is expressed by the following constraint:

$$\mathrm{coin}(x_i, y_i, x_2, y_2, r_2) \wedge (x_j = x_i) \wedge (y_j = y_2) \wedge \mathrm{not\_equal}(p_i, p_j)$$

3 Spatial Variables in Prolog

In this section we present our implementation of spatial variables in Prolog and prove that our system fully adheres to Constraint Logic Programming semantics with incremental spatial solving. A CLP($\mathcal{QS}$) program is a plain CLP program with a spatial constraint store G consisting of spatial variables V and a set of spatial constraints E. Let ϕ be a spatial oracle predicate that takes G. Invoking the oracle succeeds, $\phi(G) \equiv \top$, if the corresponding numerical optimisation problem has a global minimum $\sigma(X) = 0$. The oracle is invoked when a spatial constraint is added to E, and when spatial variables are unified.

Implementation. Spatial constraints are maintained in plain CLP via attributed variables along with real values representing the current consistent configuration. Attribute variable hooks invoke the oracle predicate that calls the external numerical optimisation solver as follows:

1. set up a fresh numerical optimisation problem over polynomial variables X in the external solver corresponding to G; assign initial values for each $x \subset X$ according to the current real value assigned to the corresponding spatial variables $v \in V$

2. run the external solver's numerical optimisation algorithm
3. *IF* the solver reports failure then clear the solver database and return *fail*
4. *ELSE* retrieve real values of the solution from the solver and assign to the spatial variables' *value* attributes; clear the solver database; return *success*

Importantly, the use of the external solver is stateless, i.e. all spatial constraints are maintained on the Prolog side. This guarantees that the integration with the external solver does not interfere with the SLD resolution procedure.

Proposition 1. *The integration between the external numerical optimisation solver and Prolog does not interfere with SLD resolution.*

Proof. A CLP($\mathcal{QS}$) program is a plain CLP program with calls to an external solver. Calls to the external solver are stateless, and thus equivalent to calling an oracle. The oracle is invoked whenever the constraint store is altered or spatial variables are unified, and thus at each step in the SLD resolution procedure the constraint store is necessarily consistent, otherwise standard SLD resolution failure occurs.   □

The cost of solving a numerical optimisation problem is measured as the number of iterations required to find the minimum. If the given problem already is minimised then the algorithm requires 0 iterations.

Proposition 2. *Spatial constraint solving is incremental, i.e. adding a new spatial constraint and solving does not require re-solving the original set of constraints.*

Proof. Let G be a spatial constraint store, and ϕ a spatial oracle that determines consistency of G by a numerical optimisation algorithm. The oracle uses the current configuration assigned to the spatial variables in G as the initial variable values of the numerical optimisation problem. Let $I(\phi(G))$ be the number of numerical optimisation iterations required to solve G. Assume G is consistent, then the current configuration in G is consistent, and therefore the initial variable values of the optimisation problem evaluate to $\sigma(X) = 0$, and therefore, $I(\phi(G)) = 0$. It follows that, for any subset of constraints $G_i \subset G$, $I(\phi(G_i)) = 0$. Let a new constraint E be added to G to give constraint store G'. Let G'_i be a subgraph of G' where the spatial variables are not reachable from E. For all such subgraphs, necessarily $G'_i \subset G$ therefore $I(\phi(G'_i)) = 0$ (i.e. no spatial constraints require re-solving that are not constrained by E). Now assume that backtracking has returned the SLD resolution procedure to a prior decision point. The constraint store is reverted to the last consistent state G'' at that decision point. G'' is necessarily consistent otherwise $\phi(G'')$ would have failed at that decision point, therefore, $I(\phi(G'')) = 0$.   □

Proposition 3. *Our qualitative spatial solver based on numerical optimisation supports the required tasks of (1) consistency, (2) configuration generation, and (3) interactive geometry.*

Proof. (1) A system of polynomial constraints over variables X is satisfiable when the sum of squares is minimised, $\sigma(X) = 0$. When such a minimum is found then the corresponding spatial constraint problem is consistent. (2) The real values assigned to variables X that minimise the sum of squares are retrieved from the numerical optimisation algorithm. These values correspond to a consistent configuration of spatial objects. (3) Polynomial variables can be marked as immutable and will not be changed by the numerical optimisation solver. Interactive geometry is implemented by assigning a new value to a spatial variable (e.g. moving a point by clicking and dragging the point in a GUI), marking the corresponding polynomial variable as immutable, and solving the spatial constraints. □

4   Empirical Examples

We have fully implemented our spatial reasoning framework within the CLP($\mathcal{QS}$) system. In this section we demonstrate applicability on problems from spatial Q/A and histopathology.[2]

Spatial Q/A. Spatial variable unification (*e.g.* $A = B$) is fully supported in our system, both with respect to resolution refutation and correct spatial semantics.

```
?- point(A),point(B),incidence(not_equal,A,B),A=B. % incidence and unification
false.
?- point(A),point(B),incidence(not_equal,A,B),A\=B. % negation as failure
true.
?- line(A,B),A=B. % lines must have positive length
false.
?- circle(C1),centre(C1,P),incidence(on_boundary,P,C1).% radius must be positive
false.
?- point(A),circle(C1),A=C1.  % Prolog facilitates syntactic type checking
false.
% Identity of two circles corresponds to topological equality
?- circle(C1),circle(C2),C1=C2,topology(Relation,C1,C2).
Relation = rcc(eq); false.
% Concentric circles cannot have the tangential-proper-part relation
?- circle(C1),circle(C2),centre(C1,P), centre(C2,P), topology(rcc(tpp),C1,C2).
false.
```

Histopathology. Figure 2(a) presents a stained tissue section of red and white blood cells from a patient with chronic myelogenous leukemia. We use CLP($\mathcal{QS}$) to build a conceptual model and interactive diagram of the objects in the image, including both semantic and qualitative spatial relations, by incorporating background knowledge about cells [7]. We employ the Gene Ontology (GO) and the Cell Ontology (CL), parsed as Prolog facts and rules, e.g., eukaryotic cells consist of cytoplasm and a nucleus (part-of mereology relations), where the nucleus is spatially contained within the cytoplasm (a topological relation). First, we segment the image, which assigns a class type to each segment, and apply standard contour detection algorithms to convert the raster image into polygons.

---

[2] CLP($\mathcal{QS}$) is implemented in SWI-Prolog, and we have integrated the geometric constraint solver FreeCAD www.freecadweb.org.

(a) Stained tissue section of (b) Contours of segmented (c) User drags cells in
red and white blood cells [1]. image.   interactive diagram.

Fig. 2. Spatial reasoning in histopathology. (Color figure online)

Figure 2(b) shows the contours of *cytoplasm* (green) and *nuclei* (blue) of mature
eosinophils cells, and enucleate erythrocytes cells (red). There is a semantic error
in the segmented image (Fig. 2(b)): a single cytoplasm region (green) contains
two nuclei (blue), as expressed in the query:

```
?- cytoplasm(Cyto), nucleus(NucleusA), nucleus(NucleusB),
 |  NucleusA \= NucleusB,
 |  spatial_representation(Cyto, CytoRegion),
 |  spatial_representation(NucleusA, NucleusARegion),
 |  spatial_representation(NucleusB, NucleusBRegion),
 |  topology(rcc(pp), NucleusARegion, CytoRegion),
 |  topology(rcc(pp), NucleusBRegion, CytoRegion).
```

Our system responds by inferring the existence of two cytoplasms, each containing one nucleus (Fig. 2(c)). The resulting conceptual model is used to generate an
interactive diagram: Fig. 2(c) illustrates an updated diagram as a user *drags* the
cytoplasm regions apart - qualitative spatial relations are automatically maintained such as the nuclei remaining inside the respective cytoplasms, and the
two cytoplasms remaining discrete.

5   Related Work and Conclusions

We have presented a framework and full implementation in CLP($\mathcal{QS}$) that efficiently exploits state-of-the-art dedicated numerical optimisation algorithms for
solving a specific class of qualitative spatial constraints natively within CLP.
Within the fields of AI and KR, a variety of frameworks have been developed
that formalise notions of *space*, and spatial relations between objects [2,3,10,12].
However, what is lacking is a systematic formal account and computational characterisation of such spatial theories as a KR language. In this direction, Raffaeta
and Frühwirth [14] develop the Spatio-Temporal Annotated CLP system for reasoning about axis-aligned cuboids. Pesant and Boyer [13] extend QUAD-CLP(R)
for constructive solid geometry with quadratic polynomial constraints. The distinction with our work is that our spatial ontology is much broader due to the
numerical optimisation formulation. Operationally, another point of departure
is that our method exploits state-of-the-art dedicated solvers in a modular and
efficient way, while still adhering to CLP semantics.

References

1. Center for genomic pathology. http://ctrgenpath.net/2011/04/slide-of-the-week-april-14/. Accessed 03 Apr 2016
2. Aiello, M., Pratt-Hartmann, I.E., van Benthem, J.F.A.K.: Handbook of Spatial Logics. Springer New York Inc., Secaucus (2007)
3. Bhatt, M., Guesgen, H., Wölfl, S., Hazarika, S.: Qualitative spatial and temporal reasoning: emerging applications, trends, and directions. Spat. Cogn. Comput. **11**(1), 1–14 (2011)
4. Bhatt, M., Lee, J.H., Schultz, C.: CLP(QS): a declarative spatial reasoning framework. In: Egenhofer, M., Giudice, N., Moratz, R., Worboys, M. (eds.) COSIT 2011. LNCS, vol. 6899, pp. 210–230. Springer, Heidelberg (2011)
5. Byrd, R.H., Lu, P., Nocedal, J., Ciyou, Z.: A limited memory algorithm for bound constrained optimization. SIAM J. Sci. Comput. **16**(5), 1190–1208 (1995)
6. Cohn, A.G., Gotts, N.M.: The 'egg-yolk' representation of regions with indeterminate boundaries. Geogr. Objects Indeterminate Bound. **2**, 171–187 (1996)
7. Duesmann, G.: Applying principles of knowledge representation and reasoning by integrating declarative spatial reasoning and computer vision: a prototype system for histopathology. Bachelor thesis, The University of Münster (2016)
8. Ge, J.-X., Chou, S.-C., Gao, X.-S.: Geometric constraint satisfaction using optimization methods. Comput. Aided Des. **31**(14), 867–879 (1999)
9. Jaffar, J., Michaylov, S., Stuckey, P.J., Yap, R.H.: The CLP (R) language and system. ACM Trans. Program. Lang. Syst. (TOPLAS) **14**(3), 339–395 (1992)
10. Kapur, D., Mundy, J.L. (eds.): Geometric Reasoning. MIT Press, Cambridge (1988)
11. Light, R., Gossard, D.: Modification of geometric models through variational geometry. Comput. Aided Des. **14**(4), 209–214 (1982)
12. Ligozat, G.: Qualitative Spatial and Temporal Reasoning. Wiley-ISTE, London (2011)
13. Pesant, G., Boyer, M.: Reasoning about solids using constraint logic programming. J. Autom. Reason. **22**(3), 241–262 (1999)
14. Raffaetà, A., Frühwirth, T.: Spatio-temporal annotated constraint logic programming. In: Ramakrishnan, I.V. (ed.) PADL 2001. LNCS, vol. 1990, pp. 259–273. Springer, Heidelberg (2001)
15. Randell, D.A., Cui, Z., Cohn, A.G.: A spatial logic based on regions and connection. KR **92**, 165–176 (1992)
16. Schultz, C., Bhatt, M.: Declarative spatial reasoning with boolean combinations of axis-aligned rectangular polytopes. In: ECAI 2014–21st European Conference on Artificial Intelligence, pp. 795–800 (2014)
17. Schultz, C., Bhatt, M.: Encoding relative orientation and mereotopology relations with geometric constraints in CLP(QS). In: 1st Workshop on Logics for Qualitative Modelling and Reasoning (LQMR 2015), Lodz, Poland, September 2015
18. Schultz, C., Bhatt, M.: Spatial symmetry driven pruning strategies for efficient declarative spatial reasoning. In: Fabrikant, S.I., Raubal, M., Bertolotto, M., Davies, C., Freundschuh, S., Bell, S. (eds.) COSIT 2015. LNCS, vol. 9368, pp. 331–353. Springer, Heidelberg (2015). doi:10.1007/978-3-319-23374-1_16
19. Wałęga, P.A., Bhatt, M., Schultz, C.: ASPMT(QS): non-monotonic spatial reasoning with answer set programming modulo theories. In: Calimeri, F., Ianni, G., Truszczyński, M. (eds.) LPNMR 2015. LNCS, vol. 9345, pp. 488–501. Springer, Heidelberg (2015)

Why Can't You Behave? Non-termination Analysis of Direct Recursive Rules with Constraints

Thom Frühwirth$^{(\boxtimes)}$

Ulm University, Ulm, Germany
thom.fruehwirth@uni-ulm.de

Abstract. This paper is concerned with rule-based programs that go wrong. The unwanted behavior of rule applications is non-termination or failure of a computation. We propose a static program analysis of the non-termination problem for recursion in the Constraint Handling Rules (CHR) language.

CHR is an advanced concurrent declarative language involving constraint reasoning. It has been closely related to many other rule-based approaches, so the results are of a more general interest. In such languages, non-termination is due to infinite applications of recursive rules. Failure is due to accumulation of contradicting constraints during the computation.

We give theorems with so-called misbehavior conditions for potential non-termination and failure (as well as definite termination) of linear direct recursive simplification rules. Logical relationships between the constraints in a recursive rule play a crucial role in this kind of program analysis. We think that our approach can be extended to other types of recursion and to a more general class of rules. Therefore this paper can serve as a basic reference and a starting point for further research.

1 Introduction

It is well known that termination is undecidable for Turing-complete programming languages. Thus, there is a long tradition in research on program analysis methods, static and dynamic, to tame the problem by semi-automatic or approximative approaches.

In this work we are interested in characterizing non-terminating computations. We do so in the context of the programming language Constraint Handling Rules (CHR) [4,5,7]. As in other rule-based languages, termination is only an issue if recursion is involved. We are hopeful that our results could be transferred to other rule-based programming languages as well, since CHR can directly embed many rule-based languages and formalisms (e.g. Chap. 6 in [4]).

We propose conditions for misbehavior, i.e. a static program analysis of a recursive rule that tells us if a given goal (or a set of goals) may not terminate or lead to failure (unsatisfiable constraints). The following program serves as a first overview of the characteristic features of CHR for those not familiar

© Springer International Publishing Switzerland 2016
J.J. Alferes et al. (Eds.): RuleML 2016, LNCS 9718, pp. 208–222, 2016.
DOI: 10.1007/978-3-319-42019-6_14

with the language. In CHR, we use a first-order logic syntax. Predicates will be called constraints. Goals and states are synonyms here, they are conjunctions of constraints. In this paper, numbers are expressed in successor term notation. The following example will be further elaborated in this paper.

Example 1. Consider a recursive user-defined constraint *double* that doubles the natural number in the first argument and produces the resulting number in the second argument:

$$double(X,Y) \Leftrightarrow X = 0 \mid Y = 0.$$
$$double(X,Y) \Leftrightarrow X = s(X1) \mid Y = s(s(Y1)) \land double(X1,Y1).$$

The first rule (for the base case) says that if X is syntactically equivalent to 0, then the result Y is also zero. The syntactic equality constraint $X = 0$ is a *guard*, a precondition on the applicability of the rule. It serves as a test. The rule is only applied if this condition holds in the current context, i.e. state. On the other hand, $Y = 0$ is a constraint that is asserted once the rule is applied. The recursive rule says that if X is the successor of some number $X1$, then Y is the successor of the successor of some number $Y1$, and $X1$ doubled gives $Y1$.

To the goal $double(X,Y)$ no rule is applicable. To the goal $double(X,Y) \land X = 0$ the first rule is applicable, resulting in the state $X = 0 \land Y = 0$. To the goal $double(X,Y) \land X = 0 \land Y = s(B)$, the first rule is also applicable, but the resulting contradiction $Y = s(B) \land Y = 0$ means failure due to these unsatisfiable equality constraints.

In logical languages like CHR, variables cannot be overwritten, but they can be without value (unbound). For example, if X is $s(A)$, where A is unbound, then X will satisfy the guard, and Y will be equated to $s(s(B)))$, where B is some newly introduced variable, and the CHR constraint $double(A,B)$ will be added to the state. Since A is unbound, the guard for the recursive goal *double* does not (yet) hold. If the variable later becomes (partially) bound in a syntactic equality, the computation of *double* may resume.

There is a simple example for a infinite computation with *double*. The goal $double(X,Y) \land X = s(X1) \land X = Y$ does not terminate. The application of the recursive rule leads to the state $X = s(X1) \land X = Y \land Y = s(s(Y1)) \land double(X1,Y1)$. Since $X = Y$, we have that $X1 = s(Y1)$. Thus the computation can proceed with another recursive rule application and so on ad infinitum. The successors that are produced for Y in the second argument will also become successors for X in the first argument, because of $X = Y$. Thus the guard of the recursive goal always holds.

The goal $double(X,Y) \land X = s(X1) \land X \geq Y$ does not terminate either. Our main theorem will allow to detect this non-termination because a misbehavior condition holds. Basically, the guard and the body of the recursive rule, $X = s(X1) \land Y = s(s(Y1))$, together with the added constraint $X \geq Y$ implies the guard of the recursive goal $X1 = s(X1')$. Another theorem will tell us that the more stricter constraint $X = Y$ will therefore inherit the misbehavior.

Related Work. Non-termination analysis has been considered for term rewriting systems [3,11], logic programming languages [6,10,12,14], and imperative languages [2,8,9,13].

The works on (constraint) logic programming are based on finding loops in abstracted partial derivation trees. In our restricted case of linear direct recursion it is sufficient to consider the recursive rule and no abstraction is necessary. However, there is also a difference to our approach: mode information about the arguments is essential in analysing logic programs. A similar type of information is also needed for non-termination of constraint logic programs [12]. It gives raise to so-called filters for abstracting states of the computation. In CHR, this information is already implicitly encoded in the distinction between guard and body built-in constraints.

In [6] a simple program transformation for recursive rules in CHR was introduced that produces one or more adversary rules. When the rules are executed together, a non-terminating computation may arise. It was shown that any non-terminating computation of the original rule contains this witness computation. Based on the adversary rules, a preliminary condition for non-termination was proposed. This condition only refers to the witness computation that starts from a particular state, it can be considered as one particular special case of the misbehavior conditions we give here.

Overview of the Paper. In the next section we define syntax and operational semantics for CHR simplification rules. Section 3 gives a first basic theorem for non-termination or failure of a specific (the most general) goal for a given linear direct recursive rule. Section 4 gives our main condition for misbehavior of a recursive rule in a generalised theorem. Another theorem shows that any goal that contains a misbehaved goal will also be misbehaved. We end the paper with conclusions and directions for future work.

2   Preliminaries

In this section we give a restricted overview of syntax and semantics for Constraint Handling Rules (CHR) [4], cut down to what is essential for this paper (namely simplification rules). We assume basic familiarity with first-order predicate logic and state transition systems. Readers familiar with CHR can skip this section. CHR is a committed-choice language, i.e. there is no backtracking in the rule applications. CHR is a concurrent language, i.e. we may apply rules in parallel.

2.1   Abstract Syntax of CHR

Constraints are distinguished predicates of first-order predicate logic. We distinguish between two different kinds of constraints: *built-in (or: pre-defined) constraints* which are handled by a given constraint solver, and *user-defined (or: CHR) constraints* which are defined by the rules in a CHR program. A *CHR program* is a finite set of rules. There are two basic kinds of rules in CHR:

$$Simplification\ rule:\ r : H \Leftrightarrow C \mid B,$$
$$Propagation\ rule:\ \ \ r : H \Rightarrow C \mid B,$$

where r: is an optional, unique identifier of a rule, the *head* H is a non-empty conjunction of user-defined constraints, the *guard* C is a conjunction of built-in constraints, and the *body* B is a goal. A *goal* is a conjunction of built-in and CHR constraints. An *empty* guard expression *true* l can be omitted from a rule.

In this paper, we are only concerned with a simple class of simplification rules, so propagation rules will be ignored from now on.

2.2 Abstract Operational Semantics of CHR

Computations in CHR are sequences of rule applications. The operational semantics of CHR is given by the state transition system. (Concurrency is not made explicit in the semantics given, since it is independent of the results of this paper.) *States* are goals. Let $\mathcal{CT}$ be a constraint theory for the built-in constraints, including the trivial *true* and *false* as well as syntactical equality $=$ over finite terms. For a goal G, the notation G_{bi} denotes the built-in constraints of G and G_{ud} denotes the user-defined constraints of G.

In the transition system, all single upper-case letters are meta-variables that stand for goals. Let the variables in a disjoint variant of a rule be denoted by $\bar{x}$. A *disjoint (or: fresh) variant* of an expression is obtained by uniformly replacing its variables by different, new (fresh) variables. A *variable renaming* is a bijective function over variables.

Simplify State Transition of CHR

If $(r: H \Leftrightarrow C \mid B)$ is a disjoint variant of a rule in the program

and $\mathcal{CT} \models \exists(G_{bi}) \wedge \forall(G_{bi} \rightarrow \exists \bar{x}(H = H_S \wedge C))$

then $(H_S \wedge G) \mapsto_r (B \wedge G \wedge H = H_S \wedge C)$

Starting with a given initial state, CHR rules are applied exhaustively, until a fixed-point is reached. A simplification rule $H \Leftrightarrow C \mid B$ that is applied removes the user-defined constraints matching H and replaces them by B provided the guard C holds. Note that built-in constraints in a computation are accumulated, i.e. they are added but never removed, while user-defined constraints can be added as well as removed. The built-in constraints allow execution in the abstract without the need to know values for variables, just their relationships are expressed as constraints.

A rule is *applicable*, if its head constraints are matched by constraints in the current goal one-by-one and if, under this matching, the guard of the rule is logically implied by the built-in constraints in the goal, provided they are satisfiable. Any one of the applicable rules can be applied in a transition, and the application cannot be undone, it is committed-choice. An expression of the form $\mathcal{CT} \models \exists(G_{bi}) \wedge \forall(G_{bi} \rightarrow \exists \bar{x}(H = H_S \wedge C))$ is called *applicability condition*. We may drop $\mathcal{CT} \models$ for convenience later on. We use $H = H_S$ by abuse of notation, since the arguments of this syntactic equality are conjunctions of user-defined. This expression means to pairwise equate the user-defined constraints on the left and right hand side and then to pairwise equate their arguments, which are terms.

In a transition (or: *computation step*) $S \mapsto_r T$, S is called *source state* and T is called *target state*. When it is clear from the context, we will drop the reference to the rule r. A *computation* of a goal G in a program P is a connected sequence $S_i \mapsto S_{i+1}$ beginning with the *initial state* S_0 that is G and ending in a *final state* or the sequence is *non-terminating (or: diverging)*. The notation $\mapsto^*$ denotes the reflexive and transitive closure of $\mapsto$.

A goal (state) is *satisfiable (consistent)* if its built-in constraints are satisfiable. A state with unsatisfiable (inconsistent) built-in constraints is called a *failed* state. A computation of a goal is failed if it ends in a failed state. If a computation of a goal is failed (non-terminaing), we may also say that the goal is failed (non-terminating).

Two states $S_1 = (S_{1bi} \wedge S_{1ud})$ and $S_2 = (S_{2bi} \wedge S_{2ud})$ are *equivalent* as defined in [1], written $S_1 \equiv S_2$, if and only if

$$CT \models \forall(S_{1bi} \rightarrow \exists \bar{y}((S_{1ud} = S_{2ud}) \wedge S_{2bi})) \wedge \forall(S_{2bi} \rightarrow \exists \bar{x}((S_{1ud} = S_{2ud}) \wedge S_{1bi}))$$

with $\bar{x}$ those variables that only occur in S_1 and $\bar{y}$ those variables that only occur in S_2. A goal (or state) S is (strictly) *contained* (or: *included*) in a goal T (or: less specific than T) if and only if there exists a (non-empty) goal G such that $(S \wedge G) \equiv T$.

Note that this notion of state equivalence is stricter than logical equivalence since it it considers multiple occurrences of user-defined constraints to be different as in a multiset. For this reason, state equivalence is defined by two symmetric implications and syntactically equates the two states.

3   A Basic Misbehavior Condition for Non-Termination

In this paper we are concerned with linear direct recursion, expressed by simplification rules of the form

$$r : H \Leftrightarrow C \mid B_{bi} \wedge B_{ud},$$

where H and B_{ud} are atomic user-defined constraints for the same predicate symbol and where C and B_{bi} are built-in constraints.

To introduce our appropach, we will start with a theorem about a condition for non-termination that only applies to a specific initial goal. It is not just any goal, however. It is of the form $H \wedge C$, i.e. it consists of the head and guard of the given recursive rule. Such a goal is the *most general state* to which the rule is applicable. This is easy to see, since removing H or replacing C by more general, weaker built-in constraints would invalidate the rule application condition of the operational semantics of CHR.

The theorem below already reflects the structure of the upcoming main theorem. Certain goals for a given recursive rule are non-terminating or failing if a certain implication between the built-in constraints of the guard and body of the rule holds. Our theorems provide an analysis that does not distinguish between non-termination and (termination by) failure of goal. This is justifiable, since in both cases the computation goes wrong. We therefore refer to the conditions in the theorems as *misbehavior* conditions.

The misbehavior condition we give is typically decidable (depending on the decidability of the underlying theory for the built-in constraints, of course). Since termination (the halting problem) is undecidable for Turing-complete programming languages, we cannot expect a sufficient and necessary condition in general. A sufficient condition suffices. Interestingly, for the most general goal $H \wedge C$ of a rule, we can give a condition that clearly separates termination from non-termination, but is agnostic to failure. This is what the first theorem is about (and it sets the stage for a more general theorem).

Theorem 1. Given a recursive rule

$$r : H \Leftrightarrow C \mid B_{bi} \wedge B_{ud},$$

and its disjoint variant with variables $\bar{x}$

$$r : H' \Leftrightarrow C' \mid B'_{bi} \wedge B'_{ud},$$

then the *basic misbehavior condition*

$$\mathcal{CT} \models \exists (C \wedge B_{bi}) \wedge$$

$$\forall ((C \wedge B_{bi}) \to \exists \bar{x} (B_{ud} = H' \wedge C')).$$

implies non-termination or failure of the goal

$$H \wedge C$$

through rule r.

If the basic misbehavior condition does not hold, then the computation of the goal

$$H \wedge C$$

through rule r terminates.

Proof. The proof can be found in the appendix of the full version of this paper that is available online via the authors homepage. It is based on the proof of a more general theorem that will be stated in the next section.   □

Note that while non-termination requires the basic condition to hold, failure of the goal may occur whether the condition holds or not. So the condition is necessary for non-termination of the goal $H \wedge C$, but does not make a statement about failure. Thus the condition is not sufficient for non-termination, but it is sufficient for misbehavior (non-termination or failure). Still it is remarkable that we can give a converse of this misbehavior condition. This will not be the case any more for the general theorem.

We now look at some examples to see applications of this first theorem.

Example 2. Here is a simple recursive rule that goes through the successors that define a natural number:

$$number(X) \Leftrightarrow X = s(Y) \mid number(Y).$$

Note that there are no built-in constraints in the body of the rule.

The basic misbehavior condition amounts to

$$CT \models \exists XY(X = s(Y)) \wedge$$

$$\forall XY((X = s(Y)) \to \exists X'Y'(number(Y) = number(X') \wedge X' = s(Y'))).$$

The first, existential part of the condition holds, while the implication in the second part does not. It is not the case that for all Y, Y is equivalent to some X' that in turn is equivalent to $s(Y')$. For example, Y may be 0. Thus the goal $number(X) \wedge X = s(Y)$ will terminate. Actually it will lead to the state $X = s(Y) \wedge number(Y)$.

Now consider a variant of the above rule that enforces the constraint that a variable must be a successor term:

$$number(X) \Leftrightarrow X = s(Y) \wedge number(Y).$$

Note that there are no built-in constraints in the guard of the rule, so the guard has been dropped. The basic misbehavior condition amounts to

$$CT \models \exists XY(X = s(Y)) \wedge$$

$$\forall XY((X = s(Y)) \to \exists X'Y'(number(Y) = number(X'))).$$

This condition holds, there fore the goal $number(X) \wedge X = s(Y)$ will not terminate or lead to failure. Actually, it will not terminate, producing a longer and longer nested term of successsors.

Next consider a variant of the first rule where the position of the variables X and Y is interchanged in the guard constraint:

$$number(X) \Leftrightarrow Y = s(X) \mid number(Y).$$

The basic misbehavior condition amounts to

$$CT \models \exists XY(Y = s(X)) \wedge$$

$$\forall XY((Y = s(X)) \to \exists X'Y'(number(Y) = number(X') \wedge Y' = s(X'))).$$

The condition holds, since for all Y that are equivalent to X', there exists a Y' such that $Y' = s(X')$. And indeed, the goal $number(X) \wedge Y = s(X)$ will not terminate.

Example 3. Consider the recursive rule for the constraint *double* from Example 1 of the introduction section:

$$double(X, Y) \Leftrightarrow X = s(X1) \mid Y = s(s(Y1)) \wedge double(X1, Y1).$$

The implication of the basic misbehavior condition is

$$\forall((X = s(X1) \wedge Y = s(s(Y1))) \rightarrow \exists(double(X1, Y1) = double(X', Y') \wedge X' = s(X1'))).$$

It does not hold. Actually, the goal $double(X, Y) \wedge X = s(X1)$ is terminating and does not fail. The rule can be applied once.

Example 4. Consider the following rule with empty guard and $X > Y$ in its body

$$p(X, Y) \Leftrightarrow X > Y \wedge p(Y, X).$$

The implication of the misbehavior condition then is

$$\forall XY((X > Y) \rightarrow \exists X'Y'(p(Y, X) = p(X', Y'))).$$

Clearly, the basic misbehavior condition holds. Actually, the goal $p(X, Y)$ will fail at the second recursive step, since the recursive call exchanges the two arguments of p but $X > Y$ and $Y > X$ contradict each other.

Example 5. Let *odd* and *prime* be built-in constraints. Consider the following recursive rule

$$c(X) \Leftrightarrow odd(X) \mid c(s(s(X))),$$

The misbehavior condition amounts to

$$\exists X\, odd(X) \wedge \forall X(odd(X) \rightarrow \exists X'(c(s(s(X))) = c(X') \wedge odd(X'))).$$

Since the successor of the successor of an odd number is always odd, the condition holds. Indeed, the goal $c(X) \wedge odd(X)$ is non-terminating.
    Now consider a variation of the above rule

$$c(X) \Leftrightarrow prime(X) \mid c(s(s(X))).$$

The condition amounts to

$$\exists X\, prime(X) \wedge \forall X(prime(X) \rightarrow \exists X'(c(s(s(X))) = c(X') \wedge prime(X'))).$$

Since the successor of the successor of a prime number may not be prime, the condition does not hold. Thus the goal $c(X) \wedge prime(X)$ terminates. It does so after one recursive step. (It will terminate for any given number X in at most two recursive steps: one of every three sequential even or odd natural numbers is a multiple of three, and hence not prime.)

4   The Main Misbehavior Condition

We are going to state a generalization of Theorem 1. It is easy to see from the CHR operational semantics and its applicability condition that any state to which a given rule is applicable must contain its head and guard. All such states are therefore equivalent to a state of the form $H \wedge G \wedge Q$, where Q is an arbitrary constraint.

To generalise our initial theorem, we could simply add Q to the premise of the implication in the basic misbehavior condition. This is, however, not sufficient to guarantee non-termination or failure. As it turns out, we also have to add an appropriate variant of Q to the conclusion of the implication. This ensures that the appropriate variant of Q holds at each recursive step. This will be our main misbehavior theorem.

We will then show in another theorem that any state that contains $H \wedge G \wedge Q$ which misbehaves is also doomed to misbehave. So both theorems together typically cover an infinite set of states that do not terminate or fail.

4.1   Lemmata

For the proof of the upcoming main theorem, we will need the following lemmata.

Lemma 1 (From [6]). Given goal C consisting of built-in constraints only and a goal H consisting of user-defined constraints only. Let the pairs (H, C) with variables x and (H', C') with variables y be disjoint variants. Then the following applicability condition holds

$$\mathcal{CT} \models \forall \bar{x}(C \to \exists \bar{y}(H' = H \wedge C')).$$

Lemma 2 *(CHR monotonicity)* (Sect. 4.2 in [4]). If a rule r is applicable to a state, it is also applicable to the state when constraints have been added, as long as this state is not failed.

$$\text{If } G \mapsto_r G' \text{ then } (G \wedge H) \mapsto_r (G' \wedge H),$$

provided $G \wedge H$ is satisfiable.

4.2   Main Misbehavior Theorem

We are now ready to state the main theorem of the paper.

Theorem 2. Let Q be a built-in constraint. Given Q and a recursive rule

$$Q, \quad r : H \Leftrightarrow C \mid B_{bi} \wedge B_{ud},$$

and their disjoint variant with variables $\bar{x}$

$$Q', \quad r : H' \Leftrightarrow C' \mid B'_{bi} \wedge B'_{ud},$$

Then the *general misbehavior condition*

$$\mathcal{CT} \models \exists (Q \wedge C \wedge B_{bi}) \wedge$$

$$\forall ((Q \wedge C \wedge B_{bi}) \to \exists \bar{x}(B_{ud} = H' \wedge Q' \wedge C')).$$

implies non-termination or failure of the computation of the goal

$$H \wedge C \wedge Q$$

through rule r.

Proof. We prove the claim by induction over the computation steps.

Base Case. The claim is that the goal $H \wedge C \wedge Q$ either is failed or there exists a computation step by applying the recursive rule r. We show that there is always such a computation step possible (and that the resulting state is not failed).

According to the abstract operational semantics of CHR, this computation step must be of the form:

$$(H \wedge C \wedge Q) \mapsto_r (B'_{bi} \wedge B'_{ud} \wedge C \wedge Q \wedge H' = H \wedge C')$$

$$\text{if } CT \models \exists (C \wedge Q) \wedge \forall (C \wedge Q \to \exists (H' = H \wedge C'))$$

We have to show that the applicability condition holds, so that we can apply the recursive rule. By the first, existential part of the general misbehavior condition we know that $\exists (Q \wedge C \wedge B_{bi})$ is satisfiable. Since this conjunction logically implies $\exists (C \wedge Q)$, we know that the source state $\exists (H \wedge C \wedge Q)$ is satisfiable, too. By Lemma 1 we know that $\forall (C \to \exists (H' = H \wedge C'))$ trivially holds. So $\forall (C \wedge Q \to \exists (H' = H \wedge C'))$ holds as well. Thus the applicability conditions holds and the recursive rule r is applicable.

The resulting target state of the transition is $(B'_{bi} \wedge B'_{ud} \wedge C \wedge Q \wedge H' = H \wedge C')$. B'_{ud} is a user-defined constraint and thus can be ignored for determining the satisfiability of the state. We already know from the applicability condition that $\exists (C \wedge Q \wedge H' = H \wedge C')$. By Lemma 1 we know that $\forall (C \wedge B_{bi} \to \exists (H' = H \wedge C' \wedge B'_{bi}))$ trivially holds. By the first part of the misbehavior condition we know that $\exists (Q \wedge C \wedge B_{bi})$ is satisfiable. Thus $(B'_{bi} \wedge C \wedge Q \wedge H' = H \wedge C')$ must also be satisfiable. Thus the target state is satisfiable.

Inductive Step. We have to show that given a state where the recursive rule has been applied, either the recursive rule is applicable again or the state is failed.

We assume such states are of the form $(G \wedge B_{bi} \wedge B_{ud} \wedge C \wedge Q)$, where G is an arbitrary constraint. This form holds for the target state of the base case.

Now consider a source state of the desired form. If it is failed, we are done. If it is not failed, we show that the following computation step is possible with the recursive rule:

$$(G \wedge B_{bi} \wedge B_{ud} \wedge C \wedge Q) \mapsto_r (G \wedge B_{bi} \wedge B'_{bi} \wedge B'_{ud} \wedge C \wedge Q \wedge H' = B_{ud} \wedge C')$$

$$\text{if } CT \models \exists (G_{bi} \wedge B_{bi} \wedge C \wedge Q) \wedge \forall (G_{bi} \wedge B_{bi} \wedge C \wedge Q \to \exists (H' = B_{ud} \wedge C'))$$

For the proof of applicability of the recursive rule we reuse the one for the base case. Instead of H', we have now B_{ud}, and there are additional constraints $G \wedge B_{bi}$ in the source state. By monotonicity of CHR (Lemma 2), we know that if a rule is applicable to a state, it is also applicable to the state when constraints have been added, as long as this state is not failed. Thus the additional constraints $G \wedge B_{bi}$ cannot inhibit the applicability of the rule, since the state is not failed.

We still have to show that the target state is of the required form. But Q' seems to be missing from it. The implication of the misbehavior condition in the theorem is

$$\forall((Q \wedge C \wedge B_{bi}) \to \exists(B_{ud} = H' \wedge Q' \wedge C')).$$

Therefore, since the target state contains $(Q \wedge C \wedge B_{bi})$, it also contains $(B_{ud} = H' \wedge Q' \wedge C')$. Thus the target state is equivalent to $(G' \wedge B'_{bi} \wedge B'_{ud} \wedge C' \wedge Q')$, when we let G' be $(G \wedge B_{bi} \wedge C \wedge Q \wedge H' = B_{ud})$.

So the target state is also of the required form.   □

Theorem 2 states an implication between the general misbehavior condition and failing or non-terminating goals. The condition is sufficient for misbehavior, but not necessary. As we will see, due to the next theorem, the converse does not hold (unlike Theorem 1).

We continue with some examples, old and new, for the application of the main misbehavior theorem.

Example 6. Consider a variation of the recursive rule from Example 5 with the opposite guard:

$$c(X) \Leftrightarrow notprime(X) \mid c(s(s(X))).$$

The basic misbehavior condition amounts to

$$\exists X \, notprime(X) \wedge \forall X(notprime(X) \to \exists X'(c(s(s(X))) = c(X') \wedge notprime(X'))).$$

Since the successor of the successor of a non-prime may be prime, the condition does not hold. By Theorem 1, the goal $c(X) \wedge notprime(X)$ thus terminates.

Let Q be $odd(X)$. The implication of the general misbehavior condition is

$$\forall X(odd(X) \wedge notprime(X) \to \exists X'(c(s(s(X))) = c(X') \wedge odd(X') \wedge notprime(X'))).$$

Again, it does not hold. The status of non-termination is undecided by Theorem 2. (Actually, there is no infinite sequence of odd numbers that does not contain a prime, therefore any computation containing $c(X) \wedge odd(X)$ will terminate.)

Now let Q be $even(X) \wedge X = s(s(s(Y)))$. This time the condition holds, since any sequence of even numbers greater or equal to three (since $X = s(s(s(Y))))$) does not contain a prime number. The corresponding goal $c(X) \wedge even(X) \wedge X = s(s(s(Y)))$ is non-terminating. (So $c(X)$ terminates for odd numbers but does not terminate for even numbers greater than two.)

The following example exhibits a non-terminating computation for a list concatentation constraint.

Example 7. Let *cons* and *nil* denote function symbols to build lists. Then we can define the concatenation of two lists $L1$ and $L2$ resulting in a third list $L3$:

$$append(L1, L2, L3) \Leftrightarrow L1 = nil \mid L2 = L3.$$
$$append(L1, L2, L3) \Leftrightarrow L1 = cons(X, L1') \mid$$
$$L2 = L2' \wedge L3 = cons(X, L3') \wedge append(L1', L2', L3').$$

The implication of the basic misbehavior condition is

$$\forall(L1 = cons(X, L1') \wedge L2 = L2' \wedge L3 = cons(X, L3') \rightarrow$$

$$\exists(append(L1', L2', L3') = append(L1'', L2'', L3'') \wedge L1'' = cons(X', L1''')))$$

This formula does not hold, because the premise of the implication does not constrain $L1''$ (which is equivalent to $L1'$) to be a *cons* term as required by the conclusion.

Regarding the general misbehavior condition, let Q be $L1' = L3$. Then the implication of the general condition amounts to

$$\forall(L1' = L3 \wedge L1 = cons(X, L1') \wedge L2 = L2' \wedge L3 = cons(X, L3') \rightarrow$$

$$\exists(append(L1', L2', L3') = append(L1'', L2'', L3'') \wedge L1''' = L3'' \wedge L1'' = cons(X', L1''')))$$

This formula does hold, because $L1' = L3$ and $L3 = cons(X, L3')$ in the premise implies $L1' = L1'' \wedge L1''' = L3'' \wedge L1'' = cons(X', L1''')$ in the conclusion, as we can choose $X' = X$ and $L3'' = L3'$. Indeed, the computation for the goal

$$append(L1, L2, L3) \wedge L1 = cons(X, L1') \wedge L1' = L3$$

is non-terminating, producing longer and longer lists.

4.3   Containment Theorem

Theorem 2 only gives us a particular goal that is non-terminating or fails. By the following theorem we can apply the theorem to any goal that contains that particular goal. Usually, there are infinitely many such goals. The proof directly follows from the previous theorem and the monotonicity property of CHR.

Theorem 3. Any goal

$$H \wedge C \wedge Q \wedge G$$

with arbitrary constraint G, where the general misbehavior condition according to Theorem 2, holds for $H \wedge C \wedge Q$, will either not terminate or fail.

Proof. We prove the claim by induction.

Base Case. The state $H \wedge C \wedge Q \wedge G$ is either failed or not. In the first case we are done. In the second case, the recursive rule is applicable to the state. Because by monotonicity of CHR (Lemma 2), we know that if a rule is applicable to a state, it is also applicable to the state when constraints have been added, as long as this state is not failed.

Induction Step. The same reasoning holds for all subsequent states in the computation: If we have a state, it is either failed or the recursive rule is applicable to it by monotonicity.

Thus the computation of a goal $H \wedge C \wedge Q \wedge G$ either fails or diverges.   □

The following example introduces some specific goals for a non-terminating computation.

Example 8. Consider a variant of the rule of Example 4 with empty guard and $X \geq Y$ in its body

$$p(X,Y) \Leftrightarrow X \geq Y \wedge p(Y,X).$$

Let Q be *true*. The implication of the misbehavior condition then is

$$\forall XY((X \geq Y) \rightarrow \exists X'Y'(p(Y,X) = p(X',Y'))).$$

This condition holds. So any computation for a goal consisting of $p(X,Y)$ and arbitrary built-in constraints either fails or is non-terminating. The computation for the goal $p(X,Y)$ is non-terminating. So is the more specific goal $p(X,Y) \wedge X = Y$. The more specific goal $p(X,Y) \wedge X < Y$ fails. So do the goals with the built-in constraints $X > Y$ and $X \neq Y$. The goal $p(X,Y) \wedge p(Y,X)$ is non-terminating as well, producing the constraint $X = Y$.

Note that while Q satisfies the misbehavior condition, $Q \wedge G$ need not do so. Thus the converse of Theorem 2 does not hold. The following example illustrates this point.

Example 9. Continuing with Example 3, let Q be $X = Y$ in the general misbehavior condition. The implication of the condition is

$$\forall((X = Y \wedge X = s(X1) \wedge Y = s(s(Y1)))) \rightarrow$$

$$\exists(double(X1,Y1) = double(X',Y') \wedge X' = Y' \wedge X' = s(X1'))).$$

It can be simplified into

$$\forall((X = Y \wedge X = s(X1) \wedge X1 = s(Y1)) \rightarrow$$

$$\exists(X1 = X' \wedge Y1 = Y' \wedge X1 = Y1 \wedge X1 = s(X1')))).$$

where $X1 = s(Y1)$ and $X1 = Y1$ are in contradiction. Thus the implication does not hold. However, the goal $double(X,Y) \wedge X = s(X1) \wedge X = Y$ does not terminate.

But there is a more general Q that shows by Theorem 3 that the computation for this goal either fails or is non-terminating. Let Q be $X \geq Y$. The implication of the misbehavior condition is

$$\forall((X \geq Y \wedge X = s(X1) \wedge Y = s(s(Y1)))) \rightarrow$$

$$\exists(double(X1,Y1) = double(X',Y') \wedge X' \geq Y' \wedge X' = s(X1'))).$$

It can be simplified into

$$\forall((X1 \geq s(Y1) \wedge X = s(X1) \wedge Y = s(s(Y1)))) \rightarrow$$

$$\exists(X1 = X' \wedge Y1 = Y' \wedge X1 \geq Y1 \wedge X1 = s(X1')))).$$

where $X1 \geq s(Y1)$ implies $X1 \geq Y1 \wedge X1 = s(X1')$. The misbehavior condition holds. So the goal $double(X,Y) \wedge X = s(X1) \wedge X \geq Y$ does not terminate or it fails. Actually it is non-terminating.

5   Conclusions

The paper introduced theorems with so-called misbehavior conditions for non-termination and failure as well as termination of linear direct recursive simplification rules in CHR. Certain goals for a given recursive rule are non-terminating or failing if a certain implication between the built-in constraints of the guard and body of the rule holds.

We proved a basic theorem for non-termination or failure of the most general goal for recursive rules that consists of their head and guard. A kind of converse also holds: If the misbehavior condition for this goal is violated, it will terminate. We then gave the main condition for misbeavior. It is parameterised with regard to suitable additional built-in constraints in the goal. Finally, a third theorem showed that any goal that contains a misbehaved goal will also be misbehaved.

Future Work. Having stated the theorems describing non-termination and failure, the immediate next question is how to find the built-in constraints that satisfy the misbehavior condition. This is very likely to be an undecidable problem due to the undecidabilty of termination itself. We can imagine an iterative approach of finding better and better approximations for suitable constraints. Another possibility is the systematic enumeration of possible built-in constraints over the involved variables, as one reviewer suggested.

One should extend our approach to a more general class of rules and to other types of recursion. Our approach readily seems applicable to CHR propagation rules. If other CHR constraints occur in the body of the rule, they would have to be abstracted to/approximated by built-in constraints. Multiple and mutual (indirect) recursion cover the standard formulations of e.g. the Fibonacci and the Ackermann function. We think that existing rule unfolding techniques for CHR will come handy to replace mutual by direct recursion.

Another open problem is if there is some kind of converse for the main Theorem 2, similar to the one for Theorem 1. A related question is if there are most general built-in constraints for Theorem 2. The answer seems to depend on the expressibility of the built-in constraints in the constraint theory.

Last but not least, it should be investigated how our approach carries over to related languages like constraint logic programming ones and the other rule-based approaches that have been embedded in CHR. In conclusion, we think this paper can serve as a basic reference and nucleus for a wealth of further research.

Acknowledgements. We thank the anonymous referees for their helpful suggestions on how to improve the paper.

References

1. Betz, H., Raiser, F., Frühwirth, T.: A complete and terminating execution model for constraint handling rules. Theor. Pract. Log. Program. **10**, 597–610 (2010)
2. Brockschmidt, M., Ströder, T., Otto, C., Giesl, J.: Automated detection of non-termination and NullPointerExceptions for Java bytecode. In: Beckert, B., Damiani, F., Gurov, D. (eds.) FoVeOOS 2011. LNCS, vol. 7421, pp. 123–141. Springer, Heidelberg (2012)

3. Endrullis, J., Zantema, H.: Proving non-termination by finite automata. In: LIPIcs-Leibniz International Proceedings in Informatics, vol. 36. Schloss Dagstuhl-Leibniz-Zentrum fuer Informatik (2015)
4. Frühwirth, T.: Constraint Handling Rules (Monography). Cambridge University Press, Cambridge (2009)
5. Frühwirth, T.: Constraint handling rules - what else? In: Bassiliades, N., Gottlob, G., Sadri, F., Paschke, A., Roman, D. (eds.) RuleML 2015. LNCS, vol. 9202, pp. 13–34. Springer, Heidelberg (2015)
6. Frühwirth, T.: A devil's advocate against termination of direct recursion. In: Proceedings of the 17th International Symposium on Principles and Practice of Declarative Programming, pp. 103–113. ACM (2015)
7. Frühwirth, T.: The CHR Web Site. Ulm University (2016). www.constraint-Phandling-rules.org
8. Gupta, A., Henzinger, T.A., Majumdar, R., Rybalchenko, A., Xu, R.-G.: Proving non-termination. ACM Sigplan Not. **43**(1), 147–158 (2008)
9. Le, T.C., Qin, S., Chin, W.-N.: Termination and non-termination specification inference. In: Proceedings of the 36th ACM SIGPLAN Conference on Programming Language Design and Implementation, pp. 489–498. ACM (2015)
10. Liang, S., Kifer, M.: A practical analysis of non-termination in large logic programs. Theor. Practi. Log. Program. **13**(4–5), 705–719 (2013)
11. Payet, É.: Loop detection in term rewriting using the eliminating unfoldings. Theoret. Comput. Sci. **403**(2), 307–327 (2008)
12. Payet, É., Mesnard, F.: A non-termination criterion for binary constraint logic programs. Theor. Pract. Log. Program. **9**(02), 145–164 (2009)
13. Payet, É., Mesnard, F., Spoto, F.: Non-termination analysis of Java bytecode (2014). CoRR abs/1401.5292
14. Voets, D., De Schreye, D.: A new approach to non-termination analysis of logic programs. In: Hill, P.M., Warren, D.S. (eds.) ICLP 2009. LNCS, vol. 5649, pp. 220–234. Springer, Heidelberg (2009)

Translation of Cognitive Models from ACT-R to Constraint Handling Rules

Daniel Gall$^{(\boxtimes)}$ and Thom Frühwirth

Institute of Software Engineering and Compiler Construction, Ulm University,
89069 Ulm, Germany
{daniel.gall,thom.fruehwirth}@uni-ulm.de
http://uni-ulm.de/in/pm

Abstract. Cognitive architectures are used to abstract and simplify the process of computational cognitive modeling. The popular cognitive architecture ACT-R has a well-defined psychological theory, but lacks a formalization of its computational system. This inhibits computational analysis of cognitive models, e.g. confluence or complexity analysis. In this paper we present a source to source transformation of ACT-R models to Constraint Handling Rules (CHR) programs enabling the use of analysis tools for CHR to analyze computational cognitive models. This translation is the first that matches the current abstract operational semantics of ACT-R.

Keywords: Computational cognitive modeling · ACT-R · Operational semantics · Source to source transformation · Constraint Handling Rules

1 Introduction

Computational cognitive modeling is a research field at the interface of computer science and psychology. It tries to explore human cognition by building detailed computational models of cognitive processes [20]. Cognitive architectures support the modeling process by offering a formal, well-investigated base that unifies various psychological theories to an abstract theory of cognition. Based upon the architecture, domain specific models are built. In the best case, cognitive architectures constrain the model space to models that are plausible, i.e. a cognitive architecture should only allow models that correspond to human behavior [21].

Adaptive Control of Thought – Rational (ACT-R) [5] is a popular cognitive architecture. It is a modular production rule system with a special architecture of the working memory that operates on data stored as so-called *chunks*, i.e. the unit of knowledge in the human brain. Although it has a well-defined psychological theory, its computational system is not described formally leading to implementations that are full of technical artifacts [4,14,19]. This inhibits analysis of cognitive models for features like confluence, termination and computational complexity. Thus, to the best of our knowledge, there are no theoretical results on (semi-)automatic methods deciding one of those computational properties

© Springer International Publishing Switzerland 2016
J.J. Alferes et al. (Eds.): RuleML 2016, LNCS 9718, pp. 223–237, 2016.
DOI: 10.1007/978-3-319-42019-6_15

for ACT-R. Nevertheless, since computational models are computer programs, those properties are important since they reveal a lot of information about the semantics of the program or model. For instance, cognitive models with exponential complexity are often implausible, when humans usually find approximate solutions with non-exponential time complexity [17].

Constraint Handling Rules (CHR)[1] [10] is a rule-based language with a strong foundation in logic. In contrast to ACT-R, it has a well-defined operational semantics [6] and even a declarative semantics – the logical reading of a program. There are many theoretical results and practical applications [11] like an automatic confluence test [2,10], an algorithm to decide operational equivalence [1,10] and semi-automatic methods for complexity analysis [9].

Due to the strong relation of logic to human deduction and the analysis features of CHR, *we want to use CHR for analysis of cognitive models.* This approach already has been used successfully for analysis of graph transformation systems [16]. In this paper we therefore build on our work in [14], where we have defined the abstract operational semantics of ACT-R. We use the abstract semantics and not an implementation semantics because it is most suitable for analysis of the aforementioned computational properties as it abstracts from details like timings or conflict resolution. Thus it captures the essence of the core transition system of ACT-R as we have shown by a soundness result between the abstract and the implementation semantics in [14]. This makes analysis of the abstract semantics meaningful for implementations.

The *main contribution of this paper* is the translation scheme from ACT-R models to CHR programs to make CHR analysis tools accessible for cognitive models. The translation is constructed such that every computation in the original ACT-R model is also possible in the translated CHR program and, vice versa, only the computations that are possible in ACT-R are possible in the CHR translation. This is important to ensure that the analytical tools of CHR can be used for cognitive models.

The work in this paper extends our prior work from [14] where we have defined the abstract semantics of ACT-R that is suitable for analysis of cognitive models due to its abstraction level. In [13] we have given a first, rough definition of the abstract semantics of ACT-R and a corresponding simple translation to CHR. However, due to differences between the semantics and errors in the previous formulations, the translation from prior work cannot be used for the current, improved semantics of ACT-R in [14]. We want to close this gap in this paper by a formally defined translation of cognitive models to CHR suiting the current operational semantics of ACT-R. This enables sound, elegant analysis of cognitive models through CHR.

2   Preliminaries

In this section we give a short description of Constraint Handling Rules and the cognitive architecture ACT-R. Therefore, we first describe ACT-R very briefly

---

[1] http://www.constraint-handling-rules.org

and then summarize our results on syntax and semantics from [14]. We concentrate on our so-called *abstract semantics* that we have first described in [13] and improved under the consideration of recent work [4] in [14].

2.1 Constraint Handling Rules

We recapitulate syntax and semantics of CHR briefly. For an extensive introduction to CHR, its semantics, analysis and applications, we refer to [10]. The syntax of CHR is defined over *constraints*, i.e. (first-order) logical predicates. There are two disjoint sets of constraints: user-defined (CHR) constraints and built-in constraints (that come from the host-language CHR is embedded in). A CHR program consists of rules of the form $H_k \setminus H_r \Leftrightarrow G \mid B$ where the heads H_k and H_r are conjunctions of user-defined constraints, the guard G is a conjunction of built-in constraints and the body B is a conjunction of both types of constraints. Note that at most one of H_k and H_r can be empty. If G is empty, it is interpreted as the built-in constraint *true*.

The operational semantics is defined by the following transition scheme over CHR states that are defined as conjunctions of constraints:

$$(H_k \wedge H_r \wedge C) \mapsto (H_k \wedge G \wedge B \wedge C)$$

if there is an instance with new local variables $\bar{x}$ of above rule in head normal form, i.e. all constants in the head of the rule are replaced by variables and respective bindings in the guard, and $CT \models \forall (C \rightarrow \exists \bar{x} G)$ for a constraint theory CT [10].

Informally, a CHR program is run on a constraint store, that is a conjunction of constraints. A rule is applicable, if the head matches constraints from the store and the guard holds. In that case, the matching constraints from H_k are kept in the store, the constraints matching H_r are removed and the constraints from B and G are added.

Throughout this paper, we use multi-set notation to describe logical conjunctions, e.g. to describe CHR states. Thereby, $\uplus$ denotes multi-set union. We also implicitly convert (multi-)sets to corresponding lists (denoted by square brackets) when using them within a constraint.

2.2 Informal Description of ACT-R

ACT-R is a modular production rule system. Its data elements are so-called *chunks*. A chunk has a *type* and a set of *slots* (determined by the type) that are connected to other chunks. Hence, human declarative knowledge is represented in ACT-R as a network of chunks. Figure 1 shows an example chunk network that models the family relations between some persons.

In Fig. 2, there is an overview of ACT-R's architecture. The modules are responsible for different cognitive features. For instance, the declarative knowledge (represented as a chunk network) can be found in the *declarative module*. The heart of ACT-R is the *procedural system* that consists of a set of *production*

226 D. Gall and T. Frühwirth

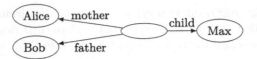

Fig. 1. A chunk network that stores some family relations. Thereby, the chunks named *Alice*, *Bob* and *Max* are of a chunk type that does not have further slots. The central chunk (not named in the figure) is of type *parent* with three slots: *mother*, *father* and *child*. If Alice and Bob had more children, there would be more such chunks connecting them to the chunks representing their other children.

rules. Those rules do not have access to all information from other modules, but only to parts of it that are stored in *buffers*. A buffer is connected to a module and can hold at most one chunk at a time. Rules match the contents of the buffer, i.e. they check if the chunks of particular buffers have certain values. If a rule is applicable, it can *modify* particular slots of the chunk in the buffer, *request* the module to put a whole new chunk in its buffer or *clear* a buffer. Modifications and clearings are available for the production rule system, whereas requests can take some time while the procedural system is continuing work in parallel.

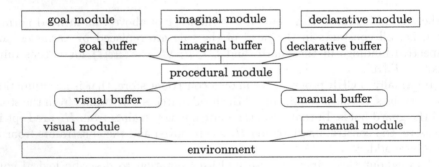

Fig. 2. Modular architecture of ACT-R. This illustration is inspired by [5,21].

2.3 Syntax

We use the term representation of the ACT-R syntax that we have introduced in [14]. This syntax can be obtained directly from the original syntax of ACT-R. However, it simplifies its handling using logical or set operators.

All terms in ACT-R are defined over two disjoint, possibly infinite sets of constant symbols $\mathcal{C}$ and variable symbols $\mathcal{V}$. An ACT-R architecture defines the set of buffers $\mathbb{B} \subseteq \mathcal{C}$ and the set of actions A. In this paper, we restrict the set of actions to $\{=, +, -\}$ for modifications, requests and clearings respectively.

An ACT-R model consists of a set of *rules* Σ, a set of type names $\mathbb{T} \subseteq \mathcal{C}$ and a (total) *typing function* $\tau : \mathbb{T} \rightarrow 2^{\mathcal{C}}$ that defines the slots for each type. A *production rule* in Σ is defined as $L \Rightarrow R$, where L is a set of buffer tests of the form $=(b, t, P)$ and R is a set of actions of the form $a(b, t, P)$ where $a \in A$ is an action symbol, $b \in \mathbb{B}$ is a buffer, $t \in \mathbb{T}$ is a type and $P \subseteq C \times (C \cup V)$ is a set of slot-value pairs.

The function $vars$ maps an arbitrary set of terms to its set of variables in V. We require $vars(R) \subseteq vars(L)$ for a production rule $L \Rightarrow R$, i.e. no new variables must be introduced on the right-hand side.

There are some further syntactic restrictions: Actions $a(b, t, P) \in R$ are only allowed for tested buffers, i.e. if $=(b, t', P') \in L$. A modification action may not change the type of the chunk, i.e. if $=(b, t, P) \in R$ then $=(b, t, P') \in L$. We also require that each test refers to another buffer. Additionally, the actions are only allowed to specify each slot at most once in their set of slot-value pairs.

In the following example, we show the syntax of an ACT-R production rule and its informal semantics.

Example 1 (Production Rules). This example builds on chunks of type *parent* as in Fig. 1. By the following rule we want to determine the parents of a given person. Therefore, we have special goal chunks of type g that represent our query. They have the slots *query, mother, father* and *state*. This means that they hold the person whose parents are of interest (*query*), the current state of the derivation (*state*) and the result (*mother* and *father*). In the beginning, a goal chunk is only connected to a person chunk by the *query* slot and has the value *start* in its state slot. The model will connect the other slots with corresponding chunks.

Our example rule starts the retrieval of the queried chunk:

$$\{=(goal, g, \{(state, start), (query, X)\})\}$$
$$\Rightarrow \{+(retrieval, parent, \{(child, X)\}), =(goal, g, \{(state, retrieval)\})\}$$

The variable X denotes the name of the child. In the actions, we state a request to the *retrieval* buffer to look for a chunk of type *parent* that has X in its *child* slot. The state is modified from *start* to *retrieval*.

To complete the computation, we would need a second rule that takes the result in the retrieval buffer modifies the mother and father slots of the goal chunk accordingly.

2.4   Operational Semantics

In this section we describe the semantics of an ACT-R model as a state transition system based on our prior work [14]. Therefore, we first introduce the notion of an ACT-R state and then give the transition relation $\rightarrowtail$.

States. ACT-R operates on a network of typed chunks that we call a *chunk store*. It is defined over a set of types $\mathbb{T}$ and a typing function τ. Chunks are defined as unique, immutable entities with a type and connections to other chunks:

Definition 1 (Chunk Store). A *chunk store* Δ is a multi-set of tuples (t, val) where $t \in \mathbb{T}$ is a chunk type and $val : \tau(t) \to \Delta$ is a function that maps each slot of the chunk (determined by the type t) to another chunk. To identify an individual chunk, we define the total function $id : \Delta \to \mathcal{C}$ that maps each chunk to a unique identifier from the set of constants that is determined by its type and slot-value pairs.

The typing function τ maps a type t from the set of type names $\mathbb{T}$ to a set of allowed slots, hence the function *val* of chunk c has the slots of c as domain. Note that a chunk store can contain multiple elements with the same values that still are unique entities representing different concepts.

We assume that there is a special type $\texttt{chunk} \in \mathbb{T}$ with $\tau(\texttt{chunk}) = \emptyset$. Additionally, there is a chunk $\texttt{nil} \in \Delta$ that is defined as $\texttt{nil} := (\texttt{chunk}, \emptyset)$.

We now define the notion of a *cognitive state* as the content of the buffers:

Definition 2 (Cognitive State). A *cognitive state* γ is a function $\mathbb{B} \to \Delta \times \mathbb{R}_0^+$ that maps each buffer to a chunk and a delay. The set of cognitive states is denoted as Γ, whereas Γ_{part} denotes the set of *partial cognitive states*, i.e. cognitive states that are partial functions and do not necessarily map each buffer to a chunk. A buffer b is called *empty*, if $\gamma(b) = \texttt{nil}$.

The delay decides at which point in time the chunk in the buffer is available to the production system. A delay $d > 0$ indicates that the chunk is not yet available to the production system. This implements delays of the processing of requests.

Definition 3 (ACT-R States). An *abstract ACT-R state* is a tuple $\langle \Delta; \gamma; \upsilon \rangle^{\mathbb{V}}$ where Δ is a chunk store, γ is a cognitive state using Δ, υ is a multi-set of first-order predicates (called *additional information*) and $\mathbb{V}$ is a set of variable bindings. The set of allowed parameter valuations Υ is defined by the concrete architecture.

The additional information is used to model the modularity of ACT-R where the procedural system does not have direct access to all information in the individual modules. For instance, it contains so-called sub-symbolic information that is used to define activation levels of chunks, e.g., to model learning and forgetting.

State Transitions. First of all, we define the notion of matchings:

Definition 4 (Matching). A buffer test $\theta := =(b, t, P)$ for a buffer $b \in \mathbb{B}$ testing for a type t and slot-value pairs $P \subseteq \mathcal{C} \times (\mathcal{C} \cup \mathcal{V})$ *matches* a state $\sigma := \langle \Delta; \gamma; \upsilon \rangle^{\mathbb{V}}$, written $\theta \sqsubseteq \sigma$, if and only if $\gamma(b) = ((t, val), 0)$ and for all $(s, v) \in P : \forall (\mathbb{V} \to \exists v' \in \mathcal{V} : id(val(s)) = v' \wedge v = v')$ for a fresh variable v'.

A rule $r := L \Rightarrow R$ matches a state σ, written as $r \sqsubseteq \sigma$, if and only if all buffer tests $t \in L$ match σ. We define the set $Bindings(r, \sigma)$ as the bindings of the variables that follow from the matching $r \sqsubseteq \sigma$.

A buffer test matches a state, if and only if all its slot tests hold in the state, i.e. the variable bindings imply that the values in the rule are the same as in the state (for the tested buffer). Note that a test can only match chunks in the cognitive state that are visible to the system, i.e. whose delay is zero. A test cannot match chunks with a delay greater than zero.

The modification of a state by a transition is defined by interpretation functions $I : \mathcal{A} \times \mathcal{S}_{va} \to 2^{\Gamma_{\text{part}} \times \Upsilon}$ of actions that determine the possible effects of an action. An interpretation maps each state and action of the form $a(b, t, P)$ – where $a \in A$ is an action symbol, $b \in \mathcal{C}$ a constant denoting a buffer, $t \in \mathcal{C}$ a type, and $P \subseteq \mathcal{C} \times (\mathcal{C} \cup \mathcal{V})$ is a set of slot-value pairs – to a tuple $(\gamma_{\text{part}}, \upsilon)$. Thereby, γ_{part} is a partial cognitive state, i.e. a partial function that assigns some buffers a chunk. The partial cognitive state γ_{part} will be taken in the operational semantics to overwrite the changed buffer contents, i.e. it contains the new contents of the changed buffers. Analogously, the additional information υ defines changes of parameter valuations induced by the action.

Note that the interpretation of an action can return more than one possible effect. For example, the declarative module can find more than one chunk matching the retrieval request. In implementations usually one chunk is returned according to certain additional information (called chunk activation which is an elementary concept of ACT-R to model learning). However, in the abstract semantics all matching chunks are regarded to find potential conflicts in a model.

From the interpretation of one action, the interpretation of a rule can be derived by combining the individual actions. Since the actions refer to different buffers, the changes of the partial cognitive state are disjoint and can be combined to a larger partial cognitive states. Additional parameters can simply be merged by multi-set union. Due to space reasons, we refer to [14] for a formal description.

We now define the transition relation $\longmapsto$ of ACT-R. The first class of transitions (*rule transitions*) is defined for a fresh variant r' of a rule $r \in \Sigma$ with $vars(r') = \bar{y}$:

$$\frac{r' \sqsubseteq \sigma \wedge \mathbb{V}^* = Bindings(r', \sigma) \wedge (\gamma_{\text{part}}, \upsilon^*) \in I(r')}{\sigma := \langle \Delta; \gamma; \upsilon \rangle^{\mathbb{V}} \longmapsto \langle \Delta \uplus \Delta'; \gamma'; \upsilon' \rangle^{\mathbb{V} \cup \mathbb{V}^*}}$$

where Δ' are the chunks added in the interpretation function. The *id* function is extended for the chunks in Δ' by fresh names from $\mathcal{C}$. γ' has the values of γ_{part} where defined or the values of γ otherwise, and $\upsilon' := \upsilon \uplus \upsilon^*$. The interpretation function I is defined as follows:

- $I(=(b, t, P), \sigma) = \{(\gamma_p, \emptyset)\}$ for modifications where $\gamma_p(b) := ((t, val_b'), 0)$. For $\gamma(b) = ((t, val_b), d)$ (from the state σ), the new values are defined as $val_b'(s) := v$ if $(s, v) \in P$ and $val_b'(s) := val_b(s)$ otherwise.
  Thus, a modification creates a copy of the chunk in the buffer with modified values as specified in P. Modifications are deterministic, i.e. that there is only one possible effect.

- $(\gamma_p, v_b) \in I(\texttt{+}(b, t, P), \sigma)$ for requests if $(c_b, v_b) \in request_b(t, P, v)$ and $\gamma_p(b) :=$ $(c_b, 1)$. Thereby, the function $request_b : \mathbb{T} \times 2^{\mathcal{C} \times (\mathcal{C} \cup \mathcal{V})} \times \Upsilon \to 2^{\Delta \times \Upsilon}$ is a function defined by the architecture for each buffer. It calculates the set of possible answers for a request that is specified by a type and a set of slot value pairs. Possible answers are tuples of a chunk and additional information.
- $(\gamma_p, v_p) \in I(\texttt{-}(b, \texttt{chunk}, \texttt{nil}), \sigma)$ for clearings where $\gamma_p(b) = (\texttt{nil}, 0)$ and

$$v_p := \{dmchunk(id(c), t) \mid \gamma(b) = (c, d) \land c = (t, val)\} \uplus$$
$$\{dmchs(id(c), s, v) \mid \gamma(b) = (c, d) \land c = (t, val) \land s \in \tau(t) \land val(s) = v\}.$$

The buffer is emptied and its chunk is added to declarative memory represented as additional information.

There are also transitions without a rule (*no rule transitions*):

$$\frac{b^* \in \mathbb{B} \land \gamma(b^*) = (c^*, d^*) \land d^* > 0}{\sigma := \langle \Delta; \gamma; v \rangle^{\mathbb{V}} \rightarrowtail \langle \Delta; \gamma'; v \rangle^{\mathbb{V}}}$$

where $\gamma'(b^*) := (c^*, 0)$. Thus, one pending request is chosen non-deterministically to be applied for one buffer b^*.

3   Translation

In this section we show how to translate an ACT-R model to a CHR program. This is the main contribution of this paper. The translation is the first that matches the current operational semantics of ACT-R.

3.1   Set Normal Form

To simplify the translation scheme, we assume the ACT-R production rules to be in *set normal form*, i.e. that each buffer test only contains each slot at most once. Every production rule can be transformed to a production rule preserving operational semantics: If a rule has (s, v) and (s, v') in one buffer test, then one of the two must be a variable or $v = v'$, otherwise the rule can never fire since one slot cannot have two different values. Let v be a variable and v' a variable or constant. Then the operational semantics will add the following bindings to the state: $v = v' = v^*$ for some constant v^* (that is the identifier of a chunk) from the state. We can now simply replace each occurrence of v by v' in the rule directly and have the same semantics.

3.2   Translation of States

An ACT-R state $\sigma := \langle \Delta; \gamma; v \rangle^{\mathbb{V}}$ can be translated to the following CHR state:

$$\biguplus_{b \in \mathbb{B}} \{buffer(b, id(c), t, d) \mid \gamma(b) = (c, d) \land c = (t, val_c)\}$$

$$\uplus \biguplus_{b \in \mathbb{B}} \{chs(id(c), s, id(v)) \mid (c, d) \in \Delta \land c = (t, val_c) \land val_c(s) = v\}$$

$$\uplus \, v \uplus \mathbb{V} \uplus \{fire\}.$$

Hence, for every buffer a *buffer* constraint with the chunk id, the type and the delay is constructed. For every slot-value pair in the valuation function of a chunk, a corresponding *chs* constraint is added to the store that keeps track of the connections of a chunk. Note that by this definition chunks that appear in more than one buffer are copied in the CHR state and have the same identifier. This is made explicit in the definition by the multi-set union over all buffers.

Additional information and variable bindings are translated to corresponding built-in constraints. As we will see in the following sections, the *fire* constraint is needed to enable translated ACT-R rules to fire. This is necessary, since our translation needs additional transitions for one original rule application. Those additional transitions must not be interfered by other rule applications.

3.3   Translation of Rules

In our translation scheme, ACT-R rules are translated to corresponding CHR rules. However, as we will see, there are some additional rules needed to achieve the same behavior in both languages.

First of all, to manage relations between newly introduced variables, we define some auxiliary functions: Both the *chunk variable function cvar* : $\mathbb{B} \rightarrow \mathcal{V}_1$ and the *modified chunk function mvar* : $\mathbb{B} \rightarrow \mathcal{V}_2$ are defined as $b \mapsto C_b$ and return a fresh, unique variable C_b for each buffer b. The codomains $\mathcal{V}_1$ and $\mathcal{V}_2$ are disjoint subsets of $\mathcal{V}$. The first function will identify the chunk of a particular buffer in the translation. The second function is needed to introduce copies of chunks in the translation. Finally, the *value function chrval* : $\mathbb{B} \times \mathcal{C} \rightarrow \mathcal{V}, (b,s) \mapsto V_{b,s}$ returns a fresh, unique variable $V_{b,s}$ for each buffer b and slot name s. Those variables are needed to identify the values of slot-value pairs. Note that in the following we implicitly translate ACT-R constants and variables from $\mathcal{C}$ and $\mathcal{V}$ to corresponding CHR variables.

We define the translation of a production rule r of the form $L \Rightarrow R$ to a CHR rule $H_k \setminus H_r \Leftrightarrow G_= \uplus G_+ \mid B \uplus B_= \uplus B_+ \uplus B_-$ in the following sections that describe the translation of the individual parts of the rule.

Tests. The tests of the ACT-R production rule roughly correspond to the head of the CHR rule, i.e. the head of the CHR rule mainly depends on the tests in L. If there is an action for a tested buffer, then the buffer constraint is removed, otherwise it is kept. We add *chs* constraints for all slots of every tested chunk to access all values. Hence, the heads of our CHR rule are defined as follows:

$$H_r := \{fire\} \uplus \{buffer(b, cvar(b), t, 0) \mid =(b, t, P) \in L \wedge a \in A \wedge a(b, t', P') \in R\}$$
$$H_k := \{buffer(b, cvar(b), t, 0) \mid =(b, t, P) \in L \wedge a \in A \wedge a(b, t', P') \notin R\}$$
$$\uplus \{chs(cvar(b), s, v) \mid =(b, t, P) \in L \wedge (s, v) \in P\}$$
$$\uplus \{chs(cvar(b), s, chrval(b, s)) \mid =(b, t, P) \in L \wedge s \in \tau(t) \wedge s \notin slots(P)\}.$$

We require the *fire* constraint and remove it, hence no other translated production rule can fire. As mentioned before, we want to ensure that certain maintenance rules that are described in the following are completed before another rule is fired. Additionally, the rule deletes the connection between the buffer and its chunk, if there is an action for this buffer on the right hand side of the rule. The removed buffer constraints are later on replaced by new constraints that are connected to other chunks. This is because actions modify a copy of the original chunk instead of modifying it in-place.

General Translation of Actions. As can be seen in the operational semantics of ACT-R, actions specify a (partial) cognitive state that describes how the contents of the buffers change. All types of actions can be described by this abstraction. We will implement this concept in CHR to handle rule actions. Therefore, we first need to solve the technical problem that we have to know how many actions a rule has to perform to make sure that no other rules interfere with the process of applying the modifications. We keep track of this information in the *actions* constraint that holds the value of pending actions. Note that this is a static information that is known at compile time. Hence, we can add this constraint in the general part of the translated rule: $B := \{actions(|R|)\}$.

The following two general rules are added to the translated program. They are needed to actually perform the actions:

$$actions(N) \wedge mod(C, []) \Leftrightarrow N > 0 \mid actions(N - 1).$$
$$actions(N) \setminus mod(C, [(S, V)|P]) \Leftrightarrow N > 0 \mid chs(C, S, V) \wedge mod(C, P).$$

The two rules add *chs* constraints for a chunk C as specified in the list of slot-value pairs until it is empty. If all actions have been performed, i.e. the execution of the rule is finished, we make system able to fire again by the following general rule that is part of the translated program: $actions(0) \Leftrightarrow fire$. In the following we describe how the particular actions are translated to such *mod* constraints.

Modifications. Modifications copy the chunk from the buffer and modify particular slots in it. The previous chunks are not removed from the chunk store, but their link to the buffer is removed by removing the *buffer* constraint if a modification of the corresponding buffer is present in the rule. Hence, a modification has to add a new *buffer* constraint that links the buffer to the modified copy of the chunk. Therefore, we call the function $completion_b : \mathbb{T} \times 2^{(\mathcal{C} \cup \mathcal{V})} \rightarrow 2^{(\mathcal{C} \cup \mathcal{V})}$ for a buffer $b \in \mathbb{B}$ a *chunk completion function* that is defined as $completion_b(t, P) := \{(s, chrval(b, s)) \mid s \in \tau(t) \wedge s \notin slots(P)\}$. The function gets a type and a set of slot-value pairs and returns the set of slot-value pairs for the slots that do not appear in P, but are part of the type t. The values in the result are variables that are generated by the *chrval* function depending on the buffer b to avoid variable name clashes.

The modification part of the translated rule is then defined as:

$$G_= := \{newID(mvar(b)) \mid =(b, t, P) \in R\}$$
$$B_= := \{buffer(b, mvar(b), t, 0) \mid =(b, t, P) \in R\}$$
$$\uplus \ \{mod(mvar(b), P \cup completion_b(t, P)) \mid =(b, t, P) \in R\}$$

The built-in constraint $newID/1$ binds a new constant name to the variable that we obtain from the $mvar$ function in the guard. This name corresponds to the new id in the operational semantics. Then a copy of the old chunk with some modified values is placed into the buffer.

Requests. Requests to a module are modeled as built-in constraints. This means that the request function from the operational semantics of ACT-R is modeled by a built-in constraint $request(b, t, c_r, T, V)$ whose answer depends on the built-in store (that corresponds to the additional information v). Hence, the following parts are added to our translated CHR rule, where for every buffer there are unique, fresh variables T_b^a and V_b^a:

$$G_+ := \{request(b, t, p, T_b^a, V_b^a) \mid +(b, t, p) \in R\} \uplus \{newID(mvar(b))\}$$
$$B_+ := \{buffer(b, mvar(b), T_b^a, 1) \mid +(b, t, p) \in R\}$$
$$\uplus \{mod(mvar(b), V_b^a) \mid +(b, t, c_r) \in R\}$$

A request simply takes the answer of the built-in request and puts it into the requested buffer. The $newID$ built-in constraint again produces a new name for the chunk.

Clearings. In ACT-R, chunks are copied to declarative memory when a buffer is cleared. To do this, we need to know the contents of all the slots that define the chunk. However, in the definition of our translation scheme of rules we do not have access to all constraints defining the chunk that is removed from the buffer. At compilation time it is not possible to know what type of chunk will be in the buffer to be cleared. However, the kind and number of chs constraints depends on that type. Thus, we have to delay the application of the clearing and handle it by introducing an extra rule for each type t of the form $H_r^t \setminus H_k^t \Leftrightarrow B^t$ with fresh CHR variables N, B, C, D, and (for all $s \in \tau(t)$) V_s:

$$H_r^t := \{actions(N), clear(B), buffer(B, C, t, D)\}$$
$$H_k^t := \{chs(C, s, V_s) \mid s \in \tau(t)\}$$
$$B_c^t := \{dmchs(C, s, V_s) \mid s \in \tau(t)\}$$
$$\uplus \{dmchunk(C, t), buffer(B, \mathtt{nil}, \mathtt{chunk}, 0), actions(N-1)\}$$

This rule is only applicable, if a buffer clearing was triggered by the last rule applied (ensured by the $clear/1$ constraint that is introduced by the rule with the clearing action as we will see). Note that due to the removal of the $fire$ constraint, only clearing rules can be applied.

Our translation of the ACT-R rule with a buffer clearing has the following body:

$$B_- := \{clear(b) \mid -(b, \mathtt{chunk}, \mathtt{nil}) \in R\}.$$

We now exemplify the translation of rules:

Example 2 (Translation of Rules). The rule from Example 1 can be translated to the following CHR rule:

$$chs(G, state, start) \wedge chs(G, query, X) \wedge chs(G, mother, M) \wedge$$
$$chs(G, father, F) \backslash buffer(goal, g, G, 0) \wedge fire$$
$$\Leftrightarrow newID(G') \wedge newID(R') \wedge request(retrieval, parent, [(child, X)], T, V, \_) \mid$$
$$buffer(goal, g, G', 0) \wedge buffer(retrieval, T, R', 1) \wedge mod(G', V) \wedge$$
$$mod(G', [(state, retrieval), (query, X), (mother, M), (father, F)]).$$

3.4   No Rule Transition

In addition to transitions by rule applications, ACT-R can also have state transitions without rule applications. This is useful for instance, if no rule is applicable (i.e. computation is stuck in a state) but there are pending requests, then simulation time can be forwarded to the point where the next request is finished and its results are visible to the procedural system. This may trigger new rules and continue the computation.

The *no rule* transition can be modeled in CHR by one individual generic rule:

$$fire \setminus buffer(B, T, C, D) \Leftrightarrow D > 0 \mid buffer(B, T, C, 0)$$

This rule application is only possible when generally a rule could fire (ensured by the *fire* constraint). This transition is possible for all requests that are pending (i.e. that have a delay $D = 1$). Hence, one request is chosen non-deterministically.

4   Discussion

We have constructed our translation such that the translated program behaves equivalently to the original ACT-R model, i.e. every transition that is possible in the ACT-R model is also possible in the translated program leading to equivalent subsequent states (soundness) and vice versa (completeness). However, our translation has the restriction that one ACT-R transition $\sigma \rightarrowtail \sigma'$ can correspond to possibly more than one but finitely many transitions in CHR: $chr(\sigma) \mapsto \ldots \mapsto chr(\sigma')$, so-called *macro-steps*. In the intermediate states no regular transitions are possible. This is ensured by the removal of the *fire* constraint in all of those translated rules. The only rules that are applicable in an intermediate state are the ones that replace *mod* constraints with their corresponding *chs* constraints (or the respective constraints for clearings), i.e. that actually apply the actions to the state described by those constraints. Each action of a rule only introduces n such constraints, where n is the number of actions of the rules. After n steps, all *mod* and *clear* constraints are removed and a new *fire* constraint is introduced leading to a state that is equivalent to σ'.

This state allows the same macro-transitions as the original ACT-R state and describes the equivalent cognitive state and additional information. The latter is argued in the translation of the particular actions. The applicability of translated CHR rules can be seen directly from the definition of matchings (c.f. Definition 4) and the applicability condition of CHR in Sect. 2.1. The set normal form of rules and the copying of chunks in the CHR state ensure that there are constraints available in the state to match the translated rule even if two buffers hold the same chunk or two slots of the same chunk are tested twice.

For the completeness, obviously only CHR states that model valid ACT-R states can be considered. In particular it is required that they contain a *fire* constraint, the functional character of a cognitive state is maintained and chunks are described completely according to their type by the respective constraints, for instance. Then it can easily be seen, that both applicability and equivalence of actions are maintained by the translation.

5   Related Work

We first want to relate the progress of this paper with our prior work. In [13] we first have presented an abstract operational semantics and a corresponding translation to CHR together with a soundness and completeness result. However, this semantics has ignored some details that are crucial for ACT-R, like the copying of chunks when they enter a buffer. The old semantics used in-place modification which does not directly correspond to how most implementations work. Furthermore, the formulation of the semantics led to complicated proofs.

In [14] we have improved our semantics and unified it with independent work from [4]. There we concentrated on the semantics that we use for the CHR translation in this paper.

Our approach abstracts from technical details that vary in different ACT-R implementations or depend on parameter settings like timings and conflict resolution. We rather capture all possible transitions non-deterministically. Those non-deterministic transitions are removed by a conflict resolution mechanism in implementations. However, when writing a model, one is often interested in the general sequence of transitions and only later in concrete timings. Our approach gives us the power to reason about the core of the procedural system of ACT-R. For instance, a model that is confluent under our abstract semantics is independent of the order of rules, initial utility values of rules (used for conflict resolution) and timings. This gives a more concise view on the model.

We model implementation details in a refined semantics that is an instance of our abstract semantics [14]. This leads to concise, flexible implementations as shown in [12] by exchanging conflict resolution in our implementation of ACT-R.

There are many implementations of ACT-R in different languages that reach from the Lisp reference implementation [7] to certain Java (e.g. [18]) or even Python implementations [19]. All of those approaches are efforts of getting rid of many technicalities that have been incorporated over time in the reference implementation, but none of them deal with formal analysis of ACT-R.

Closest to our work is F-ACT-R [3,4], a formal formulation of the ACT-R semantics together with an implementation with the aim of simplifying model analysis. However, there are no confluence or complexity analysis tools, yet.

6   Conclusion and Future Work

In this paper we have presented a translation scheme of ACT-R models to CHR programs. It is the first of its kind that suits the current definition of the abstract operational semantics of ACT-R [14] that introduced significant changes compared to the prior rough definition of the semantics from [13]. The translation does not guarantee that each ACT-R transition corresponds to exactly one CHR transition, but in finitely many steps a valid ACT-R state is reached in CHR representing exactly the ACT-R state from the original transition.

This property enables us to use analysis methods and tools from the CHR world to analyze cognitive models. For example, in CHR confluence is decidable for terminating programs [10] and there is a tool that decides it automatically [15]. Another example are methods for semi-automatic complexity analysis [9,10] that exist for CHR. Complexity is an important property of cognitive models, since it can decide if a model is plausible or not. For instance, there are cognitive tasks that can be solved by humans in short time for growing problem size (but with errors) where the best cognitive models have exponential complexity [17]. Hence, such models are not plausible, since they seem to pursue the wrong approach.

Although CHR analysis tools can now be used on the translated programs, there are some practical limitations: we want to investigate how our translation can be used for analysis of cognitive models in practice. for instance, that confluence is often too strict. Hence, the confluence criterion of CHR classifies ACT-R models as non-confluent that should be confluent since there are certain invariants on valid ACT-R states that are not considered by the confluence criterion. For example, one invariant is that there can only be one *buffer* constraint for each buffer. Therefore, we want to use *observable confluence* to improve the behavior of the confluence criterion for cognitive models [8] in future work. Additionally, we want to investigate how reasoning on declarative knowledge can be improved by a constraint system using CHR.

References

1. Abdennadher, S., Frühwirth, T.: Operational equivalence of CHR programs and constraints. In: Jaffar, J. (ed.) CP 1999. LNCS, vol. 1713, pp. 43–57. Springer, Heidelberg (1999)
2. Abdennadher, S., Frühwirth, T., Meuss, H.: On confluence of constraint handling rules. In: Freuder, E.C. (ed.) Principles and Practice of Constraint Programming CP96. Lecture Notes in Computer Science, vol. 1118, pp. 1–15. Springer, Berlin Heidelberg (1996)
3. Albrecht, R., Gießwein, M., Westphal, B.: Towards formally founded ACT-R simulation and analysis. In: Proceedings of the 12th Biannual Conference of the German Cognitive Science Society (Gesellschaft für Kognitionswissenschaft), vol. 15 (Suppl. 1), Cognitive Processing, pp. 27–28. Springer (2014)

4. Albrecht, R., Westphal, B.: F-ACT-R: defining the ACT-R architectural space. In: Proceedings of the 12th Biannual Conference of the German Cognitive Science Society (Gesellschaft für Kognitionswissenschaft), vol. 15 (Suppl. 1), Cognitive Processing, pp. 79–81. Springer (2014)
5. Anderson, J.R., Bothell, D., Byrne, M.D., Douglass, S., Lebiere, C., Qin, Y.: An integrated theory of the mind. Psychol. Rev. **111**(4), 1036–1060 (2004)
6. Betz, H., Raiser, F., Frühwirth, T.: A complete and terminating execution model for constraint handling rules. Theor. Pract. Logic Program. **10**, 597–610 (2010)
7. Bothell, D.: ACT-R 6.0 Reference Manual - Working Draft. Department of Psychology, Carnegie Mellon University, Pittsburgh, PA
8. Duck, G.J., Stuckey, P.J., Sulzmann, M.: Observable confluence for constraint handling rules. In: Dahl, V., Niemelä, I. (eds.) ICLP 2007. LNCS, vol. 4670, pp. 224–239. Springer, Heidelberg (2007)
9. Frühwirth, T.: As time goes by: automatic complexity analysis of simplification rules. In: Fensel, D., Giunchiglia, F., McGuinness, D., Williams, M.A. (eds.) KR 2002: Proceedings of the 8th International Conference on Principles of Knowledge Representation and Reasoning, pp. 547–557, April 2002
10. Frühwirth, T.: Constraint Handling Rules. Cambridge University Press, Cambridge (2009)
11. Frühwirth, T.: Constraint handling rules - what else? In: Bassiliades, N., Gottlob, G., Sadri, F., Paschke, A., Roman, D. (eds.) RuleML 2015. LNCS, vol. 9202, pp. 13–34. Springer, Heidelberg (2015)
12. Gall, D., Frühwirth, T.: Exchanging conflict resolution in an adaptable implementation of ACT-R. Theor. Pract. Logic Program. **14**, 525–538 (2014)
13. Gall, D., Frühwirth, T.: A formal semantics for the cognitive architecture ACT-R. In: Proietti, M., Seki, H. (eds.) LOPSTR 2014. LNCS, vol. 8981, pp. 74–91. Springer, Heidelberg (2015)
14. Gall, D., Frühwirth, T.: A refined operational semantics for ACT-R: investigating the relations between different ACT-R formalizations. In: Proceedings of the 17th International Symposium on Principles and Practice of Declarative Programming, PPDP 2015, pp. 114–124. ACM, New York (2015)
15. Langbein, J., Raiser, F., Frühwirth, T.: A state equivalence and confluence checker for CHR. In: Van Weert, P., De Koninck, L. (eds.) CHR 2010. K.U.Leuven, Department of Computer Science, Technical report CW 588, July 2010
16. Raiser, F., Frühwirth, T.: Analysing graph transformation systems through constraint handling rules. Theor. Pract. Logic Program. **11**(1), 65–109 (2011)
17. van Rooij, I., Wright, C.D., Wareham, T.: Intractability and the use of heuristics in psychological explanations. Synthese **187**(2), 471–487 (2012)
18. Salvucci, D.: ACT-R: The Java Simulation & Development Environment. http://cog.cs.drexel.edu/act-r/
19. Stewart, T.C., West, R.L.: Deconstructing and reconstructing ACT-R: exploring the architectural space. Cogn. Syst. Res. **8**(3), 227–236 (2007)
20. Sun, R.: Introduction to computational cognitive modeling. In: Sun, R. (ed.) The Cambridge Handbook of Computational Psychology, pp. 3–19. Cambridge University Press, New York (2008)
21. Taatgen, N.A., Lebiere, C., Anderson, J.: Modeling paradigms in ACT-R. In: Cognition and Multi-Agent Interaction: From Cognitive Modeling to Social Simulation, pp. 29–52. Cambridge University Press (2006)

Legal Rules and Reasoning

Enabling Reasoning with LegalRuleML

Ho-Pun Lam$^{(\boxtimes)}$, Mustafa Hashmi$^{(\boxtimes)}$, and Brendan Scofield

Data61, CSIRO | NICTA, Spring Hill, Australia
{brian.lam,mustafa.hashmi}@data61.csiro.au

Abstract. This paper presents an approach for the specification and implementation of translating legal norms represented using Legal-RuleML to a variant of Modal Defeasible Logic. From its logical form, legal norms will be transformed into a machine readable format and eventually implemented as executable semantics that can be reasoned about depending upon the client's preference.

Keywords: Legal reasoning · LegalRuleML · Business contracts · Defeasible logic

1 Introduction

Generally regulatory rules are written in natural language— for their automated verification, they need to be transformed into a format that machines can understand. As a result, several languages such as RuleML[1], LKIF [7], SBVR [24], PENELOPE [8], ConDec language [26], ContractLog [25], OWL-S[2], have been proposed to facilitate this process. Each of these languages offer useful functionalities but is not free from shortcomings (see [9] for some of the shortcomings of these languages). For example, RuleML is an XML based prominent industry standard language for translating rules documents into a machine readable format. It provides the features that enable users to use different types of rules (such as derivation rules, fact, query, integrity constraint, etc.) to represent different kinds of elements according to their needs. However, it lacks support for the use of deontic concepts, such as obligations (such as achievement and maintenance), permission, prohibition, and is unable to handle cases with contrary-to-duty (CTD) obligations [6] that may arise from the violations of other obligations, which frequently appear in legal contracts [10].

Grosof [18] proposed to adopt courteous logic programming as execution model for RuleML rule-base for translating the clauses of a contract, which

---

NICTA is funded by the Australian Government through the Department of Communications and the Australian Research Council through the ICT Centre of Excellence Program.

[1] RuleML: The Rule Markup Initiative, http://www.ruleml.org.

[2] The OWL services coalition. OWL-S 1.2 Release, http://www.daml.org/services/owl-s/.

© Springer International Publishing Switzerland 2016
J.J. Alferes et al. (Eds.): RuleML 2016, LNCS 9718, pp. 241–257, 2016.
DOI: 10.1007/978-3-319-42019-6_16

filled the gap among the various types of rules in RuleML; however, their approach does not consider normative effects. Later, Governatori [10] addressed the
shortcomings of [18], and extended *Defeasible Logic*(DL) with standard deontic
operators for representing normative effects as well as an operator to deal with
CTD obligations. This extended language also provides RuleML compliant data
schemas for representing deontic elements and provides constructs to resolve
some of the shortcomings that have been discussed in [9].

This paper focuses on transforming the legal norms represented using Legal-
RuleML into a variant of Modal Defeasible Logic [16]. As a consequence, our work
reported here makes it possible to use an implementation of DL as the engine
to compute the extensions on the legal norms represented using LegalRuleML
and reason on it. Due to the space limit, details of other features supported
by LegalRuleML, such as *Contexts* and *Alternatives*, will not be covered in this
paper.

The remainder of the paper is structured as follows: in Sect. 2 we tersely
discuss a short contract from [10] following which we provide some background
information on DL in Sect. 3. Section 4 discusses the mapping and procedures
to transform a legal theory represented using LegalRuleML to DL. Section 5
discusses related work, followed by some concluding remarks and pointers for
future work.

2   A Sample Contract

In this section we discuss a sample *"Contract of Services"* based on the analysis
and adapted from [10].

Contract of Services

The Deed of Agreement is entered into effects between ABC company (to
be known as Purchaser) and ISP plus (to be known as Supplier) WHEREAS
Purchaser desires to enter into an agreement to purchase from Supplier the application server (to be known as Goods) in this agreement. Both the parties shall
enter into an agreement subject to the following terms and conditions:

1. **Definitions and Interpretations**
   1.1. All prices are in Australian current unless otherwise stated.
   1.2. This agreement is governed by the Australian law and both the parties
        hereby agree to submit to the jurisdiction of the Courts of the Queensland
        with respect to this agreement.
2. **Commencement and Completion**
   2.1. The contract enters into effects as Jan 30, 2002.
   2.2. The completion date is scheduled as Jan 30, 2003.
3. **Policy on Price**
   3.1. A *"Premium Customer"* is a customer who has spent more than $10000
        in goods. Premium Customers are entitled a 5 % discount on new orders.

3.2. Goods marked as *"Special Order"* are subject to a 5% surcharge. Premium customers are exempt from special order surcharge.

3.3. ...

4. **Purchase Order**

4.1. The Purchaser shall follow the Supplier price lists on the supplier's website.

4.2. The Purchaser shall present Supplier with a purchase order for the provision of Goods within 7 days of the commencement date.

5. **Service Delivery**

5.1. ...

5.2. The Supplier shall on receipt of a purchase order for Goods make them available within 1 days.

5.3. If for any reason the conditions stated in 4.1 or 4.2 are not met, the Purchaser is entitled to charge the Supplier the rate of $100 for each hour the Goods are not delivered.

6. **Payments**

6.1. The payment terms shall be in full upon receipt of invoice. Interest shall be charged at 5% on accounts not paid within 7 days of the invoice date. Another 1.5% interest shall be applicable if not paid within next 15 days. The prices shall be as stated in the sales order unless otherwise agreed in writing by the Supplier.

6.2. Payments are to be sent electronically, and are to be performed under standards and guidelines outlined in PayPal.

7. **Disputes:** Omitted due to limited space.

8. **Termination:** Omitted due to limited space.

The agreement covers a range of rule objectives such as roles of the involved parties (e.g., Supplier, Purchaser), authority and jurisdiction (Australia, Queensland Courts), deontic conditions associated with roles (permissions, prohibition), and temporal properties to perform required actions. A contract can be viewed as a legal document containing a finite set of articles (where each article contains a set of clauses and subclauses). The above-discussed agreement includes two main types of clauses namely: (i) *definitional clauses*, which define the basic concepts contained in this agreement; and (ii) *normative clauses*, which regulate the actions of Purchaser and Supplier for the performance of contract, and include deontic notions e.g., obligations, permission etc.

3 Modal Defeasible Logic: An Informal Introduction

The following is a modal extension of DL, based on the work of [15,16]. The basic language is defined as follows. Given a set PROP of *propositional atoms*, the set Lit = PROP $\cup \{\neg p \mid p \in$ PROP$\}$ denotes the set of *literals*. If q is a literal, then $\sim q$ denotes its complement; if q is a positive literal p then $\sim q$ is $\neg p$, and if q is $\neg p$ then $\sim q$ is p. Let MOD denotes the set of modal operators. Then the set of *modal literals* is ModLit = $\{Xl, \neg Xl \mid l \in$ Lit, $X \in$ MOD$\}$.

We define a *defeasible theory* D as a structure $(F, R, >)$, where (i) F is a set of *facts* or indisputable statements, (ii) R is the set of rules, and (iii) $>$ is an acyclic *superiority relation* on R.

To enhance the expressiveness of a rule to encode chains of obligations and violations, following the ideas of [14], a sub-structural operator $\otimes$ is introduced to capture an obligation and the obligations arising in response to the violation of the obligation. Thus, given an expression like $a \otimes b$, the intuitive reading is that if a is possible, then a is the first choice and b is the second one; if $\neg a$ holds, i.e., a is violated, then b is the actual choice. That is, the $\otimes$-operator is used to build chains of preferences, called $\otimes$-*expression*, such that: (i) each literal is a $\otimes$-expression; (ii) if A is an $\otimes$-expression and b is a (modal) literal, then $A \otimes b$ is an $\otimes$-expression.

Hence, given Lbl a set of arbitrary labels, every rule in R is of the form $r : A(r) \hookrightarrow C(r)$, where:

- $r \in$ Lbl is the unique identifier of the rule;
- $A(r) = \phi_1, \ldots, \phi_n$, the *antecedent* of the rule, is a finite set of (modal) literals denoting the premises of the rule;
- $\hookrightarrow \in \{\rightarrow, \Rightarrow, \rightsquigarrow\}$ denotes the *type* of the rule;
- $C(r)$ is the *consequent* (or *head*) of the rule, which can be either a single (modal) literal, or an $\otimes$-expression otherwise.

The intuition behind different arrows is the following. DL supports three types of rules namely: *strict rules* $(r : A(r) \rightarrow C(r))$, *defeasible rules* $(r : A(r) \Rightarrow C(r))$ and *defeaters* $(r : A(r) \rightsquigarrow C(r))$. Strict rules are rules in the classical sense, the conclusion follows every time the antecedents holds; a defeasible rules is allowed to assert its conclusion in case there is no contrary evidence to it. Finally, defeaters suggests there is a connection between its premises and its conclusion(s) but not strong enough to warrant the conclusion on its own; they are used to defeat rules for the opposite conclusion(s).

DL is a *skeptical* nonmonotonic logic meaning that it does not support contradictory conclusions. Instead, it seeks to resolve conflicts. In case there is some support for concluding A but there is also support for concluding $\neg A$, DL does not conclude either of them. However, if the support for A has priority over the support of $\neg A$ then A is concluded. Here, the superiority relation $>$ is used to describe the relative strength of rules on R. When $r_1 > r_2$, then r_1 is called *superior* to r_2, and r_2 *inferior* to r_1. Intuitively, $r_1 > r_2$ expresses that r_1 overrides r_2 if both rules are applicable[3].

Provability is based on the concept of *derivation* (or *proof*) in D satisfying the proof conditions. A *conclusion* of D is a tagged literal and can have one of the following forms: (i) $+\Delta q$ meaning that q is definitely provable in D (i.e., using only facts or strict rules); (ii) $-\Delta q$ meaning that q is definitely rejected in D; (iii) $+\partial q$ meaning that q is defeasibly provable in D; and (iv) $-\partial q$ meaning that q is defeasibly rejected in D.

---

[3] A rule is applicable if all literals in its antecedent have already been proved.

Strict derivations are obtained by forward chaining of strict rules while a defeasible conclusion p can be derived if there is a rule whose conclusion is p, and its (prerequisite) antecedent has either already been proved or given in the case at hand (i.e., facts), and any stronger rules whose conclusion is $\neg p$ has prerequisite that it failed to be derived. In other words, a conclusion p is defeasibly derivable when: (i) p is a fact; or (ii) there is an applicable strict or defeasible rule for p, and either all rules for $\neg p$ are discarded (i.e., inapplicable) or every rule for $\neg p$ is weaker than an applicable rule for p.

A full description of the proof theory can be found in [2]. A useful metaphor is to imagine, the rules with conclusion p form a team that competes with opposite team consisting of the rules with conclusion $\neg p$. If the former team wins p is defeasible provable, whereas if the opposing team wins, p is non-provable or rejected from the theory.

Throughout the paper, we use the following abbreviations on set of rules: R_s (R_d) denotes the set of strict (defeasible) rules, $R[q]$ denotes the set of rules with consequent q, and for a $r \in R$, $C(r, i)$ denotes the ith (modal) literal that appears in $C(r)$.

4   LegalRuleML: The Legal Rule Markup Language

LegalRuleML [23] is a rule interchange language proposed by OASIS, which extends RuleML with features specific to legal domain [4]. It aims to bridge the gap between natural language descriptions and semantic norms [3], and can be used to model various laws, rules and regulations by translating the compliance requirements into a machine readable format [19]. Accordingly, LegalRuleML implements defeasibility as within the law where the precedent of a rule is satisfied by the facts of a case, then assumably the conclusion of the rule holds, but not necessarily [4]. The defeasibility of these legal rules can further identify exceptions and conflicts as well as mechanisms to resolve these conflicts within the norms. Additionally, LegalRuleML provides features to model various effects that follow from applying rules, such as obligations, permissions and prohibitions.

A contract written in LegalRuleML is not intended to be executed directly, but the business logic can be transformed into a target language of a rule-based system to execute. In this section we are going to explore the building blocks of LegalRuleML and propose a method to transform legal norms represented in LegalRuleML into DL theory. Since LegalRuleML is essentially an extension of RuleML, here we only highlight the differences and identify the additions to faithfully represent legal norms.

4.1   Premises and Conclusions

The first thing we have to consider is the representation of predicates (atoms) to be used in premises or conclusions in LegalRuleML. LegalRuleML extends the construct from RuleML and represents a predicate as an *n*-ary relation, and is defined using an element <ruleml:Atom>[4].

Normative effects of an atom, on the other hand, are captured by embedding the atom inside a deontic element. The legal concepts such as *obligation* (<lrml:Obligation>), *permission* (<lrml:Permission>), *prohibition* (<lrml:Prohibition), and *right* (<lrml:Right>[5]) are the basic deontic elements in LegalRuleML. Further refinements are possible by: (i) providing an iri[6] attribute of a deontic specification, or (ii) using an <lrml:Association> to link a deontic specification to its meaning with the <lrml:applyModality> element.

```
1  <lrml:Associations>
2    <lrml:Association key="asc1">
3      <lrml:appliesModality iri="ex:achievementObligation"/>
4      <lrml:toTarget keyref="#oblig101"/>
5    </lrml:Association>
6  </lrml:Associations>
7
8  <lrml:Obligation key="oblig101">
9    <ruleml:Atom key=":atom109">
10     <ruleml:Rel iri="pay"/>
11     <ruleml:Ind>Purchaser</ruleml:Ind>
12     <ruleml:Ind>receivedReciept</ruleml:Ind>
13     <ruleml:Ind>Supplier</ruleml:Ind>
14   </ruleml:Atom>
15 </lrml:Obligation>
```

Accordingly, the above listing represents a modal literal OBL *pay(purchaser, receivedReceipt, supplier)* for the clause 6.1 in the contract that is true when *purchaser* has the (achievement) obligation[7] to pay the *supplier* upon receiving the payment[8].

4.2 Rules and Rulebases

Norms in LegalRuleML are represented as collections of statements, and can be classified into four different types according to their nature, namely: *norm statements*, *factual statements*, *override statements* and *violation-reparation statements*. These can be further classified into subtypes, as depicted in Fig. 1.

---

[4] Elements from LegalRuleML and elements inherited from RuleML will be prefixed with lrml and ruleml, respectively. Information about transforming norms represented using RuleML to DL can be found in [10]. The attributes key and keyref in LegalRuleML correspond to an unique identifier of a Node element and reference to a Node element, respectively.

[5] Note that the *right* here is different from the "right" in RuleML. In LegalRuleML, it is a deontic specification that gives a permission to a party and implies there is no obligation or prohibition on the other parties [23]; while "right" in RuleML means the right hand side of a rule.

[6] An iri attribute on a Node element in LegalRuleML corresponds to an <owl:sameAs> relationship in the abstract syntax.

[7] There are several types of obligations based on temporal validity and effects they produce e.g., *achievement, maintenance* etc., see [19] for details.

[8] In this paper, we are going to use the modal operator OBL for obligation, PER for permission, FOR for prohibition (forbidden).

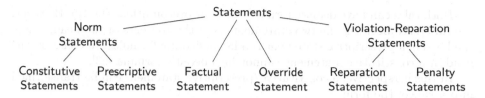

Fig. 1. Types of statements in LegalRuleML

In this section, we are going to explore different types of statements and describe how they can be transformed into rules in DL.

Norm Statements. Legal norms, in general, can be classified into *constitutive norms* (which is used to represent *institutional facts* [28] and provides definitions of terms and concepts in a jurisdiction [23]), and *prescriptive norms* (which specify the deontic behavior and effect of a legal system). These can be represented as *constitutive statements* (`<lrml:ConstitutiveStatement>`) and *prescriptive statements* in LegalRuleML (`<lrml:PrescriptiveStatement>`), respectively, to allow new information to be derived using existing rules.

The following is an example of a prescriptive statement representing the first statement of the clause 3.2 of the service contract where *goods* marked with *special order* are subject to a surcharge.

```
1  <lrml:PrescriptievStatement key="r1">
2    <ruleml:Rule key=":ruletemplate1">
3      <lrml:hasStrength>
4        <lrml:DefeasibleStrength key="str1"
5          iri="http://example.org/legalruleml/ontology#defeasible1"/>
6      </lrml:hasStrength>
7      <ruleml:if>
8        <ruleml:And>
9          <ruleml:Atom key=":atom2">
10           <ruleml:Rel iri=":specialOrder"/>
11           <ruleml:Ind>X</ruleml:Ind>
12         </ruleml:Atom>
13       </ruleml:And>
14     </ruleml:if>
15     <ruleml:then>
16       <lrml:Obligation>
17         <ruleml:Atom key=":atom3">
18           <ruleml:Rel iri=":surcharge"/>
19           <ruleml:Ind>X</ruleml:Ind>
20         </ruleml:Atom>
21       </lrml:Obligation>
22     </ruleml:then>
23   </ruleml:Rule>
24 </lrml:PrescriptievStatement>
```

Similar to the *derivation rules* in RuleML, every constitutive/prescriptive statement has two parts: *conditions* (`<ruleml:if>`), which specify the conditions (using a conjunction of formulas and may possibly empty), and *conclusion* (`<ruleml:then>`), the effects of the rule. Additionally, a separate element (`<lrml:hasStrength>`) can be used to specify the strength of the rule.

Both rules can have deontic formulas as their preconditions (body). However, the difference between the two statements is in the contents of the head, where the head of a prescriptive statement is a list of deontic formulas. In contrast, the head of a constitutive statement cannot be a deontic formula [23].

In this perspective, a constitutive/prescriptive statement can be transformed into a rule of the form:

$$label : \ body \hookrightarrow head.$$

where $label$ is the key of the statement, $\hookrightarrow \in \{\rightarrow, \Rightarrow, \rightsquigarrow\}$ is the rule type, $body$ and $head$ are the set of (modal) literals inside the <ruleml:if> and <rule:then> elements of the statement, respectively. Unless otherwise specified, due to its nature, the rule modelled using a constitutive statement will be transformed into a strict rule; while the rule modelled using prescriptive statement will be transformed into a defeasible rule. Thus, the statement above will be transformed to the defeasible rule below[9]:

$$r_1 : \ specialOrder \Rightarrow OBL \ surcharge$$

Factual Statements. Factual statements in essence are the expression of facts and can be considered as a special case of norm statements without the specification of premises. They denote a simple piece of information that is deemed to be true. Below is an example of a factual statement in LegalRuleML representing the fact $premiumCustomer(JohnDoe)$, meaning that "JohnDoe" is a premium customer.

```
1  <lrml:FactualStatement key="fact1">
2    <lrml:hasTemplate>
3      <ruleml:Atom key=":atom11">
4        <ruleml:Rel iri=":premiumCustomer"/>
5        <ruleml:Ind iri=":JohnDoe"/>
6      </ruleml:Atom>
7    </lrml:hasTemplate>
8  </lrml:FactualStatement>
```

Override Statements. To handle defeasibility, LegalRuleML uses *override statements* (<lrml:OverrideStatement>) to capture the relative strength of rules that appear in the legal norms. The element <lrml:Override> defines the relationship of superiority such that the conclusion of $r2$ overrides the conclusion of $r1$ (where $r1$ and $r2$ are the keys of statements in the legal theory, as shown below) if both statements are applicable.

---

[9] Note that in some variants of DL, new types of rules can be created for the deontic operator to differentiate between normative and definitional rules [13], for instance, the rule r_1 above will becomes: $specialOrder \Rightarrow_{OBL} surcharge$. However, we do not utilize this approach here as this will limit ourselves such that only one type of modality can appear in the head of the rule. As it is possible that different logics/semantics can be used to reason on the rules generated using the constitutive and prescriptive statements, using such approach will limit the logic that we can use when reasoning the rules. For example, in our case, we can use ambiguity blocking (of DL) for the rules generated using constitutive statements and ambiguity propagation [1] for the rules generated using prescriptive statements.

Consider again clause 3.2 of the contract where a *premium customer* is exempted from the surcharge for goods marked as *'Special Orders'*, which can be modelled as the rules below.

$$r_1 : specialOrder \Rightarrow \text{OBL } surcharge$$

$$r_2 : specialOrder, premiumCustomer \Rightarrow \text{OBL } \neg surcharge$$

In the above example, the conclusion of r_2 takes the precedence over the conclusion of r_1 (as showed above) if the order was made from a *premium customer*. The following listing illustrates this using an `<lrml:OverrideStatement>` element.

```
1  <lrml:OverrideStatement>
2    <lrml:Override over="#r2" under="#r1"/>
3  </lrml:OverrideStatement>
```

In DL terms, this construct defines a superiority relation between $r_2 > r_1$ where r_1 and r_2 are the rules generated using the statements $r1$ and $r2$ in the legal norms, respectively.

Violation-Reparation Statements. A *Violation-Reparation Statement* is the type of statement concerning what actions are required when an obligation is violated. LegalRuleML provides two constructs to model this, namely: *penalty statements* (`<lrml:PenaltyStatement>`) and *reparation statements* (`<lrml:ReparationStatement>`), as shown below.

```
1  <lrml:ReparationStatement key="reps1">
2    <lrml:Reparation key="rep1">            1  <lrml:PenaltyStatement key="pen1">
3      <lrml:appliesPenalty keyref="#pen1"/>  2    <lrml:SuborderList>
4      <lrml:toPrescriptiveStatement          3      list of deontic formulas
5              keyref="#ps1"/>                 4    </lrml:SuborderList>
6    </lrml:Reparation>                        5  </lrml:PenaltyStatement>
7  </lrml:ReparationStatement>
```

Penalty statements model sanctions and/or correction for a violation of a specified rule as outlined in the reparation statement; reparation statements bind a penalty statement to the appropriate prescriptive statement and apply the penalty when a violation occurs.

To transform these statements into DL rules, we can utilize the $\otimes$-expression that we described in Sect. 3 by appending the list of modal literals that appear in the penalty statements at the end of original rule. As an example, consider the penalty statement (in clause 6.1 of the contract) for not paying invoice within the deadline, and assume that the two model literals OBL $payWith5\,\%Interest$ and OBL $payWith6.5\,\%Interest$ are transformed from the suborder list inside the penalty statement. Then the prescriptive statement $ps1$ will be updated from

$$ps1 : goods, invoice \Rightarrow \text{OBL } payIn7days$$

to

$$ps1 : \quad goods, invoice \Rightarrow \text{OBL } payIn7days \otimes \text{OBL } payWith5\,\%Interest$$
$$\otimes \text{OBL } payWith6.5\,\%Interest$$

4.3   Other Constructs

Up to this point, the transformations described have been simple. However, there are other elements in LegalRuleML that are not particularly intuitive. We will highlight two of them in this section.

LegalRuleML provides two elements that can be used to determine whether an obligation or a prohibition of an object has been fulfilled (`<lrml:Compliance>`) or violated (`<lrml:Violation>`).

Definition 1 (Compliance and Violation [23]).

- A compliance *is an indication that an obligation has been fulfilled or a prohibition has not been violated.*
- A violation *is an indication that an obligation or prohibition has been violated.*

Consider the listing below which represents the rule:

$$ps2 :\ \text{PER}\,rel1,\ \text{OBL}\,rel2 \Rightarrow \text{FOR}\,\neg rel3.$$

```
 1  <lrml:PrescriptiveStatement key="ps2">
 2    <ruleml:Rule key=":ruletemplate2">
 3      <ruleml:if>
 4        <ruleml:And key=":and1">
 5          <lrml:Violation keyref="#ps3"/>
 6          <lrml:Permission>
 7            <ruleml:Atom key=":atom4">
 8              <ruleml:Rel iri=":rel1"/>
 9              <ruleml:Ind>X</ruleml:Ind>
10            </ruleml:Atom>
11          </lrml:Permission>
12          <lrml:Obligation key="oblig1">
13            <ruleml:Atom key=":atom5">
14              <ruleml:Rel iri=":rel2"/>
15              <ruleml:Ind>X</ruleml:Ind>
16            </ruleml:Atom>
17          </lrml:Obligation>
18        </ruleml:And>
19      </ruleml:if>
20      <ruleml:then>
21        <lrml:Prohibition key="prohib1">
22          <ruleml:Neg key=":neg1">
23            <ruleml:Atom key=":atom6">
24              <ruleml:Rel iri=":rel3"/>
25              <ruleml:Ind>X</ruleml:Ind>
26            </ruleml:Atom>
27          </ruleml:Neg>
28        </lrml:Prohibition>
29      </ruleml:then>
30    </ruleml:Rule>
31  </lrml:PrescriptiveStatement>
```

Here, we have a violation element appearing in the body as a prerequisite to activate the rule, meaning that the referenced element (*ps3* in this case) has to be violated or the rule *ps2* cannot not be utilised. Accordingly, we have two cases: either (i) the referenced element is a modal literal, or (ii) the referenced element is a rule.

Table 1. Requirements to determine whether a literal is compliant or violated.

	q	OBL q	FOR q
Compliance	q	OBL q, q	FOR q, $\neg q$
Violation	$\neg q$	OBL q, $\neg q$	FOR q, q

Case 1: Referenced Element Is a Literal. The former is a simple case. If the referenced element is a literal, essentially it acts as a precondition to activate the rule. It is practically the same as appending the violation (respectively, compliance) condition to the body of the rule, as shown below.

$$ps2: \text{ PER}\,rel1, \text{ OBL}\,rel2, \ violate(p) \Rightarrow \text{FOR}\,\neg rel3.$$

where p is the referenced literal, $violate(p)$ (respectively $comply(p)$) is a transformation, as defined in Table 1, that transforms the (modal) literal p into a set of literals that needs to be derived in order to satisfy the condition of violation (compliance). For instance, if $ps3$ is the modal literal OBL q, then the rule $ps2$ above will be updated as follows

$$ps2: \text{ PER}\,rel1, \text{ OBL}\,rel2, \text{ OBL}\,q, \neg q \Rightarrow \text{FOR}\,\neg rel3.$$

However, the case is somewhat complex when the element appears in the head of the statement, as shown in the listing below.

```
 1  <lrml:PrescriptiveStatement key="ps4">
 2    <ruleml:Rule key=":ruletemplate3" keyref=":ruletemplate2">
 3      <ruleml:then>
 4        <lrml:SuborderList>
 5          <lrml:Obligation key="obl1">
 6            <ruleml:Atom key=":atom26">
 7              <ruleml:Rel iri=":rel3"/>
 8              <ruleml:Ind>X</ruleml:Ind>
 9            </ruleml:Atom>
10          </lrml:Obligation>
11          <ruleml:And>
12            <lrml:Violation keyref="#ps5"/>
13            <lrml:Obligation key="obl2">
14              <ruleml:Atom key=":atom27">
15                <ruleml:Rel iri=":rel4"/>
16                <ruleml:Ind>X</ruleml:Ind>
17              </ruleml:Atom>
18            </lrml:Obligation>
19          </ruleml:And>
20        </lrml:SuborderList>
21      </ruleml:then>
22    </ruleml:Rule>
23  </lrml:PrescriptiveStatement>
```

Here, OBL $rel4$ (Lines 13–18) is derivable only when the modal literal OBL $rel3$ (Lines 5–10) is defeated and the reference literal $ps5$ (Line 12) is violated. However, such nested rule structure is *not* supported semantically in DL. To resolve this issue, we have to modify the statement based on its expanded form.

Definition 2 ($\otimes$-expansion). *Let $D = (F, R, >)$ be a defeasible theory, and let Σ be the language of D. We define reduct(D)=$(F, R', >')$ where for every rule*

$r \in R_d$ *with a $\otimes$-expression appears in its head:*

$$R' = R \setminus R_d \cup \{\ r : A(r),\ verify(c_1) \Rightarrow c_1$$
$$r' : A(r),\ violate(c_1),\ verify(c_1),\ verify(c_2) \Rightarrow c_2 \otimes \cdots \otimes c_n\}$$
$$\forall r', s' \in R', r' > s' \Leftrightarrow r, s \in R \ s.t. \ r' \in reduct(r), s' \in reduct(s), r > s.$$

where verify(p) is defined as:

$$\begin{cases} violate(e) & if\ a\ violation\ element\ is\ attached\ to\ the\ element\ p, \\ comply(e) & if\ a\ compliance\ element\ is\ attached\ to\ the\ element\ p, \\ \emptyset & otherwise. \end{cases}$$

where e is the literal referenced by the element attributed to p.

Here, we can first exclude the elements in the rule head and generate the rule based on $\otimes$-expression. Then, we can apply Definition 2 recursively to transform the generated rule into a set of rules with single literal in its head. Consequently, similar to the case discussed before, we can append the element to the body of the rule(s), where appropriate. Accordingly, the statement *ps4* above can be transformed into the DL rules as shown below.

$$ps4_1 : A(ps4) \Rightarrow \text{OBL}\,rel3$$
$$ps4_2 : A(ps4),\ \text{OBL}\,rel3,\ \neg rel3,\ violate(ps5) \Rightarrow \text{OBL}\,rel4$$

Case 2: Referenced Element Is a Rule. Instead, if the referenced element is a rule, then for the case of violation, we have to verify that the rule referenced is either (i) inapplicable, i.e., there is a literal in its antecedent that is not provable; or (ii) the immediate consequent of the rule is defeated or overruled by a conflicting conclusion. While for the case of compliance, we have to verify that the referenced rule is applicable and the immediate consequent of the rule is provable[10].

Definition 3 *Let $D = (F, R, >)$ be a defeasible theory. $R^b \subseteq R$ (respectively, $R^h \subseteq R$) denotes the set of rules that contains at least one element in their body (head).*

Definition 4 (Rule Status). *Let $D = (F, R, >)$ be a defeasible theory, and let Σ be the language of D. For every $r \in R^b$, r_c denotes the rule referenced by the element. We define $verifyBody(D) = (F, R', >')$ where:*

$$R' = R \setminus R_d \cup \{\ r_c^+ : A(r_c) \Rightarrow inf(r_c),$$
$$r_c^- : \Rightarrow \neg inf(r_c),$$
$$r_{cv}^- : \neg inf(r_c) \Rightarrow violation(r_c),$$
$$r_{cc}^+ : inf(r_c),\ comply(C(r_c, 1)) \Rightarrow compliance(r_c),$$
$$r_{cv}^+ : inf(r_c),\ violate(C(r_c, 1)) \Rightarrow violation(r_c),$$
$$>' = > \cup \{r_c^+ > r_c^-\}$$

---

[10] In this paper, we consider only the case of weak compliance and weak violation, and verify only the first (modal) literal that appears in the head of the rule. However, the method proposed here can be extended easily to support the verification of the cases of strong compliance [19] and strong violation [12].

For each r_c, $inf(r_c)$, $\neg inf(r_c)$, $compliance(r_c)$ and $violation(r_c)$ are new atoms not in the language of the defeasible theory. $inf(r_c)$ and $\neg inf(r_c)$ are used to determine whether a rule is *in force* (applicable). If r_c is in force, we can then verify whether the first literal that appears at the head of r_c is compliant or violated (represented using the atoms $compliance(r_c)$ and $violation(r_c)$, respectively).

Similar to the case when the referenced object is a literal, depending on where the element is in the rule, we can append the compliance and violation atoms to the body and head of the rule directly. However, unlike the case where the reference element is a literal, this time we can append the atoms required directly without any transformation.

4.4 Implementation

The above transformation can be used to transform legal norms represented using LegalRuleML into DL that we can reason on. We have implemented the above transformation as an extension to the DL reasoner SPINdle [22] — an open-source, Java-based DL reasoner that supports reasoning on both standard and modal defeasible logic. Theory reasoning starts from a set of legal norms represented using LegalRuleML, i.e., a rule base, and conclusions are generated based on the semantics of DL. At the moment, various tests have been performed on some small scale LegalRuleML theories (~ 10 statements per theory), and it takes, on average, 150 ms to transform a LegalRuleML theory into a SPINdle defeasible theory. Future versions will include optimization of the implementation of the transformation process so that it can handle large LegalRuleML theories in a more efficient manner.

We have also implemented the transformation in reverse direction, i.e., translate a DL theory back to LegalRuleML representation. However, as can be noticed from Sect. 3, LegalRuleML supports more features than DL, so only information about the legal norms, i.e., the rules, can appear in the translated theory.

As a remark, the transformation above is compliant with the current version of the LegalRuleML specification [3]. However, it should be noted that strange results may appear if a `<lrml:violation>` (or `<lrml:compliance>`) element appears at the head of a statement (i.e., the `<ruleml:then>` part of a statement). For instance, consider the case where a `<lrml:violation>` element appears as the only element at the head of a statement. Then, it will be transformed into a rule with no head literal, which is not correct. In the light of this, we believe that additional restriction(s) should be added to the specification in order to avoid this situation.

5 Related Works

The research in the areas of e-contracting, business process compliance and automated negotiation systems has evolved over the last few years. Several rules modelling languages have been developed (or improved existing ones) for representing the semantics of business vocabularies, facts and business rules [9], and rules transformation techniques have emerged.

The ContractLog [25] framework for describing the formal rules based on the contract specifications for automated execution and monitoring of the service level agreements (SLAs). It combines rule-based representation of SLAs using Horn rules and Meta programming techniques alternative to contracts defined in natural language or pure programming implementations in programming languages. A rule-based technique called *SweetDeal* for representing business contracts that enables the software agent to automatically create, negotiate, evaluate and execute the contract provisions with high degree of modularity is discussed in [17]. Their technique builds upon situated courteous logic programs (SCLP) knowledge representation in RuleML, and incorporates the process knowledge descriptions whose ontologies are represented in DAML+OIL[11]. DAML+OIL representations allow handling more complex contracts with behavioural provisions that might arise during the execution of contracts. The former has to rely upon multiple formalisms to represent various types of SLA rules e.g. Horn Logic, Event-Calculus, Description Logic—whereas the latter does not consider normative effects (i.e., the approach is unable to differentiate various types of obligations such as achievement, maintenance and permissions).

Semantics of Business Vocabulary and Business Rules (SBVR) [24] is an Object Management Group (OMG) standard to represent and fomalise business ontologies, including business rules, facts and business vocabularies. It provides the basis for detailed formal and declarative specifications of business policies and includes deontic operators to represent deontic concepts e.g., obligations, permissions etc. Also, it uses the controlled natural languages to represent legal norms [9]; however, the standard has some shortcomings as the semantics for the deontic notions is underspecified. This is because SBVR is based on classical first-order-logic, which is not suitable to represent deontic notions and conflicts. Also, it cannot handle contrary-to-duty obligations as these cannot be represented by standard deontic logic (see [6] for details). The legal knowledge interchange format (LKIF), on the other hand, is an XML based interchange format language [7] that aims to provide an interchangeable format to represent legal norms in a broad range of application scenarios, especially in the context of semantic web. LKIF uses XML schemas to represent theories and arguments derived from theories, where a theory in LKIF is a set of axioms and defeasible inference rules. In addition to these, there are other XML based rule interchange format languages e.g., SWRL [20], RIF [31], WSMO [27] and OWL-S [29] (see [9] for more details on the strengths and weaknesses of these languages).

Baget et al. [5] discuss techniques for transforming existential rules into Datalog+[12], RuleML and OWL 2 formats. For the transformation from Datalog+ into RuleML, the authors used a fragment of Deliberation RuleML 1.01, which

---

[11] DAM+OIL Reference: http://www.w3.org/TR/daml+oil-reference/.

[12] Datalog+: a sub-language of RuleML http://wiki.ruleml.org/index.php/Rule-Based_Data_Access#Datalog.2B.2F-.

includes positive facts, universally quantified implications, equality, falsity (and conjunctions) in the heads of implications. Whereas [30] transforms the association rules into Drool Rule Language (DRL) format using Lisp-Miner[13], and [21] proposes a model driven architecture based model to transform SBVR compliant business rules extracted from business contracts of services to compliant executable rules in formal contract language (FCL [11]). However, the former's transformation is limited only to existential rules; while the latter captures only the business rule (SBVR bears only business rules), which may or may not have legal standings. Whilst, LegalRuleML represents legal standings, the LegalRuleML's temporal notions of enforceability, efficacy and applicability cannot be represented with SBVR. In contrast, the approach proposed in this paper enables the translation of defeasible expressions, and various *deontic concepts* including the notion of *penalty* and *chain of reparations*.

6   Conclusions

In this paper, we have proposed a transformation such that (legal) norms represented using LegalRuleML can be transformed into DL which provides us a method for modeling business contracts and reasoning about them in a declarative way. Whilst LegalRuleML aims at providing specifications to legal norms that can be represented in a machine readable format, the major impedance now is the lack of dedicated and reliable infrastructure that can provide support to such capability.

As a future work, we are planning to incorporate our technique into some smart-contract enabled systems, such as Ethereum [32]. This will extend its language such that, instead of using programming logics, users can define their (smart-)contracts in a declarative manner.

References

1. Antoniou, G., Billington, D., Governatori, G., Maher, M.J.: A flexible framework for defeasible logics. In: Proceedings of the 17th National Conference on Artificial Intelligence, pp. 405–410. AAAI Press/The MIT Press (2000)
2. Antoniou, G., Billington, D., Governatori, G., Maher, M.J.: Representation results for defeasible logic. ACM Trans. Comput. Logic **2**(2), 255–286 (2001)
3. Athan, T., Boley, H., Governatori, G., Palmirani, M., Paschke, A., Wyner, A.: OASIS LegalRuleML. In: International Conference on Artificial Intelligence and Law, ICAIL 2013, Rome, Italy, pp. 3–12, 10–14 June 2013
4. Athan, T., Governatori, G., Palmirani, M., Paschke, A., Wyner, A.: LegalRuleML: design principles and foundations. In: Faber, W., Paschke, A. (eds.) Reasoning Web 2015. LNCS, vol. 9203, pp. 151–188. Springer, Heidelberg (2015)
5. Baget, J., Gutierrez, A., Leclère, M., Mugnier, M., Rocher, S., Sipieter, C.: Datalog+, RuleML and OWL 2: formats and translations for existential rules. In: RuleML 2015 Challenge, Berlin, Germany, 2–5 August 2015

---

[13] Lisp-Miner: http://lispminer.vse.cz.

6. Carmo, J., Jones, J.: Deontic Logic and Contrary to duties. In: Handbook of Philosophical Logic, 2nd edn., pp. 265–343. Kulwer, Dordrech (2002)
7. ESTRELLA Project: The Legal Knowledge Interchange Format (LKIF), Deliverable 4.1, European Commission (2008). http://www.estrellaproject.org/
8. Goedertier, S., Vanthienen, J.: Designing compliant business processes with obligations and permissions. In: Eder, J., Dustdar, S. (eds.) BPM Workshops 2006. LNCS, vol. 4103, pp. 5–14. Springer, Heidelberg (2006)
9. Gordon, T.F., Governatori, G., Rotolo, A.: Rules and norms: requirements for rule interchange languages in the legal domain. In: Governatori, G., Hall, J., Paschke, A. (eds.) RuleML 2009. LNCS, vol. 5858, pp. 282–296. Springer, Heidelberg (2009)
10. Governatori, G.: Representing business contracts in RuleML. Int. J. Coop. Inf. Syst. 14(2–3), 181–216 (2005)
11. Governatori, G., Milosevic, Z.: Dealing with contract violations: formalism and domain specific language. In: EDOC 2005, pp. 46–57. IEEE Computer Society (2005)
12. Governatori, G., Olivieri, F., Scannapieco, S., Cristani, M.: Designing for compliance: norms and goals. In: Palmirani, M. (ed.) RuleML - America 2011. LNCS, vol. 7018, pp. 282–297. Springer, Heidelberg (2011)
13. Governatori, G., Rotolo, A.: Defeasible logic: agency, intention and obligation. In: Lomuscio, A., Nute, D. (eds.) DEON 2004. LNCS (LNAI), vol. 3065, pp. 114–128. Springer, Heidelberg (2004)
14. Governatori, G., Rotolo, A.: Logic of violations: a gentzen system for reasoning with contrary-to-duty obligations. Australas. J. Logic 4, 193–215 (2006)
15. Governatori, G., Rotolo, A.: A computational framework for institutional agency. Artif. Intell. Law 16(1), 25–52 (2008)
16. Governatori, G., Rotolo, A.: BIO logical agents: norms, beliefs, intentions in defeasible logic. Auton. Agent. Multi-Agent Syst. 17(1), 36–69 (2008)
17. Grosof, B., Poon, T.C.: SweetDeal: representing agent contracts with exceptions using XML rules, ontologies, and process descriptions. In: The 12th International World Wide Web Conference, pp. 340–349 (2012)
18. Grosof, B.N.: Representing e-commerce rules via situated courteous logic programs in RuleML. Electron. Commer. Res. Appl. 3(1), 2–20 (2004)
19. Hashmi, M., Governatori, G., Wynn, M.T.: Normative requirements for regulatory compliance: an abstract formal framework. Inf. Syst. Front. 18(3), 429–455 (2016). doi:10.1007/s10796-015-9558-1
20. Horrocks, I., Patel-Schneider, P.F., Boley, H., Tabet, S., Grosof, B., Dean, M.: SWRL: A Semantic Web Rule Language (2004). https://www.w3.org/Submission/SWRL/
21. Kamada, A., Governatori, G., Sadiq, S.: Transformation of SBVR compliant business rules to executable FCL rules. In: Dean, M., Hall, J., Rotolo, A., Tabet, S. (eds.) RuleML 2010. LNCS, vol. 6403, pp. 153–161. Springer, Heidelberg (2010)
22. Lam, H.-P., Governatori, G.: The making of SPINdle. In: Governatori, G., Hall, J., Paschke, A. (eds.) RuleML 2009. LNCS, vol. 5858, pp. 315–322. Springer, Heidelberg (2009)
23. OASIS LegalRuleML Technical Committee: LegalRuleML Technical Committee Specifications (2015). https://www.oasis-open.org/committees/legalruleml/charter.php, retrieved 12
24. Object Management Group (OMG): Semantics of Business Vocabulary And Rules (SBVR). OMG (2008). http://www.omg.org/spec/SBVR

25. Paschke, A., Bichler, M., Dietrich, J.B.: ContractLog: an approach to rule based monitoring and execution of service level agreements. In: Adi, A., Stoutenburg, S., Tabet, S. (eds.) RuleML 2005. LNCS, vol. 3791, pp. 209–217. Springer, Heidelberg (2005)

26. Pesic, M., van der Aalst, W.M.P.: A declarative approach for flexible business processes management. In: Eder, J., Dustdar, S. (eds.) BPM Workshops 2006. LNCS, vol. 4103, pp. 169–180. Springer, Heidelberg (2006)

27. Roman, D., Keller, U., Lausen, H., de Bruijn, J., Lara, R., Stollberg, M., Polleres, A., Feier, C., Bussler, C., Fensel, D.: Web service modeling ontology. Appl. Ontol. **1**(1), 77–106 (2005)

28. Searle, J.R.: The Construction of Social Reality. Free Press, New York (1997)

29. The OWL Services Coalition: OWL-S 1.2 Release (2008). http://www.daml.org/services/owl-s/

30. Vojíř, S., Kliegr, T., Hazucha, A., Skrabal, R., Simunek, M.: Transforming association rules to business rules: easyminer meets drools. In: Joint Proceedings of the 7th International Rule Challenge, the Special Track on Human Language Technology and the 3rd RuleML Doctoral Consortium. Seattle, USA, July 2013

31. W3C RIF Working Group: RIF: Rule Interchange Format (2005). https://www.w3.org/standards/techs/rif

32. Wood, G.: Ethereum: A Secure Decentralised Generalised Transaction Ledger (2014). http://gavwood.com/paper.pdf, Accessed December

SBVR to OWL 2 Mapping in the Domain of Legal Rules

Firas Al Khalil$^{(\boxtimes)}$, Marcello Ceci, Kosala Yapa, and Leona O'Brien

Governance, Risk, and Compliance Technology Center, University College Cork,
13 Sourh Mall, Cork, Ireland
{firas.alkhalil,marcello.ceci,kosala.m,leona.obrien}@ucc.ie

Abstract. The Semantics of Business Vocabulary and Business Rules
(SBVR) is a specification created by the Object Management Group
(OMG) to provide a way to semantically describe business concepts
and specify business rules. However, reasoning with SBVR is still an
open subject, and current efforts to provide reasoning are done through
the Web Ontology Language (OWL), by providing a mapping between
SBVR and OWL. In this paper we focus on the problem of mapping
SBVR vocabulary and rulebook to OWL 2, but unlike previous mappings described in the literature, we provide a novel and unorthodox
mapping that allows to describe *legal rules* which have their own intricate anatomy.

Keywords: SBVR · OWL · Rule · Legal

1 Introduction

Following the global financial crisis of 2008, more interest has been geared
towards information systems of the financial industry as they were key con-
tributors to the failures that occurred across the industry.

The Governance, Risk, and Compliance Technology Center (GRCTC) was
established in 2012 to conduct R&D on the use of semantic technologies for GRC
in the financial industry. One of its objectives is to design and build semantic
technologies based on regulatory ontologies to enable sense-making by GRC
actors around complex regulations in order to facilitate regulatory change management in financial organizations and to help address the aforementioned problems. The main technologies used are Semantics of Business Vocabulary and
Business Rules [1] (SBVR) to capture rules from legislative text, and the Web
Ontology Language [16] (OWL 2) to perform advanced reasoning tasks which
are not supported in SBVR.

To this end, we have developed at GRCTC a Regulatory Compliance Interpretation Methodology [3] (RIM), which indicates how to extract rules from
regulations and represent them in a machine-readable knowledge base. Simply
speaking, the RIM is a collaborative methodology requiring 2 agents: (1) the
Subject-Matter Expert (**SME**), a lawyer knowledgeable of the legislative text

© Springer International Publishing Switzerland 2016
J.J. Alferes et al. (Eds.): RuleML 2016, LNCS 9718, pp. 258–266, 2016.
DOI: 10.1007/978-3-319-42019-6_17

and responsible of capturing the rules and transmitting them to the *STE*, and (2) the Semantic Technology Expert (**STE**), a knowledge engineer whose role is to translate the rules captured by the SME into an OWL ontology.

The *lingua franca* of the SME and the STE is SBVR Structured English (SBVR SE): the SME produces a regulatory vocabulary and rulebook in SBVR and transmits them to the STE [2]. The STE can ask for clarification, so the process is repeated until all ambiguities are eliminated and the STE is satisfied with the vocabulary and the rulebook.

Once the SME - STE interaction is done, the STE becomes responsible of the translation of the developed vocabulary and rulebook from SBVR to OWL 2, and this is the subject of this paper. Current mappings [5, 6, 10–12] are generic and do not take into account the unique nature of a legal rule. In our approach, a legal rule defines conditions that in turn qualify events as relevant or not, and if an event is relevant to the rule, it is considered as compliant to the rule if, and only if, it complies to a *complicance condition* (it is actually called a *deontic condition*, but more on that in Sect. 5), otherwise the event breaches the rule.

In order to support this kind of reasoning, we developed the Financial Industry Regulatory Ontology [7] (FIRO). The FIRO-H module of FIRO provides all the necessary scaffolding needed to map SBVR to OWL, while its details and its reasoning capabilities are out of the scope of this paper. We will introduce FIRO-H concepts as we require them to understand the mapping. To the best of our knowledge, this is the first mapping from SBVR to OWL that is tailored for a practical application in a specific domain.

The rest of the paper is organized as follows: Sect. 2 introduces SBVR; Sect. 3 discusses the different components of FIRO; Sects. 4 and 5 show how to map SBVR vocabulary and rulebook, respectively, to OWL using FIRO; Sect. 6 reviews the state of the art on SBVR to OWL mapping; and finally we conclude in Sect. 7.

2   SBVR

The Object Management Group (OMG) created the Semantics of Business Vocabularies and Business Rules (SBVR) specification [1] to define business concepts and rules using a *controlled natural language*, SBVR Structured English (SBVR SE). It is meant to be used by business people to describe their business activities, hence its adoption in the RIM of GRCTC: it allows non-technical experts (SMEs) to define rules using a controlled language (as opposed to legalese).

The elements of SBVR vocabulary (that are of relevance to our discussion) are:

1. General Noun Concepts. They are nouns that describe classes of objects; they classify things based on their common properties (e.g. Bank, Share, ...).
2. Individual Noun Concepts. They designate individual occurrences of things (e.g. Cork is a city in Ireland, however Cork is an individual instance, a single and unique concept).

3. *Verb Concepts.* Composed of a **verb** (technically *verb symbol*) and one or more Verb Concept Roles. A Verb Concept Role is a noun concept, either general or individual. Examples of a basic verb concepts:

   (a) Bank *transfers* Asset. *transfers* is a verb that has 2 Verb Concept Roles, namely Bank and Asset.

   (b) Bank of Ireland *issues* Share. *issues* is a verb that has 2 verb concept roles, namely the individual noun concept Bank of Ireland and the general noun concept Share.

   (c) Bank *defaults*. defaults is a verb with 1 verb concept role, namely the general noun concept Bank.

The rulebook contains *Definitional* (or *Structural*) rules and *Behavioural* (or *Operative*) rules. In the legal context, definitional rules correspond to *Constitutive Norms* that are characterized by their alethic modality (i.e. necessity, possibility, impossibility); behavioral rules correspond to *Regulative Norms* that are characterized by their deontic modality (i.e. obligation, permission, and prohibition). Every rule is a combination of: (1) a modality, and (2) one or multiple verb concepts connected with keywords. In this paper we will restrict ourselves to behavioural rules only, therefore, we will be considering deontic modalities only. Example of a rule:

It is obligatory that each **Price** *reflects* the **Prevailing Market Condition** for each Share.

The modality of the rule is expressed in "It is obligatory that" which indicates an obligation. We have 3 noun concepts: (1) **Price**, (2) Prevailing Market Condition, and (3) Share, and 2 Verb Concepts: (1) Price *reflects* Prevailing Market Condition, and (2) Share *has* Prevailing Market Condition.

The vocabulary only contains Noun Concepts and Verb Concepts. The universal quantifier each is not present in the Verb Concept, but it is present in the rule. The modality is also in the rule only. This distinction is crucial for the modeling of rules in FIRO, which we will introduce in Sect. 3.

3   FIRO

GRCTC is currently developing a set of ontologies called FIRO (Financial Industry Regulatory Ontology) to enable semantic applications such as classification, querying, and reasoning. FIRO is composed of different modules, from which we are only interested in:

FIRO-H. This ontology is a *high-level* ontology focused on the concept of regulatory compliance. It defines all the concepts and relationships necessary to represent legal and business rules, and their compliance.

FIRO-D. This ontology specializes FIRO-H by describing the concepts and the relationships expressed by a specific regulation (e.g. UK AML Regulation, MiFID, US Bank Secrecy Act). In other words, in FIRO-D we find *domain*-specific rules.

FIRO-Op. This ontology uses FIRO-H as a framework and one or multiple FIRO-Ds to support a specific GRC-related process or task. In FIRO-Op we taylor an ontology for a specific GRC *operation.*

Please note that a full discussion of FIRO, classes and relations in every module, and its reasoning capabilities are out of the scope of this paper. We will only introduce concepts of FIRO (FIRO-H more specifically) as we need them.

4   The Vocabulary

4.1   Definitions

Definition 1 (Factor). *A generic or specific entity that plays a role in an action. It is the result of the interpretation of the entities involved in the rule.*

Definition 2 (Action). *An abstract category of events that is defined arbitrarily. It is the result of the interpretation on the behaviour required by the rule.*

Definition 3 (Event). *A concrete manifestation of an abstract action.*

Action and Factor roughly correspond to *Verb Concept* and *Verb Concept Role*, respectively, in SBVR. They are defined during *rule interpretation* (intended as statutory interpretation, see [4]) which means that the same rule found in the legislative text can have multiple interpretations (that is, can be "defined arbitrarily"). An example of an action would be:

Bank transfers Asset

This action describes in an abstract manner all the events that consist in a bank transferring an asset. It does not designate a specific Bank or a particular Asset. It describes the category of actions that are qualified as Bank *transfers* Asset.

Events are actions described in data, not the rule. Examples of events relating to the *Action* Bank *transfers* Asset:

Bank of Ireland transfers Share N. 0001234
Central Bank of Ireland transfers Parcel N. 0004321

4.2   Mappings

We find in the literature different papers (e.g. [5,6,10–12]) talking about the transformation of SBVR vocabulary to OWL 2, and they are all based on the same basic notion also described in the official documentation of SBVR [1, Section 10.3]. Table 1 summarizes this translation.

In FIRO, we take a different approach. Indeed, FIRO-H describes 3 main classes:

Factor. The equivalent of a *Verb Concept Role* in SBVR.

Table 1. SBVR to OWL: the classical approach *vs* FIRO

SBVR	OWL only	OWL + FIRO
General Noun Concept	*Class*	*Class* subclass of *Factor*
Individual Noun Concept	*Individual*	*Individual* of a (*Class* subclass of *Factor*)
verb	*Object* or *Data Property*	*Individual* of *Verb*

Verb. Corresponds to the class of Verbs in SBVR. A verb (symbol) found in a verb concept is an individual of the class *Verb* and not an *Object* or *Data Property* as described in the literature.

Action. Corresponds to a verb concept in SBVR. It is composed of one or multiple Factors. The class *Action* is used in conjunction with two object properties:

hasFactor. Has a domain *Action* and ranges over *Factor*. (FIRO further specifies hasFactor into *hasSubject*, *hasObject*, etc. for more meaningful querying and reasonning).

hasVerb. Has a domain *Action* and ranges over *Verb*.

Let us take the example Bank *transfers* Asset. This verb concept would be created in FIRO-D using FIRO-H as follows: (1) Bank and Asset become OWL classes, each of them *subclassOf Factor*, (2) *transfers* becomes an individual of the class *Verb*, and (3) the whole verb concept will be defined (using the Manchester syntax [9]) as a class Bank_Transfers_Asset:

```
Class Bank_Transfers_Asset: Action and (hasSubject some Bank)
and (hasObject some Asset) and (hasVerb value transfers)
```

5   The Rulebook

5.1   Definitions

Definition 4 (Condition). *An Action used in a rule. A condition has the same properties as actions and may restrict factors by specifying (1) their scope or value, or (2) the role they play in another condition.*

Definition 5 (Rule). *A rule is made of 1 deontic modal operator, 1 deontic condition, and any number of applicability conditions.*

Definition 6 (Applicability Condition). *It is a condition that determines if a given event is relevant to a given rule or not. It corresponds to the "condition of application" of prescriptions in [8].*

Definition 7 (Deontic Condition). *It is a condition that determines if a relevant event complies/breaches a rule. It corresponds to the "legal effect" of prescriptions in [8]. A deontic condition has 1 deontic factor.*

Definition 8 (Deontic Factor). *A deontic factor of a deontic condition is a* Factor *that is the direct object/main target of the deontic modal operator. If a relevant event meets the deontic factor, it is compliant with the rule, if it does not meet it, it breaches the rule.*

Let us take the example *Action* Bank *transfers* Asset to demonstrate the types of specifications mentioned in Definition 4:

1. Bank *transfers* at least 2 Assets is a specification of scope.
2. Central Bank of Ireland *transfers* Asset is a specification of value.
3. Bank *transfers* Asset *of* Enterprise. Here Asset plays a role also in a second action Enterprise *has* Asset.

Let us take an example rule to explain Definitions 4 to 8:

It is obligatory that each Bank *transfers* less than $10'000

The *deontic modal operator* of this rule is expressed in "It is obligatory that". This rule has 1 *deontic condition*: Bank *transfers* less than $10'000. The *deontic condition* is based on the *action* Bank *transfers* Asset. An event is relevant to the rule if it is describing a bank transferring an amount of money. An event describing *a company* (other than a bank) transferring an amount of money is not relevant to this rule. If the event is relevant, and if the amount of money is less than $10'000, then the event is compliant with the rule, otherwise it breaches it. Therefore, the factor of $10'000 is the critical point that determines if an event is compliant or not; it is the *deontic factor*, the direct object of the obligation.

5.2 Mappings

FIRO-H provides the following:

Condition. Is a *subclassOf Action* used to define both *deontic* and *applicability* conditions.

hasDeonticFactor. An object property to specify the deontic factor.

RegulatoryStatement. The class of regulatory statements. Every rule is represented as an individual of this class.

DeonticModality. A class containing 3 individuals: *obligation, prohibition,* and *permission.*

hasDeonticModality. An object property with a domain *RegulatoryStatement* and a range *DeonticModality.*

To illustrate the mapping of a rule described in SBVR to OWL using FIRO-H, let us take the following example: we have a vocabulary made of the noun concepts Quote, Bid Price, Share, and Trading Venue and verb concepts Quote *include* Bid Price, Share *traded on* Trading Venue, and Share *has* Quote. The rule we are considering is:

It is obligatory that each quote (for each share *traded on* a trading venue) *include* at least two bid price

First of all, noun concepts and individual noun concepts should be created,
then, 3 verb concepts should be translated into 3 Actions as described at the
end of Sect. 4.2 (namely `Share_Has_Quote`, `Share_Traded_TradingVenue`, and
`Quote_Include_BidPrice`). Finally, we should create *rule2* as an individual of
the class *RegulatoryStatement* as follows: `rule2 hasModality obligation`.

This rule has 2 conditions expressed in 2 separate actions: (1) a share should
have a quote and be traded on a trading venue, and (2) the quote of the aforementioned share should include at least two bid prices.

If there is an event that does not satisfy the first condition, it is not relevant
to the rule; the event does not constitute a breach of *rule2*. Therefore, the first
condition is an *applicability condition*. However, the second condition is necessary
for the rule: if an event satisfies the first condition, but does not satisfy the
second one, it may constitute a breach; otherwise, the event complies to the
rule. Therefore, the second condition is a *deontic condition*.

```
Class Rule2_Condition1: Condition
equivalentClass (Share_Has_Quote and hasSubject some
  (Share and (subjectOf some Share_Traded_TradingVenue)))
Class Rule2_Deontic: Condition
equivalentClass (compliesTo rule2)
equivalentClass (Quote_Include_BidPrice
  and hasSubject some (Quote and (objectOf Rule2_Condition1)
  and hasObject min 2 BidPrice)
```

6 State of the Art

The work described in the literature dealing with the transformation of SBVR
to OWL follow the same pattern. All of them take their inspiration from the
SBVR specification [1] which gives a rather basic mapping. One of the earliest
mappings was described by Demuth and Libeau [6] who decided to translate
SBVR vocabulary to OWL and SBVR rules to R2ML [17] of the REWERSE
project. They created their own SBVR MOF representation to express SBVR
hierarchy; they also restricted the expressiveness to unary and binary facts (verb
concepts).

Cearvolo et al. [5] proposed a mapping between SBVR vocabulary and
rules to OWL. However, SBVR facts that could not be translated into OWL
were expressed in SWRL; e.g. round-trip car movements cannot be expressed
with OWL DL: defining CarMovements whose fillers of properties hasReceiving-
Branch and hasSendingBranch are the same individual would involve dynamically defined enumerated classes (with the property filler as the only member)
and this is not even possible with OWL Full.

Karpovic and Nemuraite [11] talked about the transformation from SBVR
to OWL exclusively. They presented a mapping of different concepts and fact
types (partitive, associative, property of, etc.). In a subsequent work, Kaprovic
et al. [10] presented a (detailed) reverse mapping: from OWL 2 to SBVR; the aim
of this goal was to show that SBVR can be used to describe OWL 2 concepts.

Reynares et al. [13–15] presented also a detailed mapping of SBVR to OWL 2,
however they attack the vocabulary, facts and logical operators. Rules are not

described. Moreover, they conclude by sharing the same concern of Cearvolo et al. [5], that OWL is not expressive enough to describe all kinds of SBVR semantics.

The most comprehensive mapping between SBVR and OWL 2 was described by Kendall and Linehan [12]. The goal of their work was to provide a reversible mapping between both specification without any loss of semantics. However, they restrict themselves to SBVR vocabularies only; i.e. behavioral rules are excluded.

7   Conclusion

In this paper we presented a mapping of SBVR vocabulary and rulebook to OWL 2 using the Financial Industry Regulatory Ontology (FIRO) as a framework that governs our mapping. We showed the parallels between FIRO-H and SBVR vocabulary, more precisely, we showed that in SBVR a *Verb Concept* and a *Verb Concept Role* correspond to *Action* and *Factor*, respectively, in FIRO-H. An *Action* used in a rule is a *Condition*.

We then showed how to model a rule using *Actions* as building blocks: a rule is defined by a *Deontic Modal Operator*, a *Deontic Condition* (the direct object of the modal operator), and any number of *Applicability Conditions*. Applicability conditions will qualify an event as relevant to a rule or not. The deontic condition will decide, via its *Deontic Factor*, if a relevant event is compliant to or breaching a rule.

The mapping we presented is significantly different from what has been described in the literature. The value of this approach as compared to the state of the art lies in the reasoning capabilities it enhances in terms of rules comparison and data classification. An interesting research direction would be attempting to automatically transform an SBVR logical formulation to OWL using FIRO-H as a host framework.

Acknowledgments. This work is mainly supported by Enterprise Ireland (EI) and the Irish Development Authority (IDA) under the Government of Ireland Technology Centre Programme.

References

1. Semantics of Business Vocabulary and Business Rules (SBVR) Version 1.2, April 2013. http://www.omg.org/spec/SBVR/1.2/PDF
2. Abi-Lahoud, E., Butler, T., Chapin, D., Hall, J.: Interpreting regulations with SBVR. In: Joint Proceedings of the 7th International Rule Challenge, the Special Track on Human Language Technology and the 3rd RuleML Doctoral Consortium, Seattle, USA, July 11–13, 2013 (2013)
3. Abi-Lahoud, E., O'Brien, L., Butler, T.: On the road to regulatory ontologies. In: Casanovas, P., Pagallo, U., Palmirani, M., Sartor, G. (eds.) AICOL 2013. LNCS, vol. 8929, pp. 188–201. Springer, Heidelberg (2014)

4. Araszkiewicz, M.: Towards systematic research on statutory interpretation in AI and law. In: Legal Knowledge and Information Systems - JURIX 2013: The Twenty-Sixth Annual Conference, December 11–13, 2013, pp. 15–24. University of Bologna, Italy (2013)

5. Ceravolo, P., Fugazza, C., Leida, M.: Modeling semantics of business rules. In: Digital EcoSystems and Technologies Conference, 2007, DEST 2007, pp. 171–176. Inaugural IEEE-IES (2007)

6. Demuth, B., Liebau, H.-B.: An approach for bridging the gap between business rules and the semantic web. In: Paschke, A., Biletskiy, Y. (eds.) RuleML 2007. LNCS, vol. 4824, pp. 119–133. Springer, Heidelberg (2007)

7. Espinoza, A., Abi-Lahoud, E., Butler, T.: Ontology-driven financial regulatory change management: an iterative development process. In: 2nd Semantic Web and Linked Open Data workshop (SW-LOD), Enc 2014. 5th, November, Oaxaca, México (2014)

8. Gordon, T.F., Governatori, G., Rotolo, A.: Rules and norms: requirements for rule interchange languages in the legal domain. In: Governatori, G., Hall, J., Paschke, A. (eds.) RuleML 2009. LNCS, vol. 5858, pp. 282–296. Springer, Heidelberg (2009)

9. Horridge, M., Drummond, N., Goodwin, J., Rector, A.L., Stevens, R., Wang, H.: The manchester OWL syntax. In: Proceedings of the OWLED 2006 Workshop on OWL: Experiences and Directions, Athens, Georgia, USA, November 10–11, 2006 (2006)

10. Karpovic, J., Krisciuniene, G., Ablonskis, L., Nemuraite, L.: The comprehensive mapping of semantics of business vocabulary and business rules (SBVR) to OWL 2 ontologies. ITC **43**(3), 289–302 (2014)

11. Karpovic, J., Nemuraite, L.: Transforming SBVR business semantics into Web ontology language OWL2: main concepts. In: Information Technologies' 2011: Proceedings of the 17th International Conference on Information and Software Technologies, IT 2011, Kaunas, Lithuania, pp. 231–238 (2011)

12. Kendall, E., Linehan, M.H.: Mapping SBVR to OWL2. Technical report, IBM Research Report, RC25363 (WAT1303-040) (2013)

13. Reynares, E., Caliusco, M.L., Galli, M.R.: An automatable approach for SBVR to OWL 2 mappings. In: XVI Ibero-American Conference on Software Engineering, pp. 201–214 (2013)

14. Reynares, E., Caliusco, M.L., Galli, M.R.: SBVR to OWL 2 mappings: an automatable and structural-rooted approach. CLEI Electron. J. **17**(3) (2014). ISSN 0717-5000

15. Reynares, E., Caliusco, M.L., Galli, M.R.: A set of ontology design patterns for reengineering SBVR statements into OWL/SWRL ontologies. Expert Syst. Appl. **42**(5), 2680–2690 (2015)

16. W3C OWL Working Group: OWL 2 Web Ontology Language Document Overview, 2nd edn. (2012). https://www.w3.org/TR/owl2-overview/

17. Wagner, G., Giurca, A., Lukichev, S.: A general markup framework for integrity and derivation rules. In: Dagstuhl Seminar Proceedings. Schloss Dagstuhl-Leibniz-Zentrum für Informatik (2006)

Rule- and Ontology-Based Data Access and Transformation

OBDA Constraints for Effective Query Answering

Dag Hovland[1](✉), Davide Lanti[2](✉), Martin Rezk[2](✉), and Guohui Xiao[2](✉)

[1] University of Oslo, Oslo, Norway
hovland@ifi.uio.no
[2] Free University of Bozen-Bolzano, Bolzano, Italy
{dlanti,mrezk,xiao}@inf.unibz.it

Abstract. In Ontology Based Data Access (OBDA) users pose SPARQL queries over an ontology that lies on top of relational data-sources. These queries are translated on-the-fly into SQL queries by OBDA systems. Standard SPARQL-to-SQL translation techniques in OBDA often produce SQL queries containing redundant joins and unions, even after a number of semantic and structural optimizations. These redundancies are detrimental to the performance of query answering, especially in complex industrial OBDA scenarios with large enterprise databases. To address this issue, we introduce two novel notions of OBDA constraints and show how to exploit them for efficient query answering. We conduct an extensive set of experiments on large datasets using real world data and queries, showing that these techniques strongly improve the performance of query answering up to orders of magnitude.

1 Introduction

In Ontology Based Data Access (OBDA) [18], the complexity of data storage is hidden by a conceptual layer on top of an existing relational database (DB). Such a conceptual layer, realized by an ontology, provides a convenient vocabulary for user queries, and captures domain knowledge (e.g., hierarchies of concepts) that can be used to enrich query answers over incomplete data. The ontology is connected to the relational database through a declarative specification given in terms of mappings that relate each term in the ontology (each class and property) to a (SQL) view over the database. The mappings and the database define a *(virtual)* RDF graph that, together with the ontology, can be queried using the *SPARQL query language.*

To answer a SPARQL query over the conceptual layer, a typical OBDA system translates it into an equivalent SQL query over the original database. The translation procedure has two major stages: (1) *rewriting* the input SPARQL query with respect to the ontology and (2) *unfolding* the rewritten query with respect to the mappings. A well-known theoretical result is that the size of the translation is worst-case exponential in the size of the input query [13]. These worst-case scenarios are not only theoretical, but they also occur in real-world applications, as shown in [16], where some user SPARQL queries are

© Springer International Publishing Switzerland 2016
J.J. Alferes et al. (Eds.): RuleML 2016, LNCS 9718, pp. 269–286, 2016.
DOI: 10.1007/978-3-319-42019-6_18

translated into SQL queries containing thousands of join and union operators. This is mainly due to *(i)* SPARQL queries containing joins of ontological terms with rich hierarchies, which lead to redundant unions [19]; and *(ii)* reifications of n-ary relations in the database into triples over the RDF data model, which lead to SQL translations containing several (mostly redundant) self-joins. How to reduce the impact of exponential blow-ups through optimization techniques so as to make OBDA applicable to real-world scenarios is one of the main open problems in current OBDA research.

The standard solutions to tackle this problem are based on *semantic and structural optimizations* [19,20] originally from the database area [5]. Semantic optimizations use explicit integrity constraints (such as primary and foreign keys) to remove redundant joins and unions from the translated queries. Structural optimizations are in charge of reshaping the translations so as to take advantage of database indexes.

The main problem addressed in this paper is that these optimizations cannot exploit constraints that go beyond database dependencies, such as domain constraints (e.g., people have only one age, except for Chinese people who have two ages), or storage policies in the organization (e.g., table `married` *must* contain all the married employees). We address this problem by proposing two novel classes of constraints that go beyond database dependencies. The first type of constraint, *exact predicate*, intuitively describes classes and properties whose elements can be retrieved without the help of the ontology. The second type of constraint, *virtual functional dependency* (VFD), intuitively describes a functional dependency over the virtual RDF graph exposed by the ontology, the mappings, and the database. These notions are used to enrich the OBDA specification so as to allow the OBDA system to identify and prune redundancies from the translated queries. To help the design of enriched specifications, we provide tools that detect the satisfied constraints within a given OBDA instance. We extend the OBDA system *Ontop* so as to exploit the enriched specification, and evaluate it in both a large-scale industrial setting provided by the petroleum company Statoil, and in an ad-hoc artificial and scalable benchmark with different commercial and free relational database engines as back-ends. Both sets of experiments reveal a drastic reduction on the size of translated queries, which in some cases is reduced by orders of magnitudes. This allows for a major performance improvement of query answering.

The rest of the paper is structured as follows: Preliminaries are provided in Sect. 2. In Sect. 3 we describe how state-of-the-art OBDA systems work, and highlight the problems with the current optimization techniques. In Sect. 4 we formally introduce our novel OBDA constraints, and show how they can be used to optimize translated queries. In Sect. 5 we provide an evaluation of the impact of the proposed optimization techniques on the performance of query answering. In Sect. 6 we briefly survey other related works. Section 7 concludes the paper. Omitted proofs and extended experiments with Wisconsin benchmark can be found in the extended version of this paper [12].

2   Preliminaries

We assume the reader to be familiar with relational algebra and SQL queries, as well as with ontology languages and in particular with the OWL 2 QL[1] profile. To simplify the notation we express OWL 2 QL axioms by their description logic counterpart *DL-Lite$_R$* [4]. Notation-wise, we will denote tuples with the bold faces; e.g., **x** is a tuple.

Ontology and RDF Graphs. The building block of an ontology is a *vocabulary* (N_C, N_R), where N_C, N_R are respectively countably infinite disjoint sets of *class names* and (object or datatype) *property names*. A *predicate* is either a class name or a property name. An *ontology* is a finite set of axioms constructed out a vocabulary, and it describes a domain of interest. These axioms of an ontology can be serialized into a concrete syntax. In the following we use the *Turtle syntax* for readability.

Example 1. The ontology from Statoil captures the domain knowledge related to oil extraction activities. Relevant axioms for our examples are:

`:isInWell rdfs:domain :Wellbore`	`:isInWell rdfs:range :Well`
`:hasInterval rdfs:domain :Wellbore`	`:hasInterval rdfs:range :WellboreInterval`
`:completionDate rdfs:domain :Wellbore`	
`:ProdWellbore rdfs:subClassOf :DevelopWellbore`	`:DevelopWellbore rdfs:subClassOf :Wellbore`

The first five axioms specify domains and ranges of the properties `:isInWell`, `:hasInterval`, and `:completionDate`. The last two state the hierarchy between different wellbore[2] classes.

Given a countably infinite set N_I of *individual names* disjoint from N_C and N_R, an *assertion* is an expression of the form $A(i)$ or $P(i_1, i_2)$, where $i, i_1, i_2 \in N_I$, $A \in N_C, P \in N_R$. An OWL 2 QL *knowledge base* (KB) is a pair $(\mathcal{T}, \mathcal{A})$ where $\mathcal{T}$ is an OWL 2 QL ontology and $\mathcal{A}$ is a set of assertions (also called ABox). Semantics for entailment of assertions ($\models$) in OWL 2 QL KBs is given through Tarski-style interpretations in the usual way [1]. Given a KB $(\mathcal{T}, \mathcal{A})$, the *saturation of $\mathcal{A}$ with respect to $\mathcal{T}$* is the set of assertions $\mathcal{A}_\mathcal{T} = \{A(s) \mid (\mathcal{T}, \mathcal{A}) \models A(s)\} \cup \{P(s, o) \mid (\mathcal{T}, \mathcal{A}) \models P(s, o)\}$. In the following, it is convenient to view assertions $A(s)$ and $P(s, o)$ as the *RDF triples* $(s, \texttt{rdf:type}, A)$ and (s, P, o), respectively. Hence, we view a set of assertions also as an RDF graph $\mathcal{G}^\mathcal{A}$ defined as $\mathcal{G}^\mathcal{A} = \{(s, \texttt{rdf:type}, A) \mid A(s) \in \mathcal{A}\} \cup \{(s, P, o) \mid P(s, o) \in \mathcal{A}\}$. Moreover, the *saturated RDF graph* $\mathcal{G}^{(\mathcal{T}, \mathcal{A})}$ associated to a knowledge base $(\mathcal{T}, \mathcal{A})$ consists of the set of triples entailed by $(\mathcal{T}, \mathcal{A})$, i.e. $\mathcal{G}^{(\mathcal{T}, \mathcal{A})} = \mathcal{G}^{\mathcal{A}_\mathcal{T}}$.

OBDA and Mappings. Given a vocabulary (N_C, N_R) and a database schema Σ, a *mapping* is an expression of the form $A(f_1(\mathbf{x}_1)) \leftarrow sql(\mathbf{y})$ or $P(f_1(\mathbf{x}_1), f_2(\mathbf{x}_2)) \leftarrow sql(\mathbf{y})$, where $A \in N_C$, $P \in N_R$, f_1, f_2 are function symbols,

---

[1] http://www.w3.org/TR/owl2-overview/.

[2] A wellbore is a three-dimensional representation of a hole in the ground.

$\mathbf{x}_i \subseteq \mathbf{y}$, for $i = 1, 2$, and $sql(\mathbf{y})$ is an SQL query in Σ having output attributes $\mathbf{y}$. Given Q in $N_C \cup N_R$, *a mapping m is defining Q* if Q is on the left hand side of m.

Given an SQL query q and a DB instance D, q^D denotes the set of answers to q over D. Given a database instance D, and a set of mappings $\mathcal{M}$, we define the *virtual assertions set* $\mathcal{A}_{\mathcal{M},D}$ as follows:

$$\mathcal{A}_{\mathcal{M},D} = \{A(f(\mathbf{o})) \mid \mathbf{o} \in \pi_{\mathbf{x}}(sql(\mathbf{y}))^D \text{ and } A(f(\mathbf{x})) \leftarrow sql(\mathbf{y}) \text{ in } \mathcal{M}\} \ \cup$$
$$\{P(f(\mathbf{o}), g(\mathbf{o'})) \mid (\mathbf{o},\mathbf{o'}) \in \pi_{\mathbf{x}_1,\mathbf{x}_2}(sql(\mathbf{y}))^D \text{ and } P(f(\mathbf{x}_1), g(\mathbf{x}_2)) \leftarrow sql(\mathbf{y}) \text{ in } \mathcal{M}\}$$

In the Turtle syntax for mappings, we use *templates*–strings with placeholders– for specifying the functions (like f and g above) that map database values into URIs and literals. For instance, the string <http://statoil.com/{id}> is a URI template where "id" is an attribute; when id is instantiated as "1", it generates the URI <http://statoil.com/1>.

An *OBDA specification* is a triple $\mathcal{S} = (\mathcal{T}, \mathcal{M}, \Sigma)$ where $\mathcal{T}$ is an ontology, Σ is a database schema with key dependencies, and $\mathcal{M}$ is a set of mappings between $\mathcal{T}$ and Σ. Given an OBDA specification $\mathcal{S}$ and a database instance D, we call the pair $(\mathcal{S}, D)$ an *OBDA instance*. Given an OBDA instance $\mathcal{O} = ((\mathcal{T}, \mathcal{M}, \Sigma), D)$, the *virtual RDF graph exposed by $\mathcal{O}$* is the RDF graph $\mathcal{G}^{\mathcal{A}_{\mathcal{M},D}}$; the *saturated virtual RDF graph $\mathcal{G}^{\mathcal{O}}$ exposed by $\mathcal{O}$* is the RDF graph $\mathcal{G}^{(\mathcal{T}, \mathcal{A}_{\mathcal{M},D})}$.

Example 2. The mappings for the classes and properties introduced in Example 1 are:

```
:Wellbore-{wellbore_s} rdf:type :Wellbore
← SELECT wellbore_s FROM wellbore WHERE wellbore.r_existence_kd_nm ='actual'

:Wellbore-{wellbore_s} :isInWell :Well-{well_s}
← SELECT well_s, wellbore_s FROM wellbore WHERE wellbore.r_existence_kd_nm ='actual'

:Wellbore-{wellbore_s} :hasInterval :WellboreInterval-{wellbore_intv_s}
← SELECT wellbore_s, wellbore_intv_s FROM wellbore_interval

:Wellbore-{wellbore_s} :completionDate '{year}-{month}-{day}'^^xsd:date
← SELECT wellbore_s, year, month, day FROM wellbore WHERE wellbore.r_existence_kd_nm ='actual'

:Wellbore-{wellbore_s} rdf:type :ProdWellbore
← SELECT w.wellbore_s AS wellbore_s FROM wellbore w, facility_clsn WHERE complex-expression
```

Query Answering in OWL 2 QL KBs. A *conjunctive query* $q(\mathbf{x})$ is a first order formula of the form $\exists \mathbf{y}. \ \varphi(\mathbf{x}, \mathbf{y})$, where $\varphi(\mathbf{x}, \mathbf{y})$ is a conjunction of equalities and atoms of the form $A(t)$, $P(t_1, t_2)$ (where $A \in N_C, P \in N_R$), and each t, t_1, t_2 is either a *term* or an individual variable in $\mathbf{x}, \mathbf{y}$. Given a conjunctive query $q(\mathbf{x})$ and a knowledge base $\mathcal{K} := (\mathcal{T}, \mathcal{A})$, a tuple $\mathbf{i} \in N_I^{|\mathbf{x}|}$ is a *certain answer* to $q(\mathbf{x})$ iff $\mathcal{K} \models q(\mathbf{i})$. The task of query answering in OWL 2 QL (*DL-Lite$_{\mathcal{R}}$*) can be addressed by query rewriting techniques [4]. For an OWL 2 QL ontology $\mathcal{T}$, a conjunctive query q can be rewritten to a union q_r of conjunctive queries such that for each assertion set $\mathcal{A}$ and each tuple of individuals $\mathbf{i} \in N_I^{|\mathbf{x}|}$, it holds $(\mathcal{T}, \mathcal{A}) \models q(\mathbf{i}) \Leftrightarrow \mathcal{A} \models q_r(\mathbf{i})$. Many rewriting techniques have been proposed in the literature [3, 14, 22].

SPARQL [9] is a W3C standard language designed to query RDF graphs. Its vocabulary contains four pairwise disjoint and countably infinite sets of symbols: I for *IRIs*, B for *blank nodes*, L for *RDF literals*, and V for *variables*. The elements of $C = I \cup B \cup L$ are called *RDF terms*. A *triple pattern* is an element of $(C \cup V) \times I \times (C \cup V)$. A *basic graph pattern* (*BGP*) is a finite set of joins of triple patterns. BGPs can be combined using the SPARQL operators join, optional, filter, projection, etc.

Example 3. The following SPARQL query, containing a BGP with three triple patterns, returns all the wellbores, their completion dates, and the well where they are contained.

```
SELECT * WHERE {?wlb rdf:type :Wellbore. ?wlb:completionDate ?cmpl. ?wlb:isInWell ?w.}
```

To ease the presentation of the technical development, in the rest of this paper we adopt the OWL 2 QL entailment regime for SPARQL query answering [15], but disallow complex class/property expressions in the query. Intuitively this restriction states that each BGP can be seen as a conjunctive query without existentially quantified variables. Under this restricted OWL 2 QL entailment regime, the task of answering a SPARQL query q over a knowledge base $(\mathcal{T}, \mathcal{A})$ can be reduced to answering q over the saturated graph $\mathcal{G}^{(\mathcal{T}, \mathcal{A})}$ under the simple entailment regime. This restriction can be lifted with the help of a standard query rewriting step [15].

3 SPARQL Query Answering in OBDA

In this section we describe the typical steps that an OBDA system performs to answer SPARQL queries and discuss the performance challenges. To do so, we pick the representative state-of-the-art OBDA system *Ontop* and discuss its functioning in detail.

During its start-up, *Ontop* classifies the ontology, "compiles" the ontology into the mappings generating the so-called $\mathcal{T}$-mappings [19], and removes redundant mappings by using inclusion dependencies (e.g., foreign keys) contained in the database schema. Intuitively, $\mathcal{T}$-mappings expose a saturated RDF graph. Formally, given a basic OBDA specification $\mathcal{S} = (\mathcal{T}, \mathcal{M}, \Sigma)$, the mappings $\mathcal{M}_{\mathcal{T}}$ are $\mathcal{T}$-mappings for $\mathcal{S}$ if, for every OBDA instance $\mathcal{O} = (\mathcal{S}, D)$, $\mathcal{G}^{\mathcal{O}} - \mathcal{G}^{(\mathcal{A}_{\mathcal{M}_{\mathcal{T}}}, D)}$.

Example 4. The $\mathcal{T}$-mappings for our running example are those in Example 2 plus

```
:Wellbore-{wellbore_s} rdf:type :Wellbore
← SELECT wellbore_s FROM wellbore WHERE wellbore.r_existence_kd_nm ='actual'

:Wellbore-{wellbore_s} rdf:type :Wellbore
← SELECT wellbore_s, wellbore_intv_s FROM wellbore_interval

.Wellbore-{wellbore_s} rdf:type :Wellbore
← SELECT w.wellbore_s FROM wellbore w, facility_clsn WHERE ... complex-expression
```

The new mappings are derived from the domain of the properties `:isInWell`, `:completionDate`, and because `:ProdWellbore` is a sub-class of `:Wellbore`.

After the start-up, in the query answering stage, *Ontop* translates the input SPARQL query into an SQL query, evaluates it, and returns the answers to the end-user. We divide this stage in five phases: *(a)* the SPARQL query is *rewritten* using the tree-witness rewriting algorithm; *(b)* the rewritten SPARQL query is *unfolded* into an SQL query using $\mathcal{T}$-mappings; *(c)* the resulting SQL query is optimized; *(d)* the optimized SQL query is executed by the database engine; *(e)* the SQL result is translated into the answer to the original SPARQL query. For the sake of simplicity, we disregard phase *(a)* since it goes out of the scope of this paper (cf. [10]), and phases *(d)* and *(e)* because they are straightforward. In the following we elaborate on phases *(b)* and *(c)*.

From SPARQL to SQL. In phase *(b)* the rewritten SPARQL query is unfolded into an SQL query using $\mathcal{T}$-mappings. The rewritten query is first transformed into a tree representation of its SPARQL algebra expression. The algorithm starts by replacing each leaf of the tree, that is, a triple pattern of the form (s, p, o), with the union of the SQL queries defining p in the $\mathcal{T}$-mapping. Such SQL queries are obtained as follows: given a triple pattern $p = $ `?x rdf:type :A`, and a mapping $m = $ `:A`$(f(\mathbf{y'})) \leftarrow sql(\mathbf{y})$, the *SQL unfolding* $\mathrm{unf}(p, m)$ of p by m is the SQL query SELECT $\tau(f(\mathbf{y'}))$ AS x FROM $sql(\mathbf{y})$, where τ is an SQL function filling the placeholders in f with values in $\mathbf{y'}$. We denote the sub-expression "SELECT $\tau(f(\mathbf{y'}))$ AS x" by $\pi_{x/f(\mathbf{y'})}$. The notions of "unf" and "π" are defined similarly for properties.

Example 5. Consider the triple pattern $p = $ `?wlb :completionDate ?d`, and the fourth mapping m from Example 2. Then the SQL unfolding $\mathrm{unf}(p, m)$ is the SQL query

```
SELECT CONCAT(":Wellbore-",well_s) AS wlb,CONCAT("'",year,"-",month,"-", day,"'^^xsd:date") AS d
FROM wellbore WHERE wellbore.r_existence_kd_nm = 'actual'
```

Given a triple pattern p and a set of mappings $\mathcal{M}$, the *SQL unfolding* $\mathrm{unf}(p, \mathcal{M})$ *of* p *by* $\mathcal{M}$ is the SQL union $\cup_{m \in \mathcal{M}}\{\mathrm{unf}(p, m) \mid \mathrm{unf}(p, m)$ *is defined*$\}$.

Once the leaves are processed, the algorithm processes the upper levels in the tree, where the SPARQL operators are translated into the corresponding SQL operators (Project, InnerJoin, LeftJoin, Union, and Filter). Once the root is translated the process terminates and the resulting SQL expression is returned.

Example 6. The unfolded SQL query for the SPARQL query in Example 3 and $\mathcal{T}$-mappings in Example 4 has the following shape:

$$(\pi_{wlb/\square}sql_{:\text{Wellbore}} \cup \pi_{wlb/\square}sql_{:\text{ProdWellbore}} \cup \pi_{wlb/\square}sql_{:\text{hasInterval}})$$
$$\bowtie (\pi_{wlb/\square,cmp/\Diamond}sql_{:\text{completionDate}}) \bowtie (\pi_{wlb/\square,w/\circ}sql_{:\text{isInWell}})$$

where $\square = $ `:Wellbore-{wellbore_s}`, $\Diamond = $ `'{year}-{month}-{day}'^^xsd:date`, $\circ = $ `:Well-{well_s}`, and sql_P is the SQL query in the mapping defining the class/property P.

Optimizing the Generated SQL Queries. At this point, the unfolded SQL queries are merely of theoretical value as they would not be efficiently executable by any database system. A problem comes from the fact that they contain joins over the results of built-in database functions, which are expensive to evaluate. Another problem is that the unfoldings are usually verbose, often containing thousands of unions and join operators. Structural and semantic optimizations are in charge of dealing with these two problems.

Structural Optimizations. To ease the presentation, we assume the queries to contain only one BGP. Extending to the general case is straightforward. An SQL unfolding of a BGP has the shape of a join of unions $Q = Q_1 \bowtie Q_2 \ldots \bowtie Q_n$, where each Q_i is a union of sub-queries. The first step is to remove duplicate sub-queries in each Q_i. In the second step, Q is transformed into a union of joins. In the third step, all joins of the kind $\pi_{x/f} sql_1(\mathbf{z}) \bowtie \pi_{x/g} sql_2(\mathbf{w})$ where $f \neq g$ are removed because they do not produce any answer. In the fourth step, the occurrences of the SQL function π for creating URIs are pushed to the root of the query tree so as to obtain efficient queries where the joins are over database values rather than over URIs. Finally, duplicates in the union are removed.

Semantic Optimizations. SQL queries are semantically analyzed with the goal of transforming them into a more efficient form. The analyses are based on database integrity constraints (precisely, primary and foreign keys) explicitly defined in the database schema. These constraints are used to identify and remove redundant self-joins and unions from the unfolded SQL query.

How Optimized are Optimized Queries? There are real-world cases where the optimizations discussed above are not enough to mitigate the exponential explosion caused by the unfolding. As a result, the unfolded SQL queries cannot be efficiently handled by DB engines [16]. However, the same queries can usually be manually formulated in a succint way by database managers. A reason for this is that database dependencies cannot model certain domain constraints or storage policies that are available to the database manager but not to the OBDA system. The next example, inspired by the Statoil use case explained in Sect. 5, illustrates this issue.

Example 7. The data stored at Statoil has certain properties that derive from domain constraints or storage policies. Consider a modified version of the query defining the class :Wellbore where all the attributes are projected out. According to storage policies for the database table wellbore, the result of the evaluation of this query against any database instance must satisfy the following constraints: (i) it must contain all the wellbores[3] in the ontology (modulo templates); (ii) every tuple in the result must contain the information about name, date, and well (no nulls); (iii) for each wellbore in the result, there is exactly one date/well that is tagged as 'actual'.

---

[3] i.e., individuals in the class :Wellbore.

Query with Redundant Unions. Consider the SPARQL query retrieving all the wellbores, namely SELECT * WHERE {?wlb rdf:type :Wellbore.}. By ontological reasoning, the query will retrieve also the wellbores that can be inferred from the subclasses of :Wellbore and from the properties where :Wellbore is the domain or range. Thus, after unfolding and optimizations, the resulting SQL query has the structure $\pi_{wlb/\square}(sql_1)$, with $sql_1 = (sql_{:\text{Wellbore}} \cup sql_{:\text{ProdWellbore}} \cup \pi_{\#} sql_{:\text{hasInterval}})$, where $\square$ = :Wellbore-{wellbore_s}, and # = wellbore_s. However, all the answers returned by sql_1 are also returned by the query $sql_{:\text{Wellbore}}$ alone, when these two queries are evaluated on a data instance satisfying item *(i)*.

Query with Redundant Joins. For the SPARQL query in Example 3, the unfolded and optimized SQL translation is of the form $\pi_{wlb/\square,cmp/\Diamond,w/\circ}(sql_2)$ with $sql_2 = sql_1 \bowtie sql_{:\text{completionDate}} \bowtie sql_{:\text{isInWell}}$. Observe that the answers from sql_2 could also be retrieved from a projection and a selection over wellbore. This is because sql_1 could be simplified to $sql_{:\text{Wellbore}}$ and items *(ii)* and *(iii)*. The problem we highlight here is that this "optimized" SQL query contains two redundant joins if storage policies and domain constraints are taken into account.

It is important to remark that the constraints in the previous example cannot be expressed through schema dependencies like foreign or primary keys (because these constraints are defined over the output relations of SQL queries in the mappings, rather than over database relations[4]). Therefore, current state-of-the-art optimizations applied in OBDA cannot exploit this information.

4   OBDA Constraints

We now formalize two properties over an OBDA instance: *exact predicates* and *virtual functional dependencies*. We will then enrich the OBDA specification with a constraints component, stating that all the instances for the specification display such properties. We show how this additional constraint component can be used to identify and remove redundant unions and joins from the unfolded queries.

From now on, let $\mathcal{O} = (\mathcal{S}, D)$ be an OBDA instance of a specification $\mathcal{S} = (\mathcal{T}, \mathcal{M}, \Sigma)$.

4.1   Exact Predicates in an OBDA Instance

In real world scenarios it often happens that axioms in the ontology do not enrich the answers to queries. Often this is due to storage policies not available to the OBDA system. This fact leads to redundant unions in the generated SQL, as shown in Example 7. In this section we show how certain properties defined on the mappings and the predicates, ideally deriving from such constraints, can be used to reduce the number of redundant unions in the generated SQL queries for a given OBDA instance.

---

[4] Materializing the SQL in the mappings is not an option, since the schema is fixed.

Definition 1 (Exact Mapping). *Let $\mathcal{M}'$ be a set of mappings defining a predicate A. We say that $\mathcal{M}'$ is exact for A in $\mathcal{O}$ if $\mathcal{O} \models A(\boldsymbol{a})$ if and only if $((\emptyset, \mathcal{M}', \Sigma), D) \models A(\boldsymbol{a})$.*

In practice it is often the case that the mappings for a particular predicate declared in the OBDA specification are already exact. This leads us to the next definition.

Definition 2 (Exact Predicate). *A predicate A is exact in $\mathcal{O}$ if the set of all the mappings in $\mathcal{M}$ defining A are exact for A in $\mathcal{O}$.*

Recall that *Ontop* adds new mappings to the initial set of mappings through the $\mathcal{T}$-mapping technique. For exact predicates, this can be avoided while producing the same saturated virtual RDF graph. Fewer mappings lead to unfoldings with less unions.

Proposition 1. *Let $\mathcal{M}'$ be exact for the predicate A in $\mathcal{T}$. Let $\mathcal{M}'_{\mathcal{T}}$ be the result of replacing all the mappings defining A in $\mathcal{M}_{\mathcal{T}}$ by $\mathcal{M}'$. Then $\mathcal{G}^{\mathcal{O}} = \mathcal{G}^{((\emptyset, \mathcal{M}'_{\mathcal{T}}, \Sigma), D)}$.*

Example 8. The $\mathcal{T}$-mappings for :Wellbore consist of four mappings (see Example 4). However, :Wellbore is an exact class (Example 7). Therefore we can drop the three $\mathcal{T}$-mappings for :Wellbore inferred from the ontology, and leave only its original mapping.

4.2 Functional Dependencies in an OBDA Instance

Recall that in database theory a functional dependency (abbr. FD) is an expression of the form $\mathbf{x} \rightarrow \mathbf{y}$, read $\boldsymbol{x}$ *functionally determines* $\boldsymbol{y}$, where $\mathbf{x}$ and $\mathbf{y}$ are tuples of attributes. We say that $\boldsymbol{x} \rightarrow \boldsymbol{y}$ *is over an attributes set R* if $\mathbf{x} \subseteq R$ and $\mathbf{y} \subseteq R$. Finally, $\boldsymbol{x} \rightarrow \boldsymbol{y}$ *is satisfied by a relation I on R* if $\mathbf{x} \rightarrow \mathbf{y}$ is over R and for all tuples $\mathbf{u}, \mathbf{v} \in I$, if the value $\mathbf{u}[\mathbf{x}]$ of $\mathbf{x}$ in $\mathbf{u}$ is equal to the value $\mathbf{v}[\mathbf{x}]$ of $\mathbf{x}$ in $\mathbf{v}$, then $\mathbf{u}[\mathbf{y}] = \mathbf{v}[\mathbf{y}]$. Whenever R is clear from the context, we simply say that $\mathbf{x} \rightarrow \mathbf{y}$ is satisfied in $\mathcal{I}$.

A *virtual functional dependency* intuitively describes a functional dependency on a saturated virtual RDF graph. We identify two types of virtual functional dependencies:

- *Branching VFD*: This dependency describes the relation between an object and a set of functional properties providing information about this object. Intuitively, it corresponds to a "star" of "functional-like"[5] properties in the virtual RDF graph. For instance, given a person, the properties describing its (unique) gender, national id, biological mother, etc. are a branching VFD.

---

[5] A property which is functional when restricting its domain/range to individuals generated from a single template.

- *Path VFD*: This dependency describes the case when, from a given individual and a list of properties, there is at most one path that can be followed using the properties in the list. For instance, x works in a single department y, and y has a single manager w, and w works for a single company z.

We use these notions to identify those cases where a SPARQL join of properties translates into a redundant SQL join.

Definition 3 (Virtual Functional Dependency). *Let t be a template, and S_t be the set of individuals in $G^{\mathcal{O}}$ generated from t. Let $P, P_1, \ldots, P_n$ be properties in $\mathcal{T}$. Then*

- *A branching VFD is an expression of the form $t \mapsto^b P_1 \cdots P_n$. A VFD $t \mapsto^b P$ is satisfied in $\mathcal{O}$ if for each element $s \in S_t$, there are no $o \neq o'$ in $G^{\mathcal{O}}$ such that $\{(s, P, o), (s, P, o')\} \subseteq G^{\mathcal{O}}$. A VFD $t \mapsto^b P_1 \cdots P_n$ is satisfied in $\mathcal{O}$ if $t \mapsto^b P_i$ is satisfied in $\mathcal{O}$ for each $i \in \{1, \ldots, n\}$.*
- *A path VFD is an expression of the form $t \mapsto^p P_1 \cdots P_n$. A VFD $t \mapsto^p P_1 \cdots P_n$ is satisfied in $\mathcal{O}$ if for each $s \in S_t$ there is at most one list of nodes $(o_1, \ldots, o_n)$ in $G^{\mathcal{O}}$ such that $\{(s, P_1, o_1), \ldots, (o_{n-1}, P_n, o_n)\} \subseteq G^{\mathcal{O}}$.*

The next example shows, similarly as in [23], that general path VFDs cannot be expressed as a combination of path VFDs of length 1.

Example 9. Let $\mathcal{G}^{\mathcal{O}} = \{(s, P_1, o_1), (o_1, P_2, o_2), (s, P_1, o_1')\}$, and t a template such that $S_t = \{s\}$. Then, $t \mapsto^p P_1 P_2$ is clearly satisfied in $\mathcal{O}$. However, $t \mapsto^p P_1$ is not.

A property P might not be functional, but still $t \mapsto^b P$ might be satisfied in $\mathcal{O}$ for some t.

Example 10. Let $\mathcal{G}^{\mathcal{O}} = \{(s, P, o_1), (s, P, o_2), (s', P, o_3)\}$, and t a template such that $S_t = \{s'\}$. Then, the VFD $t \mapsto^p P$ is satisfied in $\mathcal{O}$, but P is not functional.

A functional dependency satisfied in the virtual RDF graph might not correspond to a functional dependency over the database relations. We show this with an example:

Example 11. Consider the following instance of the view `wellbore`.

wellbore_s	year	month	day	r_existence_kd_nm	well_s
002	2010	04	01	historic	1
002	2009	04	01	actual	1

The mapping defining `:completionDate` (c.f. Example 2) uses the view `wellbore` and has a filter `r_existence_kd_nm='actual'`. Observe that there is no FD (wellbore_s → year month day). However, the VFD `:Wellbore-{}` $\mapsto^b$ `:completionDate` is satisfied with this data instance, since in $\mathcal{G}^{\mathcal{O}}$ the wellbore `:Wellbore-002` is connected to a single date `"2010-04-01"^^xsd:date` through `:completionDate`.

Functional dependencies satisfied in a database instance often do not correspond to any VFD at the virtual level. We show this with an example:

Example 12. Consider the table $T_1(x, y, z)$ with a single tuple: $(1, 2, 3)$. Clearly $x \to y$ and $x \to z$ are FDs satisfied in T_1. Now consider the following mappings:

:{x} P₁ :{y} ← **SELECT** * **FROM** T_1 :{x} P₁ :{z} ← **SELECT** * **FROM** T_1

Clearly, there is no VFD involving P_1.

Hence, the shape of the mappings affects the satisfiability of VFDs. Moreover, the ontology can also affect satisfiability. We show this with an example:

Example 13. Consider again the data instance D_E from Example 12, and the mappings $\mathcal{M}_E$

:{x} P₁ :{y} ← **SELECT** * **FROM** T_1 :{x} P₂ :{z} ← **SELECT** * **FROM** T_1

Consider an OBDA instance $\mathcal{O}_E = ((\emptyset, \mathcal{M}_E, \Sigma_E)D_E)$. Then the virtual functional dependencies $:\{\} \mapsto^b P_1$ and $:\{\} \mapsto^b P_2$ are satisfied in $\mathcal{O}$. Consider another OBDA instance $\mathcal{O}'_E = ((\mathcal{T}_E, \mathcal{M}_E, \Sigma_E), D_E)$, where $\mathcal{T}_E = \{P_1 \text{ rdfs:subClassOf } P_2\}$. Then the two VFDs above are not satisfied in $\mathcal{O}'_E$.

VFD Based Optimization. In this section we show how to optimize queries using VFDs. Due to space limitations, we focus on branching VFDs. The results for path VFDs are analogous and can be found in the technical report [12], as well as proofs.

Definition 4. *The set of mappings $\mathcal{M}$ is basic for $\mathcal{T}$ if, for each property P in $\mathcal{T}$, P is defined by at most one mapping in $\mathcal{M}_\mathcal{T}$. We say that $\mathcal{O}$ is basic if $\mathcal{M}$ is basic for $\mathcal{T}$.*

To ease the presentation, from now on we assume $\mathcal{O}$ to be basic. We denote the (unique) mapping for P_i in $\mathcal{T}$, $i \in \{1, \dots, m\}$, as

$$t_d^i(\mathbf{x}_i) \quad P_i \quad t_r^i(\mathbf{y}_i) \leftarrow sql_i(\mathbf{z}_i).$$

where t_d^i, and t_r^i are templates for the domain and range of P_i, and $\mathbf{x}_i$, $\mathbf{y}_i$ are lists of attributes in $\mathbf{z}_i$. The list $\mathbf{z}_i$ is the list of projected attributes, which we assume to be the maximal list of attributes that can be projected from sql_i.

Although we only consider basic instances, we show in the technical report [12] how the results from this section can also be applied to the general case.

We also assume that queries $sql_i(\mathbf{z}_i)$ always contain a filter expression of the form $\sigma_{\text{notNull}(\mathbf{x}_i, \mathbf{y}_i)}$, even if we do not specify it explicitly in the examples, since URIs cannot be generated from nulls [6]. Without loss of generality, we assume that $\mathbf{z}_1$ contains all the attributes in $\mathbf{x}_1, \mathbf{y}_1, \dots, \mathbf{y}_n$.

In order to check satisfiability for a VFD in an OBDA instance one can analyze the DB based on the mappings and the ontology. The next lemma formalizes this intuition.

Lemma 1. *Let $P_1, \ldots, P_n$ be properties in $\mathcal{T}$ such that, for each $1 \leq i < n$, $t_d^i = t_d^1$. Then, the VFD $t_d^1 \mapsto^b P_1 \ldots P_n$ is satisfied in $\mathcal{O}$ if and only if, for each $1 \leq i \leq n$, the FD $\boldsymbol{x}_i \to \boldsymbol{y}_i$ is satisfied on $sql_i(\boldsymbol{z}_i)^D$.*

Example 14. Consider the properties `:inWell` and `:completionDate` from our running example. The lemma above suggests that the VFD `:Wellbore-{}` $\mapsto^b$ `:isInWell` `:completionDate` is satisfied in our OBDA instance with a database instance D if and only if *(i)* `wellbore_s→well_s` is satisfied in $sql_{:isInWell}^D$, and *(ii)* `wellbore_s→year month day` is satisfied in $sql_{:completionDate}^D$.

From Example 7, there is an organization constraint for the view `wellbore` forcing only one completion date for each "actual" wellbore. As a consequence, the two FDs *(i)* and *(ii)* hold in any database D following this organization constraint. Therefore, the VFD in such instance is also satisfied.

We now show how VFDs can be used to *find redundant joins* that can be eliminated in the SQL translations.

Definition 5 (Optimizing Branching *VFD*). *Let t be a template. An optimizing branching VFD is an expression of the form $t \rightsquigarrow^b P_1 \cdots P_n$. An optimizing VFD $t \rightsquigarrow^b P_1 \cdots P_n$ is satisfied in $\mathcal{O}$ if $t \mapsto^b P_1 \cdots P_n$ is satisfied in $\mathcal{O}$, and for each $i \in \{1, \ldots, n\}$ it holds*

$$\pi_{\boldsymbol{x}_1, \boldsymbol{y}_i} sql_1(\boldsymbol{z}_1)^D \subseteq \rho_{\boldsymbol{x}_1/\boldsymbol{x}_i}(\pi_{\boldsymbol{x}_i, \boldsymbol{y}_i} sql_i(\boldsymbol{z}_i))^D \tag{1}$$

Example 15. Recall that the VFD `:Wellbore-{}` $\mapsto^b$ `:isInWell, :completionDate` in Example 14 is satisfied in our OBDA instance. The precondition (1) holds because (a) the properties are defined by the same SQL query (modulo projection) and (b) the organization constraint "each wellbore entry must contain the information about name, date, and well (no nulls)". Thus, the optimizing VFD `:Wellbore-{}` $\rightsquigarrow^b$ `:isInWell, :completionDate` is satisfied in this instance.

Lemma 2. *Consider n properties $P_1, \ldots, P_n$ with $t_d^i = t_d^1$, for each $1 \leq i \leq n$, and for which $t_d^1 \rightsquigarrow^b P_1 \cdots P_n$ is satisfied in $\mathcal{O}$. Then*

$$\pi_\gamma(sql_1(\boldsymbol{z}_1))^D = \pi_\gamma(sql_1(\boldsymbol{z}_1) \bowtie_{\boldsymbol{x}_1 = \boldsymbol{x}_2} sql_2(\boldsymbol{z}_2) \bowtie \cdots \bowtie_{\boldsymbol{x}_1 = \boldsymbol{x}_n} sql_n(\boldsymbol{z}_n))^D,$$

where $\gamma = \boldsymbol{x}_1, \boldsymbol{y}_1, \ldots, \boldsymbol{y}_n$.

We now show how virtual functional dependencies can be used in presence of triple patterns of the form `?z rdf:type C`. As for properties, We assume that for each concept C_j we have a single $\mathcal{T}$-mapping of the form $C_j(t^j(\mathbf{x})) \leftarrow sql_j(\mathbf{z}_j)$.

Definition 6 (Domain Optimizing Class Expression). *A domain optimizing class expression (domain OCE) is an expression of the form $t_j \rightsquigarrow_{P_i}^d C_j$. We say that $t_j \rightsquigarrow_{P_i}^d C_j$ is satisfied in $\mathcal{O}$ if $t_j = t_d^i$ and $\pi_{\boldsymbol{x}} sql_j(\boldsymbol{z}_j)^D \supseteq \rho_{\boldsymbol{x}/\boldsymbol{x}_i}(\pi_{\boldsymbol{x}_i} sql_i(\boldsymbol{z}_i))^D$.*

Definition 7 (Range Optimizing Class Expression). *A* range optimizing class expression *(range OCE) is an expression of the form* $t_j \leadsto_P^r C_j$. *We say that* $t_j \leadsto_{P_i}^r C_j$ *is satisfied in* $\mathcal{O}$ *if* $t_j = t_r^i$ *and* $\pi_x sql_j(z_j)^D \supseteq \rho_{x/y_i}(\pi_{y_i} sql_i(z_i))^D$.

Optimizing VFDs and classes give us a tool to identify those BGPs whose SQL translation can be optimized by removing redundant joins.

Definition 8 (Optimizable branching BGP). *A BGP* β *is optimizable w.r.t.* $\mathfrak{v} = t_d \leadsto^b P_1 \dots P_n$ *if* (i) $\mathfrak{v}$ *is satisfied in* $\mathcal{O}$; (ii) *the BGP of triple patterns in* β *involving properties is of the form* ?v P_1 ?v_1. …?v P_n ?v_n.; *and* (iii) *for each triple pattern of the form* ?u rdf:type C *in* β, *?u is either the subject of some* P_i *and* $t_d^i \leadsto_{P_i}^d C$ *is satisfied in* $\mathcal{O}$, *or* ?u *is in the object of some* P_i *and* $t_r^i \leadsto_{P_i}^r C$ *is satisfied in* $\mathcal{O}$.

Finally, we prove that the standard SQL translation of optimizable BGPs contains redundant SQL joins that can be safely removed.

Theorem 1. *Let* β *be an optimizable BGP w.r.t.* $t_d \leadsto^x P_1 \dots P_n$ $(x = b, p)$ *in* $\mathcal{O}$. *Let* $\pi_{v/t_d^1, v_1/t_r^1, \dots, v_n/t_r^n} sql_\beta$ *be the SQL translation of* β *as explained in Sect. 3. Let* $sql'_\beta = sql_1(x_1, y_1 \dots, y_n)$. *Then* sql_β^D *and* $sql_\beta'^D$ *return the same answers.*

Corollary 1. *Let* Q *be a SPARQL query. Let* sql_Q *be the SQL translation of* Q *as explained in Sect. 3. Let* sql'_Q *be the SQL translation of* Q *where all the SQL expressions corresponding to an optimizable BGPs w.r.t. a set of VFDs have been optimized as stated in Theorem 1. Then* sql_Q^D *and* $sql_Q'^D$ *return the same answers.*

Example 16. It is clear that the class :Wellbore is optimizing w.r.t. the domain of :completionDate and :isInWell. Since :Wellbore-{} $\leadsto^b$:completionDate, :isInWell is satisfied (c.f. Example 15), one can allow the semantic optimizations to safely remove redundant joins in query sql_1, sketched in Example 7. From Theorem 1, it follows that, $sql_{:Wellbore} \bowtie sql_{:completionDate} \bowtie sql_{:isInWell}$ can be by simplified to $sql_{:Wellbore}$.

4.3   Enriching the OBDA Specification with Constraints

We propose to enrich the traditional OBDA specification with a constraint component, so as to allow the OBDA system to perform enhanced optimization as described in the previous section. More formally, an *OBDA specification with constraints* is a tuple $\mathcal{S}_{constr} = (\mathcal{S}, \mathcal{C})$ where $\mathcal{S}$ is an OBDA specification and $\mathcal{C}$ is a set of exact mappings, exact predicates, optimizing virtual functional dependencies, and optimizing class expressions. An *instance of* $\mathcal{S}_{constr}$ is an OBDA instance of $\mathcal{S}$ satisfying the constraints in $\mathcal{C}$. Our intention is to be able to use more of the constraints that exist in real databases for query optimization, since we often see that these cannot be expressed by existing database constraints (i.e. keys). Since $\mathcal{S}$ does not necessarily imply $\mathcal{C}$, checking the validity of $\mathcal{C}$ may have to take into account more information than just $\mathcal{S}$. The constraints C may be known to hold e.g. by policy, or be enforced by external tools, e.g., as in the case mentioned in the experiments below, by the tool used to enter data into the database.

In order to aid the user in the specification of C, we implemented tools to identify what exact mappings and optimizing virtual functional dependencies are satisfied in a given OBDA instance (see [12]). The user can then verify whether these suggested constraints hold in general, for example because they derive from storage policies or domain knowledge, and provide them as parameters to the OBDA system. The user intervention is necessary, because constraints derived from actual data can be an artifact of the current situation of the database.

Optimizing VFD Constraints. We have implemented a tool that automatically finds a restricted type of optimizing VFDs satisfied in a given OBDA instance and we have extended *Ontop* to complement semantic optimization using these VFDs. This implementation aims to mitigate the problem of redundant self-joins resulting from reifying relational tables. Although this is a simple case, it is extremely common in practice and, as we show in our experiments in Sect. 5, this class of VFDs is powerful enough to sensibly improve the execution times in real world scenarios.

Exact Predicates Constraints. We implemented a tool to find exact predicates, and we extended *Ontop* to optimize T-mappings with them. For each predicate P in the ontology T of an OBDA instance $\mathcal{O}$, the tool constructs the query q that returns all the individual/pairs in P. Then it evaluates q in the two OBDA instances $\mathcal{O}$ and $((\emptyset, \mathcal{M}, \Sigma), D)$. If the answers for q coincide in both instances, then P is exact.

5   Experiments

In this section we present a set of experiments evaluating the techniques described above. In [12] we ran additional controlled experiments using an OBDA benchmark built on top of the Wisconsin benchmark [7], and obtain similar results to the ones here.

Statoil Scenario. In this section we briefly describe the Statoil use-case, and the challenges it presents for OBDA. At Statoil, users access several databases on a daily basis, and one of the most important ones is the Exploration and Production Data Store (EPDS) database. EPDS is a large legacy SQL (Oracle 10g) database comprising over 1500 tables (some of them with up to 10 million tuples) and 1600 views. The complexity of the SQL schema of EPDS is such that it is counter-productive and error-prone to manually write queries over the relational database. Thus, end-users either use only a set of tools with predefined SQL queries to access the database, or interact with IT experts so as to formulate the right query. The latter process can take weeks. This situation triggered the introduction of OBDA in Statoil in the context of the Optique project [13]. In order to test OBDA at Statoil, the users provided 60 queries (in natural language) that are relevant to their job, and that cannot be easily performed or formulated at the moment. The Optique partners formulated these queries in SPARQL, and handcrafted an ontology, and a set of mappings connecting EPDS to the ontology. The ontology contains 90 classes, 37 object properties, and 31 data properties; and there are more than 140 mappings. The queries have between 0 to 2 complex filter expressions (with several arithmetic and string operations), 0 to 5 nested optionals, modifiers such as ORDER BY and DISTINCT, and up to 32 joins.

Experiment Results. The queries were executed sequentially on a HP ProLiant server with 24 Intel Xeon CPUs (X5650 @ 2.67 GHz), 283 GB of RAM. Each query was evaluated three times and we took the average. We ran the experiments with 4 exact concepts and 15 virtual functional dependencies, found with our tools and validated by database experts. The 60 SPARQL queries have been executed over *Ontop* with and without the optimizations for exact predicates and virtual functional dependencies. We consider that a query times out if the average execution time is greater than 20 min.

Table 1. Results from the tests over EPDS.

	std. opt	w/VFD	w/exact predicates	w/both
Number of queries timing-out	17	10	11	4
Number of fully answered queries	43	50	49	56
Avg. SQL query length (in characters)	51521	28112	32364	8954
Average unfolding time	3.929 s	3.917 s	1.142 s	0.026 s
Average total query exec. time with timeouts	376.540 s	243.935 s	267.863 s	147.248 s
Median total query exec. time with timeouts	35.241 s	11.135 s	21.602 s	14.936 s
Average successful query exec. time (without timeouts)	36.540 s	43.935 s	51.217 s	67.248 s
Median successful query exec. time (without timeouts)	12.551 s	8.277 s	12.437 s	12.955 s
Average number of unions in generated SQL	6.3	3.4	5.1	2.2
Average number of tables joined per union in generated SQL	21.0	18.2	20.0	14.2
Average total number of tables in generated SQL	132.7	62.0	102.2	31.4

The results are summarized in Table 1 and Fig. 1. We can see that the proposed optimizations allow *Ontop* to critically reduce the query size and improve the performance of the query execution by orders of magnitude. Specifically, in Fig. 1 we compare standard optimizations with and without the techniques presented here. Observe that the average successful query execution time is higher

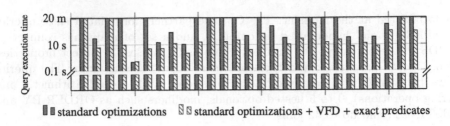

Fig. 1. Comparison of query execution time with standard optimizations. Log. scale

with new optimizations than without because the number of successfully executed queries increases. With standard optimizations, 17 SPARQL queries time out. With both novel optimizations enabled, only four queries still time out.

A total of 27 SPARQL queries get a more compact SQL translation with new optimizations enabled. The largest proportional decrease in size of the SQL query is 94 %, from 171 k chars, to 10 k. The largest absolute decrease in size of the SQL is 408 k chars. Note that the number of unions in the SQL may decrease also only with VFD-based optimization. Since the VFD-based optimization removes joins, more unions may become equivalent and are therefore removed. The maximum measured decrease in execution time is on a query that times out with standard optimizations, but uses 3.7 s with new optimizations.

6   Related Work

Dependencies have been intensively studied in the context of traditional relational databases [2]. Our work is related to the one in [23]; in particular their notion of path functional dependency is close to the notion of path VFD presented here. However, they do not consider neither ontologies, nor databases, and their dependencies are not meant to be used to optimize queries. There are a number of studies on functional dependencies in RDF [11,24], but as shown in Example 12, functional dependencies in RDF do not necessarily correspond to a VFD (when considering the ontology). Besides, these works do not tackle the issue of SQL query optimization.

The notion of *perfect mapping* [8] is strongly related to the notion of exact mapping. However there is a substantial difference: a perfect mapping must be *entailed* by the OBDA specification, whereas exact mappings are additional constraints that enrich the OBDA specification. For instance, perfect mappings would not be effective in the Statoil use case, where organizational constraints and storage policies are not entailed by the OBDA specification. The notion of *EBox* [17,21] was proposed as an attempt to include constraints in OBDA. However, EBox axioms are defined through a $\mathcal{T}$-box like syntax. These axioms cannot express constraints based on templates like virtual functional dependencies.

7   Conclusions

In this work we presented two novel optimization techniques for OBDA that complement standard optimizations in the area, and enable efficient SPARQL query answering over enterprise relational data. We provided theoretical foundations for these techniques based on two novel OBDA constraints: virtual functional dependencies, and exact predicates. We implemented these techniques in our OBDA system *Ontop* and empirically showed their effectiveness through extensive experiments that display improvements on the query execution time up to orders of magnitude.

Acknowledgement. This work is partially supported by the EU under IP project Optique (*Scalable End-user Access to Big Data*), grant agreement n. FP7-318338.

References

1. Baader, F., Calvanese, D., McGuinness, D., Nardi, D., Patel-Schneider, P.F. (eds.): The Description Logic Handbook: Theory, Implementation and Applications, 2nd edn. Cambridge University Press, Cambridge (2007)
2. Beeri, C., Vardi, M.Y.: The implication problem for data dependencies. In: Even, S., Kariv, O. (eds.) ICALP. LNCS, vol. 115, pp. 73–85. Springer, Heidelberg (1981)
3. Bienvenu, M., Ortiz, M., Simkus, M., Xiao, G.: Tractable queries for lightweight description logics. In: Proceedings of IJCAI. IJCAI/AAAI (2013)
4. Calvanese, D., De Giacomo, G., Lembo, D., Lenzerini, M., Rosati, R.: Tractable reasoning and efficient query answering in description logics: the DL-Lite family. JAR **39**(3), 385–429 (2007)
5. Chakravarthy, U.S., Fishman, D.H., Minker, J.: Semantic query optimization in expert systems and database systems. In: Proceedings of DEXA, pp. 659–674 (1986)
6. Das, S., Sundara, S., Cyganiak, R.: R2RML: RDB to RDF mapping language. W3C Recommendation, W3C, September 2012. http://www.w3.org/TR/r2rml/
7. DeWitt, D.J.: The wisconsin benchmark: past, present, and future. In: Gray, J. (ed.) The Benchmark Handbook. Morgan Kaufmann (1993)
8. Di Pinto, F., Lembo, D., Lenzerini, M., Mancini, R., Poggi, A., Rosati, R., Ruzzi, M., Savo, D.F.: Optimizing query rewriting in ontology-based data access. In: Proceedings of EDBT, pp. 561–572. ACM Press (2013)
9. Glimm, B., Ogbuji, C.: SPARQL 1.1 entailment regimes. W3C Recommendation, W3C, March 2013. http://www.w3.org/TR/sparql11-entailment/
10. Gottlob, G., Kikot, S., Kontchakov, R., Podolskii, V.V., Schwentick, T., Zakharyaschev, M.: The price of query rewriting in ontology-based data access. AIJ **213**, 42–59 (2014)
11. He, B., Zou, L., Zhao, D.: Using conditional functional dependency to discover abnormal data in RDF graphs. In: Proceedings of SWIM, pp. 43: 1–43: 7. ACM (2014)
12. Hovland, D., Lanti, D., Rezk, M., Xiao, G.: OBDA constraints for effective query answering (extended version). CoRR Technical report abs/1605.04263, arXiv.org e-Print archive (2016). http://arxiv.org/abs/1605.04263

13. Kikot, S., Kontchakov, R., Podolskii, V., Zakharyaschev, M.: Exponential lower bounds and separation for query rewriting. In: Czumaj, A., Mehlhorn, K., Pitts, A., Wattenhofer, R. (eds.) ICALP 2012, Part II. LNCS, vol. 7392, pp. 263–274. Springer, Heidelberg (2012)
14. Kikot, S., Kontchakov, R., Zakharyaschev, M.: Conjunctive query answering with OWL 2 QL. In: Proceedings of KR, pp. 275–285 (2012)
15. Kontchakov, R., Rezk, M., Rodríguez-Muro, M., Xiao, G., Zakharyaschev, M.: Answering SPARQL queries over databases under OWL 2 QL entailment regime. In: Mika, P., Tudorache, T., Bernstein, A., Welty, C., Knoblock, C., Vrandečić, D., Groth, P., Noy, N., Janowicz, K., Goble, C. (eds.) ISWC 2014, Part I. LNCS, vol. 8796, pp. 552–567. Springer, Heidelberg (2014)
16. Lanti, D., Rezk, M., Xiao, G., Calvanese, D.: The NPD benchmark: reality check for OBDA systems. In: Proceedings of EDBT (2015)
17. Mora, J., Rosati, R., Corcho, O.: kyrie2: query rewriting under extensional constraints in ELHIO. In: Proceedings of ISWC, pp. 568–583 (2014)
18. Poggi, A., Lembo, D., Calvanese, D., De Giacomo, G., Lenzerini, M., Rosati, R.: Linking data to ontologies. In: Spaccapietra, S. (ed.) Journal on Data Semantics X. LNCS, vol. 4900, pp. 133–173. Springer, Heidelberg (2008)
19. Rodríguez-Muro, M., Kontchakov, R., Zakharyaschev, M.: Ontology-based data access: Ontop of databases. In: Alani, H., Kagal, L., Fokoue, A., Groth, P., Biemann, C., Parreira, J.X., Aroyo, L., Noy, N., Welty, C., Janowicz, K. (eds.) ISWC 2013, Part I. LNCS, vol. 8218, pp. 558–573. Springer, Heidelberg (2013)
20. Rodriguez-Muro, M., Rezk, M.: Efficient SPARQL-to-SQL with R2RML mappings. J. Web Semant. **33**, 141–169 (2015)
21. Rosati, R.: Prexto: query rewriting under extensional constraints in DL-Lite. In: Simperl, E., Cimiano, P., Polleres, A., Corcho, O., Presutti, V. (eds.) ESWC 2012. LNCS, vol. 7295, pp. 360–374. Springer, Heidelberg (2012)
22. Rosati, R., Almatelli, A.: Improving query answering over DL-Lite ontologies. In: Proceedings of KR, pp. 290–300 (2010)
23. Weddell, G.E.: Reasoning about functional dependencies generalized for semantic data models. ACM Trans. Database Syst. **17**(1), 32–64 (1992)
24. Yu, Y., Heflin, J.: Extending functional dependency to detect abnormal data in RDF graphs. In: Aroyo, L., Welty, C., Alani, H., Taylor, J., Bernstein, A., Kagal, L., Noy, N., Blomqvist, E. (eds.) ISWC 2011, Part I. LNCS, vol. 7031, pp. 794–809. Springer, Heidelberg (2011)

A Framework Enhancing the User Search Activity Through Data Posting

Nunziato Cassavia[2], Elio Masciari[2], Chiara Pulice[1(✉)], and Domenico Saccà[1]

[1] DIMES, University of Calabria, Rende, Italy
{cpulice,sacca}@dimes.unical.it
[2] ICAR-CNR, Rende, Italy
{cassavia,masciari}@icar.cnr.it

Abstract. Due to the increasing availability of huge amounts of data, traditional data management techniques result inadequate in many real life scenarios. Furthermore, heterogeneity and high speed of this data require suitable data storage and management tools to be designed from scratch. In this paper, we describe a framework tailored for analyzing user interactions with intelligent systems while seeking for some domain specific information (e.g., choosing a good restaurant in a visited area). The framework enhances user quest for information by performing a data exchange activity (called data posting) which enriches the information sources with additional background information and knowledge derived from experiences and behavioral properties of domain experts and users.

Keywords: Big data · Rule based data transformation · Rule driven data presentation

1 Introduction

The impressive progress and development of Internet and on-line technologies has led to an increasing availability of a huge volume of data generated by heterogeneous sources at high production rates [7]. These massive data, referred as *Big Data* [14], exhibit a great variety and may be exploited to gather information about people, things, services and their interactions. In this respect, a great deal of attention has been devoted to the design of novel algorithms for analyzing information available from Twitter, Google, Facebook, and Wikipedia, to cite a few of the main big data producers. The availability of such unprecedented large amount of heterogeneous information sources is quite challenging and lead to the need for complex search solutions.

Despite search engines have been already proposed in the early age of Internet, the returned results are often quite far from the expected query answers from a user viewpoint. Indeed, when seeking for useful information, users may be driven by some predefined faceted features (*browsing*) or may simply formulate a query using "free" keywords (*searching*). However, most of the present systems mainly follow one of the two mentioned paradigms and only few systems offer a mix of the two of them. Thus, there is an increasing deal of interest,

© Springer International Publishing Switzerland 2016
J.J. Alferes et al. (Eds.): RuleML 2016, LNCS 9718, pp. 287–304, 2016.
DOI: 10.1007/978-3-319-42019-6_19

shared by both researchers [1] and industries [12], for the construction of *Intelligent Information Systems* (IIS) which goal is to assist end users in the search of relevant information and in the interaction with services in the net.

In this scenario, the type of query being performed plays a crucial role. Obviously enough, for well defined queries, a search engine like Google, is able to provide correct results in a few milliseconds[1]. However, in some cases users do not know exactly how to find the desired information about an object or a service (e.g. a book or a restaurant). In this case, the model leveraged by Amazon is better suited. More in detail, Amazon-like search tools, feature product categorization and recommender systems, thus making the user search experience quite interactive and iterative. Indeed, directory contents are hierarchically organized in order to guide users through a subset of documents potentially related to information being queried, thus limiting the possibility to input free text queries. In this respect, users re-think and refine their needs by learning the adjustments to the search being performed by exploiting the available choices. To better understand how directory navigation works, we resurge to accommodation booking portals analogy. Indeed, those portals offer a hierarchical navigation systems, i.e. from the home page, user can choose the desired country, then s/he can specify the city and finally the type of structure s/he is interested in. This navigation model suffers a great limitation due to ontology specification. Indeed, ontologies specified by the service designer may not meet user needs.

A solution to overcome the above mentioned limitations is the implementation of *faceted* navigation that helps users in the information "surfing" process [19,20]. More in detail, a new frontier for IIS is to combine searching and browsing by using features that are not a-priori predefined but selected for and adapted to the search context. Indeed, search results can be improved by building a custom map that, based on the initial query results, tries to learn additional knowledge about data being queried by iterative refinement of search dimensions and parameters. Upon this, in this paper we define an extension to the classical faceted navigation and consider the following challenge: *detecting on-the-fly features that are relevant in the search context and tailored to the user behavior.* The latter implies several research issues have to be addressed. First of all, data gathered by social network and search engines available on the web are inherently non structured; therefore, a data exchange task has to be performed for moving source data into a target "structured" database enabling an effective analysis of user behavior. To this end, in this paper we devise a data exchange setting for enhancing the information content of source data. More specifically, we exploit a version of data exchange called *data posting* that was first sketched in [16] and presented as an open research stream in a conference panel [6].

The following example will better clarify the problem under investigation and will illustrate each step of our approach.

Example 1. When interacting with the social network, users usually issue several queries, post comments and upload (tagged) files. For example a user may pose

---

[1] As a matter of fact, due to its quick result presentation, many users go through Google even if they exactly know the URLs of the resources they are interested in.

the following query: *Find a restaurant in Milan.* Traditional search engines will provide user results ranked on the basis of their default criteria. However, this ranking could be ineffective as users may not be satisfied by query answers as they are mainly based on proximity search and some fixed categorization (e.g. stars, price). In order to overcome this limitation, we perform a data pre-processing by clustering user comments stored in our system. As a result, we obtain a set of comment groups that may contain some new possible search categories (referred in the following as search *dimensions*) previously hidden in the data. It could therefore happen that the clustering algorithm suggests to add a new dimension to the source information that classifies the quality of dishes served at each restaurant, while matching the user query for a restaurant located in Milan area. The new dimension could be *Food Quality.* As users interact with the system and new enquiries and comments are made, some other additional dimensions could arise. For instance, the *Food Quality* could be refined by an additional dimension *fresh fish* with suitable values: *bad/good/excellent.* Data posting is used both to enrich the source raw data with the discovered dimensions and to personalize them for the current user so that the enriched information may be added to the search toolbar as soon as search keywords (e.g., "starters" or "main courses") are typed for which the dimensions are pertinent, thus enabling a faceted browsing.   □

In our architecture, data posting considers the information extracted by the clustering algorithm and tries to derive new dimensions that could be added to the initial domain scheme while preserving the information richness. Roughly speaking, the *data posting setting* $(\mathbf{S}, \mathcal{D}, T, \Sigma_{st}, \Sigma_t)$ consists of a source schema $\mathbf{S}$ (i.e. the search dimensions provided by specialized search engines), a domain schema $\mathcal{D}$ (i.e. the search domain), a target flat fact table T (i.e. the search keywords), a set Σ_{st} of source-to-target count constraints (i.e. frequency of keywords) and a set Σ_t of target constraints (i.e. conditions on keywords). The *data posting problem* associated with this setting is: given finite source instances I_S for $\mathbf{S}$ and $I_\mathcal{D}$ for $\mathcal{D}$, find a finite instance I_T for T such that $\langle I_S, I_\mathcal{D}, I_T \rangle$ satisfies both Σ_{st} and Σ_t. Main difference w.r.t. classical data exchange is the presence of the domain schema that stores "new" values (dimensions) to be added while exchanging data. The actual values to be assigned to dimensions are defined by taking into account the target constraints (e.g. the relative frequency of basic dimensions).

In sum, in this paper we focus on (i) the analysis of user's searching and comment posting activities in order to identify potentially interesting suggestions about user searches, (ii) the proposal of a novel data exchange setting that exploits them for enhancing the information contents of the source databases and (iii) the definition of a search strategy based on tailored faceted features. Our approach is motivated by the observation that both performed searches and posted comments define a quite accurate profiling of user wishes and feedbacks that can be exploited to construct background information and knowledge in an application domain for supporting advanced further searches. It is worth noticing, that commonly used search engines do not exploit such a refined information. Thus, the final result of our work is a user behavior oriented search framework for implementing new generation IIS.

Plan of the Paper. The paper is organized as follows. Section 2 introduces some background on the faceted navigation and our solution to the complex search problem. A detailed description of the data posting technique that provides the formal basis for enhancing the content of information sources is discussed in Sect. 3. Finally, Sect. 4 draws the conclusion.

2   Real-Time *Faceted* Navigation

Several techniques for browsing and navigating data in the net have been proposed over the years. In this section, we focus on faceted browsing [20] which is an exploration technique for structured datasets that allows users to find information without a-priori knowledge of their schemas.

In faceted browsing the information space is partitioned using relevant features (i.e., facets) of the data. Consider, as an example, the faceted view of a search engine depicted in Fig. 1. Starting from the home page, the user has the chance to search information about the location *and* several attributes pertaining to the search (i.e. the type of structure, the rating and so on). For example, s/he can browse the cities (*Cosenza, Scilla, . . .*), the structure types (*Hotel, B&B, apartment, . . .*) and their star rating (2, 3, 4, . . .). As a feature is selected, the user can choose other attributes among those available for the current search status. Moreover, during the browsing process, it is also possible to discard features no longer relevant to the search (i.e. user can perform *dimensional filtering*). This iterative process guides the user through the accommodation search by selecting a custom path instead of a hierarchy provided by the service designer.

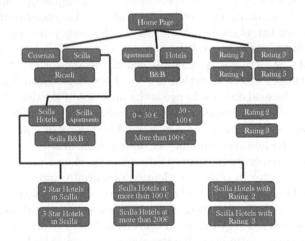

Fig. 1. Faceted navigation example

It is worth noticing that efficient faceted navigation (i.e. easy to use and providing access to richer information) relies on the availability of a meaningful feature set that characterize the domain being searched. However, as these features must be known and created in advance, important trends in the data may not be detected. In the following, we describe our ad-hoc intelligent algorithms that exploit clustering to improve on the above mentioned process.

Improving Faceted Navigation by Clustering. The faceted search pattern described above can be enhanced by exploiting a data mining approach for information enrichment. Among the plethora of data mining algorithms proposed in literature, we focused on Clustering. The rationale for this choice is described in the following. When users interact with web based systems, either for information browsing and searching or for posting comments and suggestions, they provide useful information about their behaviors. This information can be exploited for an accurate user profiling that is the basis for designing better user-oriented services. Unfortunately, no information about a possible classification of user features is easily available as no labeled examples can be collected. To overcome this limitation, we exploit clustering due to its unsupervised features. The clustering problem we address can be formalized as follows: Given a set $\mathcal{O} = \{o_1, \ldots, o_n\}$ containing n objects[2], cluster analysis aims at producing a partitioning[3] $\mathcal{C} = \{C_1, \cdots, C_k\}$ of the objects in O, such that objects in the same set C_i are maximally similar and objects in different sets are minimally similar, according to some similarity function. Consequently, each object $o \in \mathcal{O}$ is contained in exactly one set C_i. These sets $C_i \in \mathcal{C}$ are called clusters.

More in detail, given an input dataset we perform the following steps:

- Given the initial set $\mathcal{O}$ of objects, a partition $\mathcal{C}$ of $\mathcal{O}$ is provided. The feature set to be used for representing objects is derived by the data source (e.g. timestamps, location, etc.);
- We run our technique for discovering cluster labels which is based on the notion of *discriminative cluster patterns*. Discriminative cluster patterns highlight all the characteristics of a given cluster, since they are expected to lie in a specific cluster and at the same time not to lie in any other cluster;
- The initial partition is incrementally updated according to a (possibly infinite) stream $\{o_{n+1}, \ldots, o_{n+k}, \ldots\}$ of new incoming objects. In this respect, each object o_i (may) induce a new partition $\mathcal{P}_i$ that could contain a different number of discriminative features.

A detailed description of the clustering strategy is beyond the scope of this work, however, we briefly recall some basic concepts that we exploited for our purposes.

When dealing with data containing textual information, a major issue is the selection of the set of relevant terms, or *index terms*, i.e., the terms capable of best representing the topics associated with a given textual content. In order to

---

[2] For the sake of generalization we do not distinguish between query text and post as both of them can be considered as plain text objects.

[3] In this paper we refer to the hard clustering problem, where every data point belongs to exactly one cluster.

achieve this, some standard text processing operations are used [3,13], such as *lexical analysis, removal of stopwords, stemming, lemmatisation.*

Terms have different discriminating power, i.e., their relevance in the context where they are used. To weight term relevance, a common approach is to assign high significance to terms occurring frequently within a document, but rarely with respect to the remaining documents of the collection. The weight of a term is hence computed as a combination of its frequency within a document (*term frequency - TF*) and its rarity across the whole collection (*inverse document frequency - IDF*). We denote by $tf(w_j, m_i)$ the number of occurrences of term w_j within message m_i, and by $df(w_j, \mathcal{M})$ the number of messages (within a given message collection $\mathcal{M}$) containing w_j. A term w_j is denoted as an *index term* for $\mathcal{M}$ if $l \leq df(w_j, \mathcal{M}) \leq u$, where l and u represent default threshold values. The ratio here is that terms appearing in a few documents, as well as terms appearing in most documents, are less significant, and hence they should be discarded.

A widely used representation model is the vector-space model [3]. Each message m_i is represented as an m-dimensional vector $\mathbf{w}_i$, where m is the number of index terms and each component $\mathbf{w}_i[j]$ is the (normalized) *TF.IDF* weight associated with a term w_j:

$$\mathbf{w}_i[j] = \frac{tf(w_j, m_i) \cdot \log(N/df(w_j, \mathcal{M}))}{\sqrt{\sum_{p=1}^{m}[tf(w_p, m_i) \cdot \log(N/df(w_p, \mathcal{M}))]^2}}$$

After the pre-elaboration steps have been performed, many algorithms can be exploited for text clustering. An interesting solution for dealing with the big data scenario is represented by *Lingo* algorithm [15].

3   Enriching the Data: The Data Posting Challenge

As the cluster partition is obtained, we check if the discriminative terms that characterize the clusters may cause new dimensions to arise. To this end, we propose a novel approach, referred as Data Posting, that, starting from raw data and existing ontologies, can add new dimensions induced by clustering. More in detail, we store query result as a materialized data cube to be exploited for further search. These data will be used as training set for further clustering refinement that will group query results in a unsupervised way. The obtained clustering will be used for extracting features relevant to the query, that have not been neither specified by the user nor considered for building the query result. As an example consider a user searching for a restaurant in Milan. S/he will type the query "restaurant in Milan" (also many search engines will suggest this statement). Traditional search results will include restaurants located in the city along with their rank. By exploiting our approach, instead, we are able to suggest users a further interesting parameter (i.e., analysis dimension) as the rank of appetizers, main courses and sweets, allowing a more focused search.

3.1 Data Exchange

Data exchange [2,9] is the problem of migrating a data instance from a source schema to a target schema such that the materialized data on the target schema satisfies a number of given integrity constraints (mainly inclusion and functional dependencies). The integrity constraints are specified by: TGDs (Tuple Generating Dependencies), which are universal quantified formulas with additional existential quantifiers, and EGDs (Equality Generating Dependencies), which are universal quantified formulas enforcing the equality of two variables.

The classical data exchange setting is: $(S, T, \Sigma_{st}, \Sigma_t)$, where S is the source relational database schema, T is the target schema, Σ_t are dependencies on the target scheme T and Σ_{st} are source-to-target dependencies. The dependencies in Σ_{st} map data from the source to the target schema and are TGDs, which have the following format: $\forall \mathbf{X}(\phi_S(\mathbf{X}) \to \exists \mathbf{Y}\ \psi_T(\mathbf{X}, \mathbf{Y}))$, where $\phi_S(\mathbf{X})$ and $\psi_T(\mathbf{X}, \mathbf{Y})$ are conjunctions of literals on S and T, respectively, and $\mathbf{X}, \mathbf{Y}$ arc lists of variables. Dependencies in Σ_t specify constraints on the target schema and can be either TGDs or EGDs – the latter ones have the form $\forall \mathbf{X}(\psi_T(\mathbf{X}) \to x_1 = x_2)$, where x_1 and x_2 are variables in $\mathbf{X}$.

Example 2. Consider a source schema S with three relations:

1. R(N, P) (*Restaurant*) with attributes N (Restaurant Name) and P (Average Price),
2. P(I, U, N, E) (*User Review Post*) with attributes I (Post Identifier), U (User), N (Restaurant Name) and E (Evaluation) and
3. $\mathcal{D}_{\mathrm{PEC}}$(P, E, C) (*Restaurant Category*) with attributes P (Average Price), E (Evaluation) and C (Category Value) – the "special" notation for the this relation name will be clarified later.

The target schema T has two relations:

1. CR(N, C) (*Classified Restaurant*) with two attributes N (Restaurant Name) and C (Category Value), and
2. CP(I, U, N, C) (*Classified Post*) with attributes I (Post identifier), U (User), N (Restaurant Name) and C (Classified Review Evaluation).

We want that each restaurant be classified by choosing one of the evaluation reviews given for it:

$$\Sigma_{st} = \{\, \mathrm{R}(\mathrm{n}, \mathrm{p}) \to \exists\, \mathrm{C}\ \mathrm{CR}(\mathrm{n}, \mathrm{C});$$
$$\mathrm{P}(\mathrm{i}, \mathrm{u}, \mathrm{n}, \mathrm{e}) \wedge \mathrm{R}(\mathrm{n}, \mathrm{p}) \wedge \mathcal{D}_{\mathrm{PEC}}(\mathrm{p}, \mathrm{e}, \mathrm{c}) \to \mathrm{CP}(\mathrm{i}, \mathrm{u}, \mathrm{n}, \mathrm{c}) \,\}$$
$$\Sigma_t = \{\, \mathrm{CR}(\mathrm{n}, \mathrm{c}) \to \exists\, \mathrm{I}, \mathrm{U}\ \mathrm{CP}(\mathrm{I}, \mathrm{U}, \mathrm{n}, \mathrm{c});$$
$$\mathrm{CR}(\mathrm{n}, \mathrm{c}_1) \wedge \mathrm{CR}(\mathrm{n}, \mathrm{c}_2) \to \mathrm{c}_1 = \mathrm{c}_2 \,\}$$

where all low-case letter variables are universally quantified. The constraints in Σ_{st} move restaurant names and user reviews into the target database; in addition, every review evaluation is replaced by the category value associated to the pair (average price, evaluation) by the relation $\mathcal{D}_{\mathrm{PEC}}$ and every restaurant is classified with a value that is non specified but only declared by the existentially qualified C. The first constraint in Σ_t is a TGD and enforces that every restaurant be classified using any of the classified review evaluations issued for it. The second constraint is an EGD that admits at most one classification for a restaurant.   □

The target schema typically contains some new attributes that are defined using existentially quantified variables and the main issue of Data Exchange is to reduce arbitrariness in selecting such variable values. Therefore a data exchange solution is required to be "universal" in the sense that homomorphisms exists into every possible solution, i.e., a universal solution holds a sort of "minimal arbitrariness" property. Indeed, a main goal of data exchange is to single out situations for which a universal solution exists and can be computed in polynomial time. A universal solution has the benefit that the query semantics is independent from any specific solution that may be selected as target database, so that it can support certain answers, that is, the answers that occur in the intersection of a query over all "possible" target databases. In the above example, a universal solution does not bound a restaurant classification to one of its review but it generates a new review tuple for each restaurant in order to respect the principle of "minimal arbitrariness".

In our framework, the issue of "minimal arbitrariness" is not crucial for our goal, which consists in finding a "specific" solution that enriches the knowledge content of the target database instead. In the example, a specific solution can be obtained by choosing one of the issued reviews to classify a restaurant. But an arbitrary choice is not really a great achievement: the data exchange setting must provide mechanisms for making "intelligent" choices. A major step forward in this direction is to extend the data exchange setting with a new type of data dependency, called *count constraint* (an extension of cardinality constraint), first proposed in [17], which prescribes the result of a given count operation on a relation to be within a certain range. Count constraints use a *set term* that is either a constant set term or a *formula term*, defined as $\{\mathbf{X} : \exists \mathbf{Y} \psi\}$, where $\mathbf{X}$ and $\mathbf{Y}$ are disjoint list of variables, and ψ is conjunction of literals in which variables in $\mathbf{X}$ occur free (similar notation for set terms and aggregate predicates has been used in the dlv system [8]). There is an interpreted function symbol *count* (denoted by $\#$) that can be applied to a set term T to return the number of tuples in T (i.e., the cardinality of the table represented by T).

The following example is devoted to clarify how count constraints can be used to enlarge the perspective of Data Exchange.

Example 3. Consider the data exchange problem that has been modeled in Example 2. We now enrich the criteria for restaurant classification by requiring that a category can be assigned to a restaurant only if there are at least 10 reviews supporting it. If more than one category is applicable, the one which occurs more frequently in the reviews posted by distinct users is chosen. In absence of an applicable category, a restaurant gets the classification value "NA" (not applicable).

The new mapping is defined by keeping the rules in Σ_{st} and modifying the ones in Σ_t as shown next. As usual, lower-case and upper-case letters denote variables that are respectively universally and existentially quantified – in addition, dotted letters denote free variables used for defining sets.

(1): $c \neq$ "NA" $\wedge$ CR$(n, c) \rightarrow \#(\{\ddot{\text{I}} : \text{CP}(\ddot{\text{I}}, \text{U}, n, c)\}) \geq 10$.

(2): CR$(n, $"NA"$) \wedge$ CP$(\_, \_, n, c) \rightarrow \#(\{\ddot{\text{I}} : \text{CP}(\ddot{\text{I}}, \text{U}, n, c)\}) < 10$.

(3): $c \neq$ "NA" $\wedge$ CR$(n, c) \wedge$ CP$(\_, \_, n, \ddot{c}) \rightarrow \#(\{\ddot{\text{U}} : \text{CP}(\text{I}, \ddot{\text{U}}, n, c)\}) \geq \#(\{\ddot{\text{U}} : \text{CP}(\text{I}, \ddot{\text{U}}, n, \ddot{c})\})$.

(4): CR$(n, \_) \rightarrow \#(\{\ddot{\text{C}} : \text{CR}(n, \ddot{\text{C}})\}) = 1$.

All the four rules in Σ_t are count constraints. Constraint (1) states that any restaurant classification value c different from "NA" must be substantiated by at least 10 distinct users posting a review that classifies the restaurant with the value c – such reviews are collected by means of the set term with free variable $\ddot{\text{I}}$. Constraint (2) states that if a restaurant is classified with "NA", then any classification posted for must violate the previous constraint. Among the applicable categories for a restaurant, the constraint (3) choices the one with highest frequency in the restaurant reviews posted by distinct users – note that in this case, as the set term is defined by the variable $\ddot{\text{U}}$ rather than by $\ddot{\text{I}}$, reviews posted by a same user are counted only once. Constraint (4) implements the functional dependency $\text{N} \rightarrow \text{C}$ in the relation CR so that, in case of a tie in a restaurant classification, any of the values satisfying the constraint (3) is to be chosen.

As mentioned above, $\#$ is an interpreted function symbol for computing the cardinality of a set. We point out that existentially quantified variables are local in a set term, e.g., $\{\ddot{\text{I}} : \text{CP}(\ddot{\text{I}}, \text{U}, n, c)\}$ stands for $\{\ddot{\text{I}} : \exists \text{U} \; \text{CP}(\ddot{\text{I}}, \text{U}, n, c)\}$; in addition, anonymous variables, denoted by underscore, are used to define a relation projection, e.g., CP$(\_, \_, n, c)$ stands for the projection of CP on N and C. $\qquad \square$

3.2 Data Posting

The approach of using count constraints for Data Exchange has an evident drawback: the lack of a universal solution in most cases. Indeed, a universal solution is achievable only when the upper bound of a count constraint is 1, as it happens for functional dependencies. Nevertheless, as we pointed out before, our goal is finding a solution that enriches data while exchanging them, rather than preserving the correspondence with the source database in order to support certain answers. More specifically, our approach is aimed at enabling the selection of suitable values for existentially quantified variables, whereas the classical data exchange setting leave them undistinguished, except for the cases functional dependencies have to be satisfied.

Count constraints are powerful formal tools to define "intelligent" value selection. Their introduction allows us to enrich source data with new features (i.e., additional attributes[4] reflecting properties discovered during the process of data exchange), in order to construct big data tables that can be effectively queried by

---

[4] Also in OLAP analysis, attributes used to highlight properties of raw data (mainly, by categorization and grouping) are called *dimensions* – we recall that an OLAP system is characterized by multidimensional data cubes that enable manipulation and analysis of data stored in a source database from multiple perspectives (see for instance [5]).

end users. Thus, the new setting can be used for a new declination of data exchange for posting existing data with additional patterns so that the end user is enabled to extract additional information and knowledge from existing data while receiving suggestions and guidelines for making more comprehensive queries.

More in detail, through this approach, named data posting, the source database is enriched with additional tables, called *domain relations* (denoted by the symbol "$\mathcal{D}$" with subscript adornments), that store "new" values (dimensions) to be added into the target database, and count constraints are used to select such values as illustrated in Example 3. The issue of inventing new values to be included into the target relation is also one of the goals of classical data exchange setting. The main difference with data posting is the focus: to preserve the relationships with the source database, classical data exchange only considers dependencies delivering universal solutions that support certain queries, whose answers are independent from the values assigned to existentially quantified variables. Instead, data posting looks for more expressive constraints to enrich the contents of the exchanged data. This approach can be thought of as a theoretical contribution to support the so-called "faceted" navigation, described in Sect. 2.

We next introduce the formal setting for data posting. We start from the definition of the involved database schemata. Let

- $\mathbf{S} = \langle S_1, \ldots, S_n \rangle$ be a *source database schema* with relation schemes $S_1, \ldots, S_n$,
- $\mathcal{D} = \langle \mathcal{D}_1, \ldots, \mathcal{D}_m \rangle$ be a *domain database schema* with domain relation schemes $\mathcal{D}_1, \ldots, \mathcal{D}_m$ and
- $\mathbf{T} = \langle T_1, \ldots, T_q \rangle$ be a *target database schema* with relation schemes $T_1, \ldots, T_q$.

We assume that all databases on both $\mathbf{S}$ and $\mathcal{D}$ are finite. As it will be shown later in this section, any target database on $\mathbf{T}$ is finite as well, given the structure of our exchange constraints.

A *source-to-target TGD constraint* is a dependency over $\langle \mathbf{S}, \mathcal{D}, \mathbf{T} \rangle$ of the form

$$\forall \mathbf{x} \left(\phi_S(\mathbf{x} \cup \tilde{\mathbf{y}}) \rightarrow \phi_T(\mathbf{z}) \right),$$

where $\mathbf{x}$, $\tilde{\mathbf{y}}$ and $\mathbf{z}$ are lists of universally quantified variables such that $\mathbf{x} \cap \tilde{\mathbf{y}} = \emptyset$ and $\mathbf{z} \subseteq \mathbf{x} \cup \tilde{\mathbf{y}}$, the formula ϕ_S and ψ_T are conjunctions of atoms with predicate symbols in $\mathbf{S} \cup \mathcal{D}$ and in $\mathbf{T}$, respectively.

The variables in $\tilde{\mathbf{y}}$ are called *non deterministic* and occur in non-deterministic domain predicates, defined next. Given a domain relation scheme $\mathcal{D}_i$, a *non-deterministic domain predicate* is an atom occurring in ϕ_S with format $[\mathcal{D}_i(\mathbf{u}, \tilde{\mathbf{v}})]$, where the terms in $\mathbf{u}$ are either constants or variables in $\mathbf{x}$ (i.e., universally quantified in the standard way), and the terms in $\tilde{\mathbf{v}}$ are variables in $\tilde{\mathbf{y}}$, which are universally quantified within the scope of the variables in $\mathbf{x}$. The semantics of the predicate is: for every value assignment for the variables in $\mathbf{x}$, any (non-necessarily proper) subset D' of $\sigma_{\mathbf{u}}(D_i)$ is non-deterministically selected, where D_i is the the domain relation with scheme $\mathcal{D}_i$, $\sigma_{\mathbf{u}}(D_i)$ is the selection of the tuples in $\mathcal{D}_i$ that unify with the values of $\mathbf{u}$, and the variables in $\tilde{\mathbf{v}}$ are universally quantified on the projection of D' over the attributes corresponding to such variables.

We now define the semantics of any source-to-target TGD constraint $t = \forall \mathbf{x}\,(\,\phi_S(\mathbf{x} \cup \tilde{\mathbf{y}})\, \rightarrow\, \phi_T(\mathbf{z})\,)$ – say that the number of variables in $\mathbf{x}$ is n and the number of variables in $\tilde{\mathbf{y}}$ is m. Let $I = (I_S, I_D)$ be given, where I_S and I_D are finite source instances for $\mathbf{S}$ and for $\mathcal{D}$, respectively. The *active domain* D_I is the set of all values occurring in I_S and I_D. Let an *admissible instance* I_T for $\mathbf{T}$ be also given, that is an instance whose values all occur in D_I. The semantic of t states whether t is satisfied or not by $\langle I_S, I_D, I_T \rangle$. Before defining such a semantic, we need the additional notion of *non-deterministic domain mapping*, which is a function $(D_I)^n \rightarrow (2^{D_I})^m$ mapping every n-tuple of values assigned to the universally quantified variables in $\mathbf{x}$ into an m-tuple of ranges for the non-deterministic variables in $\tilde{\mathbf{y}}$. The notion of satisfiability is introduced after preliminary fixing one of the possible non-deterministic domain mappings, say f_t.

We say that $\langle I_S, I_D, I_T \rangle$ satisfies t w.r.t. f_t if for each $\mathbf{v} \in (\mathbf{D_I})^n$ and for each $\tilde{\mathbf{v}} \in f_t(\mathbf{v})$: either $\phi_S(\mathbf{x} \cup \tilde{\mathbf{y}})[\mathbf{x}/\mathbf{v}, \tilde{\mathbf{y}}/\tilde{\mathbf{v}}]$ is made false by $\langle I_S, I_D \rangle$ or $\phi_T(\mathbf{z})[\mathbf{z}/(\mathbf{v} \cup \tilde{\mathbf{v}})_\mathbf{z}]$ is made true by I_T, where the substitution $[\mathbf{x}/\mathbf{v}, \tilde{\mathbf{y}}/\tilde{\mathbf{v}}]$ assigns the values $\mathbf{v}$ and $\tilde{\mathbf{v}}$ to the corresponding variables in $\mathbf{x}$ and $\tilde{\mathbf{y}}$, respectively, in the formula ϕ_S and it induces a substitution, denoted by $[\mathbf{z}/(\mathbf{v} \cup \tilde{\mathbf{v}})_\mathbf{z}]$ for the variables of $\mathbf{z}$ in the formula ϕ_T as well, since $\mathbf{z} \subseteq \mathbf{x} \cup \tilde{\mathbf{y}}$ by definition.

Given a set Σ of source-to-target TGD constraints and finite source instances I_S for $\mathbf{S}$, I_D for $\mathcal{D}$ and I_T for $\mathbf{T}$, $\langle I_S, I_D, I_T \rangle$ satisfies Σ if for each $t \in \Sigma$, there exists a non-deterministic domain mapping f_t such that $\langle I_S, I_D, I_T \rangle$ satisfies t w.r.t. f_t.

As an example, consider the first TGD defined in Example 2: $R(n, p) \rightarrow \exists C\ CR(n, C)$. In the data posting setting, the existentially quantified variable C must be replaced by a non-deterministic variable $\tilde{c}$ ranging on the attribute C (Category Value) of domain relation $\mathcal{D}_{PEC}(P, E, C)$ (*Restaurant Category*), whose first two attributes are P (Average Price) and E (Evaluation). The TGD is rewritten as:

$$R(n, p) \wedge [\mathcal{D}_{PEC}(p, \_, \tilde{c})] \rightarrow CR(n, \tilde{c}).$$

The meaning of the rule is the following. Let us first fix the values for the variables n and p. Then we choose a non-deterministic domain mapping for defining a range for the variable $\tilde{c}$. To this end, we may proceed as follows. Let H be domain relation corresponding to $\mathcal{D}_{PEC}$. We compute: $H' = \sigma_{\$1=p}(H)$ (selection of all tuples whose first field is equal to p) and $H'' = \pi_{\$3}(H')$ (projection of H' on the third field). Then, we non-deterministically select a subset H''' of H'' as the range for the non-deterministic universally quantified variable $\tilde{c}$.

The example clarifies that our TGD constraints differ from classical ones as they replace existentially quantified variables with variables ranging on suitable finite domains.

A *count constraint* is a dependency over $\mathbf{T}$ of the form

$$\forall \mathbf{x}\,(\,\phi_T(\mathbf{x}) \rightarrow \#(\{\mathbf{y} : \exists \mathbf{z}\, \alpha(\mathbf{x}, \mathbf{y}, \mathbf{z})\}) < \text{op} > \beta(\mathbf{x})\,)$$

where ϕ_T is a conjunction of atoms with predicate symbol in $\mathbf{T}$, $< \text{op} >$ is any of the comparison operators ($=, >, \geq, <$ and $\leq$), $H = \{\mathbf{y} : \exists \mathbf{z}\, \alpha(\mathbf{x}, \mathbf{y}, \mathbf{z})\}$ is a *set term*, $\#$ is an interpreted function symbol that computes the cardinality of the (possibly empty) set corresponding to H, $\#(H)$ is *count term*, and $\beta(\mathbf{x})$ is an integer or a variable in $\mathbf{x}$ or another count term with universally quantified variables in $\mathbf{x}$. The two lists $\mathbf{y}$ and $\mathbf{z}$ consist of distinct variables that are also different from the universally quantified variables in $\mathbf{x}$, $\alpha(\mathbf{x}, \mathbf{y}, \mathbf{z})$ is a conjunction of atoms $T_i(\mathbf{x}, \mathbf{y}, \mathbf{z})$ with $T_i \in \mathbf{T}$.

To define the semantic of a count constraint, we assume that an instance I_T for $\mathbf{T}$ is given. Then, we consider the *active domain* D_I as the set of all values occurring in I_T. Given a substitution $\mathbf{x}/\mathbf{v}$ assigning values in D_I to universally quantified variables, $K(\mathbf{v}) = \{\mathbf{y} : \exists \mathbf{z} \, \alpha(\mathbf{x}, \mathbf{y}, \mathbf{z})\}$ defines the set of values in D_I assigned to the free variables in $\mathbf{y}$ for which $\exists \mathbf{z} \, \alpha(\mathbf{x}, \mathbf{y}, \mathbf{z})$ is satisfied by I_T and $\#(K)$ is the cardinality of this set. We say that I_T satisfies

$$\forall \mathbf{x} \, (\, \phi_T(\mathbf{x}) \rightarrow \#(\{\mathbf{y} : \exists \mathbf{z} \, \alpha(\mathbf{x}, \mathbf{y}, \mathbf{z})\}) < \mathrm{op} > \beta(\mathbf{x})$$

if for each substitution $\mathbf{x}/\mathbf{v}$ that makes true $\phi(\mathbf{x})[\mathbf{x}/\mathbf{v}]$, $k_1 < \mathrm{op} > k_2$ is true as well, where k_1 is the cardinality of the set $\{\mathbf{y} : \exists \mathbf{z} \, \alpha(\mathbf{x}, \mathbf{y}, \mathbf{z})\}[\mathbf{x}/\mathbf{v}]$ and k_2 is the value of $\beta(\mathbf{x})[\mathbf{x}/\mathbf{v}]$.

As an example, consider the first count constraint defined in Example 3:

$$\forall \mathsf{n}, \mathsf{c} \, (\, \mathsf{c} \neq \text{``NA''} \wedge \mathsf{CR}(\mathsf{n}, \mathsf{c}) \rightarrow \#(\{ \, \ddot{\mathsf{I}} : \exists \mathsf{U} \, \mathsf{CP}(\ddot{\mathsf{I}}, \mathsf{U}, \mathsf{n}, \mathsf{c})\}) \geq 10 \,).$$

The constraint states that if the pair (n, c) occurs in CR (i.e., the restaurant n has been classified with the value c), then there exist at least 10 posts in CP assigning the value c to the restaurant.

Observe that target count constraints extends EGD (Equality Generating Dependencies) of the classical data exchange setting. Any EGD $\forall \mathbf{x}(\, \psi(\mathbf{x}) \rightarrow x_1 = x_2 \,)$, where x_1 and x_2 are variables in $\mathbf{x}$, can be formulated by the following count constraint:

$$\forall \mathbf{x} \, (\, \phi(\mathbf{x}) \rightarrow \#(\{y : y = x_1 \vee y = x_2\}) = 1)$$

where y is a new variable not included in $\mathbf{x}$. The extension of our formalism to include the disjunction of "safe" comparison predicates such as $y = x_1 \vee y = x_2$ is straightforward. Indeed, in practice, the usage of a disjunction can be avoided by exploiting the specific structure of the formula ϕ. For instance, the rule:

$$\mathsf{CR}(\mathsf{n}, \_) \rightarrow \#(\{ \, \ddot{\mathsf{C}} : \mathsf{CR}(\mathsf{n}, \ddot{\mathsf{C}})\}) = 1.$$

introduced in Example 3, implements the functional dependency that any restaurant gets exactly one classification value.

We are now ready to formulate the data posting problem:

Definition 1. *The* data posting setting $(\mathbf{S}, \mathcal{D}, T, \Sigma_{st}, \Sigma_t)$ *consists of a source database schema* $\mathbf{S}$, *a domain database scheme* $\mathcal{D}$, *a target flat fact table* T, *a set* Σ_{st} *of source-to-target count constraints and a set* Σ_t *of target count constraints. The* data posting problem *associated with this setting is: given finite source instances* I_S *for* $\mathbf{S}$ *and* $I_\mathcal{D}$ *for* $\mathcal{D}$, *find a finite instance* I_T *for* T *such that* $\langle I_S, I_\mathcal{D}, I_T \rangle$ *satisfies both* Σ_{st} *and* Σ_t.

The main differences of the data posting setting with respect to the classical data exchange problem are four: (1) coupling the source database schema with a domain database scheme with finite instances, playing the role of a sort of ontology to enrich the exchange of data, (2) replacing existentially quantified variables with variables ranging on suitable finite domains and enabling non-deterministic choices of the values to be assigned to them, (3) restricting the usage of TGDs (tuple generating dependencies) only in Σ_{st} so that infinite relations cannot be created and (4) using only count constraints in Σ_t with the effect of losing independence from any specific possible solution to the benefit of enabling "intelligent" choices in the selection of a solution.

A meaningful example of data posting problem is illustrated next.

Example 4. We significantly extend the setting of Examples 2 and 3 as follows. Consider a source schema **S** with three relations:

1. $R_S(N, P, L)$ (*Restaurant*) with attributes N (Restaurant Name), P (Average Price) and L (Location) – the relation contains the additional attribute L w.r.t. the one defined in Example 2,
2. $P(I, U, N, E)$ (*User Review Post*) with attributes I (Post Identifier), U (User), N (Restaurant Name) and E (Evaluation) – the relation is not changed w.r.t. the one defined in Example 2,
3. $UB(U, B)$ (*User Behavior*) with attributes U (User Identifier) and B (User Behavior) – the relation stores a synthetic descriptor of the typical behavior of a user.

The domain relations in $\mathcal{D}$ are:

1. $\mathcal{D}_{PEC}(P, E, C)$ (*Restaurant Category*) with attributes P (Price Range), E (Evaluation) and C (Category Value) – the same as the one defined in Example 2 except that the average price is now replaced by a price range: the relation stores the evaluation category for any pair (price range, evaluation),
2. $\mathcal{D}_{PR}(P_1, P_2, PR)$ (*Price Range*) with attributes P_1 (Range Lower Bound), P_2 (Range Upper Bound) and PR (Price Range) – the relation fixes the interval for a price range,
3. $\mathcal{D}_{BR}(UB, LB)$ (*Behavior Relationship*) with attributes UB (User Behavior) and LB (Leader Behavior) – the relation stores pairs of behaviors (b_1, b_2) stating that a user with behavior b_1 is typically influenced by a user with behavior b_2,
4. $\mathcal{D}_{LR}(L, R)$ (*Location Region*) with attributes L (Location) and R (Region) – for each possible location, the relation stores the region it belongs to.

The target schema **T** has five relations:

1. $R_T(N, P, PR, L, R)$ (*Restaurant*) with attributes N (Restaurant Name), P (Average Price), PR (Price Range), L (Location) and R (Region) – the relation adds two dimensions (Price Range and Region) to the corresponding source relation,
2. $CR(N, C)$ (*Classified Restaurant*) with two attributes N (Restaurant Name) and C (Category Value) – the same as the one defined in Example 2,
3. $CP(I, U, N, C)$ (*Classified Post*) with attributes I (Post identifier), U (User), N (Restaurant Name) and C (Classified Review Evaluation) – the same as the one defined in Example 2,

4. $\text{UL}(\text{U}, \text{L})$ (*Follow Relationship*) with attributes U (User) and L (Leader) – the relation stores pairs of users (u_1, u_2) stating that u_1 is influenced by user u_2,
5. $\text{CRC}(\text{N}, \text{U}, \text{C})$ (*Customized Restaurant Classification*) with attributes N (Restaurant Name), U (User) and C (Classified Review Evaluation) – the relation stores restaurant classifications that are customized for a user on the basis of the reviews issued by her/his leaders.

The constraints in Σ_{st} are:

(st_1): $\text{R}_{\text{S}}(\text{n}, \text{p}, \_) \wedge range(\text{p}, \text{pr}) \wedge [\mathcal{D}_{\text{PEC}}(\text{pr}, \_, \ddot{\text{c}})] \rightarrow \text{CR}(\text{n}, \ddot{\text{c}})$
(st_2): $\text{R}_{\text{S}}(\text{n}, \text{p}, \_) \wedge \text{UB}(\text{u}, \_) \wedge range(\text{p}, \text{pr}) \wedge [\mathcal{D}_{\text{PEC}}(\text{pr}, \_, \ddot{\text{c}})] \rightarrow \text{CRC}(\text{n}, \text{u}, \ddot{\text{c}})$
(st_3): $\text{R}_{\text{S}}(\text{n}, \text{p}, 1) \wedge \mathcal{D}_{\text{LR}}(1, \text{r}) \wedge range(\text{p}, \text{pr}) \rightarrow \text{R}_{\text{T}}(\text{n}, \text{p}, \text{pr}, 1, \text{r})$
(st_4): $\text{P}(\text{i}, \text{u}, \text{n}, \text{e}) \wedge \text{R}_{\text{S}}(\text{n}, \text{p}, \_) \wedge range(\text{p}, \text{pr}) \wedge \mathcal{D}_{\text{PEC}}(\text{pr}, \text{e}, \text{c}) \rightarrow \text{CP}(\text{i}, \text{u}, \text{n}, \text{c})$
(st_5): $\text{UB}(\text{u}_1, \text{b}_1) \wedge \text{UB}(\text{u}_2, \text{b}_2) \wedge \mathcal{D}_{\text{BR}}(\text{b}_1, \text{b}_2) \rightarrow \text{UL}(\text{u}_1, \text{u}_2)$

To simplify the notation, the predicate $range(p, pr)$ is used to represent the conjunction: $\mathcal{D}_{\text{PR}}(\text{p}_1, \text{p}_2, \text{pr}) \wedge (\text{p}_1 \leq \text{p}) \wedge (\text{p} < \text{p}_2)$. Recall that an "underscore" (anonymous) term for an attribute a in a predicate p represents the projection of the relation corresponding to p that excludes the column corresponding to a. As pointed out in Example 3, lower-case and upper-case letters denote variables that are respectively universally and existentially quantified while dotted letters denote free variables used for defining sets. The scope of existentially quantified variable is inside a set definition.

Observe that non-deterministic domain predicates only occur in the first two rules and are used to choose category values for restaurant classification and for customized restaurant classification, respectively – in both cases, the post evaluations are converted into classification values on the basis of the average price charged by a restaurant. The two rules may assign more than a classification value to a restaurant but subsequent constraints will enforce that the classification of a restaurant in CR be unique, whereas the specific classification for an user may hold multiple values.

Rule (st_3) enriches the source relation for a restaurant by adding two categorization attributes: price range and region – the new attributes are "dimensions" and the target restaurant relation represents a star-schema data cube in the OLAP terminology [5].

Rule (st_4) copies the user review posts into the target database after having converted the post evaluations into classification values on the basis of the average price. Finally, the rule (st_5) constructs the target follow relationship using user behaviors and the pairs (b_1, b_2) in $\mathcal{D}_{\text{BR}}$, representing the pattern that a user with behavior b_2 is a potential influencer for a user with behavior b_1.

The constraints in Σ_t are:

(t_1): $\text{CR}(\text{n}, \text{c}) \rightarrow \#(\{\ddot{\text{I}} : \text{CP}(\ddot{\text{I}}, \text{U}, \text{n}, \text{c})\}) \geq 10$.
(t_2): $\text{CP}(\_, \_, \text{n}, \text{c})) \wedge \neg\text{CR}(\text{n}, \_) \rightarrow \#(\{\ddot{\text{I}} : \text{CP}(\ddot{\text{I}}, \text{U}, \text{n}, \text{c})\}) < 10$.
(t_3): $\text{CR}(\text{n}, \text{c}) \wedge \text{CP}(\_, \_, \text{n}, \ddot{\text{c}}) \rightarrow \#(\{\ddot{\text{U}} : \text{CP}(\text{I}, \ddot{\text{U}}, \text{n}, \text{c})\}) \geq \#(\{\ddot{\text{U}} : \text{CP}(\text{I}, \ddot{\text{U}}, \text{n}, \ddot{\text{c}})\})$.
(t_4): $\text{CR}(\text{n}, \_) \rightarrow \#(\{\ddot{\text{C}} : \text{CR}(\text{n}, \ddot{\text{C}})\}) \leq 1$.
(t_5): $\text{CRC}(\text{n}, \text{u}, \text{c}) \rightarrow \#(\{\ddot{\text{L}} : \text{CP}(\text{I}, \ddot{\text{L}}, \text{n}, \text{c}) \wedge \text{UL}(\text{u}, \ddot{\text{L}})\}) \geq 10$.
(t_6): $\text{UL}(\text{u}, 1) \wedge \text{CP}(\_, 1, \text{n}, \text{c}) \wedge \neg\text{CRC}(\text{n}, \text{u}, \text{c}) \rightarrow \#(\{\ddot{\text{L}} : \text{CP}(\text{I}, \ddot{\text{L}}, \text{n}, \text{c}) \wedge \text{UL}(\text{u}, \ddot{\text{L}})\}) < 10$.

First of all, we point out that the classification value "NA" introduced in Example 3 to represent a missing classification is not anymore necessary. In fact, a missing classification is simply notified by the absence of a classification tuple for a restaurant – this happens when the empty range is chosen for the non-deterministic domain predicate $[\mathcal{D}_{\mathtt{PEC}}(\mathtt{pr}, \_, \tilde{c})]$ in the rules (st_1) and/or (st_2).

Constraint (t_1) imposes that any restaurant classification value c must be substantiated by at least 10 distinct users posting a review that classifies the restaurant with the value c. Constraint (t_2) states that if a restaurant is not classified, then any classification posted for it violates the previous constraint. Among the applicable categories for a restaurant, the constraint (t_3) choices the one with highest frequency in the restaurant reviews posted by distinct users.

Two remarks on the negated predicate $\neg\mathtt{CR}(\mathtt{n}, \_)$ used in (t_2) to check whether a restaurant is not classified are in order. First, as the anonymous term stands for the projection of $\mathtt{CR}$ on the first column, the negation is "safe" in the sense all variables are bound by positive predicates. Second, extending our setting to handle safe and acyclic negation is a straightforward.

In the same way as in Example 3, Constraint (t_4) implements the functional dependency $\mathtt{N} \to C$ in the relation $\mathtt{CR}$ so that, in case of a tie in a restaurant classification, any of the values satisfying the constraint (t_3) is to be chosen. Observe that, here the comparison operator in the right hand side is "$\leq$" as a restaurant is not anymore required to have a classification, whereas it is "$=$" in the corresponding constraint in Example 3, where a missing classification is expressed by means of the value "NA".

Constraint (t_5) enforces that any customized restaurant classification value c for a user u must be substantiated by at least 10 distinct influencers for u posting a review that classifies the restaurant with the value c. The reverse condition that is imposed by Constraint (t_5). Observe that there is no constraint that forbids to have several customized classification values of a restaurant for the same user. □

Complexity Analysis. Next we measure the complexity of data posting according to the *data complexity* approach of [4,18] for which the program (i.e., $\mathbf{S}, \mathcal{D}, T, \Sigma_{st}$, and Σ_t) is constant while the database (the instances I_S for $\mathbf{S}$ and $I_{\mathcal{D}}$ for $\mathcal{D}$) is variable. We stress that our complexity results derives from the assumption that the domains of the attributes in $\mathbf{T}$ are finite and are part of the input.

Theorem 1. *Given* $(\mathbf{S}, \mathcal{D}, \mathbf{T}, \Sigma_{st}, \Sigma_t)$ *and finite source instances* I_S *for* $\mathbf{S}$ *and* $I_{\mathcal{D}}$ *for* $\mathcal{D}$, *the problem of deciding whether there exists an instance* I_T *of* $\mathbf{T}$ *such that* $\langle I_S, I_{\mathcal{D}}, I_T \rangle$ *satisfies* $\Sigma_{st} \cup \Sigma_t$ *is* NP-*complete under the data complexity.*

Proof. Membership to NP is obvious: it is sufficient to guess an instance I_T of $\mathbf{T}$ and to check whether or not $\langle I_S, I_{\mathcal{D}}, I_T \rangle$ satisfies $\Sigma_{st} \cup \Sigma_t$. Observe that the size of I_T is polynomially bounded by the input size as no duplicated tuples are allowed in a relation. Furthermore, it is easy to see that checking all constraints on I_T can be easily done in deterministic polynomial time.

To prove NP-hardness we next produce a reduction from the graph 3-coloring, which is well known to be NP-complete. Take any (undirected) graph $G = (N, A)$, where N is the set of nodes and $A \subseteq N \times N$ is the set of arcs. We are also given three colors, say g, r and b. We define a source scheme consisting of two relations: $\mathtt{nodes}(\mathtt{N})$, storing the nodes of the graph, and $\mathtt{arcs}(\mathtt{N_s}, \mathtt{N_e})$, storing the arcs represented as pairs of nodes. The domain scheme has a unique relation $\mathcal{D}_C$ with value $\{g, r, b\}$. The target database scheme contains three relations: $\mathtt{node_T}(\mathtt{N})$ and $\mathtt{arc_T}(\mathtt{N_s}, \mathtt{N_e})$, which are copies of respectively $\mathtt{nodes}$ and $\mathtt{arcs}$, and $\mathtt{cn}(\mathtt{N}, \mathtt{C})$, which assigns a color to a node.

The constraints are:

(1): $\mathtt{nodes}(\mathtt{n}) \rightarrow \mathtt{node_T}(\mathtt{n})$.

(2): $\mathtt{arcs}(\mathtt{n}, \mathtt{m}) \rightarrow \mathtt{arc_T}(\mathtt{n}, \mathtt{m})$.

(3): $\mathtt{nodes}(\mathtt{n}) \wedge [\mathcal{D}_C(\mathtt{c})] \rightarrow \mathtt{cn}(\mathtt{n}, \mathtt{c})$.

(4): $\mathtt{node_T}(\mathtt{n}) \rightarrow \#(\{\, \breve{\mathtt{C}} : \mathtt{cn}(\mathtt{n}, \breve{\mathtt{C}})\}) = 1$.

(5): $\mathtt{arc_T}(\mathtt{p}, \mathtt{q}) \rightarrow \#(\{\, \breve{\mathtt{C}} : \mathtt{cn}(\mathtt{p}, \breve{\mathtt{C}}) \vee \mathtt{cn}(\mathtt{q}, \breve{\mathtt{C}})\}) = 2$.

The first three constraints are the TGDs in Σ_{st}: the first two simply copy the source node and arc relation and the third one selects a color to every node. The fourth rule is a count constraints enforcing the condition that every node must have assigned exactly one color. The last rule requires the two nodes of an arc to have different colors. It turns out that the data posting problem admits a solution if and only if the graph is 3-colorable. Note the disjunction is used in the last rule, which could be however avoided by means a slightly more complicated formulation. We prefer to use this simpler format of disjunction as the extension of our formalism to include disjunction is straightforward.   □

The above proof evidences that the high complexity is determined by the presence of non-deterministic domain predicates in source-to-target TGD dependencies. This fact suggest us to single out a subclass of the data posting problem for which the feasibility check can be done in polynomial time.

Definition 2. *We say that a data posting problem is deterministic if every source-to-target TDG dependency does not contain non-deterministic domain predicates.*

Proposition 1. *Given a deterministic data posting problem* $(\mathbf{S}, \mathcal{D}, T, \Sigma_{st}, \Sigma_t)$ *and finite source instances I_S for $\mathbf{S}$ and I_D for $\mathcal{D}$, the problem of deciding whether there exists an instance I_T of T such that $\langle I_S, I_D, I_T \rangle$ satisfies $\Sigma_{st} \cup \Sigma_t$ is polynomial under the data complexity.*

Proof. As every source-to-target TGD dependency does no contain non-deterministic domain predicates, the number of tuples that can be added to the relation T is polynomial in the size of the relations and the domains that occur in the left hand side of the dependency. Once generated all possible tuples of T, the next step consists in verifying whether the tuples in T satisfy all target count constraints. This check is obviously performed in polynomial time.   □

Remarks. One of the most important features of data posting setting is coupling the source database schema with a domain database scheme with finite instances, playing the role of a kind of ontology to enrich the exchange of data. We stress that an important preliminary task for data posting is to provide domain relations containing meaningful patterns for adding properties to source tuples and enhancing the knowledge content of the target ones. The OLAP analysis [5] pursues a similar goal while adding dimensions to a data cube – we followed this approach in defining the domain relations $\mathcal{D}_{PR}$ and $\mathcal{D}_{LR}$ to add two dimensions that group prices into ranges and locations into regions, respectively. Moreover, the discovery of more hidden (some time, even surprising) properties is the goal of two important data mining techniques: *clustering* and *classification* [11]. Indeed, the two domain relations $\mathcal{D}_{BR}$ (characterizing relationships among user behaviors) and $\mathcal{D}_{PEC}$ (defining categories for restaurants) can be thought of as results of a data mining task. We recall that, in our framework, clustering is used to discovery properties that may enhance the user search on the target database.

A promising future line of research is to include some data mining techniques directly inside the data posting setting. This is coherent with our ambitious goal of posting data with high knowledge content. A main contribution to move along this line is given by the power of count constraints. Indeed, in [17] it has been first shown that a version of count constraint implementing the "group-by" SQL operator can be used to mimic another classical data mining technique: *frequent itemset mining*, that is the problem of discovering frequent itemsets in a transaction database. Later on, in [10] it has been illustrated how count constraints may play an important role in the resolution of *Inverse Frequent set Mining* (IFM), that is the problem of computing a transaction database satisfying given support constraints for some itemsets, which are typically the frequent ones.

4   Conclusion

The impressive progress and development of Internet and on-line technologies has led to an increasing availability of a huge volume of data generated by heterogeneous sources at high production rates. Therefore, the issue of devising novel solutions for analyzing big data, coming both from various information sources and from logs of user interactions and behaviors, is becoming more and more compelling in the construction of Intelligent Information Systems (IIS) to assist end users in the search of relevant information and in the interaction with services in the net. In this paper, we have presented a user behavior oriented search framework for implementing new generation IIS that offers advanced search functionalities. Our framework exploits a suite of clustering algorithms devoted to the extraction of unsupervised information hidden in the collected data and, through *Data Posting*, allows to enrich the contents by supplying additional pieces of information while moving data. A portion of enriched information (dimensions) pertinent with the keywords of the query is presented to the user into the search toolbar, enabling a faceted browsing.

References

1. Agrawal, D., et al.: Challenges and Opportunities with Big Data: A community white paper developed by leading researchers across the United States (2012)
2. Arenas, M., Barceló, P., Fagin, R., Libkin, L.: Locally consistent transformations and query answering in data exchange. In: PODS, pp. 229–240 (2004)
3. Baeza-Yates, R., Ribeiro-Neto, B.: Modern Information Retrieval. ACM Press Books, Addison Wesley, New York (1999)
4. Chandra, A., Harel, D.: Structure and complexity of relational queries. J. Comput. Syst. Sci. **25**, 99–128 (1982)
5. Chaudhuri, S., Dayal, U.: An overview of data warehousing and OLAP technology. SIGMOD Rec. **26**(1), 65–74 (1997)
6. Cuzzocrea, A., Saccà, D., Ullman, J.D.: *Panel on* big data: a research agenda. In: IDEAS, pp. 198–203 (2013)
7. The Economist: Data, data everywhere. The Economist, February 2010
8. Faber, W., Pfeifer, G., Leone, N., Dell'Armi, T., Ielpa, G.: Design and implementation of aggregate functions in the DLV system. TPLP **8**(5–6), 545–580 (2008)
9. Fagin, R., Kolaitis, P.G., Popa, L.: Data exchange: getting to the core. ACM Trans. Database Syst. **30**(1), 174–210 (2005)
10. Guzzo, A., Moccia, L., Saccà, D., Serra, E.: Solving inverse frequent itemset mining with infrequency constraints via large-scale linear programs. TKDD **7**(4) 18 (2013)
11. Han, J., Micheline Kamber, J.P.: Data Mining: Concepts and Techniques. Morgan Kaufmann Publishers, Burlington (2011)
12. Manyika, J., Chui, M., Brown, B., Bughin, J., Dobbs, R., Roxburgh, C., Byers, A.H.: Big data: the next frontier for innovation, competition, and productivity. McKinsey Global Institute, May 2011
13. Moens, M.: Automatic Indexing and Abstracting of Document Texts. Kluwer Academic Publishers, Berlin (2000)
14. Nature: Big data. Nature, September 2008
15. Osinski, S., Stefanowski, J., Weiss, D.: Lingo search results clustering algorithm based on singular value decomposition. In: Kłopotek, M.A., Wierzchoń, S.T., Trojanowski, K. (eds.) Intelligent Information Processing and Web Mining, vol. 25, pp. 359–368. Springer, Heidelberg (2004)
16. Saccà, D., Serra, E.: Data posting: a new frontier for data exchange in the big data era. In: AMW (2013)
17. Saccà, D., Serra, E., Guzzo, A.: Count constraints and the inverse OLAP problem: definition, complexity and a step toward aggregate data exchange. In: Lukasiewicz, T., Sali, A. (eds.) FoIKS 2012. LNCS, vol. 7153, pp. 352–369. Springer, Heidelberg (2012)
18. Vardi, M.Y.: The complexity of relational query languages. In: STOC, pp. 137–146 (1982)
19. White, R.W., Roth, R.A.: Exploratory Search: Beyond the Query-Response Paradigm: Synthesis Lectures on Information Concepts Retrieval, and Services. Morgan & Claypool Publishers, San Rafael (2009)
20. Yee, K.P., Swearingen, K., Li, K., Hearst, M.: Faceted metadata for image search and browsing. In: Proceedings of the SIGCHI Conference on Human Factors in Computing Systems, CHI 2003, pp. 401–408 (2003)

Rule Induction and Learning

PRIMER – A Regression-Rule Learning System for Intervention Optimization

Greg Harris[1]([✉]), Anand Panangadan[2], and Viktor K. Prasanna[3]

[1] Department of Computer Science, University of Southern California,
Los Angeles, CA, USA
gfharris@usc.edu
[2] Department of Computer Science, California State University, Fullerton, CA, USA
apanangadan@fullerton.edu
[3] Ming-Hsieh Department of Electrical Engineering,
University of Southern California, Los Angeles, CA, USA
prasanna@usc.edu

Abstract. We introduce intervention optimization as a new area of exploration for data mining research. Interventions are events designed to impact a corresponding time series. The task is to maximize the impact of such events by training a model on historical data. We propose PRIMER as a new regression-rule learning system for identifying sets of event features that maximize impact. PRIMER is for use when domain experts with knowledge of the intervention can specify a transfer function, or the form of the expected response in the time series. PRIMER's objective function includes the goodness-of-fit of the average response of covered events to the transfer function. Incorporating domain knowledge in this way makes PRIMER robust to over-fitting on noise or spurious responses. PRIMER is designed to produce interpretable results, improving on the interpretability of even competing regression-rule systems for this task. It also has fewer and more intuitive parameters than competing rule-based systems. Empirically, we show that PRIMER is competitive with state-of-the-art regression techniques in a large-scale event study modeling the impact of insider trading on intra-day stock returns.

Keywords: Regression rules · Intervention analysis · Rule induction · Event response · Time series · Intervention optimization · Rule learning

1 Introduction

Intervention analysis was introduced in 1975 by Box and Tiao [1] as a means of assessing the impact of a special event on a time series. In one example, they evaluate whether gasoline regulation in 1960 impacted smog levels in Los Angeles. The effect is not obvious in the noisy graph of monthly smog levels. However, their method is able to quantify even weak effects in such noisy time series. Their method has three steps:

© Springer International Publishing Switzerland 2016
J.J. Alferes et al. (Eds.): RuleML 2016, LNCS 9718, pp. 307–321, 2016.
DOI: 10.1007/978-3-319-42019-6_20

1. Identification – frame a model for change which describes what is expected to occur given knowledge of the known intervention;
2. Fitting – work out the appropriate data analysis based on that model;
3. Diagnostic Checking – if the model proves inadequate for inference, make necessary adjustments and repeat the analysis.

1.1 Intervention Optimization

Our research extends intervention analysis from the case of one event to the case of many events. The goal is to reliably predict which events will have the highest *impact* (defined later in this section) on their corresponding time series. We call this *intervention optimization* and have not found it previously discussed in data-mining literature. An example use-case is optimizing the impact of advertising campaigns on same-store sales for a retail business. In this case, the events include various kinds of advertising campaigns, such as locally airing a television ad or mailing fliers. Each event is expected to affect a corresponding time series, in this case, sales at the targeted store location. Another example use-case is optimizing cyclic steam injection for enhanced oil recovery in highly viscous oil fields. Pausing production periodically to send steam down an oil well warms the surrounding oil, making it easier to extract once pumping resumes. The increase in production depends on the well, the reservoir, and the characteristics of the steam job. Intervention optimization is useful in these use-cases, because it helps maximize the impact of limited resources (ad budget or steam supply).

Intervention optimization requires training a model that predicts the impact of an event based on a set of descriptive features. Modeling the highest-impact events is challenging due to the propensity to over-fit. Models that make inferences based on too-few historical high-impact examples can have low out-of-sample accuracy. Additionally, over-fitting can be caused by noise in the time series, which affects the estimation of impact. PRIMER, the intervention optimization system we propose, adapts to noisy time series by requiring more samples for inference. We evaluate PRIMER and other modeling techniques by the average impact of their top-predicted $x\%$ of intervention events, using held-out data and given only the features describing each event. The same techniques can be applied to general event studies where one has no direct control over the events, but would still benefit from a predictive or explanatory impact model.

We define the *impact* of an event as the cumulative subsequent "boost" in time series values caused by the event. Concretely, we assume a given event E occurs at time t_0 and is expected to affect time series R of realized values. In our notation, R_t refers to the value of R at time index t. The first value of R subject to the influence of E is R_{t_0}, and the value one time step after the event is R_{t_0+1}. We first calculate a baseline time series B of expected values had the event not occurred. In the simplest case, $B_t = R_{t_0-1}, \forall t : t \geq t_0$, which assumes the time series would have simply remained at the last known pre-event level. In more complex cases, B must be determined from a domain-specific model, including considerations such as autocorrelation and seasonality. We define S such that:

$$S_t = R_t - B_t \tag{1}$$

making it the unexplained residual after all known effects unrelated to E have been removed from R. If E were to have no impact, then the expectation $\mathbf{E}[S] = 0$. Finally, we define the impact of E on S over a finite period (n time steps) as:

$$impact_E(S) = \sum_{t=t_0}^{t_0+n-1} S_t \qquad (2)$$

We assume the effect of E begins at t_0, meaning the event is unanticipated in the time series: $B_t = R_t, \forall t : t < t_0$.

1.2 Interpretability

Modeling impact as a function of input variables is a regression problem, and we include state-of-the-art regression algorithms in the experiments in Sect. 4. However, our interest is in interpretable models which more easily provide insight to the user. For this reason, we also evaluate regression-rule learning algorithms, which are designed to emphasize interpretability over accuracy. Regression-rules are simple piece-wise constant models, taking the form:

$$(F_1 \wedge F_2 \wedge F_3) \longrightarrow C$$

This is understood to mean that an event containing features F_1, F_2, and F_3 would have a predicted impact of C. Some systems generate ordered rule lists where the predicted value of a sample comes from the first rule that *covers* it, meaning the first rule where the sample contains all the rule features [2,14,15]. Other systems generate unordered ensembles of rules, where *all* rules that cover a sample provide an additive contribution to the overall prediction [5].

Currently-proposed regression-rule learning systems are not specifically designed to produce rules easily interpretable for the task of intervention optimization. The ideal set of rules for this task should be:

- short, covering only the highest-impact events
- sorted in descending order of predicted impact
- free of exceptions or caveats to the predictions

Current systems do not produce rule sets with these attributes. Ensemble-based systems produce rule sets which cannot be shortened without affecting the predictions. Ensemble rule sets can be sorted in descending order of impact contribution to improve interpretability, but caveats remain in the form of rules with negative impact contribution. For example, a rule with features F_1 and F_2 may have a high impact contribution, but another rule with only feature F_1 may have a negative impact contribution. Therefore, a user cannot reliably identify high-impact events by simply remembering the high-impact rules. Likewise, ordered rule lists generated by current systems are complicated by exceptions. The rules are not ordered according to impact, but are ordered according to how well they reduce a loss function such as mean squared error. The rule lists cannot be re-sorted by impact, because the order of precedence must be maintained for accurate predictions. For example, a high-impact rule in the middle of the list with feature F_1 may be preempted by an earlier low-impact rule with feature F_2. So, a user cannot simply say that events with feature F_1 will have high impact, without also mentioning the exception for events that also contain feature F_2.

PRIMER is a rule-based system designed specifically to generate interpretable rules for intervention optimization. The rule lists generated by PRIMER are ordered according to expected impact. The user can review and retain only as many rules as needed to cover a sufficient number of events. Because of the rule ordering, predictions can be interpreted as minimum predictions. There is no concern about exceptions, because earlier rules in the list have predictions at least as high.

The requirement of using interpretable models sometimes means accepting lower accuracy. PRIMER, however, is able to maintain high accuracy by taking advantage of domain knowledge specific to the task of intervention optimization. The domain knowledge provided by the user is the functional form of the expected response pattern. By knowing the expected pattern to find in the time series, PRIMER is better able to disregard spurious fluctuations and noise. In this paper, we limit our scope to response patterns that exhibit a strong initial response that decays following the event, until eventually the effect has dissipated. The two example use-cases mentioned both have this form of response pattern. In the retail business use-case, the effect of an ad is likely to be strongest initially, before it slowly gets forgotten. In the oil recovery use-case, production is highest immediately after steam injection. As the oil cools, production gradually decays back to its original level.

PRIMER has a unique objective function designed specifically for intervention optimization. It combines three heuristics to improve out-of-sample performance: impact, coverage, and goodness-of-fit to the expected response pattern. We show its effectiveness in a large-scale event study modeling the impact of insider trading filings on intra-day stock returns. The study of market reactions to news, and filings in particular, is an active area of research in Behavioral Finance [16,20]. PRIMER has the capability of providing insight into which filing characteristics most influence the market. In our tests, we show that PRIMER is competitive with state-of-the-art regression algorithms at identifying high-impact filings, while the model output has improved interpretability.

2   Related Work

Intervention optimization is a regression problem, and we include common regression models in our experiments. Due to our emphasis on model interpretability, however, we describe only other regression-rule learning systems in this related work section:

REGENDER [5] is a system for learning an ensemble of regression rules using forward stage-wise additive modeling. Each rule is added greedily, one by one. The rules are chosen to minimize a loss function, which is either the sum of squared error or the sum of absolute error, calculated over all samples.

The number of rules to learn is an input to the algorithm which acts as the stopping criterion. The minimization technique can be specified as either gradient boosting or a least angle approach. To reduce correlation between rules as well as computational complexity, the training of each rule is done using a random subset of the training data. The fraction of samples to use for training is an input to the algorithm. The final parameter is a shrinkage factor which reduces the degree to which previously generated rules affect the generation of the successive one in the sequence. The algorithm outputs an unordered list of rules. The prediction for a given sample is calculated by summing the contributions of all rules that cover the sample.

SeCoReg [14] is a regression rule system based on the separate-and-conquer strategy [8]. The algorithm uses hill-climbing to find each rule. The objective function maximized by hill-climbing is a weighted combination of the relative root mean squared error and the relative coverage:

$$h_{cm} = \alpha \cdot (1 - L_{RRMSE}) + (1 - \alpha) \cdot relCov \qquad (3)$$

Here, the parameter α controls the trade-off between error and coverage. The stopping criterion for the algorithm is set as the fraction of samples that can be left uncovered by the rules learned. A third user-specified parameter controls the number of splitpoints found by a supervised clustering algorithm for discretizing numeric features.

Ant-Miner-Reg [2] is a version of SeCoReg with hill-climbing replaced by Ant Colony Optimization. It requires three additional user-specified parameters to control the optimization.

Dynamic Reduction to Classification [15] is a method of converting a regression problem into a multi-class classification problem. This enables the use of well-studied classification rule induction techniques. For each rule, the predicted value is the median of the values covered. The rule quality is measured by how well it identifies samples valued within one standard deviation of the predicted value. Samples valued within one standard deviation of the predicted value are set as the positive class, and all other values outside this range are considered negative. In this way, traditional classification rule heuristics can be used as an objective function. The heuristics tested by its authors include: correlation, relative cost measure, Laplace measure, and weighted relative accuracy. The algorithm uses separate-and-conquer combined with hill-climbing. The stopping criterion for the algorithm is the fraction of samples that can be left uncovered by the rules learned.

M5'Rules [12] learns rules that have a linear model in the head instead of a constant prediction. The algorithm uses separate-and-conquer to learn the set of rules, stopping when all samples are covered. Each rule is learned by first generating a decision tree and then extracting the rule corresponding to the best leaf. The best leaf is determined according to a heuristic. Its authors tested three heuristics: percent root mean squared error, mean absolute error divided by coverage, and the correlation between predicted and actual values for samples covered by a leaf multiplied by the number of samples in the leaf.

3 PRIMER

We propose a new method for intervention optimization: Pattern-specific Rule-based Intervention analysis Maximizing Event Response (PRIMER). In this section, we refer to Algorithm 1 as we describe each part of the method.

The inputs to PRIMER, as shown in Algorithm 1, include a set of events. Each event contains a descriptive set of binary features. Each also contains the corresponding response, which is a short time series segment beginning with the event at time t_0 and lasting until the impact of the event has substantially decayed. The event response is a sub-sequence of S, defined in Eq. 1.

3.1 Separate-and-Conquer with Beam Search

PRIMER uses the separate-and-conquer strategy [8] common to most rule learning systems. This strategy iteratively identifies the events not yet covered by any rule (separate), and then learns a new rule using only the uncovered events (conquer). The new rule covers additional events, which are then removed from consideration in the next iteration. This guarantees subsequent rules have diversity in coverage. Lines 1–7 in Algorithm 1 describe our implementation of this strategy. This loop is repeated until rules are discovered that cover all events, or until the empty rule is returned because no better rule could be found.

To find each new rule, PRIMER uses top-down beam search. Beam search is a greedy heuristic search method which is used by the vast majority of rule learning algorithms [9]. It finds good rules quickly, while covering only a small fraction of the search space. Beam search starts with an empty rule that covers all samples and greedily refines it by adding features as conditions. It maintains a beam of the best b rules of each rule length. To find rules of length l, each feature is successively added as a refinement to each rule in the beam for length $l - 1$. The refined candidate rules are then evaluated, and the top b rules are stored in the beam for length l. After reaching some stopping criterion, the best rule from all lengths is selected.

Limiting the beam size limits the extent of the search. Setting $b = 1$ makes beam search equivalent to hill-climbing. Setting $b = \infty$ makes it equivalent to exhaustive search. PRIMER implements top-down beam search in the FINDBESTRULE function (lines 8–21). The function returns the single highest-scoring rule discovered during the search.

3.2 Objective Function

During beam search, each candidate rule is evaluated and scored by an objective function. PRIMER's unique objective function combines three heuristics to improve out-of-sample performance: impact, goodness-of-fit, and coverage.

Impact. The goal of intervention optimization is to maximize the impact of future interventions. We evaluate rules according to the average impact of the out-of-sample events they cover, so historical impact is naturally an important heuristic. For rule evaluation, the impact for an event is defined in Eq. 2. During model training, however, PRIMER optimizes only on impact that fits the expected response pattern given by a user with domain expertise. This helps avoid over-fitting to noise or spurious fluctuations in the time series.

The key to the intervention analysis method proposed by Box and Tiao [1] is specifying the expected response pattern. Their method is able to quantify weak effects in noisy time series by relying on the use of a *transfer function*, a tentative specification of the stochastic model form. The transfer function is based on prior knowledge of the intervention, and how the time series is expected to react. Some example transfer functions they listed include linear, pulse, and step functions. PRIMER inherits the use of a transfer function from their work on intervention analysis.

With PRIMER, we have tested response patterns that exhibit an abrupt initial response at time t_0 which decays back down to the pre-intervention level within n time steps. Specifically, we have tested the exponential decay function:

$$f(t) = Ae^{-k(t-1)}, \quad t \geq 1 \tag{4}$$

and the power law function:

$$f(t) = At^{-k}, \quad t \geq 1 \tag{5}$$

In both cases, A is the scaling parameter, and k determines the rate of decay. Restricting the impact to only include the fitted area under the transfer function curve makes the algorithm more robust by down-weighting, for example, spurious spikes that occur well after t_0.

The first step in calculating the fitted impact of a rule is to average the responses of all events covered by the rule ($avgResponse$ in line 23 of Algorithm 1). The next step is to fit the transfer function to the average response by minimizing the sum of squared differences:

$$\underset{A,k}{\text{minimize}} \quad \sum_{t=1}^{n}(f(t) - avgResponse_t)^2 \tag{6}$$

$$\text{subject to} \quad A, k \geq 0$$

We use the trust-region-reflective optimization algorithm [4], which allows us to specify lower bound constraints of zero on the fit parameters.

Goodness-of-Fit. In PRIMER, we score each rule conservatively, based on the goodness-of-fit of the average response to the transfer function. In line 24 of Algorithm 1, we calculate confidence intervals for the fit parameters optimized in Eq. 6. We calculate the confidence intervals based on the asymptotic normal distribution for the parameter estimates [19]. The level of confidence used in the interval calculation is a user-specified parameter, α, which produces $100 \cdot (1 - \alpha)$ percent confidence intervals.

In line 28 of Algorithm 1, we choose the more conservative values from the confidence intervals for each fit parameter. For the scale parameter A in the exponential decay transfer function (Eq. 4) and the power law transfer function (Eq. 5), we use the lower bound confidence interval. For the rate of decay parameter k, we use the upper bound confidence interval. We calculate the rule score as the area under the transfer function using the conservative confidence interval values for parameters (line 29). This score is lower than the fitted impact due to the reduced scale and increased rate of decay. This penalizes rules with poorly-fitting average response curves which would otherwise have had high impact according to the fitted parameters.

We also use the confidence intervals as a stopping criterion. If both parameters are not significantly greater than zero according to the confidence intervals, the rule is given a score of zero. If no rule can be found with a score greater than zero, the default empty rule is chosen by the beam search, since it has been assigned a small positive score (line 10). The empty rule has no conditions and covers all remaining samples, causing the separate-and-conquer loop to terminate.

Coverage. PRIMER includes a bias toward rules with high coverage. This trade-off of impact for coverage in the objective function has the potential to improve out-of-sample performance, because high-coverage rules are less prone to over-fitting.

Due to random noise in the time series, an individual event response is unlikely to closely resemble the transfer function. A rule that covers only a small number of events will have a noisy average response. As discussed previously, a poor fit of the average response to the transfer function reduces the rule score, possibly to zero. A rule that covers many events will have a well-behaved average response where the random noise averages out. With less noise, the fit becomes better, and the rule score increases. In this way, high-coverage rules are favored. The trade-off between coverage and impact is controlled by the parameter α, which was introduced in the previous section. High α equates to low-confidence bounds, which are close to the least squares fit parameters. Inversely, low α increases confidence that the true parameters are within the intervals by widening the intervals. Effectively, lowering α reduces tolerance for noisy average responses, which then increases the bias toward rules with less noise; and rules with less noise tend to be rules with higher coverage.

Figure 1 illustrates how increasing coverage increases the score for a rule on synthetic data. This plot involves samples with the same power law decay response added to noisy time series. Adding samples smooths the average response, which raises the lower bound on the fitted curve.

Algorithm 1. PRIMER

Input:

events	▷ set of events or interventions
event.features	▷ each event has a set of descriptive features
event.response	▷ time series segment starting at the time of the event
b	▷ beam size
l	▷ max rule length
T	▷ transfer function
α	▷ alpha for calculating fit parameter confidence intervals

Output:

ruleList	▷ ordered list of discovered rules

1: *ruleList* ← [ ] ▷ initialize empty rule list
2: **repeat**
3:    *rule* ← FINDBESTRULE(*events, b, l, T, α*)
4:    *ruleList*.append(*rule*)
5:    *coveredEvents* ← events in *events* covered by *rule*
6:    *events* ← *events* \ *coveredEvents*
7: **until** *events* = ∅

8: **function** FINDBESTRULE(*events, b, l, T, α*)
9:    *emptyRule.conditions* ← {} ▷ empty rule has no conditions, covers all events
10:    *emptyRule.score* ← ε ▷ a tiny score makes it rank higher than 0-score rules
11:    *beam* ← [ ] ▷ *beam* is an array of rule lists
            ▷ *beam*[2] holds a list of length-2 rules, etc.
12:    *beam*[0] ← [*emptyRule*] ▷ initialize length-0 rule list to hold the empty rule
13:    **for** $i = 1$ to l **do**
14:       *rules* ← all refinements to rules in *beam*[$i - 1$]
15:       **for each** *rule* ∈ *rules* **do**
16:          *rule.score* ← EVALUATERULE(*rule, events, T, α*)
17:       **end for**
18:       *beam*[i] ← BEST(*rules, b*) ▷ keep b best rules of length i
19:    **end for**
20:    **return** best rule in all of *beam*
21: **end function**

22: **function** EVALUATERULE(*rule, events, T, α*)
23:    *avgResponse* ← average response of events covered by *rule*
24:    *ci* ← calculate parameter confidence intervals of T fitted to *avgResponse*
25:    **if** $\min(ci) \le 0$ **then**
26:       $score = 0$ ▷ because a parameter is not significantly different from zero
27:    **else**
28:       p_{min} ← MINAUC(*ci*) ▷ for each parameter, choose the value from
            ▷ *ci* that minimizes the area under the curve
29:       *score* ← AUC(T, p_{min}) ▷ smallest confident area under the curve
30:    **end if**
31:    **return** *score*
32: **end function**

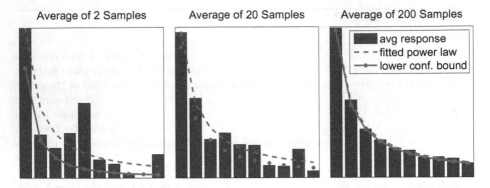

Fig. 1. Illustration using synthetic data, where each response sample is generated using the power law function with white noise added. Averaging many samples improves the goodness-of-fit, raising the lower confidence bound and increasing the score of a rule.

4   Experiments

We evaluate PRIMER on readily available data from the U.S. financial markets. Our objective is to predict which insider trading reports have the largest positive effect on intra-day stock prices. We cannot influence such financial news, so this use-case is not true intervention optimization. However, as an event study, we can evaluate PRIMER's ability to identify high-impact events.

4.1   Data

Events. For events, we use Form-4 regulatory filings disseminated by the U.S. Securities and Exchange Commission[1]. Form-4 filings are submitted by insiders (officers, directors, etc.) in publicly traded companies to disclose changes in personal ownership of company shares. We filter these down to include only purchases of common stock, which are considered more informative by analysts and market participants than sales. Insiders may sell for a variety of uninformative reasons, including diversification and raising cash for personal reasons, whereas they buy primarily because they believe company shares will rise in value. We further filter the filings down to just those that become public during business hours when the markets are open. This allows us to measure the intra-day response to each filing. Each filing has such features as:

- the insider type: director, officer, 10 % owner, or other
- the total dollar value of direct purchases, discretized
- the total dollar value of indirect purchases, discretized
- various transaction codes

We also include the market capitalization of the company prior to the filing, discretized. Our final set of events has 136 binary features covering 158,983 events from years 2004–2014.

---

[1] ftp://ftp.sec.gov/edgar/Feed/.

Time Series. For time series, we use stock returns of the company associated with each filing. We use tick data provided by Wharton Research Data Services[2]. We pre-process the data by converting it to 5-min bars, creating a time series P of the last traded price within each 5-min time period. The return time series is calculated as:

$$S_t = \frac{P_t - P_{t-1}}{P_{t-1}} \tag{7}$$

The event response listed as an input in Algorithm 1 is the length-10 sub-sequence of S beginning with the first return affected by the event:

$$event.response = [S_{t_0}, S_{t_0+1}, \ldots, S_{t_0+8}, S_{t_0+9}] \tag{8}$$

In cases with insufficient trades to calculate each bar of the response, the event is removed from the dataset. The total response is the target variable to be maximized by PRIMER.

4.2   PRIMER Settings

We choose a transfer function based on prior knowledge that the financial markets respond positively to insider purchases, and that the effect of the news decays once the information is fully disseminated and acted upon by market participants. We choose the power law decay transfer function over the exponential decay function, because it more closely fits the average response of all events in the dataset.

The parameter b for beam size varies the extent of search. For the entire experiment, we use $b = 5$. This value has been commonly used in rule learning [3,17]. Similarly low values of b have been shown to often out-perform large values when tested out-of-sample [13,18].

The parameter l constrains the maximum rule length. We set $l = 10$ for the entire experiment, a value we believe is high enough to impose minimal constraint.

The parameter α determines the confidence intervals. A low value means more emphasis on the goodness-of-fit heuristic. If the value is too low, few rules will be discovered. We experiment with three values: $\alpha = \{0.1, 0.2, 0.3\}$.

4.3   Evaluation Method

Evaluation is based on the average impact (average sum of return bars) as a function of the percent of test data covered. First, test events are sorted in descending order according to predicted impact. Then the average actual impact is calculated using the top $x\%$ of events, for $x = 1 \ldots 100$. Models are preferred which best predict the highest impact events for each given coverage percentile.

---

[2] https://wrds-web.wharton.upenn.edu/wrds/.

All experiments are evaluated using 10-fold cross-validation, where each model is trained on 90 % of the data and tested on the remaining 10 %. This is performed ten times, once for each test partition, and the results are averaged. All models are evaluated using the same ten randomly partitioned folds. For some models, we optimize a hyper-parameter by further use of 10-fold cross validation in an inner-loop. For each fold of the outer-loop, once the hyper-parameter value is chosen, it is used to train a model on the full set of training data in the fold. In total, for a model with one hyper-parameter, we run the training 110 times on subsets of data.

4.4   Baselines for Comparison

We compare PRIMER with common regression models as well as state-of-the-art regression rule learning algorithms:

- **Ridge Regression.** For linear regression with L_2-norm regularization, we use the MATLAB function `ridge`, in conjunction with cross-validation to find the optimal value for the regularization parameter, out of values: $\lambda = \{10^{-4}, 10^{-3}, \ldots, 10^5, 10^6\}$.
- **LASSO.** For linear regression with L_1-norm regularization, we use the MAT-LAB function `lasso`, which has built-in cross-validation [7]. For λ, we set the function to use a geometric sequence of ten values, the largest just sufficient to produce a model with all zeros.
- **Support Vector Regression.** For linear L_2-regularized Support Vector Regression [11], we use `liblinear` [6]. We use cross-validation to find the optimal value for the cost parameter, out of values: $c = \{10^{-4}, 10^{-3}, \ldots, 10^3, 10^4\}$.
- **RegENDER.** Regression Ensemble of Decision Rules (REGENDER) is available as a Java library which integrates with the Weka data-mining environment [10]. We run it with the parameters recommended by the authors (gradient boosting, squared-error loss function, 200 rules, $\nu = 0.5$, with resampling set to 50 % drawn without replacement) [5]. We also run it with the default parameters in Weka, which have three differences (simultaneous minimization, 100 rules, and $\nu = 1.0$).
- **M5'Rules.** We use the implementation of M5'Rules [12] included with Weka. We use the default parameters (minimum number of instances = 4, build regression tree = false, unpruned = false, use unsmoothed = false).
- **Dynamic Reduction to Classification.** Dynamic Reduction to Classification [15] also integrates with Weka. We tried numerous heuristics and found Laplace to be the best. We tried using a minimum coverage of 90 % as recommended by the authors, but found that using 100 % worked better for our dataset. In this case, we report results only for the best settings.
- **SeCoReg.** Separate-and-Conquer Regression (SeCoReg) [14] testing was inconclusive. We confirmed that the recommended parameters ($\alpha = 0.591$, minimum coverage of 90 %) worked well on small datasets. However, our dataset is too large, and we did not wait for completion.

5 Results

Table 1 and Fig. 2 both show the test results. No model performed significantly better than all others over the entire set of coverage levels. REGENDER, using its authors' recommended parameters, has the best overall performance. However, several models have similar performance, including PRIMER.

Table 1. Average total response of the events covered by the top $x\%$ of predictions of each model (top 1 %, top 5 %, etc.)

Algorithm	Average response of $x\%$ of top predictions				
	1 %	5 %	10 %	25 %	50 %
PRIMER, $\alpha = 0.1$	0.0207	0.0142	0.0099	0.0045	0.0023
PRIMER, $\alpha = 0.2$	0.0203	0.0142	0.0100	0.0046	0.0023
PRIMER, $\alpha = 0.3$	0.0204	0.0141	**0.0101**	0.0046	0.0024
Ridge regression	0.0202	0.0136	0.0097	0.0047	0.0024
LASSO	0.0202	0.0129	0.0098	0.0047	0.0024
Support vector regression	0.0161	0.0126	0.0087	0.0042	0.0023
REGENDER (authors)	**0.0214**	**0.0145**	0.0100	**0.0049**	0.0025
REGENDER (Weka)	0.0208	0.0143	0.0100	0.0049	**0.0025**
M5'Rules	0.0203	0.0141	0.0098	0.0049	0.0025
Dynamic reduction	0.0198	0.0128	0.0084	0.0040	0.0022

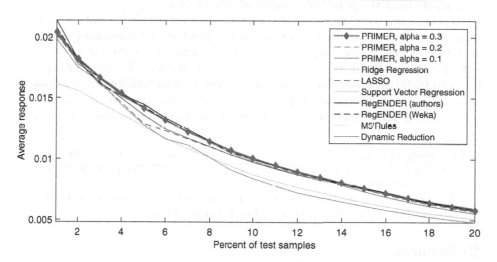

Fig. 2. Average total response of the events covered by the top $x\%$ of predictions. PRIMER is highlighted to show it is competitive with state-of-the-art models. (Color figure online)

6 Discussion

PRIMER may not work with every dataset. Ideally, the average response of the full set of events closely fits the given transfer function, despite the diluted average impact. Because PRIMER uses greedy search, an average response sufficiently fitting the transfer function must be located at least within the first search iteration (length-1 rule). Otherwise, the program will exit with only the default rule. For best results, there must be a greedy path through the search tree to find high-impact branches. The decay patterns we have studied work well in this regard. The average of two exponential decay functions is another exponential decay function if the decay parameters are the same and only the scale parameters differ. The same is true for power law functions. Even when the decay parameters are not the same, the average of two decay functions often resembles another decay function closely enough for greedy search to work.

7 Conclusion

The results of our experiments show that, with respect to impact prediction ranking, PRIMER is competitive with state-of-the-art regression techniques in a large financial event study. One advantage of using PRIMER is in the interpretability of the model. PRIMER outputs a list of rules ordered by predicted impact. This allows the top rules to stand alone without exceptions or caveats. It also allows the algorithm to be terminated early, once a sufficient number of the highest-impact rules are found. This is useful in domains where resource constraints limit the potential number of interventions.

Rule learning systems require the user to specify multiple critical operational parameters. The optimal values are domain-dependent, yet domain experts have no intuitive way of selecting values, except through trial-and-error or by using default values. PRIMER has an advantage in this regard. The most critical user input to PRIMER is the transfer function, which is likely well-known to a domain expert. The confidence interval parameter, α, has some effect on the number of rules learned. Experimental results, however, show relative insensitivity to α.

Acknowledgments. This work is supported by Chevron USA, Inc. under the joint project Center for Interactive Smart Oilfield Technologies (CiSoft), at the University of Southern California.

We would also like to thank Dr. Frederik Janssen for providing support with the SeCoReg and Dynamic Reduction to Regression algorithms.

References

1. Box, G.E.P., Tiao, G.C.: Intervention analysis with applications to economic and environmental problems. J. Am. Stat. Assoc. **70**(349), 70–79 (1975)
2. Brookhouse, J., Otero, F.E.B.: Discovering regression rules with ant colony optimization. In: Proceedings of the Companion Publication of the 2015 Annual Conference on Genetic and Evolutionary Computation, GECCO Companion 2015, pp. 1005–1012. ACM, New York (2015)

3. Clark, P., Niblett, T.: The CN2 induction algorithm. Mach. Learn. **3**(4), 261–283 (1989)
4. Coleman, T.F., Li, Y.: A reflective Newton method for minimizing a quadratic function subject to bounds on some of the variables. SIAM J. Optim. **6**(4), 1040–1058 (1996)
5. Dembczyński, K., Kotłowski, W., Słowiński, R.: Solving regression by learning an ensemble of decision rules. In: Rutkowski, L., Tadeusiewicz, R., Zadeh, L.A., Zurada, J.M. (eds.) ICAISC 2008. LNCS (LNAI), vol. 5097, pp. 533–544. Springer, Heidelberg (2008)
6. Fan, R.-E., Chang, K.-W., Hsieh, C.-J., Wang, X.-R., Lin, C.-J.: LIBLINEAR: a library for large linear classification. J. Mach. Learn. Res. **9**, 1871–1874 (2008)
7. Friedman, J., Hastie, T., Tibshirani, R.: Regularization paths for generalized linear models via coordinate descent. J. Stat. Softw. **33**(1), 1 (2010)
8. Fürnkranz, J.: Separate-and-conquer rule learning. Artif. Intell. Rev. **13**(1), 3–54 (1999)
9. Fürnkranz, J., Gamberger, D., Lavrač, N.: Foundations of Rule Learning. Springer Science & Business Media, Heidelberg (2012)
10. Hall, M., Frank, E., Holmes, G., Pfahringer, B., Reutemann, P., Witten, I.H.: The WEKA data mining software: an update. ACM SIGKDD Explor. Newsl. **11**(1), 10–18 (2009)
11. Ho, C.-H., Lin, C.-J.: Large-scale linear support vector regression. J. Mach. Learn. Res. **13**(1), 3323–3348 (2012)
12. Holmes, G., Hall, M., Prank, E.: Generating rule sets from model trees. In: Foo, N.Y. (ed.) AI 1999. LNCS, vol. 1747, pp. 1–12. Springer, Heidelberg (1999)
13. Janssen, F., Fürnkranz, J.: A re-evaluation of the over-searching phenomenon in inductive rule learning. In: SDM, pp. 329–340. SIAM (2009)
14. Janssen, F., Fürnkranz, J.: Separate-and-conquer regression. In: Proceedings of LWA 2010: Lernen, Wissen, Adaptivität, Kassel, Germany, pp. 81–89 (2010)
15. Janssen, F., Fürnkranz, J.: Heuristic rule-based regression via dynamic reduction to classification. In: IJCAI Proceedings-International Joint Conference on Artificial Intelligence, vol. 22, p. 1330 (2011)
16. Li, E.X., Ramesh, K.: Market reaction surrounding the filing of periodic SEC reports. Acc. Rev. **84**(4), 1171–1208 (2009)
17. Možina, M., Demšar, J., Žabkar, J., Bratko, I.: Why is rule learning optimistic and how to correct it. In: Fürnkranz, J., Scheffer, T., Spiliopoulou, M. (eds.) ECML 2006. LNCS (LNAI), vol. 4212, pp. 330–340. Springer, Heidelberg (2006)
18. Quinlan, J., Cameron-Jones, R.: Oversearching and layered search in empirical learning. Breast Cancer **286**, 2–7 (1995)
19. Seber, G.A.F., Wild, C.J.: Nonlinear Regression. Wiley, New York (1989)
20. You, H., Zhang, X.J.: Financial reporting complexity and investor underreaction to 10-K information. Rev. Acc. Stud. **14**(4), 559–586 (2009)

Event Driven Architectures and Active Database Systems

Rule-Based Real-Time ADL Recognition in a Smart Home Environment

George Baryannis[1](✉), Przemyslaw Woznowski[2], and Grigoris Antoniou[1]

[1] Department of Informatics, University of Huddersfield, Huddersfield, UK
{g.bargiannis,g.antoniou}@hud.ac.uk
[2] Faculty of Engineering, University of Bristol, Bristol, UK
p.r.woznowski@bristol.ac.uk

Abstract. This paper presents a rule-based approach for both offline and real-time recognition of Activities of Daily Living (ADL), leveraging events produced by a non-intrusive multi-modal sensor infrastructure deployed in a residential environment. Novel aspects of the approach include: the ability to recognise arbitrary scenarios of complex activities using bottom-up multi-level reasoning, starting from sensor events at the lowest level; an effective heuristics-based method for distinguishing between actual and ghost images in video data; and a highly accurate indoor localisation approach that fuses different sources of location information. The proposed approach is implemented as a rule-based system using Jess and is evaluated using data collected in a smart home environment. Experimental results show high levels of accuracy and performance, proving the effectiveness of the approach in real world setups.

Keywords: Event driven architectures · Activity recognition · ADL · Indoor localisation · Smart home · Multi-modal sensing

1 Introduction

In the last two decades sensors have become cheaper, smaller and widely available, residing at the edge of the Internet. A single sensor provides only partial information on the actual physical condition measured, e.g. an acoustic sensor only records audio signals. A single measurement may be useful for simple applications, such as temperature monitoring in a smart home and may be sufficient to discover very simple events, such as fire detection. However, it is often insufficient for an automated *Activity Recognition (AR)* system to infer all simple and complex events taking place in the area of interest. Therefore, a fusion of multiple sensor-related, low-level events is necessary.

The Internet of Things (IoT) paradigm offers an effective way of acquiring and delivering low-level sensor events. The strength of IoT lies in the foundations of the Internet i.e. distribution of resources, support for common naming schemas and ontologies, common access strategies and availability of computational resources, to mention a few. The challenge is to locate and fuse the

© Springer International Publishing Switzerland 2016
J.J. Alferes et al. (Eds.): RuleML 2016, LNCS 9718, pp. 325–340, 2016.
DOI: 10.1007/978-3-319-42019-6_21

right pieces of (sensor) information in order to realise AR at the best quality of information possible. There are multiple ways of approaching sensor-based AR. Chen and Khalil [3] propose a broad categorisation into data-driven approaches, exploiting machine learning techniques, and knowledge-driven approaches, leveraging logical modelling and reasoning. Both directions have their strengths and weaknesses. Machine learning techniques are criticised for not handling data conflicts well and for requiring large, annotated training datasets, while logic-based approaches are not as robust against noise and uncertainty and require carefully crafted rules.

In a multi-modal smart home environment AR usually focuses on the so-called *Activities of Daily Living (ADL)*, with the purpose of supporting *Ambient Assisted Living (AAL)* efforts, either for long-term monitoring of health-related features or for direct assistance. Such a setting brings about several requirements, such as the increased need for robustness against noise due to multiple sensors and the support for complex, uncertain and non-sequential scenarios [6]. Additionally, the user's location within the home must be recognisable with minimal user involvement (e.g. without requiring them to carry or wear a device). Inference of real-time, continuous streams of meaningful and actionable events is also a prerequisite for ADL assistance [4]. Finally, smart homes increase the difficulty in acquiring training data, since data are environment-dependent [10].

In this paper we propose a novel rule-based ADL recognition system, which is capable of reasoning over historical and real-time, multi-modal sensor data acquired in a smart home environment used as an experimental testbed. Reasoning is applied in a bottom-up, multi-level manner to support complex ADL scenarios, while rules employ non-deterministic patterns to account for missing activities. The system is capable of correcting erroneous sensor data through encoding of simple heuristics (based on expert knowledge) and cross-validating sensor readings against other sensing modalities. Such 'cleaned up' and fused sensor data are then used to achieve indoor localisation and ADL recognition. Experimental evaluation shows that high levels of accuracy and performance are achieved, in both offline and real-time modes.

The rest of this paper is organised as follows. Section 2 gives an overview of the smart home testbed that motivates our research. Section 3 provides an analysis of the offline ADL recognition system, while Sect. 4 details the modifications applied for the system to also work in real-time. Section 5 offers details about the system implementation as well as the results of the conducted experimental evaluation, Sect. 6 compares our approach to the most relevant ones in literature and Sect. 7 concludes and points out topics for future work.

2   Background

2.1   Experimental Testbed

Existing AAL systems make use of (environmental) sensor networks, wearable devices and computer vision technologies. Some research projects focus on a

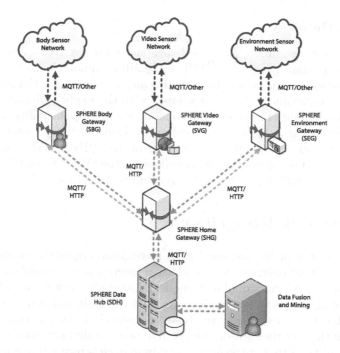

Fig. 1. An overview of the SPHERE system architecture [14]

single sensing modality, while others, such as ENSAFE[1] and eWALL [8], implement multi-modal AAL environments. The SPHERE (Sensor Platform for HEalthcare in Residential Environment) architecture attempts to combine different sensing technologies to provide a generic platform for ADL recognition. This generic, multi-modal sensor-based platform, which has been built on cutting edge infrastructure made up of commercial and prototype components, will be used to test clinical and health related hypotheses in a real life environment. The sensor-based platform has been deployed in a two-storey, two-bedroom house, converted into a fully-instrumented living lab referred to as the *SPHERE house*.

The SPHERE platform is based on three sensing technologies: an Environment Sensor Network made up of hardware sensing the home ambience; a Video Sensor Network, relying on RGB-D cameras deployed in specific rooms in the SPHERE house; and a Body Sensor Network made up of ultra low-power, wrist-wearable sensors. Environmental sensors specifically include: temperature, humidity, passive infrared (PIR) and door contact sensors; light, noise and air quality sensors; and water and electricity meters. Figure 1 provides a high-level view of the SPHERE hub and data sharing system. A detailed description of the system architecture and deployed sensors can be found in [14], along with a comparative analysis of similar multi-modal sensing platforms.

---

[1] http://www.ensafe-aal.eu.

2.2 ADL Ontology

In order to have a common, controlled vocabulary for any ADL-related effort in SPHERE, (e.g. data generation, ADL recognition, annotation of ground truth videos), an ontology has been defined, listing and categorising activities occurring in the home environment. It was developed with the explicit aim of compliance with existing models, to achieve interoperability and applicability of collected datasets beyond the project. It is based on BoxLab's Activity Labels[2] and thus extends their model. A detailed presentation of the SPHERE ADL ontology can be found in [15]; the latest version is available in the OBO[3] format from http:// data.bris.ac.uk (DOI: 10.5523/bris.1234ym4ulx3r11i2z5b13g93n7).

3   Offline ADL Recognition

The initial version of the proposed ADL recognition approach allows for offline analysis of activity patterns in a residential environment. Sensor data are pre-collected, processed and stored as facts in the recognition system. Rules identify patterns among these facts, which correspond to significant sensor events that may be linked to a specific activity. Instead of searching for patterns arbitrarily, rules exploit the fact that sensors report data periodically; patterns are identified in windows of time that correspond roughly to each sensor's reporting period.

The rule hierarchy of the ADL recognition approach is shown in Fig. 2. At the lowest level, rules rely on sensor events to derive atomic activities included in the ADL ontology, as well as location information. An intermediate level involves rules that refine initial derivations and fuse different sources of location information. Then, second and higher level rules progressively combine already recognised activities to infer complex events of increasing complexity. The defined rules rely on information reported from most environmental sensors in the SPHERE house, apart from the temperature, humidity, ambient noise and dust sensors: collected data from these sensors did not yield any AR-related patterns. Furthermore, ambient light sensors proved useful only when the effect of sunlight is minimal, i.e. when the sun is below the horizon.

The rest of this section analyses the rule base of the proposed approach, presenting rules within each distinct category in Fig. 2. Rules are expressed in a simplified syntax, where comma denotes conjunction, => denotes inference, NOT denotes negation-as-failure, while assert, retract and modify correspond to the typical fact base manipulation actions; in the case of modify, value change is denoted as `valuebefore->valueafter`. Facts are represented as predicates, starting with a capital letter; sensor data are modeled as functions, in capitals, and constant names are in lower-case letters.

---

[2] http://boxlab.wikispaces.com/Activity+Labels.
[3] http://oboedit.org.

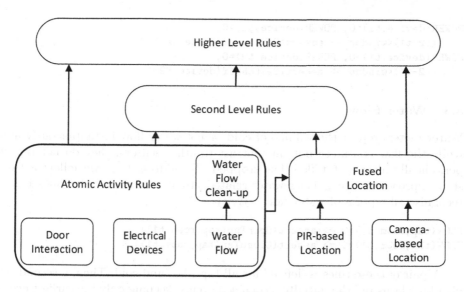

Fig. 2. Hierarchy of ADL recognition rules

3.1 Door Interaction

Door contact (DC) sensors report a zero value while the door is open and a positive value while it is shut. Reports happen either instantaneously or at a period of 10 s. Hence, activities that involve a user interacting with a door are recognised based on a change in the reported value. The first two rules below detect one or more change events within the sensor reporting window; the third ensures that all activity times refer to the earliest time when the DC sensor reported a zero value. Rules recognising door closing are defined equivalently.

```
DC(t1)=0, DC(t2)>0, (t2-t1)<window => assert(OpenDoor(t2))
DC(t1)=0, DC(t2)>0, (t2-t1)<window, OpenDoor(t3), (t3-t2)<window,
    CloseDoor(t4), t2<t4<t3 => assert(OpenDoor(t2))
DC(t1)=0, DC(t2)>0, (t2-t1)<window, OpenDoor(t3), (t3-t2)<window,
    NOT(CloseDoor(t4), t2<t4<t3) => modify(OpenDoor(t3->t2)
```

3.2 Electrical Devices

Smart meters fitted to electrical devices report consumption every 6 s. We can assume, with acceptable accuracy, that a device is switched on when the associated sensor starts reporting positive values. A pair of the rules that follow is defined for every meter-fitted device in the SPHERE house, which includes a TV, microwave, kettle, toaster and fridge. Variants of the first rule are also defined for devices that can be put on standby, such as the TV; turning on from standby is recognised when power consumption increases from a range of positive, non-zero values that correspond to standby consumption. In the case of the fridge, the recognised activities involve opening or closing the fridge door.

```
POWER(device,t1)=0, POWER(device,t2)>0,
   (t2-t1)<window => assert(SwitchOn(device,t2))
POWER(device,t1)>0, POWER(device,t2)=0,
   (t2-t1)<window => assert(SwitchOff(device,t2))
```

3.3 Water Flow

Water meters report the volume of cold or hot water flow instantaneously and while the flow continues but, in contrast to other sensors, they do not report periodically after water flow has stopped. To address this, we follow a two-step approach to recognising water-related atomic activities. The rules below recognise all reports of water flow activity:

```
FLOW(tap,room,t1)>0 => assert(OpenTap(tap,room,t1))
FLOW(tap,room,t1)=0 => assert(CloseTap(tap,room,t1))
```

A pair of these rules is defined for all taps, hot and cold. Then, a second set of rules 'cleans up' the initially recognised events, keeping only the earliest event for each distinct occurrence. The rule for cleaning up open tap events follows; the rule for close tap events is defined accordingly.

```
OpenTap(tap,room,t1), OpenTap(tap,room,t2), t1<t2,
    NOT(CloseTap(tap,room,t3), t1<t3<t2)
    => retract(OpenTap(tap,room,t2))
```

3.4 Complex Activities

Combining the activities recognised by the rules presented so far, we can recognise activities of progressively higher complexity, constructing them recursively. To express the rules, we use a subset of the event algebra defined in [5], with $\wedge$, $\vee$ and NOT denoting conjunction, disjunction and negation-as-failure, respectively and SET denoting unordered sequences of activities, following each other within a maximum time interval. All RHS in the rules imply an assert action.

Atomic activities referring to electrical appliances can be combined to create a complex activity that denotes use of the appliance. The rules below recognise such activities for all devices, with the second inferring a specially named fact for watching TV.

$$SwitchOn(device, t1) \wedge SwitchOff(device, t2) \Rightarrow Use(device, t1, t2)$$
$$SwitchOn(tv, t1) \wedge SwitchOff(tv, t2) \Rightarrow WatchingTV(t1, t2)$$

In the case of activities that involve the use of water taps, the following rules infer possible complex activities. Note that the room associated with each tap influences which activities are recognised.

$$OpenTap(tap, room, t1) \wedge CloseTap(tap, room, t2) \wedge (t1 < t2) \wedge$$
$$NOT(CloseTap(tap, room, t3) \wedge (t1 < t3 < t2))$$
$$\Rightarrow WashHands(t1, t2) \vee WashFace(t1, t2)$$
$$OpenTap(tap, bathroom, t1) \wedge CloseTap(tap, bathroom, t2) \wedge (t1 < t2) \wedge$$
$$NOT(CloseTap(tap, bathroom, t3) \wedge (t1 < t3 < t2))$$
$$\Rightarrow BrushTeeth(t1, t2) \vee BathingShowering(t1, t2)$$

In absence of further information, we cannot discard any of the inferred activities. The second-level complex activities can, in turn, be combined to infer third-level complex activities, such as a user preparing a drink or a snack:

$$SET(Use(kettle, t1, t2), CloseTap(tap, kitchen, t3))$$
$$\Rightarrow PreparingDrink(min(t1, t3), max(t2, t3))$$
$$Use(fridge, t1, t2) \vee Use(toaster, t3, t4)$$
$$\Rightarrow PreparingSnack(min(t1, t3), max(t2, t4))$$

Complex activities can also be inferred using location information, as evidenced from the following rule, which recognises the user walking from one room to another through open doors.

$$IsIn(room, t1, t2) \wedge IsIn(room2, t3, t4) \wedge t2 < t3 \wedge NOT(IsIn(room3, t5, t6) \wedge$$
$$t2 < t5 \wedge t6 < t3 \wedge OpenDoor(t7) \wedge t2 < t7 < t3) \Rightarrow WalkThroughDoors(t2, t3)$$

Note that the IsIn fact refers to the fused location information, as inferred by the rules in Sect. 3.7. Recursive construction of complex events can continue as long as there is a meaningful connection between already recognised events. The next rule recognises the fourth-level complex activity of washing the dishes:

$$(PreparingDrink(t1, t2) \vee PreparingSnack(t3, t4)) \wedge OpenTap(tap, kitchen, t5)$$
$$\wedge CloseTap(tap, kitchen, t6) \wedge min(t1, t3) < t5 < t6 < max(t2, t4)$$
$$\Rightarrow WashDishes(t5, t6)$$

3.5 PIR-based Location

ADL recognition is inextricably linked with the challenge of indoor localisation. In our approach, location information is derived from three sources: PIR sensors, video cameras and recognised atomic activities. This combination is sufficient only for single residential scenarios. The integration of wearable data, which would allow distinguishing between inhabitants is still in progress so, for the remainder of this section, we assume that all inferences refer to the same user.

The PIR sensor reports instantaneously a value of 1, when motion is detected, or 0 otherwise. Based on this, room-level location for single residential settings is inferred as follows:

```
PIR(room,t1)=1, PIR(room,t2)=0, t1<t2,
    NOT(PIR(room,t3)=0, t1<t3<t2) => assert(IsInP(room,t1,t2))
IsInP(room,t1,t2), IsInP(room,t3,t4), t3-t2<=threshold
    => modify(IsInP(t2->t4)), retract(IsInP(room,t3,t4))
IsInP(room,t1,t2), IsInP(room,t3,t4), t3-t2>threshold,
    NOT(IsInP(room2,t5,t6), t2<t5<t3), NOT(IsInP(room2,t7,t8), t2<t8<t3),
    => modify(IsInP(t2->t4)), retract(IsInP(room,t3,t4))
```

The first rule places a user in a specific room, if the corresponding PIR sensor is activated and subsequently deactivated. The next rules merge PIR activation periods in the same room by examining the temporal distance between them. If the distance does not exceed a specified threshold (e.g. roughly 60 s), then the periods are immediately considered temporally adjacent and are merged. In the opposite case, we need to ensure that no PIR sensor has been activated in a different room during that gap, before proceeding with the merge.

3.6 Video-Based Location

The second source of location information comes in the form of 2D and 3D bounding boxes detected and reported by video cameras installed in the SPHERE house. Each bounding box (BB) is linked to a specific frame id and a user id, to differentiate between boxes in a single frame. It should be stressed that cameras are only installed in the living room, kitchen and main hallway and that rules only rely on 2D and 3D coordinates, which do not carry any sensitive data whatsoever. For single residential settings, the following rules apply:

```
BB(room,frameid,userid,t1), NOT(BB(room,frameid2,userid,t2),
    frameid2= frameid-1) => assert (BBStart(room,userid,t1))
BB(room,frameid,userid,t1), NOT(BB(room,frameid2,userid,t2),
    frameid2= frameid+1) => assert (BBEnd(room,userid,t1))
BBStart(room,userid,t1), BBEnd(room,userid,t2),
    NOT(BBStart(room,userid,t3), t1<t3<t2)
    => assert(IsInV(room,t1,t2), retract(BBStart(), BBEnd()))
```

The first two rules detect starting and ending points for bounding box sequences, while the third rule places the user in the room associated with such a sequence. Note that sequences can be merged using the rules defined in Sect. 3.5.

Ghost Sequences. It is unavoidable for a video camera tracking body motion to report bounding boxes that do not correspond to an actual user or object, despite efforts in human detection research [9]. Common causes include lingering images that persist after the user has moved or vibrations applied directly or indirectly to the camera. These so-called ghost sequences can severely compromise the validity of video-based indoor localisation, even to the point that fusing other sources is not enough to filter the generated noise. Given that, it makes sense to invest effort in detecting and removing ghost sequences.

After analysing a wealth of available video camera data, we defined a set of ghost detecting heuristics that are applicable to any dataset, especially ones produced using the OpenNI Framework[4]. The simplest heuristic involves discarding any sequence of length below a minimum threshold (e.g. 30 frames, equivalent to 1 second). Integrating this heuristic into the third video-related rule above simply requires adding the conjunct `t2-t1 < threshold`. To deal with the case of ghosts caused by lingering images, the 2D bounding box coordinates are examined. If they remain fixed for longer than a maximum threshold (e.g. again 30 frames), then this stuck subset of the bounding box sequence is discarded. In cases where the user is actually not moving at all, we merge back the two subsequences that were separated by removing the stuck subset.

Other ghost detecting heuristics involve examining the 2D bounding box coordinates, along with 3D depth information. If either the width or height of the box is consistently and unjustifiably small, in correlation with depth, then it does not correspond to actual human motion. Finally, application-specific heuristics can be considered during ghost detection; for instance, heuristics for the SPHERE house include discarding specific ranges of coordinates that are known to be generated due to surrounding vibrations.

3.7 Fused Location

Having inferred location from PIR and video sensors, the final task is to fuse them into a coherent narrative for room-level indoor localisation. To be able to distinguish between actual and possibly noisy location reports, we associate a confidence value to each PIR sequence (IsInP facts) and each bounding box sequence (IsInV facts). For PIR, confidence is inversely proportional to the number of PIR sensors reporting motion. For video sequences, it depends on the probability of being a ghost, based on the heuristics defined in Sect. 3.6; A sub-sequence is flagged as a ghost while its confidence remains below a specific threshold.

The fusion process essentially infers a single location at any point in time, by combining all available sources using the rules that follow:

- If only a single source reports a location, it is assumed to hold (with a confidence level relative to the associated value)
- If both PIR and video data report the same location, it is assumed to hold (with a confidence value equal to the sum of the individual values)
- If PIR and video disagree, the correct location is the one associated with a recognised atomic activity
- If both disagreeing reports (or neither) are supported by an activity, we assume the report with the higher confidence holds (if equal, we trust PIR).

The result is an ordered temporal sequence of room-level locations, annotated with confidence values that reflect the level of agreement between the various sources. In all cases, rules take into account all possible temporal relations between two sequences, as defined by Allen's interval algebra [1].

---

[4] http://structure.io/openni.

4 Real-Time ADL Recognition

The approach presented in the previous section relies on the existence of pre-collected sensor data for the complete period of interest for ADL recognition. While the offline version can assist in diagnosing and managing healthcare and wellbeing conditions, it is unable to provide support for scenarios where emergency assistance is required. In such use cases, activities should be immediately recognised as soon as the associated sensor events take place.

To convert the offline system to a real-time one, a significant change in the nature of both rule and fact bases is required. Instead of representing the history of sensor events, facts now represent the state of each distinct sensor. For each new sensor event, the corresponding fact is modified to reflect the current state. To detect state change, each fact stores the previous state as well. In the rest of this section, we present the required adaptations to the rule base. Note that these are necessary only at the lowest level; all second and higher-level rules remain the same, since they are transparent to the way sensor events are generated.

4.1 Environmental Sensors

The state-based approach for the real-time system simplifies the definition of rules: any state change event is linked to a related atomic activity. This holds for DC sensors, electricity and water flow meters:

```
DCSensor(room,value,prev,t), value=0, prev>0
    => assert(OpenDoor(room,t))
ElecMeter(device,value,prev,t), value>0, prev=0
    => assert(SwitchOn(device,t))
FlowMeter(tap,value,prev,t), value>0, prev=0
    => assert(OpenTap(tap,t))
```

Note that there is no need, as was in the offline case, to clean up duplicate door or tap-related events; these rules fire only once when sensor values change.

4.2 PIR-Based Location

In the real-time approach, each consecutive activation/deactivation of a PIR sensor corresponds to the user being in the associated room:

```
PIRSensor(room,value,prev,t), value=1, prev=0
    => assert(PIROn(room,t))
PIRSensor(room,value,prev,t), value=0, prev=1
    => assert(PIROff(room,t))
PIROn(room,t1), PIROff(room,t2) => assert(IsInP(room,t1,t2)),
    retract(PIROn(room,t1)), retract (PIROff(room,t2))
```

Note that since PIROn/Off facts are generated and consumed in real-time, there is no need to check whether they are consecutive: if there was any other such event in between, the IsInP rule would have fired upon assertion. To decide whether subsequent activations extend the user's stay in the room, the following process is carried out (the corresponding rules are not shown for brevity):

- If activation directly follows the last deactivation, we extend immediately.
- If the elapsed time from deactivation to subsequent activation does not exceed a specified threshold, we proceed with the extension (similarly to the second rule in Sect. 3.5).
- If, in the meanwhile, no activation has taken place in a different room, we extend the already recognised period.
- If the elapsed time is greater than the threshold and there has been an activation in a different room in between, then the new activation is the beginning of a new period of stay in the room.

4.3   Video-Based Location

While the other sensors broadcast a single value, video cameras post a wealth of information, which means the state-based approach is not easily applicable; instead, each reported bounding box is stored briefly, only to be combined in facts that represent a period of time during which the user was in the room:

```
BB(room,frameid,userid,t1), NOT(IsInV(room,t2,t3,frame2,frame3),
    frame3=frameid-1) => IsInV(room,t1,t1,frameid,frameid)
BB(room,frameid,userid,t1), IsInV(room,t2,t3,frame2,frame3),
    frame3=frameid-1 => modify(IsInV(room,t3->t1,frame3->frameid))
```

The same ghost detection heuristics, as in the offline mode, are applied; a running confidence value is associated with each sequence, representing the likelihood that it is not a ghost sequence at each point in time.

4.4   Fused Location

In contrast to the offline mode, PIR sequences are not assigned confidence values relative to the number of simultaneous sequences; instead, each time a PIR sensor is activated, the system fuses available video or activity information to decide on its validity:

- If there is no active video sequence and no activity detected, there is no other choice but to assume the user caused the PIR activation.
- If the active video sequence with the highest confidence agrees with PIR, we conclude the user is in the room.
- If video reports a different room, we assume the user is in the room where the most recently recognised atomic activity was performed.

Based on these rules, we can infer room-level location for the user at any given time. Additionally, location history can also be deduced (similarly to the way the offline system reports location), provided that the previous location is stored whenever the user moves to a different room.

5   Experimental Evaluation

5.1   Implementation

Both offline and real-time modes of the ADL recognition system, analysed in Sects. 3 and 4, have been implemented in Java, using Jess [7] as a rule engine. Sensor data, which are broadcast and stored in a JSON format, are converted to Java objects, which are then connected to Jess shadow facts. The rule base was divided into several Jess modules, one for each rectangle in Fig. 2. The implemented versions of rules are designed to accommodate variable reporting periods for the sensors in the SPHERE house, since collected data indicated multiple occurrences of early or late reports.

The real-time version is built as an MQTT[5] client, since the SPHERE sensor gateways broadcast data using the MQTT protocol. In order to make sure that no sensor messages are lost, they are processed in separate threads. Whenever a new message is broadcast, it triggers an update in both the Java object associated with the sensor and the corresponding Jess shadow fact.

5.2   Data Collection

To evaluate the ADL recognition system, we used single-occupant, script-based datasets collected in the SPHERE house. Data collection involved 10 participants executing an ADL script of half-hour duration, twice. Participants were asked to visit all house locations which allowed us to observe sensor activations, temporal relationships, and so on. Recognition experiments focused on the following activity categories (a subset of the ADL ontology), included in the script: door interaction, electrical appliance interaction, water tap interaction, preparing a snack or a drink, washing hands/dishes, brushing teeth and bathing/showering. During the experiments, ground-truth data was acquired through annotation of video images collected using a head-mounted, wide-angle, 4K resolution camera. More information on data collection and video annotation can be found in [15].

5.3   Experiments Setup

The evaluation was performed on a Windows® 7 64-bit system powered by an Intel® Core™ i5-2320 processor at 3.00 GHz, with 8 GB RAM. For the real-time version, we created an MQTT server and clients, to simulate the SPHERE Home Gateway and sensor gateways, respectively (see Fig. 1). Client simulators parse precollected data and broadcast one sensor message every 5msec, one-third of the camera reporting period, the shortest out of all sensors.

The experiments focus on three aspects: performance, in terms of execution time and memory consumption for the offline mode, activity recognition accuracy, in terms of precision and recall, and localisation accuracy, i.e. the percentage of the experiment duration during which the correct room the user is in

---

[5] http://mqtt.org.

Table 1. Results of the experimental evaluation

Experiment	Exec. time (offline) (s)	Memory (offline) (MB)	Activity recognition					Localisation accuracy (%)
			FP	FN	TP	Precision (%)	Recall (%)	
1	32.045	232.4	9.5	4.5	54	85.04	92.31	97.68
2	55.907	200.8	9.5	2	55	85.27	96.49	88.44
3	45.922	129.2	7	1.5	50	87.72	97.09	88.37
4	30.808	157.8	7.5	1	44.5	85.57	97.80	97.69
5	24.548	152.6	7	4	47.5	87.15	92.23	96.14
6	32.642	234.6	9	1	48	84.21	97.96	84.35
7	67.838	179.8	4	4	54	93.10	93.10	90.91
8	26.626	186.4	4	2	51	92.72	96.23	90.90
9	29.615	79.2	3	4	41	93.18	91.11	97.14
10	36.593	149.4	8	3	52	85.95	94.55	95.53
Average	**38.254**	**170.22**	**6.9**	**2.7**	**49.7**	**87.991**	**94.887**	**92.715**

is inferred. Precision and recall are commonly defined as $precision = \frac{TP}{TP+FP}\%$ and $recall = \frac{TP}{TP+FN}\%$, where TP, FP, and FN represent activities performed and recognised, recognised but not performed and performed but not recognised, respectively. Precision and recall values are the same for both offline and real-time modes, since only the way of receiving raw sensor data changes.

5.4 Evaluation Results

The results shown in Table 1 are an average of the two times each participant performed the ADL scenario. Also, execution time and memory values are an average of 10 runs for each experiment. Performance results show that the offline version is capable of quickly processing 30 min worth of sensor information in 38 s, while requiring 170 MB, on average. Note that, in real-time mode, recognition delay is negligible due to always maintaining a small fact base.

As far as activity recognition accuracy is concerned, the proposed system shows excellent recall levels of 94.887 % on average, while precision is at the somewhat lower level of 87.991 %. This is due to the fact that, in cases where available information is not enough to distinguish between a number of possible activities, the defined rules infer them all; this ensures that all performed activities are recognised (higher recall), at the expense of recognising activities that were not performed (lower precision). Finally, the recognition system infers the correct room the user is in 92.715 % of the time on average, proving the effectiveness of both ghost detection heuristics and location fusion rules.

6 Related Work

There has been a substantial amount of research effort on activity recognition, ranging from video-based to sensor-based, and data-driven to knowledge-driven approaches. In the rest of this section, we focus on a selective subset that is more relevant to our approach, presenting the most recent and noteworthy ADL recognition approaches that incorporate logical modelling and reasoning.

Chen et al. [4] model both sensors and activities using ontologies and perform ADL recognition via equivalence and subsumption reasoning on these models. Both offline and real-time modes are supported, while recognition becomes incrementally specific, as more and more sensors are activated. Compared to our approach, this work fails to recognise atomic or lower-level activities unless higher-level ones are recognised. Also, the evaluation scenario is unrealistic, requiring users to perform activities in a predefined, strictly sequential order and fixed time intervals. Finally, the real-time system has a recognition delay of 2–3 s, which is significantly slower compared to our approach.

The COSAR system [12] proposes the integration of statistical and ontological reasoning to overcome the limitations of each approach. The statistical component incorporates historical predictions, while the ontological component filters recognitions based on the user's location. Helaoui et al. [6] propose a more tightly-coupled variant, employing a probabilistic DL reasoner. As in our approach, ADL recognition is carried out in multiple levels, building from atomic gestures towards increasingly complex activities; however, apart from the fact that the reasoner requires training data, it is also unable to reason about temporal features and works only in offline mode; also, our activity recognition system consistently outperforms these approaches, in terms of both precision and recall.

Similarly to COSAR, Skarlatidis et al. [13] extend previous work [2] on event calculus-based ADL recognition with probabilistic reasoning based on Markov Logic Networks. Experimental evaluation shows the superiority of the hybrid approach compared to purely probabilistic or event calculus ones, both in terms of recognition rates and robustness against missing data. However, their experiments focus only on posture and movement-related activities as opposed to complex ADL scenarios; also, the intervals of recognised activities are not stored, precluding the ability of inferring activities of higher complexity.

MetaQ [11] is a SPARQL-based reasoning framework for ADL recognition that relies on pattern-based descriptions of both atomic and complex activities. Sensor data are transformed into RDF graphs and native OWL reasoning is performed as an initial classification step. Then, SPARQL queries are produced based on the patterns and are applied on the graphs to realise ADL recognition. In contrast to MetaQ, our approach achieves higher recall while maintaining comparable precision levels; it also includes rules that take into account missing activities and can provide real-time inference of recognised activities.

The work presented in this paper is influenced by previous work [5] that proposed a rule-based ADL recognition system for hierarchically organised and logically consistent complex activities. However, while [5] assumes that atomic activities are already recognised and are given as input to the recognition system, our approach assumes only raw sensor data as input and rules are defined for recognition of both atomic and complex activities. Also, we focus on inferring all possible activities, in both offline and real-time settings.

7 Conclusions and Future Work

In this paper we proposed a rule-based ADL recognition system for multi-modal smart home environments that exploits a bottom-up multi-level reasoning approach to infer events of increasing complexity. The system can operate both on historical and real-time data and exploits the existence of multiple sources to achieve robustness against noise and non-deterministic activity patterns. Experiments conducted in an actual smart home setting used as a testbed prove the effectiveness of the approach and its ability to support AAL scenarios either for long-term monitoring to diagnose and manage health and wellbeing conditions or for directly assisting smart home inhabitants.

Future work involves integrating wearable sensor data to achieve three major objectives: to infer activities unidentifiable with only the other sensors; to improve localisation accuracy or provide an alternate source of location data, in scenarios where privacy is deemed more important than convenience (opting to carry or wear a device, rather than allowing cameras); to explore more complex ADL scenarios with multiple inhabitants and achieve inference of the person performing a recognised activity. Finally, we plan to address scalability issues when faced with increased amounts of sensor input, by exploring methods such as conflict detection and resolution, compression and distributed inference units.

Acknowledgments. This work was performed under the SPHERE IRC, funded by the UK Engineering and Physical Sciences Research Council (EPSRC), Grant EP/K031910/1.

References

1. Allen, J.F.: Maintaining knowledge about temporal intervals. Commun. ACM **26**(11), 832–843 (1983)
2. Artikis, A., Sergot, M.J., Paliouras, G.: A logic programming approach to activity recognition. In: Scherp, A., Jain, R., Kankanhalli, M.S., Mezaris, V. (eds.) Proceedings of the 2nd ACM International Workshop on Events in Multimedia, EiMM 2010, pp. 3–8. ACM, New York (2010)
3. Chen, L., Khalil, I.: Activity recognition: approaches, practices and trends. In: Chen, L., Nugent, C.D., Biswas, J., Hoey, J. (eds.) Activity Recognition in Pervasive Intelligent Environments. Atlantis Ambient and Pervasive Intelligence, vol. 4, pp. 1–31. Atlantis Press, Paris (2011)
4. Chen, L., Nugent, C.D., Wang, H.: A knowledge-driven approach to activity recognition in smart homes. IEEE Trans. Knowl. Data Eng. **24**(6), 961–974 (2012)
5. Filippaki, C., Antoniou, G., Tsamardinos, I.: Using constraint optimization for conflict resolution and detail control in activity recognition. In: Keyson, D.V., Maher, M.L., Streitz, N., Cheok, A., Augusto, J.C., Wichert, R., Englebienne, G., Aghajan, H., Kröse, B.J.A. (eds.) AmI 2011. LNCS, vol. 7040, pp. 51–60. Springer, Heidelberg (2011)

6. Helaoui, R., Riboni, D., Stuckenschmidt, H.: A probabilistic ontological framework for the recognition of multilevel human activities. In: Mattern, F., Santini, S., Canny, J.F., Langheinrich, M., Rekimoto, J. (eds.) UbiComp 2013, pp. 345–354. ACM (2013)
7. Hill, E.F.: Jess in Action: Java Rule-Based Systems. Manning Publications Co., Greenwich (2003)
8. Kyriazakos, S., Mihaylov, M., Anggorojati, B., Mihovska, A., Craciunescu, R., Fratu, O., Prasad, R.: eWALL: an intelligent caring home environment offering personalized context-aware applications based on advanced sensing. Wirel. Pers. Commun. **87**(3), 1093–1111 (2016)
9. Liu, J., Zhang, G., Liu, Y., Tian, L., Chen, Y.Q.: An ultra-fast human detection method for color-depth camera. J. Vis. Commun. Image Represent. **31**, 177–185 (2015)
10. Maekawa, T., Yanagisawa, Y., Kishino, Y., Ishiguro, K., Kamei, K., Sakurai, Y., Okadome, T.: Object-based activity recognition with heterogeneous sensors on wrist. In: Floréen, P., Krüger, A., Spasojevic, M. (eds.) Pervasive 2010. LNCS, vol. 6030, pp. 246–264. Springer, Heidelberg (2010)
11. Meditskos, G., Dasiopoulou, S., Kompatsiaris, I.: MetaQ: a knowledge-driven framework for context-aware activity recognition combining SPARQL and OWL 2 activity patterns. Pervasive Mob. Comput. **25**, 104–124 (2016)
12. Riboni, D., Bettini, C.: COSAR: hybrid reasoning for context-aware activity recognition. Pers. Ubiquit. Comput. **15**(3), 271–289 (2011)
13. Skarlatidis, A., Paliouras, G., Artikis, A., Vouros, G.A.: Probabilistic event calculus for event recognition. ACM Trans. Comput. Log. **16**(2), 11:1–11:37 (2015)
14. Woznowski, P., Fafoutis, X., Song, T., Hannuna, S., Camplani, M., Tao, L., Paiement, A., Mellios, E., Haghighi, M., Zhu, N., et al.: A multi-modal sensor infrastructure for healthcare in a residential environment. In: 2015 IEEE International Conference on Communication Workshop, pp. 271–277. IEEE (2015)
15. Woznowski, P., King, R., Harwin, W., Craddock, I.: A human activity recognition framework for healthcare applications: ontology, labelling strategies, and best practice. In: Proceedings of the International Conference on Internet of Things and Big Data (IoTBD), pp. 369–377. INSTICC (2016)

SmartRL: A Context-Sensitive, Ontology-Based Rule Language for Assisted Living in Smart Environments

William Van Woensel$^{(\boxtimes)}$, Patrice C. Roy, and Syed Sibte Raza Abidi

NICHE Research Group, Faculty of Computer Science,
Dalhousie University, Halifax, Canada
{william.van.woensel,patrice.c.roy,raza.abidi}@dal.ca

Abstract. To automate assisted living tasks in smart environments, the contextual and temporal aspects associated with activities of daily life (ADL) can be exploited to (1) detect and act upon inconsistent context, i.e., when an activity occurs outside of its usual context; and (2) guidance through ADL routines, by automatically executing or suggesting a next subtask at the correct context. This paper presents SmartRL, a context-sensitive rule language supporting task automation in smart environments, and applies it to an Assisted Ambient Living (AAL) use case. SmartRL realizes a number of key opportunities in this setting, such as linking the language to a domain ontology, and facilitating the detection and influencing of context; as well as considering the temporal nature of smart environment rules, the need to revert rule effects, and writing activity routines.

Keywords: Smart environments · Ontology-based · Context-aware · Assisted Ambient Living (AAL)

1 Introduction

Assisted living deals with the effects of cognitive decline, by assisting cognitively impaired people to perform activities of daily life (ADL). In particular, ambient assisted living (AAL) [1] relies on smart environments to automate assistive tasks; such as executing activities automatically (e.g., setting temperature), guiding people through ADL (e.g., via step-by-step instructions), or issuing alerts in case of unusual activities (e.g., falling, forgetting about cooking). To support task automation, one can exploit temporal and contextual aspects associated with activities; e.g., sleeping normally occurs at night in the patient's bedroom; whereas cooking typically happens in the kitchen around mealtimes. Similarly, many ADL consist of atomic activities with clear temporal interrelations: e.g., after waking up, the patient needs to wash up in the bathroom for 15–20 min; then, the patient should have breakfast in the kitchen.

To represent automated tasks in smart environments, we present a high-level, context-sensitive rule language called SmartRL, and apply it to an AAL use case. By linking SmartRL to a domain-specific ontology, we allow for high-level rule specification, reduce verboseness, and enable easy variation of rule specificity. In SmartRL rules, conditions refer to high-level context (location, activity and time), which is

© Springer International Publishing Switzerland 2016
J.J. Alferes et al. (Eds.): RuleML 2016, LNCS 9718, pp. 341–349, 2016.
DOI: 10.1007/978-3-319-42019-6_22

continuously inferred by a smart-environment middleware; whereas actions invoke smart services to perform tasks, raise alerts or instruct the user. Currently, the SmartRL parser translates (or "expands") rules into RDF triple pattern-like expressions, which are fed into our rule engine. We note that this paper focuses on presenting the SmartRL rule language, and does not detail other aspects of our system; such as the smart-environment middleware, or its rule engine implementation.

Section 2 presents our running AAL scenario. Section 3 first summarizes our domain-specific ontology, whereas Sect. 4 elaborates key SmartRL features aimed at working in smart environments. Section 5 discusses the relevant state of the art, and Sect. 6 ends with conclusions and future work.

2   AAL Scenario: Sleeping and Morning Routines

This section presents an ADL scenario that illustrates the potential of a context-sensitive AAL system (which will also be used as a running example). Sleeping and morning ADL are a recurrent set of complex activities, which patients carry out daily. Regarding sleeping, abnormal situations include cases where, at nighttime, the patient is either not in the bedroom or physically active; or where the patient is inactive and not in the bedroom at daytime. When inconsistent activities occur, the system alerts the patient or a caregiver. At the same time, allowances must be made to cases where patients e.g., shortly go to the bathroom during the night, without sending alerts.

In their morning routine, the patient goes to the bathroom to wash up, and then heads to the kitchen to prepare breakfast. In support of this, the AAL system changes ambient conditions (e.g. turn on light, heating) based on the current location, and reverts them to their initial state afterwards (e.g., a period after leaving the location). When the patient prepares their breakfast, the system guides them through the meal preparation, and possibly reminds them about the activity. For instance, the patient can choose to prepare oatmeal (using stovetop) and bacon (using oven). Instructions are shown on a screen and updated as time passes: the patient starts with cooking bacon, and after 5 min, the user should start cooking oatmeal. After 15 min, the oatmeal and bacon are ready, and the prepare breakfast activity is done. By displaying these instructions on a screen in the current room (which may differ from the kitchen), the patient is also reminded of the ongoing activity. Once the meal is done, the patient eats in the living room while e.g., watching TV or listening to the radio. In this setting, the AAL system again adapts ambient conditions according to suit the context; if the patient receives a phone call, the system turns off the volume of all devices in the room, and reverts them to their original setting after the call.

3   Smart Environment Ontology

This section summarizes the domain ontology leveraged by SmartRL, focusing on concepts from our AAL use case (Fig. 1). In addition to providing concepts referenced by rules, the SmartRL parser also uses the ontology to implement certain constructs (e.g., see Sects. 4.2 and 4.3). Technically however, SmartRL can also be made to work with other suitable ontologies, such as e.g., DomoML-env [2] or OntoDomo [3].

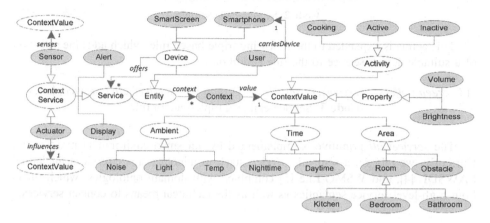

Fig. 1. Smart environment ontology

In a smart environment, an *Entity* (either a *Device* or a *User*) is associated with multiple *Contexts*; which have a particular *ContextValue,* as well as other properties (not shown) such as its certainty, related sensor, type of proximity (in case of locations), etc. *ContextValue* subclasses indicate the type of context, and include concrete *Ambient, Time, Area, Property* and *Activity* subtypes. A *Device* offers a set of *Services*, such as issuing alerts (*Alert*), displaying content (*Display*), and *Sensors* and/or *Actuators*, which sense/influence a particular *ContextValue*. Finally, a user entity can carry a smartphone with them as well (*carriesDevice*).

4   SmartRL Rule Language

This section discusses key SmartRL features, which gear the language towards smart environments, and exemplifies them in the context of our AAL use case. We show original SmartRL rules as well as their expanded RDF triple-pattern form, both to clarify their semantics and illustrate the high-level nature & conciseness of SmartRL.

4.1   Calling Smart Services

Clearly, an important requirement in smart environments is the ability to call smart services. For this purpose, SmartRL supplies the *service-call* syntax[1]:

$$\langle term \rangle : \langle service \rangle (\langle arguments \rangle)$$

Code 1. Service-call syntax

---

[1] Syntax is represented using a simplified Backus-Naur Form.

The following example action calls the "display" service on a bound screen:

$$? screen: display("start\ cooking\ oatmeal")$$

Code 2. Service-call example.

This action is expanded to the following triple-based rule, which adds the selection of a suitable device service to the rule condition:

$$(?\ screen : offers\ ?\ service), (?\ service\ a : Display) \rightarrow serviceCall(?\ service, \langle args \rangle)$$

Code 3. Service-call as a triple-pattern rule.

The *serviceCall* primitive is implemented by our smart-environment middleware. Currently, we rely on a semantic service stack to annotate smart services, including SAWSDL [4], and WSMO-Lite [5] combined with domain ontologies; which offers both high-level service semantics as well as the technical means to contact services.

4.2 Restricting User Context

Rules operating in smart environments will often invoke services depending on the user's current context. To that end, SmartRL provides the *user-context* syntax:

$$@\langle user\_context \rangle$$

Code 4. User-context syntax.

The following expressions restrict firing of the rule depending on the user's current activity (inactive), location (in the bedroom), and time (nighttime):

$$@bedroom\ \&\ @inactive\ \&\ @nighttime$$

Code 5. User-context examples.

To illustrate this, Code 6 shows the triple patterns resulting from @*bedroom*:

$$(: user : context?c), (?c : value?bedroom), (?bedroom\ a : Bedroom),$$
$$(?\ c : proxType : Inside)$$

Code 6. User-context as a triple-pattern condition.

The ontology-based nature of SmartRL enables such symbolic context references, and also allows restrictions at different levels of granularity; e.g., @*bathroom* restricts the user's current location to the bathroom, whereas @*room* simply binds the ?*room* variable to any kind of room the user is in. Further, to perform its parsing task, our system analyzes the domain ontology and determines that *Bedroom* is an *Area* (see Fig. 1), resulting in extra context properties (i.e., type of proximity; *proxyType*). This kind of ontology analysis is further illustrated in the next section.

4.3 Restricting Arbitrary Contexts

In addition to user contexts, the need often arises to restrict the symbolic contexts of any entity (such as devices). The *term-context* syntax serves this purpose:

$$\langle term \rangle (in | is) \langle term \rangle$$
Code 7. Term-context syntax.

The expression shown in Code 8 restricts *?device* to any entity inside the room the user is currently in (see Sect. 4.2) and that are currently enabled[2].

$$(?device\ in\ @room)\ \&\ (?device\ is : on)$$
Code 8. Term-context examples.

Aside from inferred, symbolic context, rules may also put restrictions on low-level context. For instance, they may refer to ambient conditions inside a room (e.g., temperature) or device context (e.g., volume), which instead have continuous values. We express such conditions by extending the syntax with property paths:

$$\langle term \rangle (.\langle name \rangle)*$$
Code 9. Term-context syntax with property paths.

Below, we show an example where the room's current temperature should be higher than 20 degrees, and a device's volume should be below 50 %:

$$@room.temp > 20\ \&\ ?device.volume < 50$$
Code 10. Term-context property paths example.

In this case, expressions are expanded to directly refer to low-level values of suitable sensor services. The SmartRL parser leverages the domain ontology to support this expansion. In particular, if the supplied *name* refers to an *Ambient* subtype (e.g., *Temp*; see Fig. 1), the expanded expression finds values supplied by suitable services, which are offered by devices inside the *term* location (only expanding relevant clauses):

$$(?sensor\ in\ @room), (?sensor : offers\ ?service), (?sensor : senses : Temp),$$
$$(?sensor\ rdf : value\ ?temp), ?temp > 20$$
Code 11. Term-context as a triple pattern condition.

Alternatively, if ⟨*name*⟩ indicates a subtype of *Property* (e.g., *Volume*), the resulting expression similarly finds services, but directly offered by the *term* device. If the name does not occur in one of these hierarchies, the parser follows "regular" relations[3]. The following condition follows the *carriesDevice* relation from the user to their smartphone (regular relation), and only fires the rule if the smartphone's volume > 0:

---

[2] Such expressions are similarly expanded as shown in Code 6.

[3] This may introduce name clashes between concepts and properties (see future work).

$$: user.carriesDevice.volume > 0$$

Code 12. Example regular and context-referencing property path.

4.4   Influencing Arbitrary Contexts

In the last two sections, we discussed how SmartRL rules may restrict user or arbitrary entity contexts. Many smart environment tasks also involve *influencing* current context; e.g., setting the temperature, turning on lights, or reducing volume. To that end, we re-use the previously introduced *service-call* syntax (see Sect. 4.1). The following expressions set the temperature in the current room and turn off a device's volume:

$$@room : temp(25), ?device.volume(0)$$

Code 13. Service-call examples that directly set context.

Comparable to when referencing arbitrary context (see Sect. 4.3), the parsing process results in expanded expressions that reference services capable of setting the indicated context. However, instead of referencing their latest values (e.g., see Code 11), these expressions call the services with the supplied arguments. Codes 18 and 19 (Sect. 4.6) show examples of rules including these kinds of conditions.

4.5   Indicating Temporal Aspects

In smart environments, and especially in AAL scenarios, temporal aspects deserve special consideration. Complex activities, such as ADL, typically involve temporal relations between lower-level activities, whereby a certain task should occur a certain timespan after the other: e.g., when cooking breakfast, one cooks oatmeal for ca. 10 min, and bacon for 15 min. In other cases, important temporal aspects relate to activities themselves, in particular, allowing reasonable timespans before rule triggering: e.g., a rule stating that sleeping occurs at night in the bedroom should allow for short visits to the bathroom. To that end, SmartRL includes a *delayed-condition* syntax:

$$[\langle condition \rangle > \langle timespan \rangle]$$

Code 14. Delayed-condition syntax.

The expressions below illustrate two examples from the AAL scenario (Sect. 2). Code 15 shows rules displaying appropriate instructions on a screen inside the current room, depending on the passed time (see Sect. 4.7 for a simplified syntax).

$@cooking =: breakfast \& ? screen\ in\ @room \rightarrow ? screen: display("cook\ beacon\ ")$
$[\ @cooking =: breakfast > 5m\ ] \& ... \rightarrow ? screen: display("cook\ oatmeal")$
$[\ @cooking =: breakfast > 10m\ ] \& ... \rightarrow ? screen: display("meal\ done")$

Code 15. Example ADL using delayed-condition syntax.

The rules in Code 16 support the sleeping activity; stating that, if unusual sleeping activities are detected, reasonable time allowances are made before e.g., issuing alerts:

$[(@nighttime \& ((not\ @bedroom)\ |\ @active)) > 30m] \rightarrow ...$
$[(@inactive \& not\ @\ bedroom) > 15m] \rightarrow ...$

Code 16. Example alert rules using delayed-condition syntax.

4.6 Reverting Task Effects

As illustrated before, smart tasks are typically performed in certain contexts to assist user activities. After leaving those contexts, these tasks' effects often need to be reverted, however. For this purpose, SmartRL includes a *cleanup-rule* syntax (together with a reserved : *init* keyword):

$\langle rule \rangle \gg \langle cleanup\_rule \rangle$

Code 17. Cleanup-rule syntax.

The rule below initially sets a room's temperature to 25° C if the user is inside for longer than 30 s; afterwards, its associated *cleanup-rule* resets the temperature to its original level, in case the user is not inside the room for longer than 1 min.

$[(@room) > 30s] \rightarrow ?room : temp(25)$
$\gg [(not\ ?room) > 1m] \rightarrow ?room : temp(: init)$

Code 18. Example cleanup-rule for setting room temperature.

Code 19 shows a rule that, when calling, reduces the volume of nearby devices; afterwards, and once the call is over, the volumes are reverted to their original setting.

$: user.carriesDevice.incomingCall \& ?device\ in\ @room \rightarrow ?device : volume(0)$
$\gg : user.carriesDevice.callDone \rightarrow ?\ device : volume(: init)$

Code 19. Example cleanup-rule when dealing with incoming calls.

To implement this feature, the *cleanup-rule* is activated after its associated rule is fired, and instantiated for each value unifying the original rule. In case the : *init* keyword is used, the system first retrieves the original context value.

4.7   Grouping Related Rules

Especially when implementing sub-activities of complex activities (such as ADL), rules will often share preconditions. To facilitate specifying such routine activities, SmartRL supports the *ruleset* syntax:

$$condition\{(\langle rule \rangle;) + \}$$

Code 20. Ruleset syntax.

This ruleset represents the cooking activity from our waking-up ADL (see Sect. 2):

```
@cooking = : breakfast & ? screen in @room {
    → ? screen: display("cook bacon") ;
    [> 5min] →? screen: display("cook oatmeal") ;
    [> 15min] →? screen: display("meal done") }
```

Code 21. Example cooking rule using *ruleset* syntax.

Similarly, the ruleset below illustrates the washing-up activity:

```
@wokenUp {
    → : bathroom : temp(25), : bathroom : light(100);
    ≫ [(not @bathroom) > 5min]
        → ?bathroom : temp(: init), ?bathroom : light(: init);
    [ > 20min] → : kitchen : temp(25), : kitchen : light(100)}}.
```

Code 22. Example wokenUp rule using *ruleset* syntax.

5   State of the Art

The literature contains a number of context-sensitive, rule-based approaches to regulate behaviors in smart environments. Here, we limit our search to works that focus on simplifying rule specification or introduce special domain-specific constructs.

In general, other authors seem to have realized the utility of relying on ontologies for high-level rule specification [3, 6, 7]. To facilitate specifying rules, some works supply a rule creation UI [3, 8]. In particular, the authors in [8] present a straightforward mobile UI, and do not elaborate on the rule format. In [3], the authors present a Protégé-plugin that allows users to select rule concepts from taxonomies. However, the resulting rules seem just as elaborate and cumbersome to write as the extended triple-pattern rules presented in this paper. In the general domain of pervasive computing, the Awareness and Notification Service (ANS) [7] rule language focuses on informing users about their environment in particular. For this purpose, the authors introduce 3 keywords: *upon* (receiving an event), *when* (a precondition is met), *do* (notify users) as well as a *scope* construct to parameterize rules. However, we were unable to find works that present an elaborate, domain-specific rule language for smart environments.

6 Conclusions and Future Work

This paper presented SmartRL, a tailored, ontology-based language for specifying context-sensitive rules in smart environments; and applied the language to an AAL use case. SmartRL includes constructs geared towards smart environments, which may call smart services, restrict the context of the user or any arbitrary entity, and directly influence device or location context. Further, we pay special consideration to temporal aspects, reverting rule effects, and specifying routines. By contrasting SmartRL rules to their expanded, triple-based format, we illustrated its high-level and concise nature.

Future work involves dealing with uncertainty; currently, our system relies on global limits for context certainty. To deal with naming clashes in property paths (see Sect. 4.3), we plan to extend our parser to detect ambiguities. Finally, we aim to evaluate additional AAL scenarios, which may result in adding new language constructs.

References

1. Rashidi, P., Mihailidis, A.: A survey on ambient-assisted living tools for older adults. IEEE J. Biomed. Health Inform. **17**, 579–590 (2013)
2. Sommaruga, L., Perri, A., Furfari, F.: DomoML-env: an ontology for human home interaction. In: SWAP, pp. 1–7. CEUR-WS.org (2005)
3. Valiente-Rocha, P.A., Lozano-Tello, A.: Ontology-based expert system for home automation controlling. In: García-Pedrajas, N., Herrera, F., Fyfe, C., Benítez, J.M., Ali, M. (eds.) IEA/AIE 2010, Part I. LNCS, vol. 6096, pp. 661–670. Springer, Heidelberg (2010)
4. Farrell, J., Lausen, H.: Semantic Annotations for WSDL and XML Schema (W3C Recommendation 2007). https://www.w3.org/TR/sawsdl/
5. Fensel, D., Fischer, F., Kopecký, J., Krummenacher, R., Lambert, D., Vitvar, T.: WSMO-Lite: Lightweight Semantic Descriptions for Services on the Web (W3C Member Submission 2010). https://www.w3.org/Submission/WSMO-Lite/
6. Bonino, D., Corno, F.: Rule-based intelligence for domotic environments. Autom. Constr. **19**, 183–196 (2010)
7. Etter, R., Costa, P.D., Broens, T.: A rule-based approach towards context-aware user notification services. In: ACS/IEEE International Conference on Pervasive Services, pp. 281–284. IEEE (2006)
8. Herbert, J., O'Donoghue, J., Chen, X.: A context-sensitive rule-based architecture for a smart building environment. In: 2nd International Conference on Future Generation Communication and Networking, FGCN 2008, pp. 437–440 (2008)

Author Index

Printed in the United States
by Baker & Taylor

Printed in the United States
By Bookmasters